Unity

KENNEBEC

Turner

COGGIN

Lewiston

WALDO

Augusta

Wales

Kennebec River

Pittston

Bowdoin

Richmond

SAGADAHOC

Green Pt. WMA

Swan I.
Dresden

Sheepscot

LINCOLN

Clary Hill

KNOX

Camden Hills SP

Bowdoinham

Merrymeeting Bay

Wiscasset

Woolwich

Salt Bay

Nobleboro

Camden

Topsham

Newcastle

Rockport

Brunswick

Damariscotta

Warren

Mark I.

Wharton Pt.

Bath

Rockland

Thomaston

Penobscot Bay

Harpswell

Hen I.

Bristol

Hog I.

Weskeag Marsh

Phippsburg

Boothbay Harbor

Port Clyde

Jenny I.

Flag I.

Reid SP

Western Egg Rock

Muscongus Bay

Graffam I.

Muscle Ridge Is.

Hermit I.
Small Pt.
Morse Mtn.
Seawall Beach
Popham Beach SP

Pond I.

Seguin I.

Damariscove I.

Pemiquid Point

White Is.

The Brothers

Eastern Egg Rock

Metinic I.

Monhegan I.

Matinicus I.

Wooden Ball I.

Matinicus Rock

N

0   10   20

Miles

Birds of Maine

Peter D. Vickery

Barbara S. Vickery and **Scott Weidensaul**
Managing Editors

Charles D. Duncan, William J. Sheehan, and **Jeffrey V. Wells**
Coauthors

Paintings by **Lars Jonsson**
and
Drawings by **Barry Van Dusen**

PRINCETON
UNIVERSITY
PRESS

NUTTALL
ORNITHOLOGICAL
CLUB

Spruce Grouse
previous page: American Woodcock

Requests for permission to reproduce material from this work
should be sent to permissions@press.princeton.edu

Published by Princeton University Press
41 William Street, Princeton, New Jersey 08540
6 Oxford Street, Woodstock, Oxfordshire OX20 1TR
press.princeton.edu

Library of Congress Control Number 2020937548

ISBN 978-0-691-19319-9
ISBN (e-book) 978-0-691-21185-5

British Library Cataloging-in-Publication Data is available

Book design by Charles Melcher and Margo Halverson, Alice Design,
Portland, Maine; with Lucian Burg, LU Design Studios, Portland, Maine

Co-published with the Nuttall Ornithological Club,
Memoirs of the Nuttall Ornithological Club, No. 25

Typeset in Adobe Caslon Pro and Open Sans

Printed on acid-free paper. ∞

Printed in Italy

10 9 8 7 6 5 4 3

This book is dedicated to the memory of Peter D. Vickery,
and to all who love Maine birds and work to ensure that
they will be here for future generations to enjoy.

This project was made possible through partnership with Maine Audubon,
and was funded in part by the Maine Outdoor Heritage Fund.

Contents

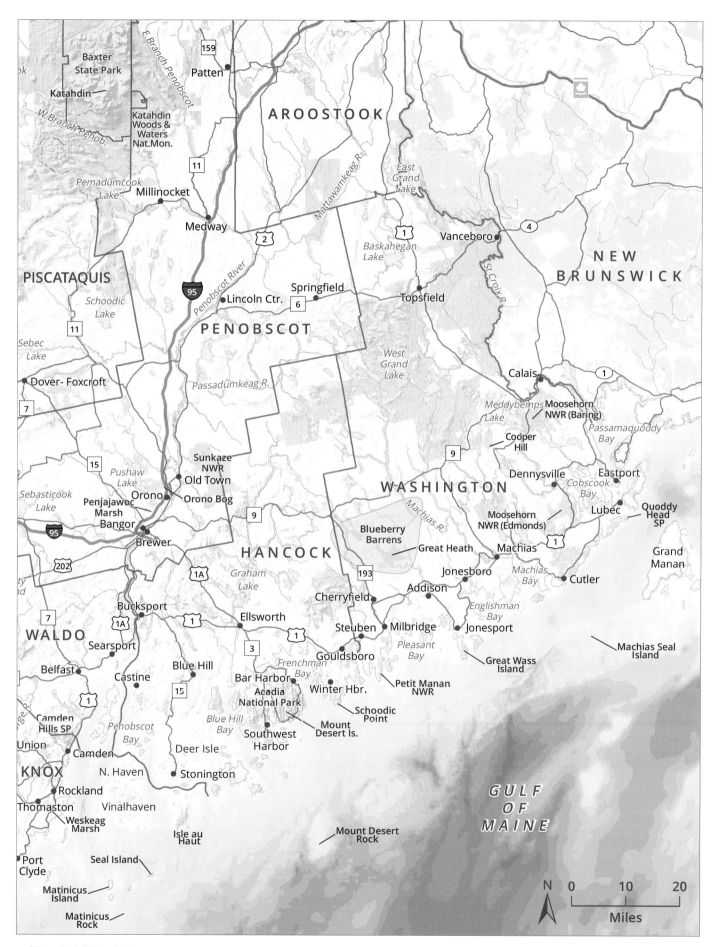

Baxter
State Park
Katahdin
Katahdin
Woods &
Waters
Nat.Mon.
E.Branch Penobscot
W Branch Penob.
159
Patten
AROOSTOOK
Pemadumcook
Lake
11
Millinocket
Medway
NEW
BRUNSWICK
Mattawamkeag R.
East
Grand
Lake
1
Vanceboro
4
PISCATAQUIS
Schoodic
Lake
95
Penobscot River
2
Baskahegan
Lake
St.Croix R.
11
Springfield
Lincoln Ctr.
6
Topsfield
PENOBSCOT
Sebec
Lake
West
Grand
Lake
Dover- Foxcroft
Passadumkeag R.
Calais
1
7
Meddybemps
Lake
Moosehorn
NWR (Baring)
Passamaquoddy
Bay
15
Pushaw
Lake
Sunkaze
NWR
Old Town
9
Cooper
Hill
Eastport
Dennysville
Cobscook
Bay
Sebasticook
Lake
Orono
Orono Bog
WASHINGTON
Lubec
Penjajawoc
Marsh
Bangor
95
9
Moosehorn
NWR (Edmonds)
Quoddy
Head
SP
Brewer
Machias R.
Machias
1
202
HANCOCK
Graham
Lake
Blueberry
Barrens
Great Heath
Machias
Bay
Cutler
Grand
Manan
1A
Searsport
7
1A
Bucksport
1
Ellsworth
193
Cherryfield
Addison
Jonesboro
Englishman
Bay
WALDO
3
Steuben
Milbridge
Jonesport
Machias Seal
Island
Belfast
Castine
15
Blue Hill
Gouldsboro
Frenchman
Bay
Pleasant
Bay
Great Wass
Island
Bar Harbor
Winter Hbr.
Petit Manan
NWR
1
Camden
Hills SP
Acadia
National Park
Schoodic
Point
Union
Penobscot
Bay
Blue Hill
Bay
Southwest
Harbor
Mount
Desert Is.
Camden
Deer Isle
N. Haven
KNOX
Rockland
Vinalhaven
Isle au
Haut
Mount Desert
Rock
GULF
OF
MAINE
Thomaston
Weskeag
Marsh
Port
Clyde
Seal Island
Matinicus
Island
Matinicus
Rock

N   0   10   20
Miles

Maine State Map – East

The Distribution of Birds in Maine

Barbara Vickery and Malcolm L. Hunter Jr.

Imagine sailing east along the coast of Maine on a long June day. With a fair wind, two distinct birding highlights could sear the day into your memory.

At dawn, you set sail near Flag Island in eastern Casco Bay, which hosts a breeding colony of Snowy Egrets, a species more typically emblematic of tropical mangrove swamps. By sunset, you reach Eastern Egg Rock in Muscongus Bay, where that icon of the North Atlantic, the Atlantic Puffin, looks quite at home nesting on a rocky, treeless island. This sailing trip exemplifies a dramatic broader phenomenon: even more than many regions, Maine is a biotic crossroads where northern and southern species mix, and where the overall richness of breeding birds is greater than one would expect in an area this size.

Twenty-three southern species reach their northern breeding range limit in Maine, and 26 northern species are at the southern edge of their breeding ranges. Many primarily western breeding species, such as Bonaparte's Gull, Sandhill Crane, Redhead, and Gadwall, reach or approach their eastern limits in Maine. Similarly, some European vagrants reach Maine, although they are seldom seen to our west. In this chapter, we will review Maine's geographic and ecological diversity with an eye to exploring the distribution of birds across the state as well as the underlying reasons for this crossroads phenomenon.

Maine's Geography

Maine is not only the largest state in New England, but it is almost as large as the other five states combined. It spans more latitude than the rest of New England, reaching farther north than any state east of the Great Lakes. Notably, Estcourt Station, at 47° 46' N on Maine's northernmost tip, is nearly the same latitude as St. Johns, Newfoundland. Maine is almost 90 percent forested, the most wooded state in the country. It is also blessed with abundant fresh water in five great river systems and innumerable streams, fast and slow; in more than 5,000 natural lakes, notably supporting a nearly statewide nesting loon population; and in more than 5 million acres (2 million ha) of freshwater wetlands comprising forested swamps, bogs, fens, marshes, and floodplains. Because of its many peninsulas, tidal streams, and thousands of islands, Maine's tidal shoreline is—depending on how it is measured—between 2,500 and 5,000 miles (4,000–8,000 km) long, 10–20 times longer than the straight-line coastal distance between Kittery and Lubec. In fact, Maine's coastline is the fourth longest in the nation. Coastal landforms range from rocky headlands to barrier beach-and-dune systems. Perhaps most exceptional are the thousands of coastal islands, many of which support important seabird nesting colonies.

Topography and Geology

Maine lies near the northern end of the Appalachian Mountains in the U.S. Its bedrock is dominated by ancient metasedimentary rocks punctuated by granitic plutons particularly evident near Sebago Lake, Mount Katahdin, and Mount Desert Island. As recently as 15,000 years ago, Maine was under ice a mile (1.6 km) thick, the Laurentide Ice Sheet. At that time, Mount Katahdin, currently 5,267 feet tall (1,605 m), was an island in a vast sea of ice. The continental glacier plucked at hilltops, then ground, scoured, and carried boulders, cobbles, and pebbles, scattering them across the landscape. Its meltwater streams concentrated the glacial debris into eskers and outwash plains. As the glacier receded, the sea inundated the land, which had been depressed by the glacier's weight; marine waters reached north to Bingham in the Kennebec River Valley and Mattawamkeag in the Penobscot River Valley. As the crust rebounded, what had been nearshore ocean bottom became today's coastal plain, now covered with a smear of marine clay. The diversity of landforms and glacial deposits from these events led to an abundance and variety of drainage patterns and soil types, creating an array of wetlands covering a quarter of the state, four times the wetland acreage of the rest of New England combined.

Climate

Latitude drives much of the climatic variation in the state, and almost inevitably, the farther north one goes the colder, longer, and snowier the winters. Furthermore, in Maine this trend is enhanced because altitude tends to parallel latitude. Notably, Moosehead Lake, 100 miles (160 km) inland, lies at 1,032 feet (315 m) above sea level; much of the land from there to Quebec is above 1,000 feet (300 m).

A third major contributor to Maine's climatic variation (unlike Vermont, for instance) is the maritime influence, which accentuates Maine's steep temperate-to-boreal gradient. The Gulf of Maine is slow to warm in spring and slow to cool in autumn. Characteristic fog and sea breezes cool the coastal areas, which are more moderate in temperature in all seasons. These coastal influences are not uniform from Eastport to Kittery, however, because of the Labrador Current, which moves south along the Atlantic Coast of Canada bringing cold water to the Gulf of Maine by way of the Scotia Shelf and the Northeast Channel. Moving in a counterclockwise gyre, it turns north into the Bay of Fundy and then circles back along Maine's Downeast coast. Its chilly and well-mixed waters make that shoreline cooler and particularly foggy in summer, enveloped in mist twice as many hours, on average, as western Penobscot Bay (Fobes 1946, in McMahon 1990). When the Eastern Coastal Current reaches Penobscot Bay, part of it turns offshore into the Gulf of Maine, making Maine's southwest coast comparatively warmer and less fog-bound (see Map 6, p. 24). Away from the coast, Maine has a classically continental climate with frigid winters and hot summers.

The climate gradient found in Maine's three degrees of latitude is spread across 20 degrees of latitude in Europe, a distance about twice the length of California (Jacobson et al. 2009). Overall, the steep climatic gradients and variety of landforms and soils contribute to the remarkable diversity of both forest and wetland types. Naturally, the avifauna reflects this, with northern species such as Atlantic Puffin, Spruce Grouse, Fox Sparrow, and Pine Grosbeak living not far from southern species like Snowy Egrets and Northern Cardinals.

Land Use

Maine's landscapes, and thus bird distribution, have been strongly shaped by human settlement and past and present land use. At the time of European arrival, Maine was populated by the Wabanaki, who were primarily hunter-gatherers on both land and sea, leaving massive middens of fish, marine mammal and bird bones, and shells in coastal areas. But they also cleared patches of land to grow corn, squash, and beans and may have set fires to enhance wildlife hunting, especially in southern and coastal areas, perpetuating the "park-like" oak and pine forests and savannahs with little understory described by many early European explorers. Native American artifacts have been found at Kennebunk Plains, for instance, and the fertile Saco River intervale in Fryeburg hosted a sizable village of the Abenaki, one branch of the Wabanaki. Downeast, Pineo Ridge was already a fire-maintained savannah dominated by blueberries (*Vaccinium angustifolium*) when first explored by European surveyors (Winne 1998). However, unlike southern New England and other areas in North America, Maine Native populations were relatively small, even before contact disease epidemics drastically reduced their numbers in the first decades of the 17th century (Mathewson 2011). Therefore, the ecological impacts of their seasonal hunting and gathering lifestyles were less intense and widespread; the composition of the forest Europeans first encountered was very similar to the mix of species found today (Barton et al. 2012).

From the 17th to 19th centuries, much of Maine was cleared for agriculture, and by the late 19th century approximately 25 percent of the state's forest was lost (Foster et al. 2017). Most clearing occurred in the southern third of the state and in eastern Aroostook County. Starting in the 1860s, many farms were abandoned as families moved west to

Map 3: *Land Use and Land Cover*

Generalized land cover classes extracted from the Northeastern Terrestrial Habitat Classification System data reveal the extension of boreal forests into eastern Maine, as well as the extent of agricultural land in Aroostook County. (The Nature Conservancy, Eastern Conservation Science 2015.)

previous page: One of Maine's thousands of lakes and ponds that provide critical nesting habitat for Common Loons, Spotted Sandpipers, Common Mergansers, Hooded Mergansers, and Wood Ducks. Baxter State Park, Piscataquis Co. (©Ian Patterson)

right: Spruce-fir forests cover much of western, northern, and Downeast Maine, providing habitat for boreal species like Spruce Grouse, Yellow-bellied Flycatcher, Boreal Chickadee, Canada Jay, Black-backed Woodpecker, Swainson's Thrush, and Magnolia Warbler. View from Number 5 Mtn., T6R7 BKP WKR, Somerset Co. (©Ian Patterson)

Boreal forests and warblers typical of northern Maine meet the ocean along the Downeast shore. Bold Coast, Cutler, Washington Co. (©Ian Patterson)

left: Twenty-foot tides on the Downeast coast create extensive mudflats, critical stopover habitat for migratory shorebirds. Gouldsboro, Hancock Co. (© Mark Berry)

below: Rocky headlands and deep coastal waters, the iconic image of the Maine coast, are often inhabited by Common Eiders and Black Guillemots. Monhegan Island. (©Mike Fahay)

bathymetry combine to bring exceptional riches of marine life to the surface and lead to an annual spectacle of thousands of migrant seabirds and hundreds of marine mammals converging to enjoy an end-of-summer feeding frenzy.

The Midcoast and Penobscot Bay Region stretches from Casco Bay to Blue Hill Bay and thus includes the many peninsulas and islands of the Midcoast and outer Penobscot Bay. The peninsulas are formed by highly metamorphosed sedimentary rocks (Osberg

et al. 1985), while granitic plutons form many of the islands such as Isleboro, Vinalhaven, and North Haven, as well as the Camden Hills and Blue Hill. Before the land rebounded from the receding glacier's weight, nearly the entire Midcoast was submerged. When the land rebounded, many valleys emerged, which, as the land subsided again, then became the bays and inlets of today's coast. Hence, it is often referred to as a drowned coastline. Covered with shallow, excessively drained sandy soils, many of the region's ridges lend

BLUEBERRY BARRENS: A BIRD HABITAT UNIQUE TO MAINE AND THE CANADIAN MARITIMES

Maine has large expanses of blueberry barrens, areas naturally dominated by wild lowbush blueberries, which are managed to enhance that commercial crop.

These barrens occur where soils are acidic and dry, often associated with glacial outwash. There is evidence that many of these were relatively open pine woodlands, shrublands, or grasslands in precolonial times because of fires set by Native Americans (Winne 1998). There are several barrens in Southern Maine, notably Kennebunk Plains, Wells Barren, and Brunswick Commons, most of which are now in conservation and no longer managed for blueberries. There are dry blueberry ridges in Waldo County in the Midcoast. However, the majority of Maine's 44,000 acres in blueberry production, and notably the largest in expanse, are in Downeast Maine where they are large enough to be apparent in satellite images.

Although management for blueberries has become more and more intensive (involving herbicides to radically reduce grass and forb cover, removal of rocks to facilitate mechanical harvest, and planting of coniferous trees as windbreaks), such barrens still provide essential habitat for several grassland-nesting birds: Upland Sandpiper, Grasshopper Sparrow, and Vesper Sparrow (see range maps in species accounts). Unlike Eastern Meadowlarks and Bobolinks, these birds do not use hayfields or pastures, but instead require areas with bunching grasses such as Little Bluestem (*Schizachyrium scoparium*) where there is some bare ground amongst the vegetation. Sandplain grasslands, which provide habitat for a number of rare plants and invertebrates, as well as grassland birds, are one of

Maine's rarest natural communities. Large commercially managed blueberry barrens are critically important for Upland Sandpipers, which are mostly restricted to areas larger than 250 acres (100 ha). Vesper Sparrows likewise are strongly associated with blueberry barrens in Maine, apparently finding enough grass and forb cover to nest along the edges even on barrens treated with herbicides (Weik 1999). In Southern Maine, barrens in conservation, now managed for wildlife rather than commercial blueberry production, also support many Field Sparrows, Prairie Warblers, and Eastern Towhees around their shrubby edges or in fields that have not recently been burned or mown.

Whimbrels have long used the Downeast barrens as a refueling stop on their southward migration; in fact, they were once known locally as "Blueberry Curlews." Large blueberry growers attempt to dissuade them with cannons, although the number of berries eaten by Whimbrels is a tiny fraction of the crop (J. Paquet, Canadian Wildlife Service, pers. com.). Northern Harriers and American Kestrels are positively associated with large blueberry barrens over other types of open lands (Weik 1999). Short-eared Owls sometimes frequent these sites and one of the few Maine records of Burrowing Owl occurred on a Downeast barren. Clarry Hill, a managed blueberry barren in Midcoast Maine, is a notable hawkwatch site, despite its relatively low elevation, because of its dramatic, unobstructed views.

BSV

OLD SOW WHIRLPOOL

The strong Fundy tides, with the largest amplitude on the Atlantic Coast, combined with the complex underwater topography of the Passamaquoddy Bay region between Maine and New Brunswick, produce the largest whirlpool in the Western Hemisphere, called the Old Sow.

On a rising (flood) tide, water can run as fast as eight knots through Lubec Narrows. When it meets water flowing in the opposite direction around Indian Island, at the western end of Head Harbour Passage, the result is a more horizontal, turbulent, and locally transient phenomenon than the familiar downward bathtub whirlpool. In fact, it involves significant upwelling, responsible for bringing nutrients and marine invertebrates to the surface and providing rich food resources to fish, marine mammals, and birds. Enormous numbers of small gulls feed on this bounty in late summer, including occasional rarities such as Sabine's, Little, and Black-headed Gulls, amid thousands of Bonaparte's. Until the mid-1980s, the spectacle was even more staggering as hundreds of thousands of Red-necked Phalaropes also congregated there.

CDD

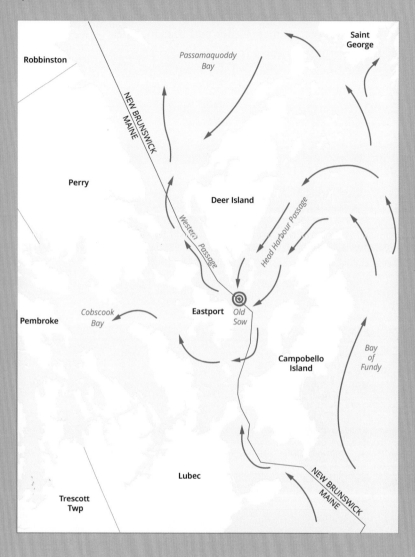

Map 5: *Old Sow Whirlpool*

themselves to wild blueberry cultivation. One of these, **Clarry Hill**, is well known as a prime raptor viewing locality during fall migration.

Vegetation of the Midcoast Region is transitional between cool spruce forests of the Canadian Maritimes and the oak-pine associations of central New England. Maine's coastal spruce-fir forests reach their southernmost extent near Harpswell. Conversely, several plant species more typical of southwestern Maine reach their easternmost extent in the region, including Shagbark Hickory (*Carya ovata*), White Oak (*Quercus alba*), and American Hornbeam (*Ostrya virginiana*).

This transitional zone exhibits a high level of species diversity. Woody species richness is higher than any other part of the state (McMahon 1990, Krohn et al. 1999). Interestingly, although this is a transition zone between northern and southern species—recall the puffin and the egret—the overall diversity of breeding birds in this region is not greater than elsewhere on the coast (Adamus 1987).

Estuaries of the Kennebec, Sheepscot, and Penobscot Rivers support tidal wetlands ranging from salt marshes to brackish and freshwater wetlands. The Kennebec River estuary, in particular, includes the largest acreage of salt marsh on the coast.

Throughout Maine, freshwater pond shores are a favorite haunt of Great Blue Herons, as well as Green Herons and Spotted Sandpipers. Kezar Pond outlet, Fryeburg, Oxford Co. (©Maine Natural Areas Program)

Merrymeeting Bay, one of the most expansive freshwater tidal marshes in the eastern U.S., is famous for the concentrations of migrant waterfowl and blackbirds (especially Bobolinks) attracted to its robust Wild Rice (*Zizania aquatica*) stands, as well as migrant shorebirds and swallows that gather there.

Seawall Beach, **Popham Beach State Park**, and **Reid State Park** are outstanding examples of barrier beach and dune systems at their northeastern U.S. range limit. These sites support nesting Piping Plovers and occasionally Least Terns, and in fall migration attract tens of thousands of shorebirds. Saltmarsh Sparrows reach their northeastern breeding limit in the salt marshes behind these barrier beaches.

The Southern Maine Region, including all of York and Cumberland Counties, along with southern Oxford and western Sagadahoc Counties, is the most developed and densely populated area of Maine. Nevertheless, there are still many diverse natural areas critically important to Maine's birds. Not surprisingly, it is also where at least least 10 species, including Blue-winged Warbler and Orchard Oriole, reach the northern limit of their ranges.

Characterized by oak, pine, and Eastern Hemlock (*Tsuga canadensis*) forests, the region is less influenced by maritime climate than the central and eastern coast, even along the immediate

shore. Its inland locations, such as the Fryeburg area, for example, often have the hottest summer temperatures in the state. The many glacial eskers and moraines create extensive wetland systems and large sand and gravel outwash deposits that provide essential aquifers. The region's largest river, the Saco, winds through extensive glacial outwash, forming Maine's largest floodplain system. Some outwash sites harbor fire-prone Pitch Pine (*Pinus rigida*) barrens and sandplain grasslands, such as **Kennebunk Plains** and Wells Barren, home to breeding Grasshopper Sparrows, Vesper Sparrows, Upland Sandpipers, and Prairie Warblers.

Maine's largest salt marshes also occur in this region, most notably **Scarborough Marsh**. The southern coast, remarkably straight compared to the Midcoast, has a series of long beaches. A few islands, including

Stratton Island, provide heronry sites for southern species, such as Little Blue and Tricolored Herons, Snowy Egret, and Glossy Ibis. **Bradbury Mountain**, Cumberland County, is the site of the state's primary spring hawkwatch. **Mount Agamenticus** in York County, a monadnock in the southern coastal plain, is one of Maine's long-standing fall hawk migration observation sites.

The Gulf of Maine

The eight ecoregions described above leave off at the ocean's edge, but the marine realm also has distinct regions. The complex interplay of seafloor topography, wide seasonal variation in water temperature, tidal amplitude, large-scale oceanic currents, and distance from shore shapes the environments that determine

Sandy beach and dunes are a southern coastal Maine habitat important for nesting Piping Plover and Least Tern and, in winter, "Ipswich" Savannah Sparrow. Seawall Beach, Phippsburg, Sagadahoc Co. (©Peter Vickery)

seabird distribution just as definitively as the landscape shapes that of terrestrial birds.

The Gulf of Maine is one of the world's most productive—and dynamic—marine ecosystems. A semi-enclosed sea, it is a deep basin bounded on the Atlantic side by the shallower Georges and Browns Banks (See Map 6, p. 24). The gulf is nourished by cold water from the Labrador Current and fresh water draining Maine and parts of Nova Scotia, New Brunswick, New Hampshire, and Massachusetts. Surface temperatures average just 2°C (36°F) in winter and 17°C (63°F) in summer, a much wider range than the waters south of Cape Cod (Maine Department of Marine Resources data). Lately it has become one of the fastest-warming waterbodies on Earth (Pershing et al. 2015). It is characterized by large diurnal tidal amplitudes reaching extremes in the Bay of Fundy and creating intense mixing of surface and deeper waters, especially Downeast. Inshore waters lie over a shallow coastal shelf less than 200 ft (60 m) deep and about six nautical miles (11 km) wide. Because of the influence of the Eastern Coastal Current, the surface waters to the east are colder, saltier, and well-mixed,

while those of the coastal shelf west of Penobscot Bay are warmer and fresher (See Map 7, p. 29).

Thousands of islands of varying sizes and vegetation cover, from tiny rocks just above the tideline to larger ones covered with spruce-fir forests, dot the inshore. Ospreys, Bald Eagles, Common Eiders, Double-crested Cormorants, and many species of warblers find these islands to be ideal breeding sites. Farther offshore, islands such as Seal Island, Eastern Egg Rock, Mount Desert Rock, Matinicus Rock, and (in waters also claimed by Canada) Machias Seal Island provide nesting habitats that are free from terrestrial predators and closer to pelagic feeding grounds. It is only here that the more southerly Roseate Tern breeds on the same islands as such northerly species as Common Murre, Razorbill, Atlantic Puffin, Black Guillemot, and Arctic Tern, also at the limits of their breeding ranges.

Still farther from shore is the truly pelagic zone with waters as deep as 1,000 ft. (300 m) in its three major basins: Jordan, Wilkinson, and Georges. Ridges, banks, and seamounts such as Cashes Ledge and Jeffreys Bank separate these basins and create

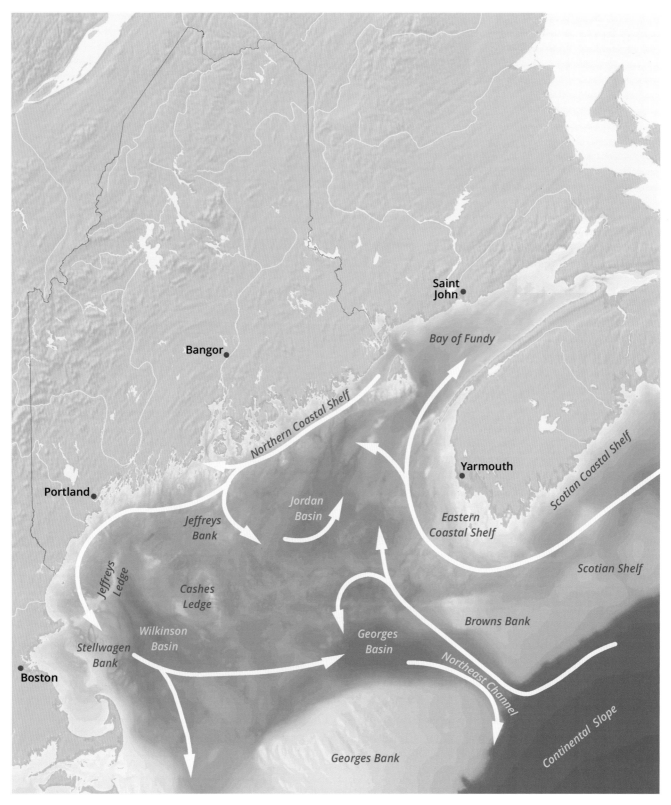

Map 6: *Gulf of Maine Bathymetric Features and Currents*

The Gulf of Maine, one of the world's most productive marine ecosystems, is a semi-enclosed deep basin bounded on the Atlantic side by Georges and Browns Banks. Within its offshore pelagic zone, the waters are deepest in its three major basins, Jordan, Wilkinson, and Georges. Seamounts such as Cashes Ledge and Jeffreys Bank create upwellings of oxygen- and nutrient-rich cold water that provide rich feeding grounds for seabirds and whales. (Data: Maine Department of Marine Resources.)

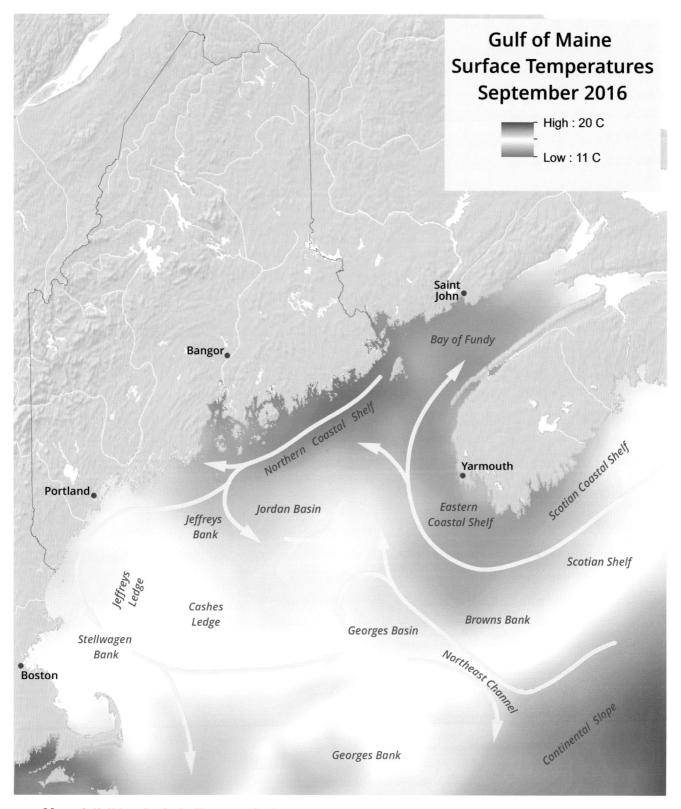

Gulf of Maine Surface Temperatures September 2016

High : 20 C
Low : 11 C

Saint John

Bay of Fundy

Bangor

Northern Coastal Shelf

Yarmouth

Scotian Coastal Shelf

Portland

Jordan Basin

Jeffreys Bank

Eastern Coastal Shelf

Scotian Shelf

Jeffreys Ledge

Cashes Ledge

Browns Bank

Stellwagen Bank

Georges Basin

Boston

Northeast Channel

Continental Slope

Georges Bank

Map 7: *Gulf of Maine Sea–Surface Temperature Gradients*

The Labrador Current brings cold water into the Gulf of Maine by way of the Scotia Coastal Shelf and the Northeast Channel. This colder water turns north into the Bay of Fundy where it is pushed to the surface, and then circles back along Maine's Downeast coast in a counterclockwise gyre. Its chilly and well-mixed surface waters make that shoreline cooler and famously foggy in summer. When the Eastern Coastal Current, running along the Northern Coastal Shelf, reaches Penobscot Bay, part of it turns offshore into the Gulf of Maine so that the surface temperatures of the southern coast are much warmer. (Data: Gulf of Maine Research Institute.)

previous page: Saco Heath, a southern example of a large raised peatland. Saco, York Co. (©Ian Patterson)

right: Blueberry barren/sandplain grasslands are a bastion for rare species like Grasshopper Sparrow and Upland Sandpiper. Kennebunk Plains, York Co. (©Patrick Higgins)

The ranges of Nelson's and Saltmarsh Sparrows overlap on the extensive salt marshes of southern Maine. Goosefare Brook, Saco, York Co. (©Maine Natural Areas Program).

upwellings of oxygen- and nutrient-rich cold water that support a robust food chain, providing ideal feeding grounds for whales and seabirds. Here, in the northern summer, austral migrants like Wilson's Storm-Petrels and Great and Sooty Shearwaters meet their boreal-breeding counterparts, Leach's Storm-Petrels and Manx Shearwaters, and jaegers ply their kleptoparasitic trade. Summer research ships and tourist cruises focused on whales provide much of the bird distribution information in this offshore zone; we know comparatively little about seabird occurrence in the Gulf of Maine in winter.

WHO OWNS MACHIAS SEAL ISLAND?

Machias Seal Island (MSI) flies a Canadian flag, its lighthouse is staffed by Canadian Coast Guard light keepers, and in summer, its seabird colony is protected by Canadian Wildlife Service (CWS) personnel. Why then, is it included in a book about Maine's birds?

Lying nine miles off Cutler, ME, and 12 miles from Grand Manan, NB, the island is integral to our understanding of Gulf of Maine birdlife. Politically, things are more complicated, because the island and surroundings are disputed territory.

The U.S. State Department claims, "Machias Seal Island has been part of the United States since the Definitive Treaty of Peace of 1783 between the United States and Great Britain. Canada has maintained a lighthouse on the island since the mid-19th century and claims that the island has become part of Canada. The United States disputes Canada's claim. We note that maintenance of a lighthouse for navigational purposes does not by itself entail a manifestation of sovereignty under international law" (USFWS, 2017, pers. com.).

Canada, for its part, points to a section of the same 1783 Treaty of Paris that excludes any island that was ever part of Nova Scotia from those transferred to the newly independent U.S. They note that Machias Seal Island is included in the 1621 Letters Patent issued by King James I establishing the colony of Nova Scotia.

A 1982 letter from the U.S. State Department to the late Captain Barna B. Norton, a colorful Downeaster who ferried birdwatchers to MSI for many years, went further, "[T]he U.S. does not recognize the Canadian claim. Canada has been informed of the U.S. view on many occasions….Canada certainly does not have the authority to impose any restrictions on your use of U.S. territory. You have the right to ignore any regulations that Canada might pretend to set for Machias Seal Island."

The island was expressly excluded from the mandate of an International Court of Justice (ICJ) chamber established in 1979 to define the maritime boundary of the two nations in the Gulf of Maine. Canadian law professor Donald McRae, a member of the ICJ, said that when the dispute between the two nations arises every few years, "they just simply try to put it aside because I don't think either side is interested in dealing with it" (Byer and Østhagen 2016).

The fortunate present situation is that MSI is simultaneously a CWS Migratory Bird Sanctuary and part of the Maine Coastal Islands NWR. In effect, both nations agree to disagree about sovereignty while communicating and cooperating for the island's management and protection.
CDD

Cordelia Stanwood was a pioneer in photographing wild birds, like this female Black-throated Blue Warbler feeding her fledglings. (Stanwood Wildlife Sanctuary)

3
Maine's Ornithological History

Jody Despres and Jeffrey V. Wells

The Early Years: Studying Birds by Shooting

"The Cormorant, Shape, or Sharke roosts by night upon some Rock that lyes out in the Sea, thither the Indian goes in his Birch-Canow when the Moon shines clear. [Having killed the birds'] watchman, he takes them up as he pleaseth, still wringing off their heads; when he hath slain as many as his Canow can carry, he gives a shout which awakens the Cormorants, who are gone in an instant."

Such anecdotes are characteristic of the observations of British gentleman-errant John Josselyn, the first known chronicler of Maine's birdlife. Based in what is now Scarborough during the 1630s and then again in the 1660s, Josselyn spent more than eight years exploring—with conspicuous delight—the natural wonders of provincial Maine and New Hampshire. He left us two volumes on the subject: *New England's Rarities Discovered in Birds, Beasts, Fishes, Serpents, and Plants of that Country* (1672) and *An Account of Two Voyages to New-England* (1674).

Along with a few less prominent passers-through, Josselyn might be considered one of Maine's first ornithologists. However, his occasional notes on Native American bird lore remind us that a long tradition of careful bird-study (most of it passed from generation to generation through oral history and never written down) existed before the first Europeans brought recorded history to this continent. While both the indigenous peoples and the Europeans were interested in birds as food, the former had deep spiritual connections with many birds. Josselyn, for instance, wrote that the kingbird is a "little black hawke highly prized by the Indians who wear them on their heads, and is accounted of worth sufficient to ransome a Sagamour [chief]; they are so strangely courageous and hardie, that nothing flyeth in the

Air that they will not bind with." Even today a few indigenous bird names are still used commonly, as in the various versions of the name "whiskey jack" or "wiskeejac" for the Canada Jay, a bird that occurs in legends of many native peoples of northern North America.

Josselyn's contributions were to be the last significant words on Maine ornithology for a long while. Alexander Wilson's nine-volume *American Ornithology* (1808–1814) added some new information, but it is not clear whether he personally ever observed birds in Maine. Another bird observer, William D. Williamson, included an annotated list of Maine birds in his *History of the State of Maine* (1832), but he listed no sources for his information, much of which was inaccurate. Whether Williamson actually birded in Maine is also questionable.

By contrast, in the very year that Williamson's list was published, John James Audubon did come to study and collect in Maine, seeking new material for his five-volume *Ornithological Biography* (1831–1839). Perhaps more significant for Maine ornithology than any bird Audubon found here was his acquaintance with young Thomas Lincoln of Dennysville, whom Audubon met while staying with the Lincoln family in the summer of 1832 looking for Spruce Grouse and gathering specimens for use in his paintings of Black Guillemot, Harlequin Duck, Red-necked Phalarope, and Winter Wren. Lincoln accompanied Audubon (who was slowed by a recent stroke) and his son on his expedition to Labrador in 1833. They hired a boat and crew and left from Eastport on 6 June 1833. On 4 July they were exploring around Natashquan (a native Innu name that means something like "place to hunt bears") on the North Shore of what is now Quebec, when Audubon heard the song of a bird and immediately knew it was a species that he had never seen or heard. He called the young men over immediately to try to procure a specimen. It was Maine's own young Tom Lincoln who collected the first—a species, ironically enough, that probably nested regularly within a few miles of Lincoln's Dennysville doorstep. In any case, Audubon graciously named it "Lincoln's finch" (now Lincoln's Sparrow). (For more on Audubon's time in Downeast Maine and his Labrador expedition, see Logan 2016.)

Between 1846 and 1857, another famous naturalist, Henry David Thoreau, made three visits to Maine, exploring Mount Katahdin, Moosehead Lake, the Allagash River, and the East Branch of the Penobscot River. No bird he saw would have made ornithological news then or now; that he found loons in the wilderness is hardly surprising, but his distinction was the wilderness he found in loons and their calls: "... a very wild sound, quite in keeping with the place and the circumstances of the traveler and very unlike the sound of a bird ... Formerly, when lying awake at midnight in these woods, I had listened to hear some words or syllables of [the woods'] language, but it chanced that I listened in vain until I heard the cry of the loon."

Thoreau's ornithology was also distinguished in another way: he rarely, if ever, collected birds or their eggs. From the 1700s until at least 1900, collecting was the *sine qua non* of ornithology. However alien this seems to our own idea of birding, birds were then hunted on so large a scale for market, sport, or decorations that hunting them for science was seldom a matter of conscience. Even after laws regulating bird hunting were on the books, they were largely ignored by those with ornithological interests. William Brewster, who collected birds in western Maine between 1871 and 1909, wrote that even game wardens saw "technical infractions of the law, if committed for some obviously necessary or worthy purpose, might often be ignored with advantage rather than detriment to its general usefulness and efficacy."

And the scientific need *was* real. Until "opera glasses" became available in the 1890s, the only optics available were small telescopes. Even if one could get a clear look at a bird, there were no field guides to aid in its identification. Those references that did exist were cumbersome, incomplete, and often inaccurate or contradictory; each might give a different name for the same species. Many species had yet to be described, and the plumages of many more had not been figured out, much less illustrated.

Probably the most comprehensive effort to solve early North American bird identification problems through collecting was that conducted by Spencer Fullerton Baird of the Smithsonian Institution. Between 1850 and 1875, Baird maintained a veritable army of collectors throughout the U.S. From 1865 on, he also maintained a summer home in Eastport. His principal source of Maine specimens was the aptly named lumber magnate, George Boardman.

Boardman lived on the banks of the St. Croix River in "Milltown," sometimes on the American side (Calais) and sometimes on the Canadian side (St. Stephen, New Brunswick). In a field of study noted both then and now for its emphasis on keeping accurate records and lists, Boardman's tendency not to distinguish his Maine bird observations from those gathered in New Brunswick was a source of headaches to ornithological writers for decades.

A number of local and state bird lists were published between 1860 and 1890. The most comprehensive of these was Everett Smith's *Birds of Maine, with Annotations of Their Comparative Abundance, Dates of Migration, Breeding Habits, etc.* which appeared serially in the outdoor sportsman's magazine *Forest and Stream* between 1882 and 1883. Although the basis for some unusual records is unclear, the list is generally credible and informative, a great improvement over Williamson's. And although the record was argued over by many ornithologists since, Smith's list provides the most plausible record of Boat-tailed Grackle in the state, still considered only hypothetical in Maine.

Ora Willis Knight, who was born in Bangor in 1874 and received a degree in chemistry from Maine State College (now University of Maine) in 1895, was an avid university-trained naturalist, although professionally employed as a chemist and microscopist. He collected specimens of birds, plants, insects, and other animals for the University of Maine and the Smithsonian and contributed many papers and observations to works of the day like Bent's *Life Histories of North American Birds*. In 1908, he published Maine's first comprehensive bird book, *Birds of Maine*, through a Bangor publishing house. Among other features, Knight's *Birds of Maine* included a descriptive key to identification, a county-by-county list of each species' status, and considerable life history information, the bulk of it gathered in Maine by Knight and his correspondents. Knight corrected and clarified many previously published records and stated the evidence for unusual records of his own.

than a thousand references, providing information that Palmer critically evaluated and wove into a very readable text that has been the foundation of the understanding of the distribution and status of birds in Maine ever since. Many of the anecdotal remarks he included are so evocative that they have been quoted liberally in this volume.

Following service in World War II, Palmer was appointed as a senior scientist of the New York State Museum and State Science Service, where he worked for 27 years. He then served as a research associate of the Smithsonian Institution for five years. In 1981, Palmer was appointed as a faculty associate in zoology and forest resources at the University of Maine at Orono and he lived the rest of his life in Tenants Harbor, Knox County, Maine, in a house he built with the help of two sons. Among the distinctive features of this house was the climate-controlled basement that housed his enormous personal library. Palmer left his reprint collection, which apparently measured 178 linear feet, to University of Maine's Fogler Library, along with several collections of rare books on Maine woods, indigenous peoples, and early explorations.

Succeeding Alfred Gross in 1953 as the ornithologist at Bowdoin College was Charles E. "Chuck" Huntington, who served in that position until his retirement in 1986. Huntington's research focused on the life history of Leach's Storm-Petrels, studying them at the Bowdoin Scientific Station on Kent Island, New Brunswick, for decades and becoming the world authority on the species. Hundreds of students were taught, inspired, and mentored by Huntington over his many years at Bowdoin. Similarly, William Drury, a noted seabird biologist and ecologist who became the ornithologist at the newly founded College of the Atlantic in Bar Harbor in 1976, trained many undergraduates in bird ecology and continued his research and management work on seabirds of Maine islands over the 16 years he held that position.

Well-known ornithologist and author of *Birds of the West Indies*, James Bond (whose name was appropriated by Ian Fleming for the character in his famous spy novels) had a strong connection to Maine. As a child he began visiting Mount Desert Island with his uncle, Carroll Sargent Tyson, a well-known artist whose series of 20 bird paintings was packaged together as *The Birds of Mount Desert Island* in the 1930s. Apparently it was his summers in Maine that inspired Bond to become an ornithologist. Bond co-authored with his uncle and then, later, authored several editions of a small book on the status of the birds of Mount Desert Island before going on to study birds of the West Indies.

A key ornithological figure at Shoals Marine Laboratory on Maine's Appledore Island was Arthur Borror, a University of New Hampshire (UNH) professor, 1961–1995. Borror not only taught thousands of UNH students about birds and ecology but also taught at the Shoals Marine Lab, run jointly by UNH and Cornell University. He supported and encouraged many generations of students to establish field studies of birds on Appledore and nearby islands and published several editions of *Breeding Birds of the Isles of Shoals*.

A lesser-known Maine ornithologist was Margaret Hundley, who received an M.A. degree from the University of Maine and called Stonington on the Deer Isle peninsula her home until her death in 1996 at age 93. Hundley was an accomplished field ornithologist and held staff positions over her lifetime with the Florida Audubon Society and the Cornell Lab of Ornithology. She contributed more than 150 articles to academic and popular bird publications and in 1998 published a book, *The Birds of Deer Isle, Maine*.

Today Maine is blessed with an amazing number of accomplished ornithologists at academic institutions, in state and federal government, with nonprofit and research institutions, and in other capacities or working on their own. Many others come to Maine as summer visitors or to carry out research projects. Their work enriches this book immeasurably.

The Modern Era

Since the publication of Palmer's *Maine Birds*, there has been a series of efforts to collect and publish ornithological records in Maine. Several of these were in publications of the Maine Audubon Society, but subsequent periodicals were begun as the need arose (see Table 2, p. 41). From 1961–1969, Maine Audubon president Christopher M. Packard, following very much in Norton's tradition, collected and curated field cards of observations as submitted by ardent birders. When Packard departed Maine Audubon in 1969 to create the Audubon Naturalist Council, the record-keeping continued, until 1973, with the publication of *Maine Nature*. Since then, several publications tracking and curating important Maine bird records

BIRD CLUBS AND SUMMER CAMPS

Knight, Brewster, Stanwood, and their contemporaries often sustained their natural history interests through their involvement in growing numbers of organizations devoted to natural history. Maine has a rich history of bird and nature organizations dating back to the founding of the Portland Museum of Natural History in 1843 and the establishment of what was first called the United Ornithologists of Maine in 1893.

The latter group had its first meeting in 1896 in the old high school in Gardiner, where there was a large group of bird enthusiasts that Knight identified in *Birds of Maine* as the "Gardiner Branch." The next year the name was changed to the Maine Ornithological Society.

Bird conservation, education, and ornithological activities were in the heyday of growth during the early decades of the 1900s as the Audubon movement took hold and a variety of other bird and nature clubs became established. The Stanton Bird Club in the Lewiston-Auburn area was established in 1919 and named after Jonathan Stanton, a beloved Bates College Latin and Greek professor who was an avid birdwatcher and bird lover. Another bird club started that year in Augusta, initially known as the Ball Bird Club after Reverend Dwight Ball. The club was renamed the

Augusta Nature Club in 1928 and remains under that name today. The Bangor Bird Conservation Club was founded in 1914, the predecessor of what is now known as the Bangor Nature Club. By 1922, Maine also had 51 Junior Audubon Clubs with more than 1,400 youth participants. Six of the 17 Audubon wardens in the U.S. were stationed on Maine nesting seabird islands. Apparently, all of this bird enthusiasm was one of the reasons why then-Governor Percival Baxter set aside 14 April 1922 as Bird Day in Maine.

Remarkably, not only do we still have our original bird and nature clubs in Maine, but we also have the statewide Maine Audubon and seven local Audubon chapters (at least one is more than 70 years old), each with its own local volunteers educating people young and old about birds and nature and advocating for

TYPICAL FIELD TRIP. AUDUBON NATURE CAMP. MEDOMAK. MAINE.

Since its founding in 1936 (when this photo was taken), the Hog Island Audubon Camp on Muscongus Bay has attracted bird enthusiasts eager to learn from the nation's best ornithologists. (Friends of Hog Island)

conservation. These organizations have been at the forefront of encouraging and developing both amateur and professional ornithologists in Maine.

Maine is justifiably famous for its many youth summer camps—lodges and cabins on lakes where kids come to swim, canoe, sail, fish, play games, sing songs around a campfire, and generally have fun. But the Maine coast is also home to several camps that are important in the history of ornithology, bird study, and conservation.

Camp Chewonki in Wiscasset, established in 1918 as a private nature-based camp, is now one of the best-known and best-loved environmental education programs in the country. Its most famous ornithological connection came in 1928 when camp founder Clarence Allen found himself without his regular nature counselor. He invited a young man named Roger Tory Peterson to come as the replacement, but Peterson had no way to get there. Legend has it that Peterson sent a telegram to Allen saying that, if Allen wanted him there, he needed to send Peterson $39.50 for a train ticket. Allen took a

leap of faith and was glad he did. Peterson worked at the camp over the next five years while painting and writing his now famous *Field Guide to the Birds*, which catapulted the hobby and sport of birding into a national pastime.

Over in Muscongus Bay near Damariscotta, the Hog Island Audubon Camp has continued to be a mecca for bird and nature enthusiasts (primarily adults) since it was established in 1936. In fact, Peterson also figured prominently there, as he was Hog Island's first birdlife instructor. Other prominent ornithologists who worked at the camp in those early years included pioneering bird photographers Allan and Helen Cruickshank and Donald Borror, a noted sound recordist from Ohio State University (and father of Appledore Island ornithologist Arthur Borror). In the years since, many of the most well-known figures in bird conservation and ornithology have either been instructors at Hog Island or got their start there as participants or interns. These include Project Puffin founder Steve Kress, Kenn Kaufman, Sara Morris, Scott Weidensaul, and Peter Vickery, among many others.

JVW

have been sustained by dedicated Maine birders, all volunteers, as *Maine Bird Life* and then *Maine Bird Notes*, arising and ceasing with the time and energies of volunteer compilers.

Our understanding of the distribution of Maine breeding birds took a critical step forward with the *Atlas of the Breeding Birds of Maine 1977–1983*. Compiled by Paul Adamus in 1987, and guided by a volunteer committee, it reflects countless thousands of hours of systematic observations contributed by more than 300 participants.

Continuing in the tradition of all-volunteer, unsponsored initiatives, the Maine Bird Records Committee (ME-BRC) was formed in 2005 to maintain an accurate record and historical archive of the state's birdlife. A nine-member committee was established and, in its first years, the committee produced the first official state bird list, developed a voting protocol, established a system for records circulation and retention, rotating terms, and methods for nomination of members to the committee. ME-

BRC continues to curate records of unusual bird sightings and maintain an up-to-date official list of bird species that have occurred in the state. It has also become a key online repository of documentation, a photo archive, and a point of access for Maine ornithological publications.

Just as the tradition of identifying birds by shooting them and examining specimens in hand gave way to observation with field guides and increasingly sophisticated optical equipment, the documentation and dissemination of bird records has undergone a comparable paradigm shift with the advent of eBird. This web-based platform, a joint project of the National Audubon Society and the Cornell Lab of Ornithology, started as a way for birders to track their own sightings through standardized checklists, share them with others, and gain access to what others were seeing. From there, it has evolved into one of the world's largest biodiversity-related citizen science projects, with more than 100 million bird sightings contributed each year by eBirders around the world. eBird does not, by itself, provide information on population sizes or breeding status; other forms of systematic observation like the Breeding Bird Survey, Christmas Bird Count, and hawkwatches are still essential. But the eBird platform is a critical tool for collecting and making available large volumes of distributional data and is the perfect site for data entry and access for the second Maine Bird Atlas effort, underway during publication of this volume. While there is no substitute for careful observations of bird behavior and habitat, as exemplified by the Maine field ornithologists of the past century, they would have found modern eBird an indispensable treasure trove.

BANDING ON APPLEDORE ISLAND

The Appledore Island Migration Station (AIMS), Maine's longest continuously running banding station, was founded in the 1970s.

It expanded into full-season fall migration monitoring in 1981, and the same for spring migration in 1990. As a long-term, constant-effort mist-netting site, the banding station has a goal of providing high-quality research that will increase the understanding of the ecology of migrant birds and improve conservation efforts on their behalf. Since 1981, the research crew has banded more than 130,000 birds on the island.

AIMS initially focused on the migration timing and stopover ecology of Nearctic-Neotropical migrants. Among the early results from the station was documentation of major differences in the stopover ecology of migrants between spring and fall migration. On Appledore, birds were more likely to be recaptured at least one day after initial capture, stay for more days, and gain more weight during fall migration than during spring migration. The station demonstrated that birds that lost mass in an experimental study had an increased likelihood of recapture in the fall, further supporting the importance of stopover sites for foraging and weight gain by migrants. Additionally, in a study of departure decisions by migrants in the spring, lean birds were more likely to remain on the island while fatter birds were more likely to initiate migratory flight.

Beyond its initial work, AIMS has contributed to a number of other studies related to migration and migratory birds. Because the station has been in operation for almost four decades, Appledore's

capture data have been used to investigate changes in the timing of migration across years, showing that spring migration is becoming earlier in Maine. In a study that compared the Appledore results to those obtained on Star Island, just a mile away, species distributions and stopover ecology varied between the two islands, reflecting differences in vegetation (Appledore has higher, denser vegetation, while Star's vegetation is lower, and the island has more open areas). Interestingly, despite more than 10,000 birds banded in that particular study, only 42 were found to have moved between the islands, suggesting strong habitat selection at the end of migratory flights. Studies of the effects of a residential wind turbine on birds found limited mortality among songbirds and seabirds and behavioral avoidance of the turbine by birds in the area. In conjunction with researchers at the Maine Medical Center, AIMS has also shown that birds have contributed to the expansion of Lyme disease by moving ticks that carry the disease-causing bacteria from other locations.

As part of its normal operation, the station has also captured (and thus documented) a number of rare species in Maine, including Chuck-will's-widows, Painted Buntings, Summer Tanagers, and Cerulean Warblers. The AIMS research team continues to work on projects that further our knowledge of migration and that find additional uses for the dataset it has amassed.
Sara Morris

Chronology of Maine Bird Record Publications

(In addition to Knight 1908; Brewster, 1924, 1925, 1937, and Griscom 1938; Palmer 1949; Adamus 1987)

1899–1911	***Journal of Maine Ornithological Society*** (*JMOS*), vols. 1–13*.
1921–1930	***The Maine Naturalist*** (*TMN*), vols. 1–10.
1945–1955	***Bulletin of Maine Audubon Society*** (*BMAS*), vols. 1–11, ed. by C. Packard.
1956–1961	***Maine Field Observer*** (*MFO*), formerly *BMAS*, vols. 1–6, ed. by C. Packard.
1956–1963	records published in ***Maine Field Naturalist*** (*MFN*), vols. 12–17(1, 2), 18(1–12), 19(1–8), 20(1); the latter, published in Jan 1964, covered bird records of Dec 1963.
1964	No bird records for this year were published in Maine journals.
1965	Jun–Nov records in *MFN* vol. 21(1-6); Jan–May and Dec 1965 records not published.
1966	Jan–Jul records in *MFN* 22(1–8); Aug–Oct records not published; Nov–Dec 1966 records in *NMAS*, see below. (1968–1971 *MFN* continued, but vols. 24–27 no longer included bird notes.)
Nov 1966–Dec 1969	***Newsletter of Maine Audubon Society*** (*NMAS*), ed. by C. Packard.
Jul 1969–Aug 1973	***Maine Nature*** (*MN*); published by C. Packard as part of newly created Audubon Naturalist Council, after Packard's departure from Maine Audubon Society. (It appears that the first issue of *MN* was Jul 1969 [vol. 1(1)], which probably had Jun 1969 records that were possibly also included in *NMAS*. Jul 1969 bird records appeared in the second issue of *MN* [*MN* vol. 1(2)].)
1972–present	***Guillemot*** has a continuous run. This publication has been the single-handed effort of Bill Townsend (W.C. Townsend) as a publication of the Sorrento Scientific Society, covering everything from astronomy to insects, herptiles, mammals, and birds. Its coverage is skewed to the Downeast part of Maine, whereas all others listed here are statewide.
1973–1974	No Maine publication that documented bird records other than *Guillemot*.
Jan 1975–Jan 1981	***Maine Audubon News*** *(MAN)* included a Field Notes page for at least the first several years.
1978–Dec 1978	Only records appeared in ***Maine Bird Life*** (*MBL*, aka *Maine Birdlife*).
1979–May 1985	***Maine Bird Life*** *(MBL)**.
Jun 1985–Feb 1987	No records other than those in *Guillemot*.
Mar 1987–Mar 2000	***Maine Bird Notes*** *(MBN)**. Last issue, 11(1).

There are also Maine Audubon Society Field Cards (MASFC) from 1951, 1955, 1957–1961, 1963–1967, and 1969–1972.

Chronology of Regional and National Publications

1945–1968	***Records of New England Birds*** (*RNEB*), vols. 1–24.
1950–1970	***Audubon Field Notes*** (*AFN*), vols. 1–24.
1971–1994	***American Birds*** (*AB*, incorporating *AFN* and continuing volume numbers).
1994–1999	***Field Notes*** (*FN*, incorporating *AB*).
1999–present	***North American Birds*** (*NAB*, incorporating *Field Notes*).
2007–2018	Reports of the Maine Bird Records Committee began appearing in ***Bird Observer*** in 2007 with the first report (*Bird Observer* 35[3]: 155–158) and continuing at least through 2018 with the 7th report.

**Journal of Maine Ornithological Society, Maine Bird Notes,* and many issues of *Maine Bird Life* are available on ME-BRC website.

MAINE'S FIRST REBORN RIVER

One of the nation's first successful river restoration projects took place in Maine with stunning implications for bird populations.

Edwards Dam was built in 1837 at the head-of-tide on the Kennebec River in Augusta. For the next 162 years, the dam stopped a migration cycle that had been part of the river's lifeblood for thousands of years. The dam created a wall in the faces of teeming millions of fish trying to spawn in upstream rivers, lakes, and ponds. These fish descended downriver as juveniles, spent years in the ocean feeding and growing into adults, before returning upriver during spring migration, ready to start a new generation. It's hard to imagine the impact this had, not only on fish-eating birds suddenly with millions fewer fish available to them, but also on the entire aquatic ecosystem that was abruptly deprived of the annual flush of ocean nutrients swept up from the sea by masses of Alewives (*Alosa pseudoharengus*), Atlantic Salmon (*Salmo salar*), American Shad, (*Alosa sapidissima*), and other sea-run migrant fish.

After many years of unwavering pressure from a coalition of conservation groups (American Rivers, Atlantic Salmon Federation, Natural Resources Council of Maine, and Trout Unlimited), the Federal Energy Regulatory Commission ruled that the environmental benefits of removing Edwards Dam outweighed the economic benefits of maintaining what was then an old and inefficient facility. This ruling is historic—the first of its kind in the U.S., setting in motion removal of the dam. More than a thousand people lined the banks of the Kennebec River on July 1, 1999, to celebrate as the dam was breached.

After that day, thousands of fish that had gathered at the base of the dam each year, following an ancient tug compelling them to swim farther upriver, were at last able to fulfill that primal instinct to find the spawning grounds of their ancestors. Just like that, a vast area of breeding habitat blocked from sea-run fish for so many years was part of the ecosystem again.

The results have astounded even the most optimistic conservationists. In 2011, more than three million Alewives were counted passing through the upstream fish-elevator in Benton; by 2018 that reached a mind-boggling five million. Birders began seeing a difference in the numbers of fish-eating birds even earlier. For decades, it was hard to find a Bald Eagle along the Kennebec between Augusta and Gardiner at any time of year. Within a few years after the dam removal, I stood on the banks of the Kennebec near the boat landing in Hallowell one June morning and, in one sweep of the binoculars, counted eight Bald Eagles, 10 Ospreys, eight Great Blue Herons, 20 Double-crested Cormorants, and dozens of Herring and Ring-billed Gulls enjoying the newfound bounty of fish. In 2014, biologists counted an astounding 58 Bald Eagles along a stretch of the Sebasticook River where fish once again migrate as the result of a second dam removal upriver on the Kennebec.

Today, the river teems with fish-eating birds. Each year in March thousands of Common Mergansers use the river as a staging area before migrating farther north to breed. From April through June, Bald Eagles; Ospreys; Great Blue Herons; Double-crested Cormorants; and Herring, Ring-billed, and Great Black-backed Gulls can be seen pursuing, catching, eating, or fighting over the abundant Alewives. Lakes, ponds, and streams are less algae-filled as migratory fish and their young feed, taking up excess phosphorus and carrying it to the ocean when they return to the sea. Now, there are abundant hatches of aquatic insects crucial to early-returning food-stressed migrant birds such as Tree and Barn Swallows, Eastern Phoebes, and Palm and Yellow-rumped Warblers.

This remarkable river restoration was repeated on New England's second largest river system, the Penobscot, with the removal of two dams, a bypass on a third, and a fish lift completed in 2016 on a fourth. This had similarly astonishing results, passing 1.2 million river herring, including Alewives, in 2017.

JVW

The Gulf of Maine is warming faster than almost all other saltwater bodies on Earth (Pershing et al. 2015), as well as experiencing high levels of ocean acidification, with profound implications for birds, discussed in greater detail below. The Gulf also suffers from rising levels of contaminants and sediments, and the spread of invasive species. The Gulf of Maine Council on the Marine Environment has highlighted sewage, land-based nutrients, and mercury as the three contaminant issues of greatest concern in the Gulf, but there are many more, and very little is known about their potential impacts on birds. Mercury has been found at high and increasing levels in a number of marine birds in Maine: Common Eiders, Leach's Storm-Petrels, Black Guillemots, and Double-crested Cormorants (Stenhouse et al. 2018). Excessive levels of nutrients, especially nitrogen, phosphorus, and dissolved organic matter, cause algal blooms and oxygen depletion that degrade coastal ecosystems and habitats. Important sources of these nutrients include agricultural lands, sewage treatment plants, paper mill effluent, and suburban and urban runoff (Cawley et al. 2012, Liebman et al. 2012). While best-known for causing closures of shellfish harvests and beaches, nutrient overloads and algal blooms also render these ecosystems less able to support healthy populations of birds and other wildlife. A 2012 assessment found that seven of 12 estuaries along the Maine coast showed moderate to high levels of problem indicators related to algal blooms (Liebman et al. 2012).

Recently, the ubiquitous presence of plastics in the world's oceans has been in the spotlight. Plastic containers and packaging account for the majority of the world's marine pollution, which has increased tenfold since 1980, according to a recent Intergovernmental Science-Policy Platform on Biodiversity and Ecosystem Services report (IPBES 2019). When these and many other household products break down into microparticles, they are ingested by virtually every marine organism. Shaw Marine and Environmental Research Institute, based in Blue Hill, found an average of 177 pieces of microplastic in each Blue Mussel (*Mytilus edulis*) they examined in 2014. We have little idea as yet of what impact this has on survival and reproduction of mussels and the species that eat them, but the fact that such plastics, when ingested, bring with them a load of additional toxins makes this worrisome.

Given Maine's rich coastal bird heritage and the substantial changes underway as a result of climate change, actions to identify, abate, or adapt to these threats and their underlying sources must be a high priority for governments, partnering with nonprofit conservation organizations and informed by appropriate research institutions.

Pesticide and Pollution Impacts

It is difficult to estimate the impact of pesticides and contaminant pollution on birds. Only a handful of the tens of thousands of synthetic chemicals in use around the world have been investigated for their effect on birds or other living things. We do know from experience that unintended impacts can be disastrous. However, there are few studies that specifically link chemical pollutants to bird health.

As noted earlier, nitrogen and phosphorus pollution have resulted in the degradation of some lakes, ponds, rivers, estuaries, intertidal, and nearshore marine habitats in Maine. Mercury, produced by industrial sources (especially coal-fired power plants and incinerators), continues to be an issue in the Northeast U.S., including Maine, where a number of bird species, such as Common Loon and Rusty Blackbird, carry some of the highest levels of mercury ever recorded in those species (Evers et al. 2007, Evers et al. 2011). In Maine's lower Penobscot River watershed, mercury contamination as the result of an industrial chemical plant operating there from 1967 to 2000 continues to be evident in the environment and in many bird species (Sullivan and Kopec 2018, Kopec et al. 2018).

The fight to ban DDT is a benchmark in environmental history, but more than 40 years later, DDT and its breakdown products continue to show up in the bodies of birds. Meanwhile, the volume of pesticides (including herbicides, insecticides, and fungicides, as well as the incorporation of insecticides into crop plant genes) used globally has climbed dramatically. In Maine there has been no publicly available tracking of pesticide use and sales since 1995, although it is estimated that more than 200,000 acres of Maine crops are treated with pesticides each year (Jennings 2004). Tens of thousands of acres of commercial forest are sprayed annually and pesticide application is likely to increase if the coming Spruce Budworm outbreak intensifies. Recent studies have found that agricultural pesticide use may explain much of the loss in the number of grassland birds in the U.S. (Mineau and Whiteside 2013, Stanton et al. 2018). Sublethal effects from pesticides and pollutants, which sicken but do not immediately kill birds (thus indirectly increasing mortality rates and lowering reproductive success), are only beginning to be studied (Stanton et al. 2018).

While much of the focus on pesticide effects on birds deals with direct impacts, the real story may be the catastrophic effects these chemicals have on the food chains that support birds. Massive declines in insect abundance and diversity, especially of flying insects, are now being documented around the world (Hallman et al. 2017, Lister and Garcia 2018, Sánchez-Bayo and Wyckhuys 2019). These declines are thought to be the

Land Conservation and Bird Habitat

Maintaining large areas of the habitats birds depend upon to breed, feed, and rest in migration and winter is the most important conservation action we can take on their behalf. Ensuring the continuation of large unfragmented areas of natural habitat will also support resilience to impacts from a changing climate and other human perturbations.

While not specifically focused on birds, land conservation efforts have made significant gains in Maine in recent decades, protecting habitat that supports literally millions of birds. Early 20th century land conservation milestones in the state include the donation of lands that became Maine's first state park (Aroostook State Park), Acadia National Park, Baxter State Park, and acquisitions of the first national wildlife refuge in the state (Moosehorn) in 1937. Despite these benchmarks, the proportion of Maine's land base in conservation remained relatively minor—less than 250,000 acres (100,000 ha), or about one percent of the state—until the late 1980s (Irland 2018). Investigative journalist Bob Cummings revealed in 1972 that Maine still held ownership rights to

---

Both MDIFW and USFWS are part of the **Gulf of Maine Seabird Working Group** (GOMSWG), a collaborative partnership among state and federal agencies, national and state Audubon organizations, universities, non-governmental organizations, and private citizens from Canada to Massachusetts that monitors, manages, and restores populations of colonial nesting seabirds in the Gulf of Maine. GOMSWG includes private organizations such as **Maine Audubon** and **National Audubon's Seabird Restoration Program** (including **Project Puffin**), which provides on-the-ground staff for management of many island seabird and wading bird colonies.

Maine Audubon is contracted by MDIFW to provide on-the-ground staff to monitor and protect endangered beach-nesting Piping Plovers and Least Terns, and to monitor migrating shorebirds. The organization conducts an annual survey of loons on Maine lakes through hundreds of volunteers. Maine Audubon also identifies, maps, and describes Important Bird Areas in the state; promotes forest management "with birds in mind" through its Forestry for Maine Birds program; hosts birding field trips and educational programs for the public on bird identification, ecology, and conservation; engages the public in citizen science projects, including the Breeding Bird Atlas; and provides advocacy to the Maine legislature and other decision-makers on various bird conservation matters.

The Natural Resources Council of Maine advocates for public policies that address the major issues impacting bird populations, including climate change, pollution and toxins, land-use planning, river restoration, wetlands protection and water quality.

Biodiversity Research Institute is a private research group based in Maine that does research on birds around the globe. Most relevant to Maine is its extensive research on mercury contamination in loons and tracking select marine birds.

Sporting groups, such as **Sportsman's Alliance of Maine**, **Ruffed Grouse Society**, **Wild Turkey Federation**, and **Ducks Unlimited**, educate their members and the public about game birds and waterfowl. They also advocate for and sometimes undertake habitat conservation and management projects for these species.

Universities and colleges: Most University of Maine branches and private colleges in Maine have at least one professor who is actively engaged in bird research.

Conserved Lands: Federally protected lands in Maine include National Wildlife Refuges, White Mountain National Forest, Acadia National Park, the Appalachian Trail corridor, and Katahdin Woods and Waters National Monument. Maine's public lands are owned and managed by the **Bureau of Parks and Lands** (currently within the Maine Department of Agriculture, Conservation and Forestry), **MDIFW**, and the **Baxter State Park Authority**. In addition, private organizations such as **The Nature Conservancy**, **Maine Coast Heritage Trust**, **Forest Society of Maine**, and **more than 70 local and regional land trusts** own fee and conservation easements on thousands of parcels. Some towns also own land. Together, these public and private agencies protect more than three million acres that provide essential habitat for Maine's breeding birds and migrants.

BSV

hundreds of thousands of acres set aside for public use when Maine was still part of Massachusetts. These lots were essentially forgotten and treated as private forest lands after the state granted one-time harvest rights to private timbering operations circa 1870. A lawsuit in the 1970s, and further negotiations in the 1980s, culminated in the consolidation of 600,000 acres (250,000 ha) into today's Public Lots.

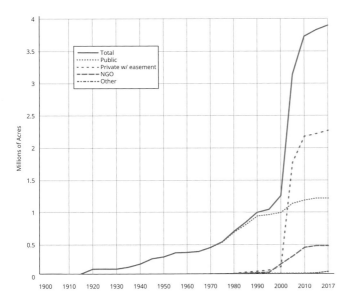

Figure 2. Progress in Land Protection

Conserved land in Maine increased dramatically with the advent of large easements on private land, 2000–2010. The timeline does not include approximately 9% of acreage for which we have no year of protection. Adapted from Lilieholm et al. (2013).

One of the most significant land conservation initiatives in Maine history has been the Lands for Maine's Future (LMF) program, established in 1987. Funded by a series of voter-approved bonds, LMF awards grants to land trusts, nonprofits, and municipalities to purchase or secure easements on the most important conservation and recreational lands. To date, the LMF program has protected more than 591,000 acres (239,000 ha) by providing $132 million (Irland 2018, Land Conservation Task Force 2019). These and other funding sources, including the federal Forest Legacy Program, federal Land and Water Conservation Fund, and private philanthropic donations, have allowed nonprofits to purchase fee title or easements for 2.2 million acres (890,00 ha) of conservation lands. As of 2018, there were 930,400 acres (376,500 ha) of fully protected land (4.7 percent of Maine's land area), including designated ecological

reserves on public land (see Map 8 p. 65). Another 3.2 million acres (1.3 million ha, 16.1 percent of Maine) are public conservation land or private land covered by easements that typically allow forestry and recreational uses but prevent most forms of development and natural resource extraction (TNC data).

However, southern Maine counties, where development threats are highest, have the smallest percentage of their land base in conservation (Irland 2018); the combined 11 southernmost counties having only 8 percent in conservation status. Aroostook County, on the other hand, has 17 percent of its land base in conservation—although only 3 percent is in strictly protected reserves (S. Meyer, pers. com.). Maine's more than 75 land trusts are increasingly important in land protection efforts, especially in southern and coastal areas that have already experienced the greatest loss and are expected to bear the brunt of development in the coming decades (Lilieholm et al. 2013, Meyer et al. 2014). In 2019, a land conservation coalition recommended increased land conservation efforts in Maine, including the issuance of a $75 million bond to further support the Land for Maine's Future program (Land Conservation Task Force 2019).

These are important steps in the right direction, but recent science suggests the key to maintaining biodiversity is maintaining 40–80 percent of the landscape in natural, intact condition (Noss et al. 2012, International Boreal Conservation Science Panel 2013, Carlson et al. 2015, Wilson 2016, Dinerstein et al. 2017). The U.N. Convention on Biodiversity has a 2020 benchmark that all signatory nations protect at least 17 percent of their lands. The U.N. is advocating for a new 2030 treaty benchmark to protect at least 30 percent of land. Clearly, more land conservation is needed in Maine, especially in southern and coastal parts of the state.

Map 8: *Conserved Lands*

More than 20 percent of Maine is protected from development by fee ownership or conservation easement held by federal, state, municipal, or private nonprofit entities (bright green). Forest harvesting is permitted on roughly 80 percent of this land. (Data: Maine Department of Agriculture, Conservation and Forestry.)

Christmas Bird Count Annual Trend Estimates (continued)

Species Name	1966-2017 Trend (%)	2007-2017 Trend (%)
Black Guillemot	2.2	2.5
White-breasted Nuthatch	2.0	7.3
Red-breasted Nuthatch	1.8	5.0
Red-throated Loon	1.7	2.0
Brown Creeper	1.3	3.0
Black-capped Chickadee	1.1	1.7
Blue Jay	1.0	9.3
Hairy Woodpecker	1.0	3.6
Golden-crowned Kinglet	0.7	-10.8
Northern Shrike	0.7	9.6
Downy Woodpecker	0.4	2.2
American Tree Sparrow	0.4	6.9
Common Raven	-0.8	-0.7
Yellow-rumped Warbler	-1.4	-15.2
Northern Goshawk	-1.4	-1.8
Horned Grebe	-1.6	-1.5
Glaucous Gull	-1.9	-1.8
Ruffed Grouse	-1.9	-4.0
Barrow's Goldeneye	-2.0	-3.9
Dovekie	-2.2	-49.5
Common Goldeneye	-2.2	-2.2
Great Cormorant	-2.7	-2.0
House Sparrow	-3.0	1.5
Pine Grosbeak	-3.2	76.4
Herring Gull	-3.4	-3.4
Canada Jay	-4.1	-4.7
Greater Scaup	-4.3	-6.7
Great Black-backed Gull	-4.4	-6.2
Fox Sparrow	-5.1	3.2
King Eider	-5.8	-5.8
American Kestrel	-6.3	-6.5
Red-winged Blackbird	-6.4	-3.9
White-winged Crossbill	-6.7	-31.9
Common Grackle	-7.5	-7.7
Boreal Chickadee	-8.2	-5.5
Evening Grosbeak	-8.3	67.4
Ring-necked Pheasant	-8.3	-9.2
Brown-headed Cowbird	-17.8	-18.2
Increasing significantly	19	25
Decreasing significantly	23	12

Major Historical Events Relevant To Maine Birds

Time Period	Conservation/Societal Activities	Habitat Condition/Change	Major Changes in Bird Populations
Pre-European Settlement	Native American hunting, fishing, small-scale agriculture, and burning.		
1600s	Subsistence hunting by Wabanaki. First European settlers. Wabanaki population decimated by diseases brought by Europeans.	Small scale forest clearing. Egging on coastal islands.	?
1700s	Widespread colonization of southern Maine. Hunting increases.	More forest clearing. First minor dams for small mills.	?
1800–1865	Maine becomes a state (1820). Northern townships surveyed; beginning of industrialization. Market hunting for waterfowl and upland birds. Portland Society of Natural History founded (1843).	Peak of agricultural clearing in southern Maine.	Extinction of Great Auk. Decline of waterfowl.
1865–1900	Railroad to northern Maine. Journal of Portland Society of Natural History begun (1864). Rumford and Millinocket paper mills open. Boom in river dam construction. Hunting season on caribou closed (1899).	Forestland acreage reaches lowest point (1872, 64% of state). Extensive fires in northern Maine. Switch from pine to spruce-fir for pulp production. Growth of agriculture in Aroostook Co. Southern Maine farmland begins to revert to shrub and forestland. Access to spawning grounds for most anadromous fish effectively blocked.	Extinction of Labrador Duck, Heath Hen, and Passenger Pigeon. Continued decline of waterfowl and many other bird species due to hunting for food and millinery trade.
1900–1950	Passage of Migratory Bird Treaty Act (1918). Establishment of National Audubon Society (1905), White Mountain National Forest, Acadia National Park, and Baxter State Park created. Growth of pulp and paper industry. Palmer's *Maine Birds* published (1949).	Acadia National Park (1916), Baxter State Park (1931), and Moosehorn NWR (1937) established. Marketable volume in Maine forests at lowest point (1933). Extensive fires in southern Maine and on Mount Desert I.	Recovery of waterfowl. Bald eagle population at lowest point due to DDT.
1950–1970	Maine Chapter of The Nature Conservancy (1951), Natural Resources Council of Maine (1959). PSNH and Maine Audubon merge (1961). Most Maine Christmas Bird Counts initiated. Rachel Carson's *Silent Spring* published (1962).	Suburbanization of southern and coastal Maine begins. Rachel Carson NWR established (1966). Advent of factory trawlers in offshore waters leads to high discard of small fish by-catch.	Reintroduction of Canada Goose. Increase in gull populations.

Major Historical Events Relevant To Maine Birds (continued)

Time Period	Conservation/Societal Activities	Habitat Condition/Change	Major Changes in Bird Populations
1970–1980	First Earth Day (1970); federal Clean Water Act, DDT banned (1972); federal Endangered Species Act (1973). River log drives end (1975). Maine Non-Game program initiated. Atlas of Breeding Birds of Maine (1978–1983). Settlement of Indian Lands Claim and Public Lots cases lead to consolidation of northern forest ownerships and public lands.	North woods road network developed. Spruce Budworm outbreak 1976–1981, with salvage clear-cuts in response. Prohibition of untreated discharge from towns and food processing plants. Continued development and fragmentation in southern Maine.	Recovery of Bald Eagles and Peregrine Falcons. Re-establishment of Atlantic Puffins. Wild Turkeys reintroduced. Population spike of some boreal budworm specialists.
1980–2000	Land for Maine's Future funding established (1987). Break-up of some forest products companies, separation of mills and land. Advent of timber investment by corporate owners with shorter time horizons. Significant land conservation. Forest Practices Act passed (1999).	End of clear-cutting; shift in forest practices. Decline in spruce-fir area following budworm salvage harvests. Decline in old age class in northern forest due to harvests. Municipal open-burning dumps closed. 200-mile (320 km) offshore fishing limit enforced; end of foreign factory ships, reduction in by-catch; advent of domestic mid-water trawlers focused on herring. West Nile virus first detected in Maine birds. Conservation land comprises 4.1% of state (1987).	Red-necked Phalarope crash in Passamaquoddy Bay. Recovery of Piping Plovers, terns; decline in Herring and Great Black-backed Gull populations, Purple Martin colonies.
2000–present	Dams removed on Kennebec and Penobscot rivers. Bald Eagles removed from federal Endangered Species list (2009).	Percent of forestland reaches near pre-settlement levels but sawlog harvest drops precipitously. Decline in spruce-fir acreage and patch size. Increased access by anadromous fish to spawning grounds, with 100-fold increase in Alewives. Warming of the Gulf of Maine documented. Conservation land grows to >20% of the state by 2018.	Bald Eagle population booms; Great Blue Herons, Great Cormorants, Common Eiders decline. Ospreys move inland. Impacts on boreal breeding birds from changes in forest practices unknown. Carolina Wrens, Red-bellied Woodpeckers expand north. Canada Goose population expands to nuisance levels. Wild Turkeys expand to northern border of Maine.

Table 6. *Timeline of Maine's history as related to the state's bird life and conservation.*

5
Introduction to Species Accounts

We include accounts for each of the 464 species documented as having occurred in Maine as of 1 January 2019, which comprise the official list of the Maine Bird Records Committee (ME-BRC). These include species now extinct or extirpated. We also include accounts for 13 species whose occurrence in Maine is considered hypothetical by ME-BRC or are failed introductions. Names and taxonomic sequence follow the American Ornithological Society's *Check-list of North American Birds* (American Ornithologists' Union [AOU], 7th edition, 1998) as amended through the 60th supplement (July 2019). For those species with relatively recent name changes, former names are noted.

The geographic boundaries of this book follow those of the state of Maine. However, we include sightings from Gulf of Maine offshore waters without respect to state versus federal jurisdiction; from Isles of Shoals, although Star Island in that archipelago is in New Hampshire; from Machias Seal Island, which is claimed by both Canada and the U.S. (see sidebar: Who Owns Machias Seal Island?, p. 29); from Lake Umbagog, straddling the New Hampshire border; and from the St. Croix River, which forms a section of the Maine and New Brunswick boundary.

Species Account Outline

A brief overview of the bird families represented in Maine's avifauna is followed by species accounts for that family. Each species account includes the following sections:

Status in Maine: Summarizes the species' current distribution and abundance in Maine and serves as an abstract for the account as a whole. We use the abundance and frequency of occurrence terms currently used by the American Birding Association:

Rare: Occurs in low numbers but annually.

Casual: Not recorded annually but with six or more total records, including three in the last 30 years, reflecting a pattern of regular occurrence.

Accidental: Five or fewer records in Maine or fewer than three in the last 30 years.

Maine Conservation Status: This section is included if the species is listed as endangered, threatened, or a species of special concern by the Maine Department of Inland Fisheries and Wildlife (MDIFW).

Historical Status in Maine: Summarizes what we know of the species from Palmer's (1949) and Knight's (1908) comprehensive surveys of Maine birds and other historical sources relevant to the species' Maine residence, breeding or migratory status, abundance, distribution, and arrival and departure dates. In the case of species that experienced significant population changes in the years after Palmer was published, this section also summarizes records from 1950 to modern times. Unless otherwise noted, all references to Palmer and Knight in the species accounts are to the 1949 and 1908 publications.

Global Distribution: Leads with the broad zoogeographic region, such as Cosmopolitan, Holarctic, Nearctic, Neotropical, or Palearctic, and provides a thumbnail sketch of breeding and wintering distribution. This section is also where the existence of other subspecies may be noted.

Global Conservation Status: Status is only included if the species carries a status above "least concern" by global and national standards, including International Union for Conservation of Nature (IUCN), U.S. Fish and Wildlife Service (USFWS), Endangered Species Act (ESA), Partners In Flight (PIF), U.S. Shorebird Conservation Plan (USSCP, 2nd ed.; Brown et al. 2001), and North American Waterbird Conservation Plan (NAWCP; Kushlan et al. 2002).

facing page: Razorbills

Remarks: Does not appear in every account and is often anecdotal. In some cases, additional material of interest is in an associated text box.

Seasonal records: We have generally assigned records from March, April, and May to spring; June, July, and August to summer; September, October, and November to fall; and December, January, and February to winter. However, the months included in the season may differ among species; in cases of some migrants through Maine, such as many shorebirds, the migration seasons do not neatly correspond to astronomical divisions of seasons and may more appropriately be thought of as northbound and southbound migration records. Except for accidental or casual visitors, in which case all relevant sightings are included, the seasonal records are not intended to be comprehensive but rather to provide examples to illustrate general patterns of distribution, abundance by season, and trends over time. Each spring section generally begins with arrival dates, then goes to maxima, both organized regionally. Summer describes breeding range in the state, if relevant, and often includes abundance and trends indicated by Breeding Bird Surveys (BBS; referencing Sauer et al. 2017 unless noted otherwise) or MDIFW surveys. Fall follows a similar pattern as spring, starting with arrivals, build-up, and then departures of migrants, in chronological order. Winter includes records of overwintering, and frequency and maxima on Christmas Bird Counts (CBC, Sauer et al. 1996, National Audubon-maintained website [netapp.audubon.org/cbcobservation]).

With rare exceptions, we include records only through 31 December 2018.

Both town and county are usually cited for observation localities; however, for places cited frequently, town or county may be omitted, and the reader is referred to the regional maps on pages xviii–xxi and the list in Appendix 1. For coastal locations and especially islands, see endpapers. Note that those islands shown in red are locations of coastal seabird nesting colonies. These are also shown on Map 18 with accompanying table on page 280. Readers will notice some localities are cited much more often than others. This uneven representation may be due to an actual frequency of birds, or to a concentration of birders (and thus records). Reports from some localities are included because of a long history of regular observation in that place allowing for comparison over time. Lake Umbagog serves that purpose in western Maine

because of William Brewster's careful and consistent observations there from 1871 to 1909 (Brewster 1924, 1925, 1937, and Griscom 1938). There have been decades of bird banding on Appledore Island by David Holmes, Sara Morris, and others. Monhegan Island is cited frequently because of its high rate of vagrant sightings; it is a well-known migrant trap that attracts many birders, especially in fall and, with such consistent observation effort, records cover many decades (see Monhegan Island sidebar page 82). Scarborough Marsh, the state's largest salt marsh and also within easy flight distance of Maine's primary wading bird colonies, is a critical place for many resident, migrant, and accidental coastal birds. For this reason, and also its proximity to population centers on the southern Maine coast, it attracts many observers year after year. Seawall Beach in Phippsburg similarly provides a long-running record of shorebirds, particularly because of regular visits by Peter Vickery. Jody Despres' many years of observations in a part of Maine much less birded helped put Turner on our map, and Bill Sheehan's decades of devoted observation of the waterfowl of northern Maine highlight the importance of Lake Josephine and Christina Reservoir (see sidebar, page 90).

Regions of Maine: When distribution is described in the text we use the formal ecoregion name when referring to that specific area of Maine, especially Midcoast or Downeast. See Chapter 2 for a map and descriptions of all ecoregions. However, we frequently use "northern Maine" to encompass Northwest, Aroostook Hills and Lowlands, parts of Central and Western Mountains and Eastern Lowlands regions. Likewise, "eastern Maine" may include parts of Eastern Lowlands as well as Downeast Maine. Central Interior Region is often shortened to "central Maine," and Central and Western Mountains to "western Maine."

Account and Sidebar Authorship: The author of each account is indicated below the account by initials. Unless otherwise noted, blue text boxes were written by the author of the accompanying species account. Co-authors: PDV, Peter D. Vickery; WJS, William J. Sheehan; JVW, Jeffrey V. Wells; CDD, Charles D. Duncan; CSW, C. Scott Weidensaul; BSV, Barbara S. Vickery. Editing and research assistants who drafted accounts: TE, Tamara Enz; RLP, Rachel L. Prestigiacomo; PD, Paul Dougherty; RVJ, Richard V. Joyce; IM, Isaac Merson; HF, Heidi Franklin; IC, Ian Carlsen. Authors of sidebars are similarly indicated, with the addition of Jeremiah Trimble and Sara Morris.

Range Maps

For most species that reach a breeding range limit in Maine, a range map accompanies the account; those breeding species found throughout the state are not mapped. Range maps are are based on data from the *Atlas of Breeding Birds in Maine* 1978–1983 (*ABBM*, Adamus 1987); the first year of the current Maine Bird Atlas (2018–2022) survey effort; Breeding Bird Surveys (BBS); MDIFW records for tracked species; records cited in the account; eBird observations during appropriate breeding months; and the authors' judgment based on personal experience and knowledge of Maine's biogeography. For a few maps, we are indebted to published articles, which are cited in the species account text. A map of the coast on page 280 indicates breeding locations for colonial birds nesting on coastal islands based on information from USFWS and MDIFW. There is also one map of winter distribution: Purple Sandpiper.

Like all maps, these represent approximations and generalizations based on current knowledge. As with any range map, it should be assumed that the bird is only likely to be found breeding within the range indicated in appropriate habitat and season. On some maps, we have further indicated the pattern of distribution within the range. "Local" shows that the species occurs in some but not all appropriate habitats and is usually found in the same localities most years but is not so confined to those few reliable locations that it would warrant using locality dots, as we do for Grasshopper Sparrow, for instance. Species where we use "Local" for all or part of the range include Field Sparrow, Fish Crow, Northern Mockingbird, Red-shouldered Hawk, Northern Rough-winged Swallow, and Vesper Sparrow. We used "Occasional" to indicate that the species occurs within this range spottily and not reliably in the same localities from year to year. The species may not be found even in appropriate habitat. Species for which we use this label include Cooper's Hawk, Eastern Towhee, Indigo Bunting, and House Wren. It should be noted that these maps do not reflect abundance within range. For some birds whose populations in Maine have declined, the maps do not reflect that change because their range within the state remains the same. We have tried to distinguish between confirmed breeding versus breeding season observations (mostly from eBird), which may imply, but do not confirm, breeding. Because the maps reflect range limits, they are likely to change both in the short and long terms. We anticipate results from the ongoing, second Maine Bird Atlas will further improve and update the understanding of both breeding and wintering ranges for many species.

When the information was available, we used it to show changes in the species' range over recent decades. For species whose ranges are expanding, such as Tufted Titmouse, mapping colors are darkest where the species began its expansion and continues to be common, fading to areas most recently colonized. For species with contracting ranges, for example Rusty Blackbird, the colors are darkest where the species currently is found and lighter in previous range extents.

Migration Tracking Maps

We also include maps of migration pathways for a sampling of individual birds tracked using technologies developed in recent decades. These new tracking approaches hugely augment the information we could once glean only through observation and the recapture of banded birds. (see Migration Tracking sidebar on p. 78.) These reveal astonishing feats of migration and the sometimes surprising ways birds link Maine to distant parts of the world.

Sources of Data
(see also History of Maine Ornithology chapter and Works Cited)

Data used for the species accounts come from many sources. For information about the species' global distribution and status beyond Maine we frequently consulted Birds of North America Online. For waterfowl, *Ducks, Geese and Swans of North America* (Baldassarre 2014) was a regular general reference. Regional and national journals that provided Maine occurrence records include *Bulletin of New England Birdlife, Records of New England Birds, Audubon Field Notes, American Birds, Field Notes,* and most recently, *North American Birds*. Since the publication of *Maine Birds* (Palmer 1949), there have been 11 publications devoted to Maine bird records, as well as Field Cards maintained by Maine Audubon Society (see Table 2, p. 41), all of which were thoroughly combed for notable records. We did our best to confirm observer name or volume and page numbers for all records; in the case of journals for which we could find no local archive, and which are not available

TRACKING THE MOVEMENT OF INDIVIDUAL BIRDS

The movement of individual birds has fascinated humans for centuries, and a variety of methods have been developed to track them.

Recent technological developments, especially miniaturization, have allowed significant advances in our understanding of bird migration. Those in modern use are described here in approximate order from oldest to newest.

METAL BANDS: This tracking technique was first used in Denmark in 1899. Researchers place an aluminum band (sometimes called a ring) on a bird's leg. Bands bear an inscribed numerical code and sometimes contact information for reporting if found. The bird must be recovered to read the band (often requiring glasses or a hand lens), making this method best for hunted species and those specifically targeted for recapture. Data from recovered banded birds can tell us the point-to-point travel distance from banding location to recapture site and the length of time since banding. Banding recoveries can sometimes determine a bird's age, but the migration route taken cannot be known from banding data. Banding is still used, even for birds carrying any of the subsequent markers (see American Woodcock map).

MARKED FLAGS: Small, inexpensive plastic leg tags, called flags, make it possible to identify marked birds with a spotting scope or telephoto camera. Fitted around one leg, usually above the "knee" (which is actually the ankle), the tag's background color indicates the country of origin, and a unique 2- or 3-character code identifies the individual. This method is successful with shorebirds, which often return to certain locales in large flocks that are easily scanned. For larger birds such as waterfowl, plastic collars may be used, while gulls, raptors, and other large birds are sometimes marked with wing tags. Observers can report flagged birds at bandedbirds.org to learn where the bird was tagged.

SATELLITE AND GSM TELEMETRY: Platform transmitter terminals (PTTs) are fitted with a harness, in the form of a backpack, or implanted. Communicating with orbiting Argos satellites, PTTs provide latitude and longitude fixes. Some PTTs use a data logger to store data until the bird is recaptured, while others transmit the data via satellite. GSM units communicate through the cellular network, storing data when out of cell range. Device weight should not exceed 3% of the bird's weight; this limitation creates pressure to develop the smallest, lightest PTTs possible. Currently, the most common small solar-powered transmitters weigh 0.34 oz. (9.5 g)–suitable for birds no lighter than a Rock Pigeon or small duck. Newer models weighing half that amount are expanding the possibilities of use (see Harlequin Duck, Great Shearwater, Hudsonian Godwit, Whimbrel, Snowy Owl, and Great Blue Heron maps).

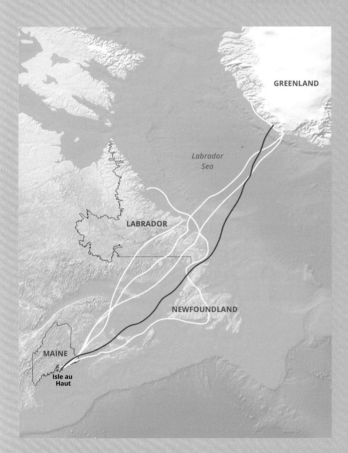

Map 9: Harlequin Duck Migration

Spring migratory routes of four male Harlequin Ducks (yellow) and a fall return migratory route of one of the ducks (red) as tracked by satellite transmitters implanted in the birds at Isle au Haut, ME, in April 2001. Males traveled to the coast of northern Labrador or Greenland in July to molt and remained there through the fall before migrating south again to winter at Isle au Haut (Robert et al. 2008).

LIGHT-SENSITIVE GEOLOCATORS: In a modern version of ancient navigational techniques, small sensors placed on a bird's leg or back record light levels every few minutes. From these data the sunrise and sunset times, and thus daylength, can be determined, allowing calculation of the corresponding latitude. Moreover, since solar noon is midway between sunrise and sunset, the longitude can also be determined. While geolocators are light enough to use on small birds, they do not broadcast data—that requires heavier batteries and additional weight. The data, sometimes several years' worth, are stored onboard, requiring recapture for data retrieval; this is a serious limitation. This method is less precise in constant daylight within the Arctic and Antarctic Circles, on dates near the equinoxes when daylength is 12 hours at all latitudes, and in deep forests. But, as with PTTs, when all goes well we learn the bird's location every day, without any bias from whether the location was visited by human observers (see Arctic Tern, Red-necked Phalarope, and Willet maps).

NANOTAGS: Tiny VHF radio transmitters, weighing as little as 0.01 oz. (0.2 g), can be placed on small birds. A thin antenna broadcasts individually distinctive radio pulse patterns every few seconds. Battery life is typically 60–180 days, and up to three years with larger, heavier tags. For shorebirds, nanotags are generally glued to the back feathers, so are shed when the bird molts (typically twice per year), while most passerines are harnessed with leg loops. Solar-powered nanotags with potentially longer lives are currently being tested and are attached as a harness. For long-distance migrants, which put on prodigious amounts of fat as fuel, it is a challenge to fit a harness for a nanotag or PTT properly. While the cost of a nanotag is similar to that of a geolocator, it has the advantage that the bird need not be recaptured (see "Ipswich" Savannah Sparrow map).

Receivers are as important as transmitters. Researchers participating in the Motus Wildlife Tracking System ("motus" is Latin for "movement") have erected and maintain receiver stations with directional antennae across the Western Hemisphere (Taylor et al. 2017). When a bird is pinged (detected) by any receiver, the data are shared cooperatively across the network. Typical detection range is 10 miles (16 km).

Although by 2019 some 950 receiver sites had been erected, the paucity of receivers poses a significant challenge for tracking birds migrating through remote areas of the Arctic, for example, or the interior of South America. Some towers may be intermittently offline or even removed. Other challenges include relatively low geographic precision unless the signal is simultaneously detected by multiple towers, allowing triangulation; reduced detectability for birds on the ground or in thick vegetation compared to those in flight; and short battery life for units light enough to be put on the smallest birds.
CDD

Map 17: Arctic Tern Migration, Track of Single Bird

The track of a single Arctic Tern (band #21269), one of 14 fitted with geolocators in 2010 by USFWS and National Audubon Society researchers on Eastern Egg Rock and Metinic Island, showing seasonal details. After being tagged, the bird made several lengthy forays to and from the breeding site (green tracks). Then, in late July it began southbound migration (red track), moving down the West African coast and crossing the Atlantic Ocean to the Patagonian Shelf off Uruguay and Argentina before continuing south to the coast of Antarctica where it spent the next five months (shown in blue). The northward trip to its breeding site in the Gulf of Maine took almost two months (yellow). (USFWS, unpublished data).

online, we noted "ref. unk." Peter Vickery relied heavily on his own bird journals as well as those of others, such as Bill Sheehan and Mark Libby. Records from Maine Audubon bird alerts (cited as fide the then-current editor), and more recently the Southern Maine rare bird alert (cited as fide D. Lovitch) were also included. We consulted BBS and CBC records extensively. More recent sightings largely come from eBird. Observations of accidental species are documented by ME-BRC on their website; the reports of their decisions are published in *Bird Observer* and are available through the ME-BRC website. When a sighting was documented photographically and the photo is archived with ME-BRC, it is noted as "ph. archive."

MDIFW data used for several graphs of population trends was gathered with support from federal Pittman-Robertson and State Wildlife Grant programs, USFWS Section 6 funds, Maine Outdoor Heritage Fund, and the Maine Endangered and Nongame Wildlife Fund.

Ultimately, this book is based on the observations of hundreds of birders who kept careful track of what they saw and shared their records with others. The advent of eBird has facilitated and amplified this process of crowd-sourcing and has magnified the benefits to collective knowledge.

Observers cited by initials include the co-authors: Peter D. Vickery, PDV; Charles D. Duncan, CDD; Bill Sheehan, WJS; and Jeff Wells, JVW. Others so cited are Jan Pierson, JEP, and Liz Pierson, ECP, both members of the team that brought this book to publication; and Davis W. Finch, DWF, who, although a New Hampshire resident, earned the abbreviation for the frequency of his contributions to knowledge of Maine's avifauna and the fact that he was Peter Vickery's early mentor and regular birding companion for more than four decades.

Streamside wetlands, where Alder Flycatchers, Swamp Sparrows, and Northern Waterthrushes occur in summer, are typical of northern and Downeast Maine. Old Stream, Washington Co. (©Joshua Royte)

ABBREVIATIONS AND ACRONYMS USED

AB	*American Birds*
ABBM	*Atlas of Breeding Birds of Maine*
AFN	*Audubon Field Notes*
ANP	Acadia National Park
AOS	American Ornithological Society—formerly American Ornithologists' Union (AOU)
BBS	Breeding Bird Survey
BMAS	*Bulletin of Maine Audubon Society*
BoM	*Birds of Maine* (Knight 1908)
BSP	Baxter State Park
CBC	Christmas Bird Count
COA	College of the Atlantic
fide	according to, or reported by
FN	*Field Notes*
HMANA	Hawk Migration Association of North America
ISS	International Shorebird Survey
JMOS	*Journal of Maine Ornithological Society*
KWWNM	Katahdin Woods and Waters National Monument
MAN	*Maine Audubon News*
MASFC	Maine Audubon Society Field Cards
MB	*Maine Birds* (Palmer 1949)
MBL	*Maine Bird Life*
MBN	*Maine Bird Notes*
MCZ	Museum of Comparative Zoology, Harvard University
MDIFW	Maine Department of Inland Fisheries and Wildlife
ME-BRC	Maine Bird Records Committee
MFN	*Maine Field Naturalist*
MFO	*Maine Field Observer*
MN	*Maine Nature*
m.ob.	multiple observers
NAB	*North American Birds*
NAS	National Audubon Society
NAWCP	North American Waterbird Conservation Plan
N.F.	National Forest
NMAS	*Newsletter of Maine Audubon Society*
NWR	National Wildlife Refuge
PIF	Partners In Flight
Plt.	Plantation (a designation of some unorganized towns)
PMNH	Portland Museum of Natural History
RNEB	*Records of New England Birds*
SGCN	Species of Greatest Conservation Need
S.P.	State Park
SWAP	State Wildlife Action Plan
TMN	*The Maine Naturalist*
TNC	The Nature Conservancy
Twp.	Township (a designation of some unorganized towns)
UMaine	University of Maine
unk. ref.	unknown reference
USFWS	U.S. Fish and Wildlife Service
USSCP	U.S. Shorebird Conservation Plan
VCES	Vermont Center for Ecosystem Studies
WMA	Wildlife Management Area of MDIFW

Standard two-letter abbreviations for states and provinces are used. NFLD, as opposed to NL, is used when the species is known to occur in Newfoundland but not in Labrador.

MONHEGAN ISLAND: A MECCA FOR BIRDS AND BIRDERS

Monhegan Island—a speck in the Gulf of Maine, not quite halfway up the coast between Kittery and Lubec—has a long and rich history.

Its fame, in broader circles, is due to its storied fishing culture, particularly lobstering, and the undeniable attraction of its stark beauty and stunning landscapes to artists for more than 200 years. On the low-lying western side of the island, the village, with its homes, yards, trees, and gardens, appears to blend directly into the sea and the surrounding woodlands. On the eastern and northern shores, the formidable headlands rise high out of the ocean and create a constant chorus of crashing waves, an unforgettable landscape.

Perhaps it was these charms that, in 1954, first attracted Tom Martin, a 31-year-old tool-and-die maker from Manhattan, to the island, for it was not known as a birding site. Tom soon began finding bird species thought not to occur regularly in Maine, most famously Clay-colored Sparrow, but his reports were met with skepticism by the New York City birding establishment. Tom's excellent photos soon removed any doubt, and the former skeptics began to visit for themselves. Tom's warmth and enthusiasm endeared him to the islanders and made this curious hobby of birdwatching acceptable. With those same traits, Tom welcomed virtually every birdwatcher who visited during spring or fall over the next six decades of his life, enhancing the island's attractiveness as a destination not only for birds but for birders. His yard became the island's epicenter, not only for birds but also for the dissemination of bird knowledge. Dozens of Tom's photos of birds on Monhegan were published in the Audubon Society field guides of the late 1970s and early 1980s. Many of his photos still hang in The Monhegan Museum, informing visitors to the island of the important place that Monhegan is for birds and birding.

Monhegan's location, 10 miles (16 km) off the coast of Maine, is on the migration route for thousands of migratory songbirds every autumn and spring. Indeed, during parts of May and September, the island's trees, bushes, and rocky beaches seem to overflow with a remarkable variety of migrants.

There are many reasons why Monhegan is so good for both attracting and viewing birds. For landbirds, food, water, and rest are critical to their survival as they undertake monumental migrations. Monhegan offers all of these. The island's position, far enough out to sea (a salty, watery desert for such species), yet close to their normal migratory route, means that it can serve as an important stopover. This is important enough under normal conditions, but in harsh and inclement weather Monhegan becomes a life raft in a turbulent and dangerous sea. Monhegan offers a variety of habitat types that cater to the island's avian diversity, especially in migration, including intertidal beaches, ponds, grassy meadows, marshes, open deciduous woodlands, and deep spruce forests.

Weather is an important factor when considering a birding trip to Monhegan Island, because conditions (especially wind direction) will determine the number of birds that make landfall. In the spring, generally southerly winds, especially with a westerly component, are the best. Northbound migrants get pushed offshore and, with few other options, find Monhegan a suitable stopover. If such conditions are accompanied by low cloud layers or timely precipitation (i.e., after migrants have already started their northward nocturnal flight), there is potential for large numbers of birds to be grounded on Monhegan. In the fall, the weather is generally less critical as southbound migration of passerines (and some raptors) tends to be more coastal than in spring. Still, westerly and northwesterly winds generally deliver more birds to this offshore oasis.

In the spring, Monhegan's many apple trees offer feeding opportunities for warblers, orioles, tanagers, and more. Their white and pink blossoms not only beautifully accent the picturesque village and contrast with the deep evergreen forests that cover most of the island, but also attract numerous insects. In the fall, birds are attracted to these same trees, along with the island's many grasses, wildflowers, and fruiting shrubs that provide food and shelter.

Songbirds are not the only migrants that visit the island. Peregrine Falcons are a famous feature of the island, attracted by the abundant prey and rugged cliffs. Some fall days, 10 or more of these impressive hunters can be seen soaring over the island or dotting the cliffs in search of their next meal. I fondly remember standing on the eastward-facing cliffs of Monhegan one day in

more than 40 species of waterfowl, more than 120 other species of birds have been observed around Christina Reservoir and Lake Josephine. Other uncommon breeders include Northern Harriers, Short-eared Owls, Common Gallinules, American Coots, and Green Herons. Great Horned Owls, Pied-billed Grebes, American Bitterns, and Common Loons also nest. Migrants regularly seen include nearly 20 species of shorebirds, along with Merlins and Peregrine Falcons that prey on these concentrations.

Though the area remains primarily in the control of local industry, public access is allowed. The location has been the setting for a number of environmental and waterfowl habitat studies and hundreds of waterfowl are trapped and banded here annually by the Maine Department of Inland Fisheries and Wildlife. It is exceptional that such a historically, recreationally, and biologically significant location occurred by accident, that it remains accessible to recreationists and researchers, and is available and important to the birds of Maine.

WJS

stubble and harvested potato fields, 22 Oct–1 Dec 2006, until cold weather and deep snow forced it to move (WJS). Late records (other than lingering overwintering birds detailed in *Winter* below): 3 adults at Trafton L., Limestone, 21 Nov 2010 (WJS); adult present 2 Oct–5 Dec 2008 at Thornhurst Farm in N. Yarmouth and Cumberland (A. Stackhouse, D. Lovitch, et al.); and 1 at Berwick 28 Oct–5 Dec (K. Couture). Other records: immature reported at Hancock, Hancock Co., 23–25 Oct 1979 (W. Townsend, *AB* 34: 139); immature at Old Orchard Beach, 22 Oct–9 Nov 1990 (S. Pollack, m.ob.; *AB* 45: 75); 1 at Mount Desert Narrows, Trenton, Hancock Co., 11 Oct 1995 (C. Witt); 1 at Union, 17–21 Nov 2003 (PDV et al.); adult on Cobbosseecontee L., Monmouth, 11 Nov 2012 (PDV); and one flying with a flock of Canada Geese, Unity Pond, Unity, 12 Nov 2018 (L. Bevier).

High count: 5, including 1 adult and 4 juveniles in family group, identified as *A. a flavirostris* by A. Fox., seen with Canada Geese on Puddledock Pond, Ft. Fairfield, 18 Oct 2008 (WJS).

No records of banded Greater White-fronted Geese recovered in ME, but waterfowl hunters have taken at least 5: 1 in Frenchboro, 22 Oct 1978, adult *gambelli* (now *frontalis*) shot by local hunter, in S. Grierson collection; 1 adult *flavirostris* shot and ph. on Sebasticook L., Newport, 29 Oct 1999 (fide D. Mairs, *NAB* 54: 27); 2 others shot early Nov 2008 in Bridgewater (W. Graves); and 1 shot in Grand Isle, 1 Oct 2013 (fide R. Mount).

WINTER: Rare but increasingly regular along southern coast in winter. First overwintered in 2011–2012 in Cumberland Co. during an exceptionally mild season. A wide-ranging adult in Portland, Westbrook, Falmouth, and Cumberland from 26 Nov 2011 through at least 15 Mar 2012 (N. Gibb, R. Romano, D. Hitchcox, m.ob.). May have been same adult observed at Thornhurst Farm which lingered, with another immature white-front, late Oct–6 Dec 2011 (R. Speirs). Another adult continued in same Portland area through fall 2014 to at least 3 Jan 2015 (R. Romano). An immature tallied on the Greater Portland CBC on 18 Dec 2010 (N. Houlihan, E. Hynes) lingered in Falmouth through 22 Dec (R. Speirs). Other records: immature recorded

on Eastport CBC, 26 Dec 1981, described as N. Am. ssp. *frontalis* with pink bill (*AB* 36: 379); 1 reported off Rte. 127, Arrowsic, Sagadahoc Co., 9 Feb 2002 (B. Lawson); lingering adult with 540 Canada Geese, Collins Pond, Nov–1 Dec 2006 (WJS); adult *A. a. flavirostris* in N. Fryeburg, Oxford Co., 8 Dec 2006 (B. Crowley); adult in Vinalhaven, 12 Dec 2006 (K. Gentalen); 1 immature at Thornhurst Farm, 4–11 Dec 2012 (F. Mitchell, eBird); 2 immatures at Saco R., Saco and Biddeford, 5–7 Dec 2012 (D. Hitchcox); adult at Cumberland, Cumberland Co., 4–6 Dec 2013 (R. Speirs).

WJS

Pink-footed Goose
Anser brachyrhynchus

European vagrant only recently documented in Maine

Status in Maine: A casual, but increasingly expected vagrant. There are 12–14 records of Pink-footed Goose in Maine. The first report occurred in 2009 and the species has since been documented in Aroostook, Cumberland, Knox, Lincoln, Sagadahoc, and Washington Counties.

Global Distribution: Palearctic. Breeds on arctic tundra in Greenland, Iceland, and Svalbard. Winters in nw. Europe.

Remarks: Pink-footed Geese in ME are likely vagrants from the burgeoning Greenland breeding population (A. Fox, pers. com.). The recent increase in Pink-footed Goose records in New England, QC, Maritime Provinces, and NFLD is probably tied to the increase in population and colonization of Greenland by Canada Geese, which migrate to e. U.S. bringing occasional vagrants with them (Sherony 2008).

SPRING: One adult Pink-footed Goose at Great Salt Bay Farm Wildlife Preserve, Damariscotta, 25 May 2013 (M. Fahay). In the days preceding this occurrence, large low-pressure system off U.S. East Coast and Maritime Provinces produced strong and persistent northeasterly winds. Bird possibly European or United Kingdom migrant blown southwest of intended course. Bird may also have been one of several that overwintered in NY, NJ, and PA the previous winter, now returning northward. Juvenile in Rockland from 1–3 Apr 2017 (L. Parker, C. Todd) thought to be one of pair noted in Winter below. Sight report of 1 at Readfield, Kennebec Co., 8 Apr 2017, not accepted by ME-BRC due to lack of detail.

FALL: Eight records from last week of Sep–Oct in north; lingering to Dec at coastal locations. All records: 1 feeding with flock of >300 Canada Geese and 2 blue-morph Snow Geese, Thornhurst Farm, N. Yarmouth, 29 Sep 2009 (T. Persons). Positively identified following day by D. Lovitch and seen by m.ob. 30 Sep–1 Oct 2009. Accepted as ME's first record (ME-BRC #2009-01). Three birds, same location 2 weeks later, 14 Oct 2009 (R. Speirs, m.ob.). These geese, also associated with Canada Geese, lingered through 6 Dec 2009. Wandered locally, foraging in hay fields and pastures in N. Yarmouth, Falmouth, and Cumberland. Photographs determined this group did not include single goose seen earlier at same location. One with flock of Canada Geese at Willey District Rd., Cherryfield, 5–27 Nov 2012 (J. Wilcox, m.ob.). One adult, Collins Pond, Caribou, 19 Oct 2013 (WJS et al.). One adult, Puddledock Pond, Ft. Fairfield, 13–15 Oct 2014 (WJS, J. Wyatt, J. Smith, C. Hardy), with >100 Canada Geese in town park pond. Seen same day as a Barnacle Goose and Greenland-race Greater White-fronted Goose, indicating an influx of geese from Greenland. One adult with several hundred Canada Geese on small, in-town impoundment, which provided refuge from hunters, Mars Hill Pond, 28–31 Oct 2015 (WJS, K. Lima). A series of observations in early fall 2017 probably related to a single, widely-ranging individual in Aroostook Co.: 26 Sept and 7 Oct at Collins Pond (WJS); 4 Oct 2017 at Peterson's Pond, Presque Isle (WJS); and 16 Oct 2017 at Mars Hill Pond (N. Houlihan, P. Moynahan). One on L. Josephine on 5 Oct 2018 (WJS).

WINTER: Three records: a late-fall/winter record, an adult at Mill Cove, W. Bath, Sagadahoc Co., 14–15 Dec 2013 (R. Robinson, M. Fahay, et al.). Found on salt water with Canada Geese during a CBC, initially identified as a Greater White-fronted Goose. It was relocated and ph. the following day. One adult seen with Canada Goose flock, Great Salt Bay, Nobleboro, 22–28 Dec 2014 (N. Graffam); and an adult and juvenile at Rockland, 2 Jan–8 Feb 2017 with Canada Geese and a single Snow Goose; juvenile lingered through 25 Feb 2017 (D. Reimer, ph., and m.ob.).

WJS

Brant
Branta bernicla

A small goose common as a coastal spring migrant

Status in Maine: Brant have been recorded in all Maine counties except Androscoggin and Waldo. However, they are most common as spring migrants on coastal waters. Occasionally, nonbreeders are found lingering through summer on offshore islands, and a small population overwinters along the southern coast. Brant are uncommon but regular inland, with records primarily along larger river valleys in spring and fall. All reports appear to be of the light-bellied "Atlantic" Brant (*B. b. hrota*) subpopulation.

Historical Status in Maine: Palmer indicated that most Brant moved across the Gulf of ME to the Bay of Fundy during spring migration, mostly bypassing ME, and noted only one inland spring record. He also described Brant as abundant in fall but did not list the species as overwintering in ME.

Global Distribution: Holarctic. Breeds across N. Am. Arctic. Winters along both coasts. Some breed in Canadian high Arctic and winter in Ireland. Atlantic Brant found in ME breed in Foxe Basin of Canadian Arctic; winter primarily along Atlantic Coast, MA south to NC. A dark form, "Black" Brant (*B. b. nigricans*), nests in w. Canadian Arctic and AK; winters along Pacific Coast from AK to Baja California. Another population, "Dark-bellied" Brant (*B. b. bernicla*), nests in Russian Arctic and winters in coastal w. Europe, France, and Great Britain. "Black" Brant rarely found in East; records in MA, NY, and NJ but none of this form in ME.

Remarks: It is evident that Brant have altered fall migration routes through ME since early 20th century. Smaller populations in mid-1900s are attributed to loss of favored eelgrass (*Zostera* spp.) beds in the 1930s, though it is unclear if eelgrass provided abundant food source along much of ME's rocky coastline. Palmer noted that strong tidal currents in the Bay of Fundy prevented growth of eelgrass there. Sea lettuce (*Ulva* spp.) may provide a more significant food source in much of ME.

There is little evidence that Brant were ever significantly sought by waterfowl hunters in ME and take by hunters appears incidental. As of 2003, five banded Brant, all banded in NU, had been recovered in ME, though none were recovered by hunters.

Trumpeter Swan
Cygnus buccinator

A graceful swan and the largest extant waterfowl species

Status in Maine: Accidental. The Trumpeter Swan was considered hypothetical in Maine based on a sight record from the mid-19th century, a specimen at the New York Zoological Park (now the Bronx Zoo) "found exhausted" on 25 November 1901 that may or may not have been taken in Maine (Palmer 1949, 64). However, a record of an adult with a missing eye at Etherington Pond, Biddeford, York, from 8–15 April 2011 (N. McReel, D. Doubleday, P Morelli, et al.) was accepted by the Maine Bird Records Committee in 2019 as the first fully documented record of the species in Maine. The individual (identified by its injury) was subsequently relocated in Prince Edward Island and later that spring in western Quebec, indicating a widely ranging bird.

Historical Status in Maine: Palmer (1949, 64) listed Trumpeter Swan as hypothetical in ME although he appeared to believe the mid-1800s Trumpeter Swan sight report by an experienced waterfowler to be reliable. Quoting Smith (1882), Palmer reported, "Some years ago (prior to 1868) a swan was seen at Scarboro, Maine during several consecutive days. The late Caleb G. Loring Jr., to whom the common swan (*C. americanus* Aud. [currently called Tundra Swan]) was well known, observed this bird repeatedly fly from the [Saco] bay and circle about over the marsh high in the air, uttering cries which led Mr. Loring to believe the bird to be a trumpeter swan." No further details or comments regarding this record are available. Unfortunately, there is no indication of the season in which this observation was made. At that time waterfowl were hunted year round in ME.

Global Distribution: A strictly N. Am. species, Trumpeter Swans breed in n. cen. Great Plains states, north through AB, BC, and into AK. Alaskan and Canadian flocks typically migratory, primarily wintering in coastal BC. Flocks in U.S. tend to be sedentary or migrate short distances.

Remarks: It is evident that Trumpeter Swans were part of New England's presettlement avifauna. Capt. John Smith (1630) mentioned encountering swans in the summer and fall of 1614. Though these were not identified to species, Tundra Swans generally vacate their wintering areas along the East Coast by mid-Apr and move north to nesting areas north of tree line in the Arctic and subarctic tundra. They are also late-fall migrants, remaining north until freeze-up. It is assumed this was also the case in the late 17th and early 18th centuries. Thus, it is more likely that swans encountered in summer in New England and ME would be molting or postbreeding Trumpeter Swans rather than Tundra Swans.

Palmer noted that Rosier reported seeing swans in Knox Co. or adjacent waters in May or Jun 1605. Though he listed this record under the Tundra/Whistling Swan account in *MB*, timing of this observation makes it more likely these birds were trumpeters.

Trumpeter Swans breeding in e. N. Am. may have wandered into the Maritime Provinces. According to Lumsden (1984), explorers and fur traders reported swans present and sometimes abundant on St. Lawrence R., L. St. Clair area, and Hudson Bay Lowlands of MB, ON, and QC. Many of those records were probably trumpeters, which are not known to have bred in the East for more than a century. Their bones have been found in a number of archaeological sites, the easternmost being Port au Choix, NFLD. The second richest find of trumpeter bones in N. Am. is a Jesuit mission in Ste. Marie-among-the-Hurons, Midland, ON. Trumpeter Swans were recorded breeding in cen. QC in 2005 and NY in 2015 (Groves 2017).
WJS

Tundra Swan
Cygnus columbianus

An Arctic breeder that rarely occurs in Maine during migration

Status in Maine: Rare. The primary migratory routes of this species are well west of Maine, but occasional stragglers are seen in spring and fall, and rarely winter. There are records for Hancock, Penobscot, Lincoln, Cumberland, Oxford, Waldo, Washington, and York Counties. The only recent sighting was in Stockton Springs, Waldo County, in 2014 (eBird).

Historical Status in Maine: Though this large waterfowl species was hunted in N. Am. since colonial times, it is doubtful Tundra Swan occurrence in ME was ever frequent. Mention was made of swans in accounts of European explorers' early visits along ME's coast. According to Palmer, J. Rosier reported seeing "Swannes" during Weymouth's voyage and explorations along coastal Knox Co., May–Jun 1605. J. Josselyn noted that he encountered swans in the Scarborough area during his two stays at Black Pt. in the mid-1600s. Neither of these early observations can be attributed to Tundra Swans with certainty, but it is clear that large white waterfowl were seen early in ME's published ornithological history. Eighteenth-century accounts were likewise ambiguous regarding the specific identity of swans reported but provided some specific locations where swans were said to occur regularly. Some of these water bodies, such as Lovewell Pond in Fryeburg and Highland L. in Westbrook, Cumberland Co., have hosted Tundra Swans more recently.

Global Distribution: Holarctic. Breeds in tundra habitat from n. QC around Hudson Bay to se. NU, west through n. YT, and northern and western coasts of AK extending into Aleutian Is. Eastern breeding populations of Nearctic subspecies *C. c. columbianus* winter along Atlantic Seaboard, primarily NJ–NC. Rare stragglers occur to n. New England, NB, NS, and NFLD. Palearctic subspecies, *C. c. bewickii*, breeds across n. Russia. Winters in n. Europe, n. Middle East, e. China, Korean Peninsula, and Japan.

Remarks: Tundra Swans are the "Whistling Swan" of older literature. Long-lived birds travel and winter as family groups. As noted by Palmer, the word "swan" is part of place names for islands, lakes, a hill, and brooks in ME. There is little evidence these were named for the waterfowl. Rather, the label appears to be a shortened form or mispronunciation of the Abenaki term "sowangan" for the Bald Eagle (Eckstorm 1941).

Interestingly, this species, despite its rarity, appeared at the same location more than 100 years apart. Reference to a pair of swans visiting Duck Pond (now Highland L.) in Westbrook–Windham in the early 18th century was found in an early history of Portland (Goold 1886). As noted above, a Tundra Swan was found at this same pond in 2009.

SPRING: An early-spring migrant in ME. Spring records primarily mid-Mar to Apr. Aside from overwintering Tundra Swans noted below, earliest spring record: 2 adults off New Harbor, Bristol, 9 Mar 1993 (L. Sawyer). In 1984, a late lingerer was observed at Lincolnville, Waldo Co., 28 May (fide ME Audubon), then at Pushaw L., Orono, on 13 Jun (fide I. Boyd), and again at Bucksport for several days to 17 Jun (M. Brown, E. Danforth, B. Bochan).

FALL: Earliest arrival reported late Sep; generally, migrants appear in mid-Nov to early Dec. Earlier documented fall records: 3 on Auburn L., Androscoggin Co., 27 Oct 1917. Flock grew to 18 birds overnight; 2 were collected and sent to ME State Museum in Augusta. Flock increased still more to high count of 49 birds by 31 Oct (Miller 1918). Other early counts: 8 at Lower Kimball Pond, Fryeburg, 9 Nov 2009 (R. Crowley, S. Mirick); an immature at Godfrey's Cove, York, 11–17 Nov 1991 (G. Carson); 1 bird at Sandy Pt. WMA, Stockton Springs, Waldo Co., 13 Nov 2014 (W. Nichols et al., eBird).

WINTER: Fall migrants occasionally linger into early winter but rarely overwinter in ME. Eight on Androscoggin R. in Brunswick lingered 26 Nov–25 Dec 1978 (obs. unk.). Two adults and 2 immatures off of Mackworth I., Falmouth, 21 Dec 1985 (R. Eakin, G. Sharpe), and 3 or more stayed in Presumpscot R. mouth through 7 Jan 1986 (PDV).

Notable exceptions: group of adult Tundra Swans spent parts of 9 winters at Brandy Pond and Sebago L. in Naples, Cumberland Co., in the 1990s; 3–5 swans reported by m.ob. for most of each winter 1991–2000 (fide ME Audubon, J. Frank, W. Howes et al.); group of 3 seen by R. Crowley on 5 Jan 2000 was the last reported occurrence of the wintering Tundra Swans at Naples.

WJS

Whooper Swan
Cygnus cygnus

A powerful flier rarely recorded in Maine

Status in Maine: Accidental. There are only six accepted Maine records of Whooper Swan. Most reported birds are likely escaped domestic waterfowl rather than wild vagrants.

Historical Status in Maine: Well covered in Knight and Palmer, the earliest record for ME is a specimen collected 10 Sep 1903 at Mud L. in Alexander, Washington Co. The bird was shot by C. Hunnewell on a small lake in the northwestern corner of the township. It was purchased shortly thereafter by C. Clark of Lubec for his bird collection. J.M. Swain first reported the swan in *JMOS* (6: 1–3). Swain noted that the taxidermist that prepared the specimen noted that it "... bore no marks of captivity."

Clark (*JMOS* 7[23]: 21) identified the swan as a whooper, noting the specimen had "... yellow covering of the lores, and extending over the larger portions of the upper mandible, while its near relative [c]olumbianus has the yellow only on the lores, and

Cumberland Co. Palmer described the "American Pintail" as an occasional to regular transient, and thought that "a few birds now winter occasionally east of Casco Bay . . ." (1949, 82). Neither author listed the duck as nesting in ME.

Global Distribution: Holarctic, circumpolar. Most abundant Arctic-breeding dabbling duck and among N. Am.'s most numerous duck species. Core breeding area western provinces and n. Great Plains; smaller numbers breed in East. Winter concentrations primarily in CA, LA, and Mexico; few birds winter in North. In East, breeds in relatively small numbers in scattered locations along St. Lawrence valley, e. Maritime Provinces, and northward to NL and e. QC. East of Mississippi R., winters primarily in South with hardier individuals sparsely distributed along Eastern Seaboard to New England and Maritime Provinces.

Remarks: Northern Pintails are most commonly found in large, open wetland complexes in ME. They generally avoid timbered and brushy wetlands and prefer sheltered, shallow waters with mud or sand bars. Merrymeeting Bay, Scarborough Marsh, and L. Josephine are the best locations to find this species. Often found in association with Mallards and, to a lesser degree, American Black Ducks, they occasionally feed in harvested grain fields (oat and barley stubble), especially if a puddle or watercourse is nearby.

Though not specifically sought by waterfowl hunters, Northern Pintail is an uncommon but regular portion of the annual waterfowl harvest in ME. Pintails made up 1.2% of ducks examined by MDIFW from 1948–1957 (Mendall and Spencer 1961). These data were collected primarily at Merrymeeting Bay. Pintails made up a similar percentage in the 1970s but USFWS survey data estimated that they comprised only 0.5% of the 2007 ME duck harvest. Of ME Northern Pintails reported to USFWS Waterfowl Parts Collection Survey, 25% were shot in Sagadahoc Co., the location of Merrymeeting Bay. Cumberland and Kennebec Cos. were also significant sources of records for this hunter survey.

More than half of the 37 banded Northern Pintails recovered in ME through 2007 were originally banded in QC or NB. Two recoveries from more distant banding locations: hatch-year female banded in AB, 12 Aug 1967, shot in n. Somerset Co., 12 Oct 1967; and after-hatch-year female banded at Mattamuskeet NWR, NC, 20 Jan 2004, shot on 6 Oct 2004 in Bowdoin, Sagadahoc Co.

Eleven Northern Pintails banded in ME recovered elsewhere. While most recovered in QC, New England, and Mid-Atlantic states, a few were significantly wider ranging. Notable among these: female banded 22 Sep 1961 near Turner shot on 22 Nov 1964 on LA coast e. of New Orleans. Another female, banded as a hatch-year bird, 21 Sep 1961, in Pittsfield, Somerset Co., was shot near Horicon NWR, WI, 15 Oct 1970. This bird was nine years old when it was recovered and was the longest-lived of banded ME pintails.

SPRING: Early migrant waterfowl, movement coincident with snowmelt. First arrivals usually appear mid-Mar in the south and early Apr northward. Pair formation begins on wintering grounds; expectedly, many spring records are for pairs or groups of pairs. Some early Mar records certainly represent overwintering birds. Early records thought to be transients: pair shot by E. Spinney in Phippsburg on 5 or 6 Mar 1901 (Palmer 1949); 4 in Damariscotta Mills, 4 Mar 1979 (obs. unk.); 1 in Spruce Head, Knox Co., 6 Mar 1982 (obs. unk.); 1 on Carvers Pond, Vinalhaven, 3 Mar 2015 (M. Fahay, eBird).

Peak northward movement earlier than most waterfowl species in ME. High counts typically last week of Mar–early Apr, numbers quickly diminish late Apr–early May.

Northern Pintails regularly congregate in spring at Abagadasset R. mouth on Merrymeeting Bay, Bowdoinham. Highest counts here >80 (48 males, >32 females) seen on 1 Apr 2004; 80, 8 Apr 2008; 59 on 11 Mar 2016; >55 on 4 Apr 2003 (all PDV); 43 on 10 Mar 2016 (H. Heuer, eBird); 42 males (only males counted), 18 Mar 1991 (D. Anderson); and 30, 11 Apr 1958 (obs. unk.). Spring season high counts at other ME localities: 55 at Kennebunk Beach, 2 Apr 1966 (obs. unk.); 38 at Scarborough, 8 Apr 1973 (obs. unk.); maximum of 24 at Cobbosseecontee L., Monmouth, 30 Mar 1985 (S. Weston, A. Curtis); >24 at Scarborough Marsh, 31 Mar 1991 (L. Brinker); and 29 on Pleasant Pond, Richmond, 10 Apr 2007 (PDV, WJS).

At breeding location near L. Josephine in Easton, 13 Northern Pintails seen 30 Apr 2003 (WJS), a notable high count.

Later records for spring migrants in south: 9 May 1945, (H. Mendall); >20 on Merrymeeting Bay, 23 Apr 1962 (obs. unk.); and 1 drake, Collins Pond, N. Windham, Cumberland Co., on 17–18 Apr 2008 (J. Scher). Later migrants away from nesting sites in n. ME: drake at Frenchville, Aroostook Co., on 15 May 1994 (WJS); 2 in Masardis, Aroostook Co., on 3 May 1973 (obs. unk.); a pair at Barren L., Caribou, 30 Apr 2004 (WJS); and 5 males and 2 females with >300 other ducks, Grand I., 26 Apr 2007 (WJS).

SUMMER: Rare breeder at single location: nests occasionally in large wetland complex near L. Josephine. First breeding record: female with 6 young discovered 23 Jul 1991 by WJS and N. Bagley. Confirmed following day by R. Hoppe (*MBN* 5[2]: 16).

Two broods, females with 9 and 4 young, seen at this location 11 Jul 1993 (WJS). Record cited in *AB* 47: 1089 erroneously lists number of birds as 17, describes locality as "Fort Fairfield" and "where *last year's* first Maine nesting record for N. Pintail was obtained." Though young not seen at this location since, a pair seen here 21 Jun 2008 (WJS). Recent summer observations: pair on L. Josephine, 21 Jun 2008 (WJS, eBird); 1 on Christina Reservoir, 25 Jun 2016 (N. Houlihan, eBird); and 1 on Ship I., Hancock Co., intermittently 3–15 Jun 2015 (M. Baran, eBird).

Single males in mid-Jun at Palmyra, Somerset Co., and Brownfield Bog during field efforts of *ABBM*, 1978–1983 (Adamus 1987). However, evidence of breeding never detected during this time and atlas lists Northern Pintail among ". . . species never documented breeding in Maine." Three midsummer records listed in Palmer.

Northern Pintails also early southbound migrants and vanguard regularly appears mid- to late Aug. Earliest records of transient birds: 1 immature at Weskeag Marsh, 13 Aug 1992 (D. Reimer); 2 molting from eclipse plumage, Mars Hill, 24 Aug 2003 (WJS); and 3 in Durham, Androscoggin Co., 28 Aug 1970 (obs. unk.); 1 at Scarborough Marsh, 20 Aug 2012 (C. Caron, eBird); and 3 at Simpson's Pt. Landing, Brunswick, 22 Aug 2017 (G. Smith, eBird).

FALL: Among earliest southbound migrants appearing by late summer. In contrast to spring movement, fall migration extended affair with migrants moving late Aug–late Nov. In addition to Aug records listed previously, earliest fall record for s. ME, 2 females in Back Cove, Portland, 2 Sep 1984 (R. Eakin).

Peak numbers typically mid–late Sep. Larger fall migration groups: >15 on Merrymeeting Bay, 20 Sep 1959 (obs. unk.); 17 at Sabattus Pond, 21 Sep 1960 (*MFO* 5: 96); >12 in Scarborough, 21 Sep 1962 (obs. unk.); and 36 on Merrymeeting Bay, 26 Sep 1970 (obs. unk.). More recent groups, all fide eBird: 27 at Green Pt. WMA, Dresden, 24 Sep 2008 (M. Fahay); 16 at Camp Ellis jetty, York Co., 20 Sep 2008 (M. Iliff); 14 at Eastern Rd., Scarborough Marsh, 20 Sep 2017 (L. Fuller, G. Butcher, L. Blutstein); 7, Sanford Lagoons, 27 Sep 2013 (D. Rankin).

WINTER: Uncommon, but regular wintering duck along entire coast. Rarely found inland from tidal waters in winter.

First winter record: 15 Feb 1912 at Falmouth and Portland (Norton 1912). Norton also noted increasing numbers overwintering in Back Cove, Portland, starting 1927–1928. By 1930–1931, 85 on 1 Dec 1930 and "about 50" on 18 Jan 1931. By mid-1950s, wintering numbers dwindled to ~10; single digits seen at this location recently. Species recorded on almost every coastal CBC but not annual on any individual count. Most CBC records for singles or pairs. Highest counts regularly on Freeport–Brunswick CBC with 48 birds on 2002 and 2003 counts. Drakes decidedly more common winterers in ME.

Twenty Northern Pintails behind Popham Beach on 21 Jan 2006 (PDV), an unusually large wintering group. C. Bartlett noted few pairs overwintering annually in Eastport and Perry, Washington Co., winters 2006–2010. Bartlett found them "often hanging with Mallards wherever fresh water trickles over mud flats." Recent Washington Co. winter records, fide eBird: 1–2 on Half Moon Cove, 17–18 Dec 2015; 1 on Boyden's L., Perry, 20 Dec 2014; 2 at Carrying Place Cove, Eastport, 20–21 Jan and 15 Feb 2017 (all C. Bartlett); 6 on marsh near Machiasport, 10 Jan 2015 (L. Seward).

WJS

Green-winged Teal
Anas crecca

Maine's smallest dabbling duck

Status in Maine: Found throughout the year, Green-winged Teal regularly breed in the state and are common and locally abundant spring and fall migrants. They sometimes linger into early winter and occasionally overwinter.

Historical Status in Maine: Palmer reported Green-winged Teal as common in spring and even more numerous in fall migration. He reported occasional summer residents but only surmised breeding in Penobscot, Hancock, and Washington Cos. He found only two winter records.

Global Distribution: Holarctic. Three subspecies worldwide, *A. c. carolinensis* treated here. Green-winged Teal breed across n. N. Am. to tree line. Breeds throughout ME and Maritime Provinces; locally in VT, NH, and more commonly in MA; locally through s. Great Ls.; and south to NJ on Atlantic Seaboard. Southern breeding range n. CA and NV east to northernmost NM, and north through NE and IA. Winters in s. U.S. and Mexico south of breeding areas, Pacific Coast north occasionally to AK. In east, winters north to CT and MA, depending on seasonal severity.

Green-winged Teal

Remarks: Most migratory flights are made at night. Species will travel in large flocks up to several hundred ducks. ME's smallest dabbling duck prefers shallow water and exposed mud for feeding. Best locations for observing large numbers in ME include larger tidal marshes such as Scarborough and Weskeag Marshes, and Merrymeeting Bay near the Abagadasset R. mouth, as well as lakes drawn down in fall such as Cobbosseecontee and Sebasticook Ls. Green-winged Teal are an important duck in ME's waterfowl harvest when the species' status is good and open season overlaps the early migration.

Two-hundred and eleven Green-winged Teal banded in ME were recovered: 98 locally, remainder (113) encountered out of state. Of 412 banded birds recovered in ME by 2007, over 75% (313) banded out of state (USGS). Most banded in e. Canadian provinces: QC (138), NL (37), NB (26), NS (16), and PEI (11).

Seventy-four Green-winged Teal recovered in ME banded at favored wintering areas in Mid-Atlantic states (VA, NC, and SC). Recovery locations most distant from ME include LA (6) and FL (10).

Green-winged Teal show little wintering site fidelity (homing) and males, in particular, may wander widely between breeding seasons. Adult male teal banded in Easton, Aroostook Co., on 5 Aug 1979 was recovered in AR on 18 Nov 1979. Hatch-year male banded at Petit Manan Pt. on 29 Sep 1989 was shot 8 years later in sw. MB. Adult drake Green-winged Teal, banded at Agassiz NWR in Marshall Co., MN, on 25 Sep 2005, was recaptured and released by MDIFW waterfowl biologists in Easton on 12 Sep 2007.

SPRING: First arrives in s. coastal ME early to mid-Mar; highest numbers pass through in early Apr. Species common in coastal areas early Apr to mid-May. Moves inland with spring thaw and as open water becomes available. Green-wings typically appear in n. ME by third week of Apr.

Records for early coastal arrivals: 2 in Milbridge, 5 Mar 1984 (N. Famous); 3 males at Scarborough Marsh, 5 Mar 2000 (R. Eakin); and unreported number at Scarborough Marsh, 4 Mar 2004 (G. Carson). Earliest arrivals inland: 1 in Winthrop, Kennebec Co., week ending 9 Mar 2004 (N. Famous) and pair in Mars Hill, 19 Mar 2010 (WJS).

Species congregates in large flocks at preferred locations in spring. High counts: 300 in Scarborough Marsh off Eastern Rd., 15 Apr 1997 (G. Carson); 150 on Abagadasset R., Merrymeeting Bay, Bowdoinham, 16 Apr 2001 (PDV); and 310 on L. Josephine, 30 Apr 2002 (WJS).

Though difficult to separate from locally breeding birds, latest migrants linger through late May in n. ME.

SUMMER: Nesting recorded in all counties except Androscoggin. Green-winged Teal first documented breeding in ME in 1940s with breeding population in ME increasing since. Date of first confirmed breeding is matter of confusion in literature. Breeding first confirmed when 1 of a brood of 6 juvenile Green-winged Teal was collected on 25 Jul 1940 on Dead Stream in Twp. 33 (now Great Pond) in Hancock Co. (Mendall and Gashwiler 1941). However, it wasn't until 1947 that a Green-winged Teal nest was discovered in ME at Moosehorn NWR (presumably in Baring or Calais). Palmer cited Mendall and listed the nest discovery date as 18 Jun 1947. Smith (*BMAS*) noted the nest was first discovered by a game warden and refuge staff member on 16 Jun 1947.

FALL: Postbreeding dispersal and movement of local birds away from natal locales occurs in early Aug. First migrants arrive in n. ME by last days of Aug and in coastal areas by second week of Sep. Numbers build rapidly through early autumn; peak abundance early Oct–early Nov from north to south. Teal congregate in large numbers in localities with plentiful food during fall and particularly favor spots with extensive areas of muddy shoreline. High counts number in hundreds: 140 at Cobbosseecontee L. in E. Monmouth on 2 Nov 1982 (PDV); 200 or more at Pine Pt., 5 Oct 1991 (L. Brinker); 200 at Sebasticook L. in Newport, 10 Oct 1999 (D. Mairs); and >400 at Sherman Marsh, Newcastle, 9 Nov 2005 (PDV).

May travel offshore over open ocean during migration. Three ducks >20 mi. offshore at Mount Desert Rock, 19 Sep 1999 (L. Brinker et al.). Another individual at same location on 3 Oct 2006 (C. Whitney et al.).

Local flocks disappear overnight at inland locations as preferred shallow water sites freeze. Most Green-winged Teal depart northern portions of the state by late Nov. Latest record for n. ME: 2 on L. Josephine on 24 Nov 2003 (WJS).

Commonly hunted in fall and represented ~10% of all ducks taken by hunters in 2007 ME hunting season.

WINTER: Small numbers linger into early winter in ME, increasingly in recent years. As of 2007, species found on 22 CBCs. Though some found inland near ice-free locations along large rivers, most Green-winged Teal tallied on coastal CBCs in tidal waters.

Drake Green-winged Teal linger later into winter than females. Two males wintered at Reid S.P. in Georgetown from Dec 1952–Mar 1953 (*BMAS* 9: 39–40). One male seen by m.ob. at W. Elm St., Yarmouth, week ending 19 Jan 1999–week ending 23 Feb (L. Woodard). Another male wintered inland at Fairfield, Somerset Co., 1988–1989 (W. and B. Sumner).

WJS

"EURASIAN" GREEN-WINGED TEAL (*ANAS CRECCA CRECCA*)

Currently treated as a subspecies of the Green-winged Teal by the AOS, the "Eurasian" Green-winged Teal is a rare but regular visitor to ME. The breeding range extends from northern Asia west through Europe and the United Kingdom to Iceland. Palmer listed only three records for the state but the form has since been recorded in the state more than 30 times. Almost all known records occurred in spring, primarily around ice-out and in association with flocks of "American" Green-winged Teal, which are typically migrating into the area at that time.

Though morphologically very similar to the North American form, males are distinguished by a horizontal white stripe along the scapulars, between the gray flanks and the back, and the lack of the vertical white line observed on drakes of the native subspecies. Females are nearly indistinguishable in the field and, expectedly, have not been reported in the state.

Most records from late Mar through the middle of Apr. The subspecies was particularly widespread in 2013: up to 3 at Abagadasset R., Bowdoinham, 20 Mar–20 Apr (S. Walsh, PDV, et al.); 1 at Wharton Pt., Brunswick, 20 Mar (G. Smith); 1 at Orrington, Penobscot Co., 27 Mar (J. Smith);

1 at Green Pt. WMA, Dresden, 28 Mar–22 Apr (M. Fahay, PDV); 1 at Boom Rd., Saco, 5–13 Apr (D. Rankin et al.); 1 at Shawmut Dam, Kennebec R., Kennebec Co., 10 Apr (L. Bevier); and 1 very late on L. Josephine, 19 May (WJS, J. Saucier, R. Waikar).

Notable record for w. ME: 1 drake observed with 3 pairs of "American" Green-winged Teal near the mouth of Meadow Brook, Aziscohos L., Parkertown Twp., 21–27 Apr 2012 (A. Johnson, DWF, and D. Green).

Latest records in s. ME: 1 drake ph. at Wells Beach on 17 May 2017 (C. Kesselheim) and 1 at Scarborough Marsh, lingering until 23 Jun 2010 (D. Lovitch, M. Fahay). Latest in north 19 May as noted above.

One winter record: 1 in Green Cove, North Brooksville, Hancock Co., 28 Dec 1971 (E. Thompson).

Intergrades of the "Eurasian" and "American" Green-winged Teal have been recorded in ME: 1 at Abagadasset R., Bowdoinham, 4 Apr 2011 (D. Lovitch et al.); 1 at Green Pt., Dresden, 10 Apr 2011 (PDV); 1 at Abagadasset R., 20 Apr 2013 (PDV); 1 on L. Josephine, 6 May 2014 (WJS); and another at Abagadasset R., 17 Mar 2016 (PDV, WJS).

Canvasback

Aythya valisineria

A large diving duck, rare but widespread during migration

Status in Maine: Rare but regular during fall, winter, and spring along the coast of Maine west of Penobscot Bay, Canvasbacks prefer shallow bays and estuaries. While rare inland and Downeast, Canvasback records from 12 of the 16 Maine counties indicate it is relatively widespread in migration.

Historical Status in Maine: Palmer described Canvasbacks as rare in fall, recorded only once in spring near Calais, and once in winter at Back Cove, Portland. Further, he noted in 1949 that there were no records at all since 1942 when 25 were seen on the St. Croix R.

Global Distribution: Nearctic. Widely distributed in West during nesting season. Core breeding area AB and SK in w. and cen. Canada, extending north to AK, YT, and NWT, and southward into U.S. prairie pothole regions. Widely scattered in WA, OR, and nw. CA, south through n. NV, UT, and into cen. CO.

Irregular breeding records from Central Valley, CA; Bosque del Apache NWR, NM; Cheyenne Bottoms NWR, KS; and east to se. MI along L. Erie and Montezuma NWR in cen. upstate NY. Winters along both coasts and throughout Mississippi R. basin. Concentrations in Puget Sound, WA, and San Francisco Bay, CA. On Atlantic Coast, winters from MA to FL, concentrating in Chesapeake Bay and coastal NC in Currituck and Pamlico Sounds.

SPRING: Palmer reported 1 spring record for ME. Since 1940s, 50 or more spring records, majority from Cumberland Co. in Portland and Scarborough areas. High number of records may be due to number of active birders in this area. Notable spring records elsewhere: 1 female on Merrymeeting Bay, 4 Apr 1957 (obs. unk.); 1 in Boothbay Harbor, 18 Mar 1977 (obs. unk.); 1 drake at Frankfort Marsh near Penobscot R., Waldo Co., 9–21 Mar 1979 (G. Freese); 1 in Belgrade, Kennebec Co., 8 Apr 1984 (P. Adamus); 3 males, Perkins Cove, Ogunquit, 10–14 Mar 2008 (fide E. Hynes); 1 male, Meadow Dam, Sedgeunkedunk Stream, Orrington, Penobscot Co., 25 Mar–7 Apr 2008 (J. Smith); 1 on Royal R., Yarmouth, 11–12 Mar 2010 (m.ob., eBird); 1, Scarborough Marsh, 2 Mar 2012 (J. Stevens, eBird); 1–2 Presumpscot R., Westbrook, Cumberland Co., 18–29 Mar 2014 (m.ob., eBird); and unknown number at Fortunes Rocks Beach, York Co., 20 Mar 2017 (D. Lovitch).

Basic (eclipse) Common Goldeneye drakes in mid- and late summer and in prealternate molt in early fall often show a partial cheek patch expressed as a white crescent in the lores. This often leads to misidentification as Barrow's Goldeneyes.

Four records of Common x Barrow's Goldeneye hybrids recorded 1984–2005. The earliest record was in Stockton Springs, Waldo Co. (*MBN* 6[1]: 7); the most recent is from Winslow Park, S. Freeport (*Guillemot* 33[1]: 15).

SPRING: Barrow's Goldeneyes move north as soon as melting ice and open water conditions allow. Most movement occurs in Mar–early Apr; late birds linger through mid-Apr. Late dates: 2 remaining to 24 Apr 1963 in Bangor (obs. unk.); 1 in Lincoln, 24 Apr 1979 (PDV); 10 at Hadley Pt., Bar Harbor, 20 Apr 1997 (C. Witt); and 1 male, Stillwater R., Old Town, Penobscot Co., 21 Apr 1999 (E. Grew). Occurs through first week in May in n. ME. Latest date on L. Josephine, 8 May 2011 (C. Kesselheim).

As of 2007, only 3 Barrow's Goldeneyes banded in ME: after-hatch-year (adult) male banded by MDIFW in Dresden, 8 Apr 1949, shot following Nov on n. shore of St. Lawrence R. southwest of Quebec City in Sainte-Anne-de-la-Perade, QC. Two other banded birds not recovered.

SUMMER: One published summer record, an apparent eclipse male described in Roque Bluffs, 14 Aug 1988 (T. Preston, J. Anthony), although descriptions provided in *MBN* and *AB* do not eliminate more likely eclipse drake Common Goldeneye. "Watched for about 25 minutes . . . [m]edium-sized duck, surface feeding rather than diving . . . curved white crescent mark behind the bill; small white speculum on the wing; brown head, white or yellow eye, white breast . . ." (*MBN* 2[3]: 22). "A Barrow's Goldeneye seen at Roque Bluffs, ME, Aug 14 was quite early (TP, JA). It was described as a female but with a white crescent behind the bill. Almost certainly it was a male in eclipse, a plumage seldom seen in this Region" (*AB* 43: 62).

FALL: Arrival in ME begins last week of Oct. Though Palmer recorded a drake shot in Maquoit Bay, Brunswick, on early date of 18 Sep 1927, earliest birds recorded at inland locations and in lower Penobscot R.: 1 male at Brewer on 19 Oct 2009 (J. Smith); 2 at Bangor Dam, Bangor, on 19 Oct 1979; 9 at Bangor Dam on 24 Oct 1982; 1 shot in Greenbush, Penobscot Co., 22 Oct 1987 (fide B. Burgason, *AB* 42: 233); and 2 drakes with 24 Common Goldeneyes, Long L., St. Agatha, 25 Oct 2007 (WJS).

Most southward movement occurs through Nov with Barrow's Goldeneye appearing along sw. ME coast by late month. Fall high counts recorded in Nov at Bangor Dam area on Penobscot R., Penobscot Co., in 1960s and 1970s: 46 seen in Bangor, 7 Nov 1965; 30 at Bangor Dam, on 4 Nov 1974; 59 on Penobscot R., Bangor, 14 Nov 1976.

WINTER: During winter, Barrow's Goldeneye found primarily in lower, ice-free sections of rivers, estuaries, and bays. Some also known to winter in protected locations on coastal islands. Areas of concentration include Harraseeket R. in Freeport, New Meadow's R. in Bath and Brunswick, St. George R. below Thomaston, Carver's Harbor in Vinalhaven, Belfast Harbor, Penobscot R., Bangor-Old Town, Englishman Bay off Jonesport, and St Croix R. in Baileyville–Calais. Surveys for wintering Barrow's conducted by MDIFW in 2008–2009 found species at 27 locations in ME. Most counts in single digits.

Barrow's Goldeneyes found on nearly all coastal and some inland CBCs in ME. On average, during 20 years prior to 2008–2009 count, ME CBCs tallied <60 Barrow's. Counts ranged from 15 on 1991–1992 count to 128 on 2002–2003 count. Inland locations along lower reaches of Penobscot R. produced highest counts of Barrow's Goldeneyes found on CBCs in ME: 72, 34, and 32 on Orono/Old Town count in 2002, 1994, and 1997. Other high CBC numbers: 28 on 1994 Freeport–Brunswick count, 19 on 1989 Greater Portland count, and 20 on 1976 Mount Desert I. count. High count of 120 recorded for former Castine (Hancock Co.) CBC in 1971 was unprecedented within ME; it is likely an error.

Other high winter counts: 70 in Bucksport, 3 Feb 1980; 48 in Belfast, winter 1993–1994 (fide W. Townsend, *FN* 48: 182); 16 on St. Croix R. in Calais on 4 Jan 2004 (fide MDIFW); and 18, Kenduskeag Stream, Penobscot Co., 12 Jan 2014 (S. Rune, eBird).

In addition to 1937 Enfield record in Palmer, occasional inland winter records: 1 drake in Howland, Penobscot Co., 1–10 Jan 1960 (Freese, *MFO* 5[1]: 5); 4 drakes in Houlton, 2 Dec 1961 (obs. unk.); 4 drakes in Caribou, 27–28 Feb 1962 (obs. unk.); 2 in Magalloway Plt., Oxford Co., 18 Jan 1970 (*MN* 1[8]: 6); 1 male at Caribou Dam, Aroostook R., Caribou, 1 Jan 2004 (WJS). Recent inland reports: 1 on China L. Boat Launch, Vassalboro, Kennebec Co., 31 Dec 2015 (L. Benner, eBird); 1, Shawmut Dam, Kennebec R., Kennebec Co., 18 and 21 Dec 2016 (L. Bevier, D. and K. Lima; eBird); 2–4, Stillwater R., Orono, intermittently 1–9 Dec 2017 (S. Mierzkowski et al., eBird); and 2, Benton, Kennebec Co., 5 Feb 2013 (D. Potter).

WJS

Hooded Merganser
Lophodytes cucullatus

Maine's smallest merganser has increased simultaneously with Maine's recovering beaver populations

Status in Maine: A locally common cavity nesting duck, the Hooded Merganser is most abundant in interior and northern Maine. A common spring and fall migrant, it sometimes winters along the coast and occasionally inland.

Hooded Merganser

Historical Status: Hooded Mergansers were probably common before European settlement but by the early 1900s the species declined to near-rarity as a breeder and migrant (Brewster 1924). Hooded Mergansers recovered slowly following increased protection from indiscriminate hunting. Perhaps more importantly, reversion and reforestation of cleared land along streams and rivers, and the concurrent re-establishment of beaver populations, created preferred nesting habitat. Palmer listed Hooded Mergansers as common summer residents and migrants in all northern and eastern regions and casual in early winter but felt they had recovered only a fraction of their former abundance.

Global Distribution: Nearctic. In e. N. Am., breeds from ne. U.S. and Maritime Provinces westward to Canadian plains. In West, breeds from Queen Charlotte I., south through BC and nw. U.S. Most common as breeder around Great Ls. (Dugger et al. 2009). Eastern populations winter primarily in southeast from s. New England west to ON and Great Ls. and south to FL and Mississippi R. valley. Found irregularly south to n. Mexico and in n. Bahamas and Greater Antilles. Western populations winter primarily in Pacific Northwest.

Remarks: Hooded Mergansers and Common Goldeneye share breeding habitat and sometimes compete for nesting cavities. Palmer noted a hybrid Hooded Merganser x Common Goldeneye shot by C. Loring at Scarborough on 2 May 1854. The specimen was mounted and retained in the collection of the Boston Society of Natural History (now the Boston Museum of Science). It was described by Cabot (1856) and described and photographed by Ball (1934).

An apparent hybrid Hooded Merganser x Common Goldeneye drake was photographed in Southwest Harbor on 16 Dec 2006 during the Mount Desert I. CBC (C. Kesselheim et al.) The bird returned and wintered annually for another 6 years and was last reported on 21 Jan 2013. Another apparently different drake hybrid of the same parent species was seen on the E. Machias R. in E. Machias during the same span of years as the Southwest Harbor bird. First reported in 2006 (E. Raynor), it was reported nearly annually in late winter and early spring through 2013 (C. Bartlett). Photographs taken on 5 Feb 2010 by Bartlett show a different head pattern than the Southwest Harbor bird.

SPRING: Migrants arrive along coast early Mar, moving inland when open water is available. Most migrants seen mid-Mar to end of Apr; peak movement early Apr. Early records, fide eBird: 2, Caribou Dam, Aroostook Co., 12 Mar 2016 (WJS); 2, Weskeag Marsh, 6 Mar 2012 (W. Nichols); 11, Tremont–Bernard Bridge, Hancock Co., 3 Mar 2017 (R. MacDonald and S. Benz); and 10, Pennamaquan R., Washington Co., 4 Mar 2017 (W. Gillies). Straggling (typically nonbreeding) individuals continue through May. Spring high counts typically lower than fall but an exceptional flock of >400 (80% male) observed on Kennebec R., Richmond, 25 Mar 2000 (PDV).

SUMMER: Rare along coast and islands but regular inland at small ponds and beaver flowages. Breeds nearly statewide where natural cavities or nest boxes available. Between 1970 and 1986, Hooded Mergansers accounted for 38% of duck nests in boxes in 24 wetlands in cen. ME (Allen et al. 1990). An early nester; most broods appear late May–late Jun. In n. ME,

Pied-billed Grebe

SPRING: Nearly annual in late Mar, undoubtedly because inland lakes, marshes, and ponds now thawing at an earlier date. First Mar records reported in 1969, 1 each: Yarmouth, 28 Mar; York, 29 Mar; and Danforth, Washington Co., 30 Mar. (obs. unk.). More recent mid-Mar reports, 1 each: Topsham, 18 Mar 1991 (D. Anderson); Freeport, 14 Mar 2007 (D. Lovitch); Warren, 19 Mar 2006 (D. Reimer); Belgrade, Kennebec Co., 19 Mar 2006 (N. Famous); Penjajawoc Marsh, Bangor, 10 Mar 2012 (P. Corcoran, eBird); Lovejoy Pond, Kennebec Co., 27 Mar 2016 (T. Aversa, eBird). Pied-billed Grebes reported east to Orrington, Penobscot Co., 30 Mar 1989 (J. Hinds) and 2 on 27 Mar 2000 (J. Smith), and on Pennamaquan R., Washington Co., 27 Mar 2011 (C. Bartlett, eBird). Exceptionally early records: 1 in Naples, Cumberland Co., 21 Feb 1998 (M. Jordan); 1 on Presumpscot R., Portland, 27 Feb and 7 Mar 1993, the latter certainly not overwintering because it was not present in Jan (S. Pollock, pers. com.). Widespread in breeding areas by Apr; usually appear in Aroostook Co. by third week of Apr. Earliest occurrences: 1 in Ft. Fairfield, 12 Apr 1981 (M. Holmes); 1 at Barren L., Caribou, on 14 Apr 2002; and 2 calling at ice-out on Christina Reservoir in 14 Apr 2006 (both WJS); 1 in Houlton, week ending 17 Apr 2001 (L. Little); 1 at Puddledock Pond, Ft. Fairfield, 20 Apr 2008 (WJS, eBird).

SUMMER: Reclusive behavior and difficulty in accessing appropriate habitat probably account for relatively small number of nesting records. The *ABBM* (Adamus 1987) confirmed Pied-billed Grebes breeding at 18 sites spread throughout the state south to Cumberland Co. The *ABBM* was unable to confirm nesting in York Co., despite Palmer's assertion that the species bred there. Recent observations confirmed nesting in Lincoln and Piscataquis Cos.: 1 adult with 3 half-grown young in Sheepscot, Lincoln Co., 25 Jun 1992 (J. Hamlin); and 6 grebes (3 adults, 3 juveniles), in Dover-Foxcroft, Piscataquis Co. (A. Larrabee). In Aroostook Co., 55 Pied-billed Grebes reported on Christina Reservoir, about two-thirds juveniles of varying ages/sizes, on 30 Jul 2011 (WJS, eBird); and following year at same locality 62 grebes, "high count lots of juvies," on 27 Jul 2012 (WJS, eBird). Since 2012, regular counts of 1–9 Pied-billed Grebes recorded there in Jul. Despite reclusive behavior, grebes common in large shallow wetland complexes: >10 pairs present, and 1 nest and 2 fledged young observed on Douglas Pond, Palmyra, Somerset Co., 16 Jun 1978 (PDV); 9 grebes seen at Christina Reservoir, Ft.

Fairfield, 6 Aug 1989 (M. Trombley); 15 individuals, including 4 broods, observed at Penjajawoc Marsh, Bangor, 14 Jul 1999 (D. Mairs); 10 grebes seen on Daigle Pond, New Canada, Aroostook Co., 23 Aug 2005.

Gibbs, Longcore et al. (1991) found Pied-billed Grebes preferred larger wetlands in e. and cen. ME; they did not occupy sites <12 ac. (5 ha) but were found regularly in sites >24 ac. (10 ha). Palmer listed the following egg dates from Portage L., Aroostook Co.: 4 eggs, 8 Jul 1939; 8 eggs, 19 Jun 1943; 5 eggs, 15 Jun 1945; sets of 4, 5, and 6 eggs, 20 Jun 1947.

FALL: Prolonged fall migration, starting in late Aug, continuing until freshwater ponds and marshes freeze in Nov. Most birds migrate in late Sep–Oct when regularly found on small ponds and streams where they do not breed. Late Aug–early Sep aggregationxs appear to reflect successful local breeding and pre-migratory flocking. Notable concentrations: 26 on Messalonskee L., 26 Aug 1978 (PDV); 50 in Easton, Aroostook Co., 20 Aug 1992 (*AB* 47: 62); 18 at Christina Reservoir, 12 Sep 1999 (M. Trombley); 20 at same locality 23 Aug 2004, and 31 on 30 Aug 2015 (both WJS, eBird); 20 at E. Monmouth, Kennebec Co., 15 Sep 1984 (*AB* 39: 25); 12 on Cobbosseecontee L., Monmouth, 9 Sep 1999 (D. Mairs). At same locality, 12 birds on 6 Nov 1988 notably late (W. Howes). Uncommon on Monhegan I. in Sep–Oct; observed on Appledore I. on only 2 occasions: 12 Sep 1990 and 19–29 Sep 1999 (both D. Holmes).

WINTER: Pied-billed G.rebes rare in winter prior to 1956. Since 1956, occasional, occurring in varying numbers in Dec, primarily along or near southern coast. Although there are no records of Pied-billed Grebes surviving winter in ME, this may change in coming decades with moderating winter conditions. Palmer listed a single winter record observed below Bangor Dam, Bangor, 4 Jan 1943 (Weston). Second winter record from Lisbon, Androscoggin Co., 7–8 Dec 1953 (obs. unk.). In Dec 1956, 7 individuals reported along southern coast: northernmost in Augusta, 28 Dec 1956, and latest in Bath, 2 Feb 1957 (*MFO* 2[3]: 24). Eastern records: 1 in Manset, Hancock Co., 14 Jan 1960 (*MFO* 5: 5); 1 in Lamoine, Hancock Co., 2 Jan 1970 (*MN*[8]: 6); 1 in Danforth, 22 Dec 1970–3 Jan 1971 (*MN* 2: 47); 1 in Rockland, 26 Dec 1971 (*MN* 4: 6); 1 on Danforth CBC, 1 Jan 1972; 2 on Mount Desert I. CBC, 30 Dec 1972; 1 at Reid S.P., 1 Dec 2007 (B. Marvil, eBird); 2 on Schoodic Peninsula, ANP, 9 Dec 2013 (S. Benz, eBird).

Additional Jan records, 1 bird each: Windham, 6 Jan 1957 (obs. unk.); N. Gorham, Cumberland Co., 31 Jan 1960 (*MFO* 5: 5); Scarborough, 1 Jan 1966 (Anderson, *MFN* 2[(3]: 45); Kennebunkport, 7 Jan 1966 (Reeve, *MFN* 22[3]: 45); Biddeford Pool, 2 Jan 1970 (*MN* 1[8]: 6); Biddeford Pool CBC, 1 Jan 1973; Scarborough, 6 Jan 1973 (*MN*, Jan 1973); Orono, 11 Jan 1977 (*AB* 31: 305); Yarmouth, 21 Jan 1998 (L. Brinker); Saco, 26 Jan 2002 (M. Jordan); Old Port Rd., Kennebunk, 1 Jan 2013 (L

Woodard, eBird); Sedgwick, Hancock Co., 5 Jan 2015 (R. Fogler, eBird). Three grebes reported in Georgetown, Sagadahoc Co., 17 Jan 1970, with 2 remaining through 7 Feb 1970 (*MN* 1[9]: 6). Additional Feb records: 1 in Bath, 2 Feb 1957 (Emery, *MFO* 2[3]: 24); 1 specimen in Brewer, 8 Feb 1967 (obs. unk.); and 1 in Presumpscot R., Portland, 27 Feb 1993 (B. Hosmer, fide S. Pollock; *MBN* 6[2]: 34). Rare inland records: 1 on Brandy Pond, Naples, 19 Jan 1997 (G. Carson, *FN* 51: 728); 1 in Naples, 21 Feb 1998 (M. Jordan).

PDV

Horned Grebe

Podiceps auritus

Globally vulnerable Horned Grebes are seen in Maine throughout the year

Status in Maine: Uncommon but regular inland, Horned Grebes are common spring and fall migrants along the coast, occasionally occurring in large flocks. They are occasional to rare summer residents in coastal Maine. There is one hypothetical breeding record from Somerset County in 1954 (A. and W. Foerster). Horned Grebes are common along the coast in winter, preferring protected bays, coves, and inlets where they congregate in small numbers (two to 12 individuals).

Historical Status in Maine: Knight erroneously indicated Horned Grebes once bred in Washington Co. on the basis of Boardman's (1903, 242) account of this species breeding in Milltown, NB: "The Horned and the Dab Chick [Pied-billed Grebe] are the most common, while a few Red-necked breed." Palmer clarified this error, indicating that Horned Grebes were common to abundant transients in spring and fall, common in winter and rare in summer.

Palmer's statement remains generally correct, though these grebes may be less abundant in spring and fall than they were in 1949. There has also been a shift southward in the Horned Grebe winter population since 1975: CBC data indicate the species generally increased in s. ME and decreased from Mount Desert I. through Washington Co. at the same time (Figure 4). Reasons for the distribution shift remain uncertain. ME CBC counts, 1976–2017, range from 329 per year in 1989 to 1,344 in 2011. Three counts >1,000 since 2010. Recent counts returned to more typical range: 548, 451, and 454, 2015–2017, respectively.

Global Distribution: Holarctic. Breeds in n. Europe, Russia, and Asia. In N. Am., primarily Hudson Bay through cen. Canada to AK, south to ND and MT; nests rarely on Magdalen I., QC. Winters along Atlantic Coast, Gulf of ME, and NS to FL, also inland throughout South; on Pacific Coast from AK to Baja California.

Global Conservation Status: IUCN: Vulnerable; NAWCP: High Concern.

SPRING: Occurs regularly in small numbers (3–15 birds) along coast until late Apr; occasionally occurs in larger flocks, >60–300 individuals, late Mar–Apr. Congregations appear most frequently in s. ME in waters with sandy substrate. Large counts: >350 at Biddeford Pool, 30 Mar 2000, diminished to 52 birds by 25 Apr 2000 (N. McReel, *NAB* 54: 260); >300 in Brunswick, 15 Apr 1958 (*MFO* 3: 46); >65 off Seawall Beach, 11 Apr 1982 and >70 observed at same locality, 19 Apr 1996 (both PDV); >100 in Saco, 11 Apr 1998 (P. Comins); 164 at Indian Pt. Blagden Preserve, Bar Harbor, 18 Apr 2009 (C. Kesselheim, eBird). In Blue Hill Bay, Moseley reported 118 on 17 Feb 2008, 28 on 25 Feb 2008, and 30 on 13 Mar 2008. In Washington Co., largest flock numbered 36 birds at Machias Bay, 7 Mar 2000 (N. Famous). Late records: Biddeford Pool, 21 May 1994 (L. Brinker); Bar Harbor, 21 May 2001 (W. Townsend); Old Orchard Beach, 23 May 1998 (P. Comins); Parson's Beach, Kennebunkport, 6 Jun 1993 (J. Dwight); Wonderland Trail, ANP, 3 Jun 2017 (M. Good, m.ob.; eBird); Camp Ellis jetty, Saco, 29 Jun 2014 (J. Krasne, eBird). Few inland spring records: 2 in W. Gardiner, Kennebec Co., 29 Mar 1970 (obs. unk.); 1 at Locke Mills, Greenwood, Oxford Co., 18 May 1983 (C. Gorman); 1 at L. Auburn, Androscoggin Co., 26 Apr 1996 (M. Schuler); 8 on Unity Pond, 14 Apr 2012, and 1 there on 23 Apr 2017 (both T. Aversa, eBird); 1 at McCrae Farm Flat, Aroostook Co., 28 Apr 2012 (WJS, eBird); and a late bird on L. Josephine, 14 Jun 2012 (WJS, eBird).

SUMMER: Birds linger along coast until mid-Jun; occasional to rare in late Jun–Jul. Two in Muscongus Bay all summer 1956 (A. Cruickshank); 1 at Crescent Surf Beach, Kennebunk, Jul–Aug 1988 (JVW et al.) and 25 Jul 2011 (K. O'Brien, eBird); 1 at Higgins Beach, Scarborough, 25 Jun 2002 (S. Bloomfield). Single birds observed at Parson's Beach, Kennebunkport, on 4 Jul 1996, 26 Jun 1998, 28 Jun 2000 (all J. Dwight); 1 at Sand Beach, ANP, 30 Jun 2013 (G. and J. Leavens, eBird); 1 in Wells, 18 Jul 2012 (F. Mitchell, eBird); and 3 at Biddeford Pool on 9 Jul 2013 (J. Scott and B. Crowley, eBird). Only summer inland record: L. Josephine, 27 Jul 2004 (WJS).

Adult Horned Grebe and "one young almost as large as the parent bird" on 2 Jun 1954 recorded from Hog I., Wood L., Attean Twp., Somerset Co. On 5 Jun, the young grebe observed swimming alone (A. and W. Foerster, *BMAS* 10: 48). Birds not ph. or carefully described leaves possibility that young bird may not have been a Horned Grebe. Thus, breeding record viewed as hypothetical.

FALL: Small numbers appear in Aug but unclear whether species regularly undergoes annual fall molt migration similar to Red-necked Grebes. At present, no evidence Horned Grebes congregate at preferred sites during this period. Early records: Coyle's Beach, Cliff I., Cumberland Co., 5 Aug 2013 (M. Fischel, eBird); Hadley Pt., Bar Harbor, 15 Aug 2015 (D. and K. Lima, eBird); 8 in Stonington, 22 Aug 1979, and 14 at Deer Isle, 21 Aug 1980 (both M. Hundley); 2 in Cutler, 25 Aug 1999 (D. Mairs); 1 off Bailey I., Harpswell, 26 Aug 2005 (fide ME Audubon); 2 at Eastern Bay, Bar Harbor, 4 Sep 1996 (C. Witt). Early inland records: 1 seen in Alfred, York Co., 18 Aug 2001 (D. Tucker); 1 on 24 Sep 2013 and 2 on 28 Sep 2015 at Windover at Great Pond, Kennebec Co. (M. and K. Veins, eBird).

The main migration takes place in Oct when larger flocks occur along the coast: >30 off Pine Pt., 3 Oct 2001 (PDV); >50 in Eastern Bay, Lamoine, Hancock Co., 3 Oct 1998 (D. Mairs); 27 in Stockton Springs, Waldo Co., 10 Oct 2006 (J. Smith); >50 in Eastern Bay, Bar Harbor, 18 Oct 2006 (R. McDonald); >60 along Mount Desert Narrows, 5 Nov 2005 (S. Lewis, eBird); and >400–600 at same locality in late Oct 2004; >100 off Pine Pt., 11 Nov 2007 (D. Lovitch).

Uncommon but regular inland at this season. Regular off Hog I., Wood L., Attean Twp., Somerset Co., 1948–1954: 1 on 5 Aug 1949 and 1 on 18 Aug 1953 are early records; 1 ph. off Hog I., Wood L., 19–22 Sep 1946; 4 calling together on 28 Sep 1948; 1 on 7 Sep 1949; and 6 on 10 Oct 1953 was the latest record (all A. and W. Foerster). In Smithfield, Somerset Co., W. Sumner observed 2 individuals on 16 Oct 1996, 4 on 17 Nov 1997, and 3 on 14 Nov 2001. In Franklin Co., 1 seen in Rangeley through Nov 1976 (obs. unk.). In Aroostook Co.: several pairs on Portage L., 2 Oct 1958 (obs. unk.); 1 on Madawaska L., T15 R6 WELS, 6–10 Nov 2003, and 1 on Long L., Sinclair, 6 Nov 2004 (both WJS). In n. Penobscot Co.: "at Lee, Maine on October 18, 1958, I was shown the results of the morning's shoot, and was shocked to find four of the eight "ducks" were Horned Grebes" (*MFN* 14: 88). In Androscoggin Co., Horned Grebes regular in small numbers at Sabattus Pond since 1994: 1–7 individuals nearly annual from 27 Sep into Nov when ice covers the pond; 17 Nov 1998 is the latest record (PDV, D. Mairs, L. Seitz et al.). A single bird observed in Auburn, 21 Nov 2000 (J. Suchecki). Large inland concentrations: 15 grebes on Lower Kimball Pond, Fryeburg, 17 Nov 1998 (R. Crowley); 9 in Auburn, 16 Nov 1991 (G. Therrien).

WINTER: Common in winter along coast. Rare inland except for L. Auburn, where species recorded regularly on CBCs since 1984 with a maximum of 10 individuals recorded in 1996. Large concentrations uncommon but reported primarily from southern coast: 163 at Scarborough, 11 Dec 1957 (*MFO* 3[1]: 6); 68 in Saco, 11 Dec 1957 (*MFO* 3: 4); 57 in Biddeford Pool, 27 Dec 1959 (*MFO* 4[10]: 114); 260 at ANP, 18 Jan 1987 (B. Milardo, *AB* 41: 254); 156 in Georgetown, Sagadahoc Co., 15 Jan 1989 (PDV, *AB* 43: 283); 51 off Jonesport, 9 Feb 1999 (N. Famous).

PD

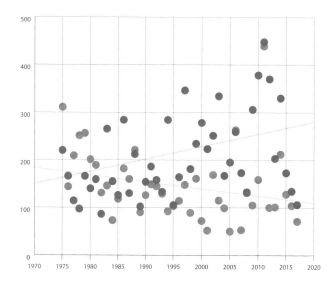

Figure 4. Horned Grebe on Christmas Bird Counts

Total number of Horned Grebes as counted on representative Maine coastal CBCs. While there was a slight increase in the overall number of grebes recorded, it was not uniform along the coast. Those counted on representative southern coastal CBCs increased (Biddeford–Kennebunk, Greater Portland, and Thomaston–Rockport; in blue), while counts on representative eastern coastal CBCs decreased (Mount Desert I., Schoodic Pt., and Eastport; in green) (NAS 2019a).

Red-necked Grebe
Podiceps grisegena

A large coastal grebe whose numbers are increasing

Status in Maine: Red-necked Grebes are common fall migrants; 80–140 individuals occur regularly at favored localities in open bays and outer headlands by mid- to late September. The species remains common along the coast through early January, but it appears to migrate farther south in late January and is less numerous in February and early March. The species is rare inland in winter. Spring migration occurs from mid-March through early May. Red-necked Grebes are uncommon to occasional along the coast in summer and are rare inland.

Historical Status in Maine: Palmer considered Red-necked Grebes uncommon to common in spring and fall on salt water. He cited spring dates between late Mar and early May; this migratory pattern has not changed appreciably since 1949. Rare inland in summer, with fall migration late Sep into Nov. Prior to the 1950s, Red-necked Grebes were regular in small numbers along the coast in winter; more recent observations reveal substantial increases since 1975 and suggest that the species clearly prefers several specific bays and coastal headlands.

Global Distribution: Holarctic. In N. Am. breeds primarily from cen. ON and MN west to AK, south to MT and e. OR. Winters in w. Atlantic Ocean from NL, Maritime Provinces, ME, south to NC; in e. Pacific Ocean from coastal AK to CA, also on Great Ls.

Global Conservation Status: NAWCP: Moderate Concern.

SPRING: In general, number of records and size of spring concentrations not as large as flocks observed in fall. Numbers increase in Mar: >100 off Scarborough, 9 Mar 1966 (Perrys, *MFN* 22[3]: 79); 91 off Mount Desert I., 29 Mar 1967 (E. Thompson); 48 in Cape Neddick through Mar 1970 (*MN* 1[10]: 6); 18 at Nubble Light, York, 28 Mar 1989 (L. Phinney); 25 at Biddeford Pool, 25 Mar 2000 (L. Brinker); and 29 at same locality on 7 Apr 2012 (S. Davis and L. Davis, eBird). Largest spring concentrations arrive in Apr: 35 at Pemaquid Pt., 18 Apr 2000, and 42 recorded at same locality, 1 Apr 2006 (both M. Libby); 22 at Blue Hill Falls, Hancock Co., 25 Apr 2014 (C. Moseley and T. Bjorkman, eBird). Off Biddeford Pool, 99 observed on 15 Apr 1999 (*AB* 46: 394) and 118 seen on 24 Apr 1995 (S. Pollock). Other concentrations: 75 at Reid S.P., 4 Apr 2004 (T. Allen); 200 off Stratton I., Saco, 11 Apr 1998 (P. Comins); 130 off Mount Desert I., 18 Apr 2003 (O. Barden); and 42 off Dyer Pt., 23 Apr 2006 (D. Lovitch).

Occasional to rare inland in spring: 3 on Long L., 17–20 Apr 1999 (J. Preis, S. Pollock); 2 at Camp Truda, Otisfield, Oxford Co., 28 Apr 2017 (M. Barber, eBird); 2 in Caribou, week ending 6 May 1997 (WJS); 1 at N. Shore Dr., North Pond, Somerset Co., 10 May 2013 (L. Bevier, eBird); 7 in Smithfield, 11 May 1994 (W. Sumner). Brewster reported a pair in breeding plumage on NH side of L. Umbagog, 21 May 1897 (Brewster 1924).

SUMMER: Occasional to uncommon as individuals or small groups along coast. s. and cen. ME: 2 birds on Stratton I., Saco, 26 Jun–6 Aug 1993 (S. Benz, T. Gaine); 4 in Falmouth, 15 Jun 1988 (*AB* 42: 1268); 6 in Rockport on 16 Jun 1990 (*AB* 44: 1112) and 3 at same locality, 22 Jun 1991 (*AB* 45: 1092); 1 off Popham Beach, 17–26 Jun 2006 (PDV); 3 nonbreeding birds in Rockland, 19 Jun 1993 (*AB* 47: 1088); 1 at East Pt. Sanctuary, Biddeford Pool, 19 Jun 2013 (L. Bevier and M. Viens, eBird); 2 off York, 30 Jun 1991 (D. Abbott); 2 in Camden, 8 Jul 2008 (D. Reimer, ph.); 3 in Falmouth, 11 Jul 1995 (*FN* 49: 907); 1 in breeding plumage at Prout's Neck, Scarborough, 15 Jul 1990 (W. Sumner, *AB* 44: 1112); 2 in Cape Elizabeth, 18 Jul 2008 (PDV, JEP); 1 in breeding plumage at Biddeford Pool, 21 Jul 1991 (*AB* 45: 1092), 1 at same locality on 19 Aug 1990 and on 21 Jul 1991 (both W. Sumner); 1 at Curtis Farm Preserve, Harpswell, 23 Jul 2016 (G. Smith, eBird); 1 in breeding plumage in Ogunquit, 2 Aug 1991 (*AB* 46: 61). Farther east, 1 off Isle au Haut, 1 Jul 1919 (Palmer 1949); 2 birds at Mount Desert Narrows, Trenton, Hancock Co., 3

Jun 1996 (J. Markowsky); 2 in Southwest Harbor, 11 Jun 1996 (A. Bacon), and 1 at same locality, 6 Jul 1994 (fide A. Bacon); 1 at Schoodic Pt., Winter Harbor, 8 Jul 1999 (*NAB* 53: 363); 1 in Southwest Harbor, 9–16 Aug 1995 (E. Hastings); 3 at Petit Manan Pt., 15 Aug 1995 (R. Widrig); 1 in breeding plumage at Biddeford Pool, 27 Aug 1995 (W. Sumner); 2 near Mistake I., Jonesport, 28 Aug 1995 (PDV, CDD et al.).

Generally rare inland in summer but recent records suggest species more regular than previously reported: 1 in Bridgton, 20 Aug 1998 (J. Preis, fide K. Gammons); 1 on Wassookeag L., Dexter, Penobscot Co., 1 Jul 1999 (J. Markowsky); 1–4 individuals on Christina Reservoir, 6–27 Aug 1989 (M. Trombley; *AB* 44: 55); 1 in Easton, Aroostook Co., 1–3 Jun 2007, and another at same locality, 27 Jul 2007 (WJS); 1 in Ft. Fairfield, 8 Aug 2008 (WJS); 1 on Christina Reservoir, 3 Jun 2011 and 24 Jul 2015 (both WJS, eBird).

FALL: Uncommon on inland lakes, but common fall migrants along coast preferring outer headlands and open bays rather than the inner protected bays and harbors favored by Horned Grebes. First Red-necked Grebes appear locally in Frenchman Bay and Penobscot Bay in Aug. Early migrants arrive in breeding plumage and molt into winter plumage. Paucity of inland records in Aug may indicate these early birds make nonstop flights from Great Ls. and breeding grounds farther west in Canada. Species regular at Mount Desert Narrows, separating Bar Harbor and Trenton: >100 individuals, 31 Aug 1986 (K. Jones, *AB* 41: 53); 225 in same area, 4 Sep 1996 (C. Witt, *FN* 51: 23); and as many as 250 on 26 Oct 1995 (*FN* 50: 20). Additional early records: 1 in Muscongus Bay, 8 Aug 1952 (obs. unk.); 2 in Rockport, 13 Aug 1989 (W. Sumner).

Widespread and common along coast Oct–Nov. Typically large concentrations: 357 at The Bluffs, Bar Harbor, 29 Nov 2015 (M. Good, eBird); 250 off Hadley Pt., Bar Harbor, 26 Oct 1995 (*FN* 50: 20) and 50 on 18 Sep 2011 (M. Good, eBird); 160 in Biddeford, 12 Nov 1988 (*AB* 43: 61), and 102 at same locality, 18 Nov 1997 (*FN* 52: 29); 87 at Petit Manan NWR, 16 Nov 1988 (*AB* 43: 61); 98 in Cutler, 25 Nov 1988 (*AB* 43: 61) and 119 at same locality, 11 Nov 1989 (*AB* 44: 55); 150 at Owl's Head, Knox Co., 28 Nov 2004 (C. Fichtel); and >200 at Reid S.P., 29 Nov 1999 (D. Mairs).

First fall inland record collected at L. Auburn, Androscoggin Co., 8 Oct 1899 (*JMOS* 2: 32). Uncommon to occasional inland since 1990 where it occurs in small numbers: minimum 8 records of 1–6 birds at Sabattus Pond, 1990–2008, the latest a single bird on 16 Nov 1990 (J. Despres). In Aroostook Co., single birds seen in Ft. Fairfield, 1 Oct 1989 (M. Trombley), and latest observed on Arnold Brook L. in Presque Isle, 21 Nov 2006, and at Long L., 15 Nov 2015 (both WJS, eBird). In Somerset Co., 1 on Moose R., 12 Oct 2014 (J. Kauffman, eBird), and 4 birds reported in Smithfield, 6 Nov 1996 (W. Sumner).

WINTER: Long-term coastal CBCs show increase in winter counts 1975–2017 (Figure 5). Since 2000, several coastal CBCs regularly record 130 individuals: Bath area (232 in 2006), Biddeford (171 in 1998), Machias Bay (414 in 1998), Pemaquid–Damariscotta (164 in 1996), and Schoodic Pt. (135 in 2005).

Reid S.P. long recognized as concentration area with at least 100 individuals recorded annually. Large counts: 185 birds on 18 Feb 1977 (*AB* 31: 304); 156 on 15 Jan 1989 (PDV, *AB* 43: 283); 265 on 12 Jan 2001 (M. Libby); >220 on 23 Dec 2007 (D. Lovitch); 218 on 19 Dec 2009 and 207 on 17 Jan 2011 (both M. Fahay, eBird); 105 at Griffith's Head, Reid S.P., on 12 Dec 2014 (M. Ostrowski and R. Ostrowski, eBird); and 241 on 19 Dec 2016 (J. Berry, eBird). Also concentrate around Mount Desert I., not only in early fall but also in Dec: >300 observed on 14 Dec 1998 (W. Townsend) and >300 recorded near One Squeak Harbor, Schoodic Pt., 12 Dec 2006 (C. Moseley). Concentrations diminish by late Jan. Red-necked Grebes become numerous as winter progresses; it appears species makes an early to midwinter movement south of the Gulf of ME.

Occasional to rare inland in winter. Aroostook Co. winter records: 1 dead in Ft. Fairfield winter 1929–1930, picked up on the ice (*BMAS* 5: 44) and 1 in Presque Isle, 2 Dec 2006 (WJS). Only Somerset Co. winter record found in Smithfield, 2 Dec 1992 (W. Sumner). Single birds observed on Augusta CBC in 1985 and 1997 and an individual was seen in Auburn, 16 Dec 2006 (*Guillemot* 36[6]: 53).

PDV

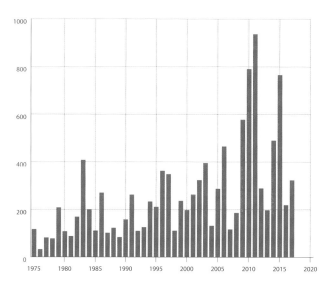

Figure 5. Red-necked Grebes on Christmas Bird Counts

Red-necked Grebe records increased across representative coastal CBCs with a notable high count of 937 in 2011. CBCs included: Biddeford–Kennebunkport, Eastport, Greater Portland, Mount Desert I., Schoodic Pt., and Thomaston–Rockport (NAS 2019a).

Eared Grebe
Podiceps nigricollis

Dazzling red eyes and unique facial feathers make this coastal visitor stand out

Status in Maine: Eared Grebes are casual visitors on the coast, usually in the winter. There are fewer than 10 records since 1977.

Historical Status in Maine: There were five records for this species 1965–1977, all of which occurred in winter. The first state record was at Wells Beach on 31 Dec 1965 (*AFN* 20: 400); another was observed off Stonington, Deer Isle, on 24 Dec 1968 (E. Thompson, *AFN* 23: 448). There are three reports of single birds from Schoodic Pt.: 2 Feb 1969 (*AFN* 23: 448 and MASFC), 14 Jan 1973, and 6 Mar 1977 (all W. Townsend). All of these were seen by one observer, and none were photographed.

Global Distribution: Global. Complex regional distribution in N. Am. Breeds from MN and MB west to e. BC and south to CA, CO, and n. TX. Winters from sw. BC along coast to CA and TX through much of Mexico, with isolated populations in Southeast U.S. Species reported from NS, NB, CT, VT, MA, RI, and NH.

SPRING: Unusual spring records: 1 described off Rt. 179, Waltham, Hancock Co., 14 May 2001 (K. Emerson, *NAB* 55: 274); more recently, 1 seen in Roque Bluffs, 9-13 Apr 2005 (J. Markowsky, F. Marenghi). "The angular head shape (like a Lesser Scaup, not the rounded head shape of a Greater Scaup/Horned Grebe type), straw yellow feathers in a fan shape eliminating [sic] from the red eye made this bird unmistakable . . ." (D. Chaffin).

SUMMER: Single bird summer at Sanford Lagoons, May-Sep " 2009 and again in 2010 (m. ob., eBird).

FALL: Few fall records: 1 at Sanford Lagoons, intermittently, 2–10 Sep 2006 (L. Brinker)), and 1 at Simpson's Landing, Brunswick, intermittently, 16 Sep–7 Oct 2012 (L. Bevier, m.ob.; eBird).

WINTER: Four winter reports in past 30 years; first remains hypothetical, 1 at Sprague Neck, Cutler, 16 Dec 1993 (N. Famous, fide PDV). Other records: 1 at Long Wharf, Portland, week ending 17 Feb 1998 (G. Neavoll, fide K. Gammons); 1 at Wells Harbor, 11 Jan 2003 (C. Dorsey). An astonishing 34 Eared Grebes were recorded on the 1991 York Co. CBC without accompanying comment.

RDP

Western Grebe

Aechmophorus occidentalis

This snappy-looking grebe is North America's largest

Status in Maine: This species is casual in Maine, with nine carefully documented records since 1981. Reports are usually single birds, although two birds were reported together in 1981, 1982, and 1989. With the exception of a record from Roque Island, Jonesport, in November 1996, all are from southern Maine. Additionally, there are seven undocumented reports from the southern Maine coast. Reports occur throughout the year but are most common in winter. Recent reports, all fide eBird: Portland Head Light, 20 January 2017 (R. Garrigus); Sears I. on 26 January 2017 (J. Wyatt); Owl's Head Harbor, Knox County, on 11, 17, and 19 February 2016 (M. Fahay, S. Hall, and N. Houlihan); Simpson's Point Landing, Brunswick, 17–24 April 2016 (m.ob.); and Saco Bay, 9 November 2007 (B. Pfeiffer).

Historical Status in Maine: First recorded in ME when two birds were seen during the Bath CBC at Reid S.P. on 18 Dec 1977. Remarkably, one of these birds returned for 17 consecutive winters. Usually appearing the last week of Nov, it was reported as early as 6 Nov in 1982. Typically staying through Mar, it remained until 18 Apr in 1993. The fact that it was not seen in the winter of 1994–1995 was noted in *Field Notes*: "Georgetown, ME's venerable W. Grebe failed to appear after 17 consecutive winters" (*FN* 49: 126).

Global Distribution: Nearctic. Breeds inland through w. N. Am. from WI and MN to WA, including MB west to BC, south to CA. Winters along coast, s. BC to Mexico, with resident populations in cen. Mexico. Documented in NB, NS, and all New England states.
PDV

Clark's Grebe

Aechmophorus clarkii

The classic grebe of the West finds New England

Status in Maine: Accidental. There is one record in Maine, a single bird seen and photographed off Owl's Head Light State Park, Knox County, 4–22 March 2005 (K. Gentalen, PDV, D. Lovitch; *BO* 35: 155). This was the first New England record.

Historical Status in Maine: Not previously recorded in ME. Third Atlantic Coast record for this species:

an individual returned several years, 2000–2005, to the Chesapeake Bay mouth in VA, and one bird was seen along Outer Banks, NC, in Mar 2003 (both Fiala and Carlson, eBird).

Global Distribution: Nearctic. Breeds in w. U.S. and s. Canada from SK to NE west to WA, OR, NV, and CA. Resident in CA, parts of AZ, and cen. Mexico.

Remarks: The Owl's Head individual was first reported as a Western Grebe, but the bright yellow-orange bill and sharply defined white supraloral face pattern were consistent with Clark's Grebe instead. Photographs that document this individual's identity are on file (ph. arch.).
PDV

ORDER
COLUMBIFORMES

Pigeons and Doves (Columbidae)

This worldwide family of 310 species includes the extinct Passenger Pigeon, once an extraordinarily abundant migrant to Maine's deciduous forests, where even the earliest European explorers noted its staggering numbers. Five other species of this agile and fast-flying family have been recorded in the state, two of them introduced.

Rock Pigeon

Columba livia

Perhaps the most ubiquitous and well-known bird in the world

Status in Maine: Introduced. This domesticated species was first introduced to North America in the early 1600s and is now an abundant resident near cities, towns, and farms, where their chief competitors are House Sparrows. Although included in BBS and CBC records, and in complete checklists uploaded to eBird, this ubiquitous species is most frequently noted as an object of prey for raptors.

Historical Status in Maine: Palmer reported that Rock Pigeons were feral and numerous residents in Portland since at least 1858 and that the population may have decreased somewhat in the preceding 20 years. As with House Sparrows, their decline in the

Orono, 31 Oct 2004 (J. Markowsky); and 1 in Cape Elizabeth, 25 Oct 2010 (PDV et al.). Though not reported in Nov, likely a few individuals occur in late fall, as Brewster's observations suggest.

WINTER: Although Soras reported irregularly on coastal CBCs in NH and MA, there is only 1 known winter record for ME: a Sora observed for 3 days, 26–28 Dec 1973, prior to the Thomaston–Rockland CBC, not located during count.
PDV

Purple Gallinule
Porphyrio martinicus

A vibrant visitor from southern locales

Status in Maine: This species is casual in Maine, with seven records in the past 30 years. Palmer listed 13 occurrences, most along the coast in spring and fall. Since 1949, there are 16 records (one involving two birds) following that pattern.

A surprising number of observations and specimens were collected far out of range in late fall 2013 and winter 2014 (L. Bevier et al.; eBird). Three occurred in Maine: one at Seal Island National Wildlife Refuge on 17 November 2013 (J. Roushdy, J. Drury); one in Trenton, Hancock County, on 8 January 2014 (M.J. Good); and one long-dead specimen at Kettle Cove, 29 January 2014 (fide R. Jones, G. Armistead).

Historical Status in Maine: Palmer noted that records prior to 1949 fell into two periods: late Mar–late Apr (five records) and late Sep–mid-Dec (six records). More recent reports support this pattern, but spring occurrences continue into May (three records) and Jun (two records). All spring reports are birds in adult (alternate) plumage. Recent fall reports occur in Oct (two reports) and Nov (two) and are birds in immature plumage. Additionally, there are six winter records, Dec (two) and Jan (four). A single adult at Bar Harbor, Mount Desert I., 10–15 Aug 1979, did not fit this pattern.

Global Distribution: Primarily Neotropical. Breeds along coast from SC to FL and Gulf Coast; resident in FL, Caribbean, coastal Mexico, and most of S. Am. Despite southern breeding distribution, species has long history of wandering north to New England and e. Canada. Reported from all New England states except VT and all Canadian provinces.
PDV

Common Gallinule
Gallinula galeata

This threatened waterbird would be better named Uncommon Gallinule

Status in Maine: Common Gallinules are uncommon and local breeders, nesting regularly at several localities in southern and central Maine. The species is an uncommon to rare spring and fall migrant primarily along the coast, except in Washington County, where the species is casual and not known to breed. There are no winter records. In 2011, the former species known as Common Moorhen (*G. chloropus*) was taxonomically split into the Common Gallinule (*G. galatea*) in the New World and Common Moorhen (*G. chloropus*), which has not occurred in Maine, in the Old.

Maine Conservation Status: Threatened.

Historical Status in Maine: Knight (1908, 145) reported this species appeared to "straggle along in spring and fall" in ME. He listed two spring and two fall records but noted the species was sometimes "brought into the taxidermist shops."

Palmer (1949, 189) listed this species as a "visitant or transient, rare in spring and fall, usually near the coast; two summer records, one of breeding." He noted four spring records (two known dates, 3 May 1925 and 5 May 1883), and eight fall records (20 Sep–26 Oct). All are coastal records, including two fall records from Merrymeeting Bay. The single breeding record cited by Palmer was reported by H. Mendall, who observed an adult with young in the summer of 1938 at a tributary of Sebasticook L.

Global Distribution: W. Hemisphere. Breeds from MA through NY, into s. QC and ON, Great Ls. to MN, and south to OK and TX. Resident along East Coast from MA to FL, Gulf Coast, and Southwest U.S., including most of CA. Also, resident through Mexico, Cen. Am., and much of S. Am. Winters primarily in Mexico and Cen. Am.

Remarks: Common Gallinules are uncommon on outer islands (two records for Appledore I. and ~10 records for Monhegan I.) and often found in unusual circumstances: one "stumbled across the road" on Monhegan I., 2 Oct 1983 (B. Nikula). On another occasion, an adult was observed departing Monhegan I. in a southerly direction only to be pursued by ~80 large gulls. The gallinule quickly alit on the ocean, some 650 ft. (200 m) from shore, and then swam back towards the island, constantly rebuffing aggressive attacks by the gulls. When it was within 160 ft. (50 m) of the island, it took flight, gulls in pursuit, and disappeared among some White Spruce (*Picea glauca*) (PDV).

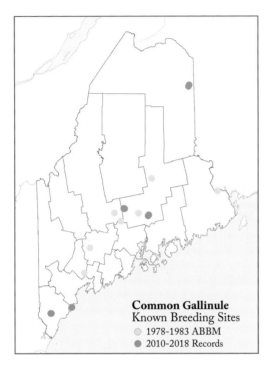

Common Gallinule
Known Breeding Sites
○ 1978-1983 ABBM
● 2010-2018 Records

SPRING: Earliest arrive mid- to late Apr: 1 on Monhegan I., 18–30 Apr 1960 (*MFO* 5: 34); 1 in York, 25 Apr 1968 (obs. unk.); 1 on Pennamaquan R., Washington Co., 25 Apr 2011 (C. Bartlett, eBird). Found at known breeding sites by late Apr–early May. At Penjajawoc Marsh: 1 on 27 Apr 1990 (S. Hedges, fide J. Hinds), an unreported number on 2 May 1995 (E. Grew), 1–2 on 4 May 1996 (E. Grew, fide A. Bacon), 2 on 9 May 1998 (E. Grew); and in Easton, Aroostook Co., 29 Apr 1990 (M. Trombley, *AB* 44: 396). Other migrants usually coastal, recorded throughout May: 1–10 May (8 reports), 11–20 May (6 reports), 21– 31 May (6 reports). Possible breeders: 1–2 birds, 6–11 May, Alder Stream Pond, Corinna, Penobscot Co. (m.ob., eBird). Noteworthy occurrences: 1 adult in Ft. Fairfield, 9 May 2000 (WJS); adult in Lisbon, Androscoggin Co., 31 May 1954 (D. Morse, *BMAS* 10: 60). High counts: 9 and 11 on Sebasticook L., 28 Jul 2012 and 27 Jun 2014 (both R. Lambert, eBird). Recent reports: 1–2, Alder Stream Pond, Corinna, 6–11 May 2017 (m.ob., eBird); 1, Mount Desert I., 25 May 2017 (S. Benz, R. MacDonald, and D. Lima; eBird); and Mount Desert I. High School, 26–29 May (m.ob., eBird).

SUMMER: Confirmed breeding at 4 localities (Adamus 1987). Common Gallinules first observed in Easton in 1987; confirmed

nesting at this locality in 1988, northernmost breeding site for this species in New England. Since 1987, found at several additional localities, and regularly at 2 of these sites: Stratton I., Old Orchard Beach (1991–2004); and Penjajawoc Marsh, Bangor, where listed as probable breeders in *ABBM* (Adamus 1987). Intermittent observations at Penjajawoc Marsh continue: Aug–Sep 2009–2010, including 1 adult and 1 juvenile recorded 18 Sep 2009 (J. Smith, eBird) and a recently fledged juvenile 5 Aug 2014 (J. Smith, eBird). Two juveniles on Alder Stream Pond, Corinna, 3, 5, 7 Aug 2016 (S. Mierzykowski et al.; eBird). Probably regular at several other sites, Douglas Pond, Palmyra, Somerset Co. Other nesting locations: Hampden, Penobscot Co., in 1977 (M. Lucey); Great Pond, Cape Elizabeth in 1991 (J. Berry, *AB* 45: 1094); and Brewer in 2005 (J. Markowsky). All these sites are large wetland complexes with extensive cattail stands and large areas of open water. Birds usually resident at nest sites until late Aug–Sep: 1 in Easton 7 Sep 1999 (M. Trombley, *NAB* 54: 27); 4 at Penjajawoc Marsh, 17 Sep 1996 (J. Markowsky); and 4 at same locality, 9 Sep 2000 (D. Mairs). One to 8 birds observed intermittently 1 Aug–14 Oct 2009 (m.ob., eBird), including 2 juveniles with "horizontal stripe developed" on 10 Aug 2009 (M. Fahay, eBird). Recent observations, fide eBird: 1, Machias Seal I., 15 Jun 2017 (M. Baran) and 1, Sebasticook R. Reservoir, Corinna Bog, 16 and 22 Aug 2017 (J. Fecteau, L. Bevier, and T. Aversa; eBird).

FALL: Unclear whether fall records constitute southerly migrations or dispersal from south and west. Appear mid- to late Sep: Sabattus Pond, 17 Sep 1985 (J. Despres, P. McWilliams); Appledore I., 19 Sep 1998 (D. Holmes et al.); Moosehorn NWR, Baring, 26 Sep 1967 (obs. unk.). Continue to arrive through mid-Oct: 1 in Phippsburg, first week of Oct 1984 (P. Donahue); 2 at ANP, Mount Desert I., 6 Oct 1985 (fide W. Townsend, *AB* 40: 256); 1 on Monhegan I., 2 Oct 1993 (B. Nikula); 1 at Capisic Pond, Portland, 16 Oct 1993 (L. Brinker); 1 at same locality, 17 Oct 1997 (R. Eakin); 1 bird in Penjajawoc Marsh, 5, 9, and 21 Oct 2009 (P. Corcoran, eBird). A single bird on Long I., Casco Bay, 12–13 Nov 1972 (*MN*, Dec 1972) was unusually late.

PDV

American Coot
Fulica americana

This distinctive but rare spring migrant is locally numerous in the fall

Status in Maine: Most abundant in southern Maine, American Coots are rare spring migrants and local, although sometimes numerous, fall migrants. Uncommon local breeders, coots are occasional in winter along and near the coast.

Maine Conservation Status: Species of Special Concern.

Historical Status in Maine: Knight (1908, 146) reported that American Coots were not known to breed in ME and were generally seen in Oct and Nov but "very seldom indeed in April and May." Knight also noted that Spinney considered this species common in fall in Sagadahoc Co., presumably because they occur regularly in Merrymeeting Bay. Palmer (1949, 190) stated this species was "transient, rare in spring and rather common in fall, occurring mostly near the coast; rare in summer (may breed) and winter." Palmer noted that the species formerly was much more numerous than in 1948, when he finished his volume.

Global Distribution: Nearctic. Breeds from NS through Canada to s. NT and YT, south through cen. U.S. to CO, KS, and MO. Resident in s. cen. U.S. from AR and LA to West Coast, including BC, and south through Mexico to Nicaragua and Caribbean. Winters on East Coast from MA to FL and Gulf Coast states. West Coast from s. coastal AK to Cen. Am.

SPRING: Rare spring migrant recorded along coast late Mar: Mercy Pond, Portland, 13 Mar 2012 and Falmouth, 26 Mar 1977, 1 each (obs. unk.). More regular in Apr: 6 in York, 25 Apr 1968 and 1 in Biddeford, 28 Apr 1961 (obs. unk. for both). Exceptionally early migrants, 1 bird each, all on 7 Mar: Camden Harbor, Knox Co., 2014 (J. Smith); Dover-Foxcroft, 1963, found dead 11 Mar and taken to UMaine, Orono.

SUMMER: Although observed in appropriate nesting habitat in many localities, few confirmed breeding records. In Palmyra, Somerset Co., 2 nests at Douglas Pond, May 1978, appear to be first confirmed records (Adamus 1987). In Easton, Aroostook Co., adult coots observed "carrying grass to a cattail hillock three times on 28 June 1988" (M. Trombley, *AB* 42: 1269). Northernmost ME breeding record 3 adults and 3 young, 3–20 Jul 1988 (M. Trombley, *AB* 42: 1269). Pair observed with 3 partially grown young in Benton, Kennebec Co., 22 Jul 2005 (L. Bevier). One bird through breeding season on Stratton I., 14 Jun–30 Jul 2013 (Project Puffin Data) apparently did not breed.

FALL: Annual fall migrants generally uncommon and locally distributed in s. cen. ME. Regular at Sabattus Pond (Sabattus and Wales), Merrymeeting Bay, Chickawaukie Pond (Rockland and Rockport), Sebasticook L., and Corinna watershed area (Penobscot Co.). Irregular elsewhere. Migration protracted: first birds appear late Aug–Sep, 1 each: Stratton I., 3–6 Aug 2013 (Project Puffin Data, eBird); York, 24 Aug 1967 (obs. unk.); Penjajawoc Marsh, 10 Sep 2015 (R. Ostrowski, eBird). Largest concentration: 6 at Christina Reservoir, 24 Sep 2004 (WJS). Main migration occurs Oct–Nov, flocks generally number <20 individuals.

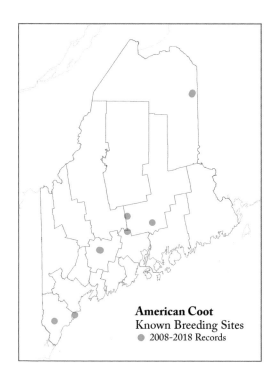

American Coot
Known Breeding Sites
● 2008–2018 Records

Occasional large flocks at favored migration sites: at Chickawaukie Pond, Rockland, 34 on 11 Nov 1985 (obs. unk.); 35 on 3 Nov 1990 (M. Plymire, *AB* 45: 76), 48 on 8 Nov 2005 (M. Libby, eBird), and largest concentration reported in ME, 860 on 29 Oct 2011 (M. Iliff, eBird). Other records: 69 at Merrymeeting Bay, 22 Oct 1972 (obs. unk.) and 500 at same locality, 12 Nov 1966 (*RNEB* 22: 7). Generally, 2–20 reported on Sabattus Pond, occasional high counts: 32 on 22 Oct 1990 (J. Despres, *AB* 45: 76) and 387 birds, 16–21 Nov 1994 (*FN* 49: 21).

Rare fall migrants in w. ME: 1 at Moose R., near Jackman, 22 Sep 1962 (obs. unk.); 10 at Old Dead R. Rd., Flagstaff L., 26 Nov 2016 (G. Vigna); 1 in Newfield, York Co., 10 Dec 1983 (W. Hancock). Occasional in Aroostook Co: Ft. Fairfield, 1 captured and released after identification in fall 1932 (*BMAS* 5: 47); 3 on 19 Oct 1985 (M. Trombley); and 3 on 1 Oct 2004 (WJS). One in Presque Isle, 30 Oct 2003 is latest record. Occasional in Washington Co.: most easterly, 7 in Calais, Oct 1967 (obs. unk.); 2 at Moosehorn NWR, Baring, 23 Oct 1972 (obs. unk.); 1 in Roque Bluffs, 10 Nov 1989 (P.K. Donahue, T. Wood, fide CDD; *AB* 44: 57); 1 in Cutler, 11 Nov 1989 (*AB* 44: 57).

WINTER: Numbers diminish in Dec as freshwater ponds freeze; a few linger on open water, usually along coast. Regular in high numbers in Chickawaukie Pond, fide eBird: 630, 30 Dec 2011 (PDV); 130, 14 Dec 2012 (B. and D. Witham); 150, 20 Dec 2014 (F. Kynd); 100, 19 Dec 2015 (G. Presley); 300, 2 Jan 2012 (S. Hall). Inland records more common in recent years: 18 birds on L. Auburn, Androscoggin Co., 2 Dec 1965 (obs. unk.); 15 in E. Auburn, 26 Nov 2011 (S. and E. Lewis, eBird); 12, Essex Woods, Bangor, 5 Nov 2011 (P. Blair, eBird). Unlikely American Coots winter successfully in ME. Most Jan records restricted to coast (>7 records), except for 1 at Moosehorn NWR, Baring, 8

Jan 1972 (obs. unk.), and ~22 birds in Rockland through 31 Jan 1991 (B. Cadbury, *AB* 45: 251). Two known Feb records, both eBird: 1, Narramissic R., Orland, Hancock Co., 7 Feb 2013 (J. Smith) and 1 in Camden Harbor, 22 Feb 2014 (T. Duddy and L. Woodard). Lingering birds either fly south or succumb to harsh winter conditions, as there are only 2 Feb reports: 1 "caught alive in slush ice by small boys on February 1, 1924, in Back Cove, Portland, and brought to Norton who released it" (Palmer 1949, 190); 2 individuals in Camden, 6 Feb 1952 (obs. unk.).
PDV

Cranes (Gruidae)

Fifteen species of cranes are found on five continents, including two in North America. The Whooping Crane, never recorded in Maine, plummeted to the brink of extinction in the 1940s and remains endangered. Sandhill Cranes, known for their elaborate mating dances and spectacular migration through the Midwest, now breed in Maine's central Interior.

Sandhill Crane
Antigone canadensis

Direct from America's heartland, this species is a recent addition to Maine's avifauna

Status in Maine: Sandhill Cranes were first confirmed nesting at Messalonskee Lake in July 2000 (Melvin 2002); the first breeding record in New England. They remain uncommon migrants and rare breeders in open wetlands in central Maine. While the species sometimes lingers into fall, it has successfully overwintered only once.

Historical Status in Maine: Although Palmer knew of no 20th century records, he considered Sandhill Cranes hypothetical in ME because of good evidence that this species occurred prior to European settlement. Knight ignored this species, and simply included Sandhill Crane as part of his account for Great Blue Herons; presumably he felt there was confusion over historical records for cranes.

The first modern record appeared in Brunswick, 9 Oct 1961, with three additional records in fall 1966. Since 1966, the species has become annual, with >40 reports of one to two birds from numerous localities in s. and cen. ME. The first crane record for Aroostook Co. was a bird photographed in Ashland (and Masardis and Scopan Twp.) in summer 1967 (E. Searway, J.S. Greenlaw, ph.). There are three records (one spring, two fall) for Washington Co. and two for w. ME.

Global Distribution: Nearctic, Neotropical, and Palearctic. Breeds throughout Canada from ON and NU to AK and BC, in U.S. from Great Ls. to MT, WY, CO, UT, NV, and OR. Winter range more limited, including FL, TX, CA, and AZ into n. Mexico. Resident in parts of FL and Cuba. Observed in all New England states, NB, NS, NL, and QC. (Gerber et al. 2014).

Remarks: Palmer (1949, 181) cites ([Reprint] 1887, 103) who surveyed the Georges Is., Knox Co., 19 May–16 Jun 1605. Rosier recounted:

> "Upon this Iland [? Allens Island], as also upone the former [Monhegan], we found (at our first coming to shore) where fire had beene made: and about the place were very large egge shelles bigger than goose egges, fish bones, the bones of some beast. Here ere espied Cranes stalking on the shore of a little Iland adjoyning [? Benner Island]; where we after saw they used to breed."

Palmer accepted the validity of these crane observations because Rosier had distinguished between cranes and herons in his list of birds, although Palmer questioned whether cranes nested on these islands and thought it more likely that these were nesting Great Blue Herons. He noted there are only three types of birds that lay eggs notably larger than a goose: swans, Great Auk, and cranes. Swans were not known to nest in ME, certainly not on coastal islands, and it seems equally unlikely that Sandhill Cranes nested along the coast, leaving the possibility and likelihood that "these very great egge shelles" were more probably those of the Great Auk (see Great Auk account, pp. 253-254).

SPRING: Southern and cen. ME arrival 15–30 Apr (more than 11 records) and 1–15 May (at least 5 records). Earliest reports: 4 in Hallowell, Kennebec Co., 31 Mar 2007 (JVW, E. Wells); 6, Mt. Agamenticus, 3 Apr 2017 (A. Aldrich, eBird); 2 in Smithfield, Somerset Co., 8 Apr 2004 (W. Sumner, fide D. Mairs); 3, Fields, Hancock Co., 8 Apr 2014 (R. MacDonald, eBird); 1 in Durham, Androscoggin Co., 9 Apr 2001 (B. Pearson); and 2 in Winthrop, Kennebec Co. 10 Apr 2004 (S. Turney). Fewer birds reported in latter half of May (3 records) and early Jun (3 records). No migrants reported in Mar. Washington Co. spring record: 1 in Perry, 30 Apr 1977 (*AB* 31: 974). Arrival dates in n. ME somewhat later: 1 in Medway, 26 Apr 1997; 1 in Eagle L., Aroostook Co., 3 May 1984 (LeBoueff, fide S. and G. Flagg); 2 in T17 R5 WELS, Aroostook Co., 12 Jun 2004 (WJS); 2 in Winthrop, 3 Apr 2007 (B. Skapa); and 1 observed in Sedgwick, Hancock Co., 23 Apr 2007 (C. Moseley).

Upland Sandpiper

Bartramia longicauda

An observer of Upland Sandpiper chicks remarked he was seeing 'downy uppies'

Status in Maine: Although reduced in number since the mid-19th century, Upland Sandpipers (known to birders as "uppies") are uncommon and local breeders on large agricultural fields, blueberry barrens, and even airports throughout much of Maine. While absent from the Western Mountain region of Somerset and Franklin Counties, they are common Downeast in Washington County and since the 1970s have increased along with the expansion of blueberry agriculture. Spring migrants arrive mid-April to mid-May and fall birds generally depart by late August or early September.

Maine Conservation Status: Threatened because of small populations, regional population declines, and diminishing habitat in the Northeast.

Historical Status in Maine: Upland Sandpipers experienced serious population declines in the late 19th–early 20th centuries because of extensive market hunting in N. Am., Argentina, and other parts of S. Am. For example, in 1890, two game dealers in Boston received more than 9,000 Upland Sandpipers for sale (Mackay 1891) and some 50,000–60,000 Upland Sandpipers were shipped annually from New England from the late 1870s to 1890 (Houston and Bowen 2001). Knight (1908, 178) noted this decline, "though this species formerly occurred commonly during the migrations and was not rare as a summer resident of various portions of the State, it is now decidedly less common and the number of breeding birds which occur in the State are very few." Palmer (1949, 212) stated, "by 1912, the species was rare in the Portland–Scarborough area . . . The records for the state were few indeed from then until after 1920." Brewster (1925) did not record Upland Sandpipers in the L. Umbagog region.

Global Distribution: Nearctic. Breeds NB, w. NS, and ME, locally throughout New England to s. QC and ON, west through MI, MN, s. SK, MB, and AB, south to PA, NJ, w. VA (scarce), IN, IL, KS, ne. CO. Separate population nests in AK and NT, also rarely in OR. Winters in S. Am. primarily in Argentina, Uruguay, Paraguay, and Suriname. Migrates north mainly through mid-continent; southerly migration more easterly.

Upland Sandpiper

Remarks: Blueberry barrens provide essential habitat for Upland Sandpipers in Midcoast and e. ME, largely because they provide extensive open areas that are critical for this species' breeding (Vickery et al. 1994). In Knox, Lincoln, and Waldo Cos., the only known regular Upland Sandpiper breeding sites have been on blueberry barrens at Clarry Hill, Union, where three to six pairs nested regularly from 1982 to at least 2000 (M. Libby and PDV), and on Appleton Ridge, Appleton, where two to three pairs were reported, Jun 1989 (PDV). Likely small numbers have nested on other large barrens in this area; J. Smith reported a pair in Stockton Springs, Waldo Co., in 2008 and 2009. In Hancock Co., Upland Sandpipers breed on blueberry barrens on Blue Hill Peninsula, in Sedgwick (C. Moseley), Surry (PDV), and probably elsewhere. With more and larger blueberry barrens east of Ellsworth, Upland Sandpipers are now common throughout these barrens. In Washington Co., the species has increased substantially since 1970. ME's 2006 species assessment found the number of breeding pairs in ME in the 1990s (the latest data they cite) probably exceeded 160 pairs "although the exact number is unknown and undoubtedly varies annually" (MDIFW 2006; Shriver et al. 2005a). By 2008, N. Famous estimated >500 pairs in e. Hancock and Washington Cos., 50 in Columbia on 8 Jul 1997 and 13 Jul 1999; 40 in T25 MD BPP on 30 Jun 1998 and 9 Jul 2002. However, many locations in mid-ME that once supported breeding Upland Sandpipers no longer do.

SPRING: Arrival 15 Apr–15 May, but dates vary annually. From 1982–2005, J. Despres reported 81% of Upland Sandpipers first appeared in Turner 25 Apr–10 May with earliest arrival 20 Apr 2005 and latest on 18 May 1986. In Somerset and n. Kennebec Cos., first migrants consistently arrived 27–30 Apr from 1995–2000, earliest arrival in Clinton, 21 Apr 2009 (W. Sumner). In Aroostook Co. birds arrive early to mid-May: 7 Sandpipers in Limestone, 16 May 2009 (WJS). Exceptionally early: 1 in S. Thomaston, 26 Mar 1983 (M. Libby); 1 in Portland, 29 Mar 2000 (R. Eakin); 2 birds in Bangor, 6 Apr 1980 (fide W. Townsend); 1 on E. Egg Rock, 6 Apr 1984 (S. Kress). Migrants continue until late May: single birds on Monhegan I., where rare, on 23 May 1997 (L. K. Brinker) and 28 May 1989 (JVW).

SUMMER: Since 1950s, Upland Sandpipers have diminished across s. and cen. ME, and are currently restricted to limited number of breeding sites except in Hancock and Washington Cos. In York Co., sandpipers bred regularly in Dayton until late 1970s: 13 reported, 20 Jul 1969 (*MN* 1: 7) and maximum of 22 noted on 24 Jul 1971 (*MN* 3: 14). Adult reported from Windham, Cumberland Co., 13 Jun 1966 (*MFN* 22: 135). Species has been breeding at Kennebunk Plains for decades; regular censuses since 1984 counted 6–12 pairs at this site. Similar grassland bird inventories recorded Upland Sandpipers at Wells Barren (1–3 pairs), although breeding since 2007 is doubtful (J. Mays), and 1–5 pairs also recorded at Sanford Airport (PDV, JVW, L. Brinker, et al.). Upland Sandpipers present at Portland Jetport from late 1970s, when it was considered a possible nester (Adamus 1987), to late 1990s; at least 2 reported at this site in 1995 (L. Brinker) and 1997 (PDV).

In Cumberland Co., 5–6 pairs recorded nesting along runways at Brunswick Landing (formerly Brunswick Naval Air Station), Brunswick, 17 Jul 1985 (PDV and P.K. Donahue), where they may remain, although midsummer records are few; one pair reported in aerial display, 12 Jun 2015 (M. Fahay, eBird). On territory in blueberry barrens along Maquoit Rd., Brunswick, 3–4 pairs also found Jun–Jul 1988 (PDV and G. Therrien). However, it appears they no longer breed at this site because a high school was constructed on the barren. One pair along Rt. 201 in n. Topsham, Jun 1988, present for a few years (PDV), and 1–2 pairs in Pownal, 16 Jul 1995, did not return in subsequent years (D. Nickerson).

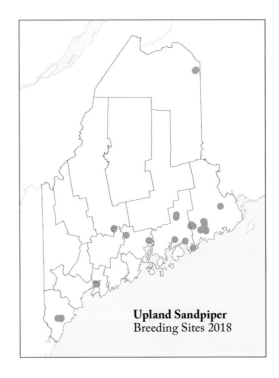

Upland Sandpiper
Breeding Sites 2018

During ABBM period, 1978–1983, this species not reported in Oxford and Franklin Cos., and was found at few localities in s. Somerset and Piscataquis Cos. (Adamus 1987). In s. Somerset and n. Kennebec Cos., Upland Sandpipers bred in Canaan, Skowhegan, Norridgewock (2 adults and 1 young in Norridgewock, 9 Jul 1966; *MFN* 22: 135), Mercer, Clinton, Benton, Waterville, and Sidney in 1970s (Adamus 1987) with birds persisting to 1990s (W. Sumner, D. Mairs). As of 2010, they continued only at Waterville Airport and in Benton and Clinton (L. Bevier and W. Sumner).

In Penobscot Co., Upland Sandpipers bred in Corinth, 8 Jun 1966 (G. Freese) and most consistently at Bangor International Airport, from ~1982 (JVW) to present (M. Lucey, J. Markowsky, B. Barker et al.). It seems likely this species once bred in agricultural fields northwest of Bangor in Dexter and Charleston, as well as the area now occupied by the Bangor Mall shopping centers built in 1977 (J. Wells, pers. com.). In Aroostook Co., the old Loring Air Force Base, now Aroostook Co. NWR, in Limestone, is only site where they still nest regularly: 20 on 15 Jul 1997 and 7 adults on 16 Jun 2012 (both WJS). Species may have nested in hayfields at Christina Reservoir, Ft. Fairfield, as well as Presque Isle and Houlton airports but these sites vacant in recent years (WJS).

In Washington Co., Upland Sandpipers are seen in multiple blueberry barrens, all fide eBird: 10 in Columbia, 5 Jun 2017 (M. Longabaugh); 8 in Columbia Falls, 1 Jun 2014 (P. Trueblood); and 8 in Deblois, 30 Jun 2017 (S. Surner).

FALL: No conspicuous fall migration pattern with large flocks concentrating at predictable staging areas; some birds depart nesting areas by mid-Jul while others linger into early Sep. Small pre-migratory aggregations, 15–25 birds, seen at large

17 Jul 1995 (PDV); 10 in Biddeford, 5 Aug 1995 (L. Brinker); 20 in Biddeford, 19 Aug 1997 (P. Comins); 12 on Stratton I., 1 Aug 1998 (L. Brinker); 7 in Biddeford, 10 Aug 1999 (P. Moynahan). Continued decline in 2000s; highest counts: 10 at S. Portland, 4 Oct 2011 (M. Viens and A. Perko, eBird); 8 in Biddeford, 3 Aug 2000 (P. Moynahan); 6 on Stratton I., 1 Aug 2002 (Project Puffin, eBird); 6 at Scarborough Marsh, 26 Sep 2003; and 5 in Biddeford, 21 Aug 2005 (P. Moynahan).

PDV and CDD

Marbled Godwit
Limosa fedoa

A large, striking shorebird with an even more striking upturned bill

Status in Maine: The Marbled Godwit is a strictly coastal species in Maine, a casual transient in spring and an uncommon, but regular, fall migrant east to Camden, Knox County. It is occasional farther east in fall. There are two winter records, one in Portland and one, lingering from late summer, in Biddeford.

Historical Status in Maine: Knight (1908, 171) considered this species a "rare fall migrant," and listed only four specimen records taken at Scarborough in Aug–Sep and 1 collected in Phippsburg, 13 Sep 1900. Palmer listed two spring records and considered the species rare in fall in Cumberland and York Cos., and very rare in Lincoln and Piscataquis Cos. He also listed a single inland record, now considered doubtful (see *Remarks*).

Global Distribution: Nearctic. Breeds in central prairies of MB; SK; e. AB; to James Bay, ON; w. MN; south to ND; SD; and MT. Winters along Atlantic Coast from NC to FL, TX, and Mexico; on Pacific Coast, from WA and OR (local), CA, Mexico to Panama.

Remarks: The only inland record is dubious, "one seen at close range on September 10, 1944, on the tableland on Mt. Katahdin (M. Linton, fide Palmer 1949, 233)." The bird was not carefully described and may have been a Short-billed Dowitcher. A spring record from Steuben, 10 May 1991 (*AB* 45: 417) should be disregarded.

SPRING: Casual spring vagrant: ~6 records, 4 since 1989. Palmer reported 2 from Scarborough Marsh: 1 taken 20 Apr 1865 and 1 collected late May 1884. Additional spring records: 1 at Scarborough Marsh, 22 May 1989 (W. Howes et al, *AB* 43: 450), inaccurately described as "apparently Maine's first spring record

for the species" (*MBN* 3: 6); 1 at Old Orchard Beach, 28–29 May 2000 (G. Carson et al., *NAB* 54: 261); 1 at Reid S.P., 10 Jun 2004 (J. Adams et al.; *Guillemot* 34: 25); 1 in Yarmouth, 2 May 2009 (D. Lovitch et al.; ph.).

FALL: Rare annual fall migrants along coast, total of 1–4 birds, sometimes present for weeks, at preferred areas at Scarborough, Biddeford Pool, Wells, and Phippsburg beaches. High counts: 5 at Scarborough, 25 Aug 1862 (Palmer 1949), and, more recently, 4 at Lubec, 5 Sep 2010 (PDV, eBird). Single godwits exceptionally early at Reid S.P. on 13–15 Jul 2017 (D. Lovitch) and at Biddeford Pool, 25 Jun 1961 (*MFO* 6: 62). Ten records 20–31 Jul. Notably, 3 from seabird nesting islands: 1 adult at E. Egg Rock, 24 Jul 1991 (B. North); 1 on Stratton I., 30 Jul 1993 (T. Gaine, fide S. Benz) and another there 29 Jul 2017 (Z. Smith, eBird). Regular along southern coast Aug to mid-Sep. Three seen by Cruickshank on W. Egg Rock, Lincoln Co., 6 Aug 1947 considered unusual (Palmer 1949). Less frequent in Hancock and Washington Cos. In Lubec, reported 22–29 Aug 1983 (PDV and P. Weld, fide W. Townsend); 14–26 Aug 1999 (D. Crockett, *NAB* 54: 28); one on 9–10 Oct 2008 (C. Bartlett, ph.); as well as 2010 high count given above. Additional Washington Co. reports: Milbridge, 16 Aug 1995, and Cutler, 1 Aug 1998 (N. Famous). Casual in late Oct–Nov: 1–2 at Pine Pt., 28 Oct 1996 (G. Carson, *FN* 51: 25); 1 at Back Cove, Portland, 3–4 Nov 1960 (D. Edgarton); 1 at Wells Harbor, 21–23 Nov 2003 (F. Pratt and L. Brinker).

Migration timing in ME inadequately known, appears adults comprise early migrants. First positively identified juveniles reported 7–12 Aug 1994 at Scarborough Marsh (L. Brinker, PDV, et al.) and 7 Aug 2010 at Seawall Beach (G. Smith, eBird). Juveniles probably make up most records after 15 Aug, but not studied carefully. Latest known record: adult reported at Biddeford on 29 Aug 2013 lingered until at least 13 Sep 2013 (ISS, eBird).

WINTER: 2 records: 1 at Back Cove, Portland, 1 Jan 1974 (G. Sharpe, ph.; *MAS*, Jan 1974); and an immature at Biddeford, first seen 26 Aug 2016 and reported almost daily until 15 Dec of that year (L. Eastman, m.ob., eBird).

PDV and CDD

Ruddy Turnstone
Arenaria interpres

A shorebird that avoids mudflats in favor of rocky and sandy beaches, overturning pebbles and seaweed with its unique, upturned mandible

Status in Maine: Ruddy Turnstones are common spring migrants, arriving in early to mid-May and remaining until early June. Regular but rare in summer on offshore seabird-nesting islands; elsewhere, summering appears to be irregular, but this warrants further investigation to distinguish between migrant and resident birds. Southbound migrants appear, albeit rarely, as early as late June; most birds, and the largest flocks, are seen in August. Numbers decrease through the end of September. Turnstones are rare in winter along the coast, although regular at Biddeford Pool.

Historical Status in Maine: Both Knight and Palmer considered this species a common spring migrant in s. ME and abundant along the coast in fall. This has not changed appreciably since 1908, although Ruddy Turnstones appear to be less numerous fall migrants since the 1980s, mirroring the species' overall decline. Neither Knight nor Palmer mentioned turnstones wintering in ME.

SPRING: Earliest arrive late Apr–early May with 2–70 along York Co. coast: 20 at Biddeford Pool, 16 Apr 1982 (JEP) increased to 70 by 26 Apr 1982 (PDV); 70 at Biddeford Pool on 26 Apr 2012 (PDV, eBird) and 32 there 22 Apr 2008 (N. McReel, eBird). Spring high counts usually last week of May–early Jun: 308 and 257 at Stratton I. on 30 May 2011 and 26 May 1996, respectively (both Project Puffin Data, eBird); 300 at Biddeford Pool on 4 Jun 1961 (*MFO* 6: 62) and 175 there on 22 May 1968 (obs.unk.); and 200 at Scarborough Marsh, 22 May 2008 (M. Resch). Only large spring turnstone numbers in Washington Co. reported from Great Wass I., were 40 birds on 22 May 1983 and 35 on 27 May 2006 (both N. Famous). Ruddy Turnstones remain into first 2 weeks of Jun: flock of 54 birds notable at Reid S.P., 5 Jun 2006 (fide D. Lovitch). Accidental inland in spring, 2 records: 18–21 at Lower Richardson L., Twp. C, Oxford Co., 31 May 1987 (J. Chivers) and 1 ph. at Plymouth Pond, Penobscot Co., 2 Jun 2005 (B. Bagley).

Ruddy Turnstones and Red Knots

Global Distribution: Holarctic. Breeds in N. Am. in high Arctic from n. Canada to coastal AK; also n. Greenland, n. Europe, and Russia. Broad winter range: w. Atlantic from NS, s. ME, and MA to FL, Caribbean, Cen. Am. and S. Am. to Tierra del Fuego; on Pacific Coast from n. CA (locally in WA), to Mexico, Cen. Am., and S. Am.

Global Conservation Status: USSCP: High Concern because of significant threats and population declines, the latter estimated at more than 80% since 1970s (L. Niles, pers. com.).

SUMMER: Rare on rocky offshore islands, especially Stratton I. and E. Egg Rock, fewer than 10 each year in late Jun. Elsewhere, challenging to distinguish summering birds from late-spring and early-fall migrants, since spring migrants seen until 10 Jun and fall migrants appear in late Jun. Actual frequency of summering birds probably underestimated.

FALL: Common along coast Jul–Aug, most birds departing by late Sep. Few birds linger Oct–Nov and rarely Dec at limited preferred sites along southern coast (Scarborough, Biddeford Pool, Kittery Pt., Stratton I.). Juveniles appear mid- to late Aug–Sep.

Occurs in small numbers to mid-Nov. Late adults at Seawall Beach, 8 Oct 1995 (PDV), and in Benton–Clinton, 8 Nov 2008, exceptionally late (L. Bevier, ph.). Large flocks of late migrants: 56 at Kittery Pt., 23 Oct 1972 (H. Card); 50 in Thomaston, 9 Nov 2002 (M. Libby); >24 in Scarborough, 9 Nov 2008 (E. Hess); 17 in Scarborough, 21 Nov 1990 (L. Brinker); and again 15 Nov 2013 (PDV, eBird). Latest of all: 5 at Scarborough on 27 Nov 2013 and singles at Biddeford on 28 and 30 Nov 2017 (all J. Fecteau, eBird); and at Schoodic Peninsula, Hancock Co., on 8 Dec that same year (S. Benz, eBird).

Juveniles appear inland more regularly than adults, along lakes and ponds and wet margins. Brewster (1925, 245–246) recorded small numbers (1–9) regularly at L. Umbagog in Oct, noting, "Once (October 26, 1883), I found nine of them near the mouth of Cambridge River, two days after the entire region had been covered with snow to a depth of seven inches." In Somerset Co., 3 birds in Fairfield, 29 Oct 1997 (W. Sumner), locally rare. In Aroostook Co., 1 on Long L., St. Agatha, 13 Oct 2008 (WJS); Christina Reservoir, on 6 Sep 2009 and again 31 Oct 2015 (both WJS, eBird); 7 at L. Josephine, 10 Nov 2003, "seen during a snowstorm when the lake was largely covered with ice," and 1 at same locality, 16 Nov 2009 (WJS). Reported regularly in Orono, Newport, and Sabattus in Oct and early Nov. Large inland flocks: >40 at Cobbosseecontee L., 21 Oct 1984 (PDV and JVW), and 150 birds at Sabattus Pond, 27 Oct 1989 (J. Despres and P. McWilliams).

PDV and CDD

Buff-breasted Sandpiper
Calidris subruficollis

A distinctive "grasspiper" and an especially long-distance migrant

Status in Maine: The Buff-breasted Sandpiper is a rare fall migrant occurring in small numbers (usually one to six birds) from late August–late September along the coast and occasionally inland to central Maine. Single birds are typically found associating with American Golden-Plovers, yellowlegs, Pectoral Sandpipers, and Least Sandpipers, and occasionally in small intraspecies groups of two to six birds. The species is commonly found on sandy beaches and short grassland habitats such as wet hay fields, stubble fields, athletic fields, golf courses, airports, and turf farms. It also occurs irregularly at shorebird roosts such as Sprague Neck in Cutler. Buff-breasted Sandpipers are rarely seen on salt marshes and tidal mudflats, but occasionally on gravelly Lubec Flats. Rare inland, they are sometimes seen at turf and dairy farms. The species has not been observed in Aroostook

County despite suitable habitat and extensive surveying (WJS, pers. com.). Indeed, there are no records north of Orono.

Historical Status in Maine: Buff-breasted Sandpipers were more common in ME before 19th century market hunting substantially reduced the population. There are no records of small flocks 1915–1940. Knight was unfamiliar with the Buff-breasted Sandpiper but said that Brown considered it a regular fall migrant in the Portland area Aug–Sep, having shot as many as four in a single day. Palmer apparently gave little credence to Brown's observations and ignored them, reporting only 23 records (15 collected, 8 sight records), Aug–Sep 1845–1940. He did recognize as valid Norton's observation of six together in Portland, 20 Aug 1940. Baird et al. (1884), relying on Boardman's comments, said Buff-breasted Sandpipers were found in the Calais area in spring and fall. That spring status seems mistaken as there are but a handful of recent spring records in the entire northeast U.S. and none in NB and NS.

Global Distribution: Breeds in high Arctic Canada, AK, and far e. Russia. Winters in s. S. Am., primarily pampas of coastal se. Brazil, cen. Argentina, and Uruguay (Lanctot et al. 2010); migrates north and south primarily through cen. N. Am. with fewer migrants regular along Atlantic Coast in fall.

Global Conservation Status: IUCN: Near Threatened; USSCP: High Concern.

Remarks: At the end of the 1800s, the population was estimated from hundreds of thousands to more than one million. The current population estimate for Buff-breasted Sandpipers is 35,000–78,000 (Wetlands International 2019). This indicates a massive decline from the end of the 1800s to the present.

SPRING: A bird well-ph. and videotaped at Clinton, 22–23 May 2017, is the only spring record (eBird).

SUMMER: 3 records, all adults: 1 ph. on Popham Beach, 26–29 Jul 2011 (M. Fahay, eBird); 1 ph. at Fryeburg Harbor, 6 Aug 2017 (A. Robbins, eBird); and one in S. Portland, 12 Aug 1995 (L. Brinker, *FN* 50: 22). All birds seen after 20 Aug are bright juveniles.

FALL: Juveniles regular and nearly annual in small numbers along coast during fall migration: 1–6 usually late Aug–third week of Sep. Maximum in one season: 30 in 2011, including 11 n. of Berwick, York Co., on 10 Sep 2011. Main migration 21 Aug–20 Sep, peak ~1 Sep. Earliest fall juveniles observed at Scarborough

Marsh, 18 Aug 1984 (JVW) and 18 Aug 2001 (P. Moynahan, eBird). Latest fall migrant: 20 Oct 1990 at Biddeford Pool (S. Pollock). Sightings of multiple birds: in Cutler, 3 on 28–30 Aug 1985 (CDD, PDV), 4 on 4 Sep 1994 (L. Brinker), 4 on 7 Sep 2009 (B. Southard); 3 in Lubec, 28 Aug 1983 (CDD); 3 in Steuben, 10–14 Sep 1989 (R. Widrig); in S. Portland: 4 on 2 Sep 1995 (L. Brinker), 4 on 28 Sep 2006 (L. Brinker), 3–5 on 4–5 Sep 2011 (L. Bevier, B. Cole, and D. Hitchcox; eBird); 3 at Reid S.P., 26 Aug 2005 (fide ME Audubon); 4 at Winding Brook Turf Farm, Lyman, 8 Sep 2006 (B. Southard); 6 at Moody Beach, York Co., 7 Sep 2006 (K. Jones); 3 at Falmouth H.S. fields, Cumberland, Cumberland Co., 14 Sep 2007 (L. Seitz); 3 at Scarborough Marsh, 2 Sep 2012 (eBird). Inland: annual late Aug–early Sep at Berwick, Clinton, and Fryeburg. Others: 5 in Bangor, 29 Aug–2 Oct 1970 (G. Freese et al.); 4 at Little Falls, Cumberland Co., 7–9 Sep 2017 (T. Fennel et al.; eBird); 1 in Orono, 18–21 Sep 1976 (N. Famous et al.; ph.); 1 in Turner, 3 Sep–7 Oct 1994 (J. Despres et al.); 2 in Gray, Cumberland Co., 6 Sep 2006 (obs. unk.); 2 at Sebago L. S.P., 12 Sep 2006 obs. unk.); 2 in Gray, 12–14 Sep 2007 (fide E. Hynes); 1 on Clarry Hill, Union, 12 Sep 2007 (PDV).

PDV and CDD

Pectoral Sandpiper
Calidris melanotos

A long-distance migrant of the Central Flyway whose numbers in Maine vary greatly from year to year

Status in Maine: Although their main migration passes through central North America, Pectoral Sandpipers are regular spring migrants in Maine. They arrive in small numbers in spring, primarily between mid-April and mid-May, and are more frequent along the coast than in fall when they are common to locally abundant. The first fall migrants arrive in mid-July with numbers increasing into September and October when flocks of 30–50 birds are occasionally reported. They are more numerous on inland lakes and ponds during the fall.

Historical Status in Maine: Knight reported that, as now, Pectoral Sandpipers were regular fall migrants, common at Sabattus Pond in Oct of 1897 and 1899, where the species remains common in season to the present. At L. Umbagog, Brewster (1925) considered Pectoral Sandpipers to be common to abundant fall migrants in late summer and fall. He reported small numbers of adults in Jul–early Aug and larger numbers of juveniles Sep–Oct, when he saw up to 100 birds at a time. Similarly, Palmer considered the

species rare in spring and common to abundant in fall, particularly along the coast, and irregular inland.

Global Distribution: Nearctic. Breeds in Arctic from Hudson Bay west through n. Canada to n. and w. AK, and n. Russia. Winters primarily in Peru, Bolivia, Chile, Argentina, and Uruguay, also in Australia and New Zealand.

Global Conservation Status: USSCP: High Concern because of high threats and population declines.

Remarks: Pectoral Sandpipers were called "creakers" by 19th-century gunners for their "*cr-rr-rr, cr-rr-rr*" flight notes (Brewster 1925).

SPRING: Rare but annual in past decade with curious exception of 2010, occurring in small numbers (1–8) late Mar–early Jun. Most spring records 15 Apr–15 May. At least 8 records 25–30 Mar: earliest at Scarborough, 25 Mar 2008 (R. Lambert) and, notably because inland, 2 in Augusta, 26 Mar 1999 (R. Spinney). In 2006, migration was generally earlier than usual with reports from Sanford (1 on 1 Apr, A. Aldrich), Buxton, York Co. (1 on 2 Apr, R. Harrison), and Scarborough (9 on 6 Apr, D. Lovitch). Late-spring migration records at Scarborough Marsh: 1 on 30 May 2006 (E. Hess), 1 on 1 Jun 2008 (D. Lovitch), and 2 on 5 Jun 1957 (*MFO* 2: 71). Later records, all from seabird islands, possibly nonbreeding birds: 7–9 Jun 2002 at Seal I. NWR and 1 at E. Egg Rock, 19–21 Jun 2011 (Project Puffin, eBird).

Spring occurrence of Pectoral Sandpipers on East Coast highly variable. No ME reports in spring of 1987, 1989, 1990, 1994, and 2000. Unprecedented flight in 1981 brought >1,000 to Newburyport, MA, 20 Apr 1981, and large flocks observed elsewhere in s. New England (R. Heil; Veit and Petersen 1993). Unusually large numbers in ME that year (1981): 23 in Orono on 7 Apr (B. Bochan); 15 in Wells, 11 Apr (obs. unk.); 10 in Kennebunk, 9 Apr (J. Ficker); 10 in Trenton, Hancock Co., 9 Apr (W. Townsend); 9 in Whiting, Washington Co., 23 Apr (N. Famous). Other large spring counts: 27 at Scarborough 27 Apr 1986 and 14 there on 26 Apr 1982 (both PDV), and 12 at same locality, 16 Apr 2006 (E. Hess).

Fewer records for eastern counties than coastal s. ME: in addition to N. Famous records above, 7 birds particularly unusual in Roque Bluffs, 7 Apr 1979 (T. Preston, Jr.). Casual inland: 5 observed in Brownfield Bog, 23 May 1984 (P. Richards); 1 seen in Orono, 8 May 1984 (J. Markowsky). Rare in n. and w. ME, with few Franklin Co. records: 1 in New Sharon on 1 May 1996 (obs. unk.); in Clinton: 1 on 8 May 1996, 1 on 16 May 2002, and 1 on 3 May 2003 (obs. unk.); 1 in Farmington on 5 May 1997 (W. Sumner); 1, Fryeburg, 20–21 May 2013 (B. Crowley, J. Scott, eBird). Although Palmer, citing Kilburn, considered this species a rare spring migrant on Aroostook R., there is only one spring

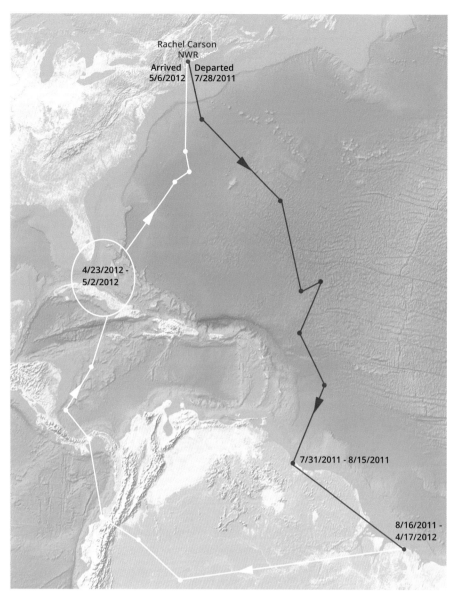

Rachel Carson
NWR

Arrived | Departed
5/6/2012 | 7/28/2011

4/23/2012 -
5/2/2012

7/31/2011 - 8/15/2011

8/16/2011 -
4/17/2012

Map 14: Willet Migration

Fall (red) and spring (yellow) migration tracks of one of the three Willets tagged with light-sensitive geolocators at Rachel Carson NWR in 2011 and 2012. All three left during the third week of July, making nonstop, over-water flights of more than 5,000 miles (8,000 km) to northern South America where they wintered. In April, the bird depicted here flew inland across n. South America, while the other two tracked more along the Venezuelan coast. They then spent several weeks at various sites in the Caribbean and along the Florida coast. (The oval suggests a likely range, as it was not possible to refine the location of these stopovers precisely.) All three returned to their breeding sites within three days of one another in early May (K. Regan, Biodiversity Research Institute, pers. com.).

and most reports do not distinguish between subspecies. "Western" Willet first recognized in ME when 8 birds identified in Wells, 8–16 Sep 1972 (DWF); likely several late-fall records 1953–1970 pertain to subspecies: 2 in Biddeford, 8 Nov 1953 (obs. unk.); 12 recorded in E. Sullivan, Hancock Co., 16 Oct 1967, an unusually high number (obs. unk.); 2 in Trenton, Hancock Co., 29 Sep 1970 (obs. unk.). "Western" Willet regular in small numbers along s. ME coast but

appears occasional in Washington Co. Earliest report for "Western" Willet of single juvenile at Biddeford Pool, 9 Jul 1993 (L. Brinker). Reports of 1–3 birds of this subspecies reasonably widespread in Aug with occasional higher counts: 12 at Scarborough, 2 Sep 1993 (PDV); 27 at Biddeford Pool, 7 Aug 2005 (D. Lovitch). Washington Co. records of W. Willet probably incomplete: 2 in Lubec, 20 Sep 1998 (N. Famous); 1 in Robbinston, 28 Aug 2007 (PDV, ph.).

The few reports that separate "Eastern" and "Western" Willets indicate they co-occur mid-Jul to early Sep: 171 "Eastern" and 1 "Western" at Biddeford Pool, 18 Jul 2008 (D. Lovitch); 11 "Eastern" and 1 "Western" on Little Stratton I., York Co., 8 Aug 2006 (R. Lambert); 6 "Eastern" and 2 "Western" Willet juveniles, 14 Aug (PDV, yr. unk.); 2 "Eastern" and 1 "Western" Willet juveniles, 7 Sep 2000 (L. Brinker). Appears "Eastern" Willets become uncommon by mid-Aug and most late Aug–Sep records pertain to "Western" *T. s. inornatus*. Latest documented "Eastern" Willet: adult in alternate plumage, reported on 22 Sep 2010 (PDV, JEP, ph.). Other reports of late "Eastern" Willets at Scarborough: 18 on 24 Aug 2010 (D. Hitchcox and N. Lund, eBird), 12 on 4 Sep 2010, and 2 on 12 Sep 2010 (both D. Lovitch). Careful observations that identify Willets to subspecies or more tagging studies of ME-breeding birds would help clarify this issue.

One contemporary inland fall record: single bird seen in T18 MD BPP, Washington Co., 25 Aug 2006 (N. Famous).

WINTER: 4 winter reports, none identified to subspecies: 1 in Rockland, 1 Jan 1987 (*AB* 41: 255); 1 in Machias, 11 Dec 1991 (R. Hunt, *Guillemot* 20: 58); 1 at Pine Pt., 4 Dec 2004–9 Jan 2005 or later (J. Adams); and 1 at same locality on 13 Dec 2007 (fide E. Hynes).

PDV and CDD

Greater Yellowlegs

Tringa melanoleuca

Common, widespread, and surprisingly little-studied

Status in Maine: Greater Yellowlegs are common spring and fall migrants in a variety of wetland habitats. The species typically arrives by early April and remains through early June. A few yellowlegs appear to remain through the summer, but this is difficult to determine with certainty because migrations for spring and fall nearly overlap. Fall migrants appear by early July with the largest numbers recorded from late July through September. Greater Yellowlegs are found regularly in small numbers into November, and there are five winter records. With few exceptions, high counts in the past decade have not equaled older ones.

Historical Status in Maine: Knight (1908, 172) suggested that Greater Yellowlegs bred in ME, saying "there seems no reason to doubt that it does nest in small numbers in the Woolastook Valley [Aroostook County] where I have observed it in early July." Knight came to this conclusion by assuming, incorrectly, that early Jul was too early for fall migrants. He also failed to describe any breeding behavior, which is notably conspicuous in this species. Palmer disagreed with Knight, contending that the species did not breed in ME; he considered it a regular spring and fall migrant that was regular inland. He reported a flock of 50 at Merrymeeting Bay, 13 Apr 1933.

Global Distribution: Nearctic. Breeds in muskeg and wet boreal habitats from n. NS, NL, and QC, n. ON, cen. SK, MB, AB, BC, to s. and cen. AK. Winters on Atlantic from NY to FL, TX, and Mexico; and along Pacific, from WA (local) to s. OR, CA, Baja California; also Mexico, Cen. and S. Am., and Caribbean.

Remarks: Palmer reported that a single gunner shot 999 Greater Yellowlegs, 1842–1854. A single Greater Yellowlegs at the tarn atop Tumbledown Mtn., Twp. 6, north of Weld, Franklin Co., 6 Jul 1990, was not in typical habitat (D. Reimer).

SPRING: Greater Yellowlegs appear early Apr generally in flocks of 2–12; occasionally many more. High counts: 200 at Weskeag Marsh, 15 May 2000 (Z. Smith, ISS), and 92 there on 7 May 1985 (ISS, eBird); 110 at Scarborough Marsh on 2 May 1983 and again 30 Apr 1985 (both PDV, eBird); and 59 birds in Phippsburg, 6 May 2009 (M. Fahay).

Common on coastal marshes, in wet fields, and along inland lakes Apr–May, occasionally lingering into early Jun. Evidence this species arrives earlier than historical records, 19th to mid-20th century. Since 1970, at least 10 records, all coastal, March 24–31, whereas Palmer cited 7 Apr. as earliest date for Scarborough. Inland, species recorded annually mid- to late Apr in past decade. Historically, arrived in n. and w. ME early May. Recent first Aroostook Co. records demonstrate now regular last week of Apr, all fide eBird: 6 at Mattawamkeag L. on 23 Apr 2010 both earliest and highest count of 9 records in Apr. for Aroostook Co. (J. Getchell); 1 in Presque Isle, 24 Apr 2008 (WJS); and 3 in Ft. Fairfield, 28 Apr 2009 (C. Kesselheim). These observations approximately 1 week earlier than M. Trombley's reports of first arrivals from late 1980s: 2 in Ft. Fairfield, 4 May 1987, and 2 there on 1 May 1988. Other early inland records, 1 each: Bethel, 25 Apr 1980 (P.A. Cross); Kenduskeag, Penobscot Co., 20 Apr 1997 (B. Barker); Clinton, 23 Apr 1997 (W. Sumner); in recent years dozens of inland Apr records (eBird).

SUMMER: Numerous records 1–10 Jun may represent late migrants northbound or summering birds that failed to migrate farther north. Few records last half of month, likely of latter category, possibly including earliest of southbound migrants, which are likely birds with failed nesting attempts. Late Jun records at Scarborough Marsh: 6 on 15 Jun 2003 (C. Marantz); 1 on 20 Jun 2004, 5 on 19 Jun 2005, 1 on 18 Jun 2006, 2 on 28 Jun 2007, 1 on 15 Jun 2010, and 3 on 20 Jun 2010 (all D. Lovitch). Additional summer lingerers: 1 in St. George, Knox Co., 21 Jun 1988 (M. Plymire), and 2 at Weskeag Marsh, on 23 Jun 2007 (D. Reimer).

FALL: eBird data show numbers rising by early Jul as southbound migrants arrive. Widespread by mid-Jul. Highest numbers typically at preferred roosting areas mid-Jul to mid-Sep: Spirit Pond, Phippsburg, 107 on 4 Aug 2017, 100 on 28 Jul 2010, 94 on 16 Aug 2016, 89 on 2 Sep 2009 (all M. Fahay, eBird); at Weskeag Marsh, 200 on 25 Jul 1979 (PDV), 100 on 14 Aug 2001 (C. Ogan, eBird), and 85 on 12 Aug 2009 (ISS Data, eBird); at Scarborough Marsh, 150 on 13 Aug 1984 (PDV), 115 on 17 Sep 1999 (L. Brinker), and 100 on 29 Aug 2000 (R. Crowley). Downeast: 75 at Hog Bay, Franklin, Hancock Co., 31 Jul 2005, and 98 at Hog Bay, 2 Sep 2006 (M. Good, S. Perrin); Machiasport: 100 on 17 Sep 1995 and 80 on 27 Jul 1999 (both N. Famous); Milbridge, Back Bay: 100 on 8 Aug 1994 (MDIFW, eBird); Whiting, Looks Cannery, Washington Co.: 95 on 5 Oct 1994 (MDIFW, eBird). Other large counts: 200 at Sherman L., Newcastle, 13 Nov 2005 (M. Mahnke); 120 at Stratton I. on 19 Jul 2005 (S. Hall and Project Puffin data, eBird).

Common in Oct, declining numbers into mid-Nov when still regular in small numbers along southern coast. Notably late records: 6 in Bar Harbor, 21 Nov 1970 (W. Townsend); 12 in Scarborough, 9 Nov 1970, 1 remaining to 25 Nov 1970 (*MN* 2[5]: 38); 14 at Pemaquid, Bristol, 23 Nov 2005 (M. Libby); 1 in S. Thomaston, 27 Nov 1991 (D. Reimer and M. Libby, *AB* 46: 63); 1 in Scarborough, 29 Nov 2009 (D. Lovitch); at least 1 record each year, 20–30 Nov, 2010–2017, except 2015 (eBird). Late inland records: 1 in Orono, 9 Nov 2003 (S. Smith); 1 in Penobscot, 19 Nov 1989 (W. Sumner).

WINTER: Five winter records, 1 each: Brandy Pond, Naples, Cumberland Co., 2 Dec 1993 (L. Brinker); Harpswell, 29 Dec 1970 (E. Gamble, *MN* 2: 47), and 5 Dec 2012 (M. Fahay, eBird); Machiasport, 3 Jan 2006 (N. Famous); and 9 Dec 2015–1 Jan 2016, possibly later, near Nonesuch R., Scarborough (A. Hancock, eBird).

PDV and CDD

Wilson's Phalarope
Phalaropus tricolor

A bird of western potholes and saline lakes, recently a regular visitor in Maine

Status in Maine: Prior to 1960, Wilson's Phalaropes were accidental in Maine, with four (or perhaps five) records. Since then, this species has become more common in south coastal Maine and is now regular there both in spring and fall annually. Wilson's Phalarope has summered irregularly at Scarborough Marsh since 1988 and was confirmed nesting on the marsh in 2002. This species remains rare inland and in eastern Maine. There are no winter records.

Historical Status in Maine: Accidental. Knight (1908, 150) considered Wilson's Phalarope to be "a very exceptional straggler" with two records: three together with one collected on Scarborough Marsh, 9 Jun 1881, and one shot at Sabattus Pond in "September or October" 1906. Palmer added two records: an adult female above Middle Dam on Lower Richardson L., Twp. C, Oxford Co., 20 May 1881 (Brewster 1925), and one he saw at Maquoit Bay, Brunswick, on 24 Aug 1941. Palmer also mentioned Brewster's "probable" inland record of four birds together at the Cambridge R. mouth in Upton, Oxford Co., 28 Aug 1873.

Global Distribution: Nearctic. Breeds from s. QC and ON, west throughout prairie states and provinces north to AB and s. NU, south to n. CA, UT, and CO. Since 1970, also irregularly and locally nests from NB, ME, MA, and NY. Winters primarily in cen.

Andes Mtns. from Peru south to Argentina and Chile. Species expanding its breeding range in eastern states and provinces, and also west in AK.

Remarks: As with many shorebirds, it is difficult to distinguish between late-spring migrants, summering individuals, and early-fall migrants. Late-spring migrants may linger until 10 Jun but do not remain in the same area. Similarly, early-fall adult migrants can arrive by mid-Jul, with juvenile birds appearing early to mid-Aug.

SPRING: Accidental in spring until 1960s. Apparently, no spring records 1941–1961, until 1 female observed in Kenduskeag, Penobscot Co., 8 Jun 1961 (G. Freese). Reports increased 1961–1982, including several inland records, much like Brewster's early observation: 1 in Glenburn, Penobscot Co., 18–19 May 1971 and 1 in Ashland, 26 May 1973.

Coastal records 1961–1982: 1 on Little Green I., Knox Co., 29 May 1967; 1 at Biddeford, 15 May 1973; 1 in Wells Harbor, 2 Jun 1973 (obs. unk.). Since 1982, Wilson's Phalaropes annual or nearly annual along southern coast, particularly at Scarborough Marsh. Observations of multiple birds similarly increased here since 1983: male and female, 2–11 May 1983 (PDV); 3 birds on 25 May 1985 (fide ME Audubon); 5, all-time maximum, on 31 May 1985 (ISS, F. Cyr; eBird); 2 on 4 Jun 1988 (K. Disney); and 2–4 birds reported regularly at Scarborough Marsh since 2001. Species now arrives in ME 15 May–1 Jun; earliest record: single bird in Wells, 30 Apr 1988 (K. Disney, J. Lortie).

Elsewhere along coast: Cumberland Co. (other than Scarborough); 1 at Maquoit Bay, 6 May 1984 (JEP). Sagadahoc Co.: 1 female at Popham Beach S.P. on 14 May 2016 (M. Fahay, eBird); 1 female in Phippsburg, 16 May 1982 (PDV); and 1 female in Georgetown, 27 May 2000 (J. Frank). Multiple spring records at Weskeag Marsh, the first a female on 7 May 1984 (PDV); since 1999, Wilson's Phalaropes regular and nearly annual at this site (L. Bevier, D. Reimer, M. Libby et al.). In Washington Co.: 1 at Petit Manan NWR, 19 May 1989 (R. Widrig); 1 in Machiasport, 1 May 1996 (P. Donahue, *FN* 50: 255), and 2 in Machias, 5 Jun 2008 (B. Southard).

Casual on offshore islands: Appledore I., 1 on 20 May 1997 (fide D.W. Holmes) and adult female, 19–31 May 2012 (m.ob., eBird). Reports of single birds from Stratton I.: 11–12 Jun 1994 (ISS and L. LaCasse, eBird); and 25 Jun–1 Jul 2012 (Project Puffin, eBird). At Seal I. NWR, 1 on 18–19 May 2017 (K. Yakola and W. Kennerley, eBird). Inland, single phalaropes observed in Aroostook Co. at L. Josephine on 15 May 2009 (WJS) and at Washburn Wastewater Lagoons on 31 May 2012 (WJS, eBird); at Penjajawoc Marsh, 11 May 1993 (J. Markowsky, N. Famous); at Flood Brothers Dairy, Clinton, males seen on 26 May 2016 and on 16 May 2017 (m.ob., eBird).

SUMMER: Documented throughout summer at Scarborough Marsh in 1988, 2–4 birds seen regularly early Jun–Aug. Four birds, 2 males and 2 females, observed in courtship flights on 23 Jun 1988 (K. Disney) and it appeared birds were nesting on this marsh. Juvenile observed 13 Aug 1988 (JVW) and an adult with 2 juveniles noted 17 Aug 1988 (PDV); no more specific evidence of nesting noted.

Summering females observed at Scarborough Marsh in 1996, 1997, and 1998 (various observers), when juvenile on 1 Aug 1998 appeared too early to be a fall migrant (L. Brinker). G. Shriver, present daily at Scarborough Marsh in 1999, reported 2 males and a female regularly 16 Jun–early Aug 1999 and observed behavior suggestive of breeding; however, no juveniles observed. First nesting confirmed by L. Brinker in 2002 when he flushed incubating male and found nest with 3 eggs along Jones Creek, 14 Jun 2002. A second nest with 4 eggs found approximately 100 meters from first, 21 Jun 2002 (L. Brinker, PDV). Male observed attending juvenile in central Scarborough Marsh, 1 Aug 2002, probably represented a third breeding effort (S. Hall, L. Brinker). Multiple adults in 2005 and 2006 possibly represented additional breeding attempts. One or more phalaropes observed sporadically through summer at Weskeag Marsh in 2008 and 2009. This marsh may provide second breeding locality in ME, although no subsequent summer records.

FALL: First fall migrants appear in coastal s. ME marshes mid-Jul; species regular by mid- to late Aug. Impossible to distinguish migrants from residents unless phalaropes absent for majority of Jun. Earliest unambiguous fall migrants reported from Atkin's Bay Marsh, Phippsburg, 1 Jul 2004 (PDV), and at Weskeag Marsh on 2 Jul 2008 (D. Reimer) and 25 Jul 1979 (PDV). Jul migrants at Scarborough Marsh: 2 adults on 16 Jul 1992 (JVW), 2 females on 17 Jul 1995 (PDV), 1 on 26 Jul 1998 (D. Abbott), and 2 on 27 Jul 2003 (L. Brinker).

Numbers peak 10 Aug–15 Sep; species regular in smaller numbers through ~20 Sep after which few records. Scarborough Marsh: 1 on 23 Sep 1962 (obs. unk.) and 1 on 25 Sep 1992 (S. Pollock); 1 on 26 Sep 1996 (G. Carson); 1 from 18–22 Sep 2013 (m.ob., eBird). One reported without further description or documentation on 30 Oct 2006 was the latest by far (M. Goldfarb, eBird).

Despite regularity in coastal s. ME, species occasional to rare in fall in Washington and Hancock Cos., with <10 records: 1 in Pembroke, Washington Co., 6 Aug 1972 (S. Bahrt); 1 in Perry, Washington Co., 13 Aug 1980 (PDV); 1 in Steuben, 23 Aug 1989 (R. Widrig); 1 juvenile in Addison, 23 Aug 2008 (D. Mitchell); 1 at Sprague Neck, 31 Aug and 1 Sep 1988 (CDD); and 1 at Pleasant Pt., Washington Co., 1 Sep 2016 (C. Bartlett and W. Gilles, eBird).

Casual to rare inland until recently; species observed occasionally at Sanford Lagoons since 1999. Other notable records: 2 ph. at Carpenter Pond, T7 R11 WELS, n. Piscataquis

Co., 14 Aug 1980 (fide PDV); 1 in Easton, Aroostook Co., 28 Jul 1991, earliest of any inland records (M. Trombley); 1 in Newport, 1 Oct 1988 exceptional both for date and inland locality (W. Sumner, *AB* 43: 64).
PDV and CDD

Red-necked Phalarope
Phalaropus lobatus

Once abundant in Maine waters, but where are they now?

Status in Maine: Red-necked Phalaropes are common to abundant spring migrants between mid-May and early June. This species occurs primarily in offshore waters and is uncommon to occasional on inshore waters in spring and fall. Fall migrants appear in mid- to late July and are common in late July and August, especially offshore. Red-necked Phalaropes were once overwhelmingly abundant in the Passamaquoddy Bay area, off Washington County and adjoining New Brunswick, numbering from hundreds of thousands to >2 million individuals. After the early 1980s, these enormous concentrations declined to the point of complete disappearance (Duncan 1996b), most likely from "severely reduced abundance of [their main prey] the zooplankton species, *Calanus finmarchicus*, in surface waters during the time phalaropes migrate through the area" (Brown et al. 2010).

Maine Conservation Status: Species of Special Concern.

Historical Status in Maine: Knight (1908, 149) had a rudimentary knowledge of Red-necked Phalaropes and provided little evidence to support his assertion that this species was "not rare along the coast from September to November and in April and May, occasionally also in late winter." Norton (1907, 81) described "thousands feeding" between Deer Island and Campobello I., NB, just a few mi. from Eastport. Palmer (1949, 238–239) described phalaropes as "transient, in spring, abundant in offshore and inshore waters of the Maine–New Brunswick boundary, straggling inshore farther westward, and rare inland, and in fall, a similar status except that more stragglers come ashore to the westward and inland." He characterized them as regular from the third week of Jul to 22 Sep with several hundred thousand present at W. Quoddy Head. At L. Umbagog, Brewster (1925) observed this species once in spring and on at least eight occasions 1874–1898.

The enormity of the Red-necked Phalarope spectacle in eastern ME and the speed with which it disappeared in the late 1980s are hard to grasp. Finch et al. (1978, 282) reported annual occurrences in late summer and early fall in lower Passamaquoddy Bay "where up to three million have been estimated in late August. . . similarly immense numbers gather in areas of upwelling around Mount Desert Rock, where more than two million birds have been estimated in early September." In an earlier draft of this account, PDV wrote, "Having witnessed some of the remarkable Red-necked Phalarope concentrations in the 1970s, I can attest to the size of these huge flocks. It was essentially impossible to accurately count the numerous vast flocks that shifted back and forth with the tides. The dizzying spectacle of uncountable flocks of phalaropes and thousands of Bonaparte's Gulls at The Old Sow was one of the most remarkable avian events in e. N. Am." While the enormous one-day numbers of the 1970s must be considered coarse guesstimates, Mercier and Gaskin (1985) made careful, systematic population estimates in 1981 and 1982. Their estimate of the total passage population for Passamaquoddy Bay for all of 1982 came to 1 million. Numbers started to decline in the early 1980s: only 100,000 reported on the single day 1 Aug 1982 (N. Famous), and 300,000 phalaropes in mid-Aug 1983 was considered a low count (*AB* 38: 177). CDD visited these waters regularly in subsequent years, eventually almost daily; his one-day maxima were 20,000 in 1985, 8,000 in 1986, 2,000 in 1987, 200 in 1988, just 20 in 1989, and none the following two years (Duncan 1996b). None were reported in 1991 (*AB* 46: 63–64) and no counts have exceeded 500 individuals since 1991.

Global Distribution: Holarctic. Circumpolar breeding distribution. Nests from s. Labrador, Greenland, Baffin I., west to n. ON, across n. Canada to nw. AK; also in Siberia, n. Scandinavia, n. Scotland, Ireland, and Iceland. Winter distribution in Atlantic not well known; small numbers off GA and FL. Fennoscandian and Russian breeders migrate overland to the Arabian Sea/Indian Ocean while those from Scotland, Iceland, and Greenland migrate over ocean through the Bay of Fundy and Gulf of ME, crossing over s. Cen. America to Pacific Humboldt Current off S. Am., south to Chile. Notably, they are the only nw. Atlantic seabird that does so (see Map 15).

While the migratory routes for Nearctic (Alaskan or Canadian) breeders remain unknown, it is likely that, as for the palearctic phalaropes, there is a "migratory divide" where more westerly breeders move directly south along the Pacific Coast while those to their east make a stopover in the Bay of Fundy and Gulf of ME.

Global Conservation Status: USSCP: Moderate Concern for steep population declines.

SPRING: Common—previously abundant—spring offshore migrants. Most numerous and regular on offshore waters Monhegan I. to Mount Desert Rock, east to Eastport. Although previously routine to see 100–500 off Monhegan I. in late May, highest count this century is 12, on 20 May 2011 (D. Hitchcox, eBird). High counts: 5,000 on 24 May 1985 (S. Surner, *AB* 39: 271) and 1,500 on 27 May 1973 (M. Libby). Farther east: >750 in Penobscot Bay off Matinicus Rock, 31 May 1985 (JEP); 50,000 off Mount Desert Rock, 24 May 2008 (C. Propst and T. Schottland); in Washington Co., 40,000 observed near Head Harbor Passage, off Eastport, 26 May 1980 (N. Famous). Observations for coastal York and Cumberland Cos. usually limited to 1–12, smaller numbers along immediate coast: 11 off Dyer Pt., Cape Elizabeth, 26 May 2005 (D. Lovitch); and 150 total off Outer Green I., Casco Bay, 25 May 2005, unusually large flock (R. Lambert). Rare inland in spring: 2 on L. Umbagog, 20 May 1881 (Brewster 1925); 1 ph. at Douglas Pond, Palmyra, Somerset Co., 28 May 1977 (G. Ball); 3 at Weskeag Marsh, 13 May 2006 (M. Libby, D. Reimer); 2 at Scarborough Marsh, 14 May 2006 (E. Hess); 5 at Sanford Lagoons, 19 May 2011 (A. Aldrich, eBird), and 1 female ph. there 23 May 2017 (m.ob., eBird); 1 at L. Josephine, 28 May 2012 (T. Day and L. Seitz, eBird). One male and 1 female at Seawall Beach, 27 May 1976, unique for being on the beach (PDV, eBird).

Red-necked Phalarope

Almost all spring records 15 May–10 Jun. Earliest confirmed record: 1 shot in Milo, Piscataquis Co., 3 May 1897 (Palmer 1949); 4 off Monhegan I., 7 May 1981, also notably early (M. Libby). Count of >75 off Matinicus Rock, 9 Jun 1957 (M. Libby) unusually high for early date.

SUMMER: More than 12 reports, 3 or fewer birds (when number is specified), off coast in last half of Jun. Too late to be considered spring migrants and unlikely to be early-fall migrants. Reports onshore at Scarborough Marsh on 22 Jun 1984 (J. James, eBird) and Ferry Beach, Saco 29 Jun 2017 (L. Harlan, eBird) are particularly unusual.

FALL: Prior to population collapse, flocks of 40–200 commonly observed offshore beginning in Jul. Early reports: 5 from MV *Bluenose* ferry, 4 Jul 1978 (PDV, eBird); 3 on Bar Harbor whale/pelagic trip, 4 Jul 2015 (D. Hollie, eBird); 11 at W. Quoddy Head, Lubec, 8 Jul 1984 (A. Farnsworth, eBird); 46 off Mount Desert I., 14 Jul 1989 (B. Agler); 70 on Bar Harbor whale/pelagic trip, 14 Jul 2017 (T. Graves, eBird); 25 off Monhegan I., 18 Jul 1960 (*MFO* 5: 72). Species remains in Gulf of ME through mid-Sep, uncommon into early Oct. Large concentrations, routinely hundreds of thousands of birds, occurred historically in Eastport–Lubec area, Washington Co., and off Mount Desert Rock, Hancock Co., but no longer found (see boxed text). Extraordinarily large counts: 2 million birds estimated on 21 Aug 1977 (DWF, PDV, *AB* 32: 176); >500,000 between Eastport and Deer I., NB, 19 Aug. 1979 (N. Famous and M. McCollough); and 1 million on 13 Aug 1980 (PDV, *AB* 35: 158).

Occasional to rare inland, though Brewster (1925) observed this species on L. Umbagog, Oxford Co., on 8 or more occasions 1874–1898. Inland records: Aroostook Co.: 1 in Houlton, 8 Sep 1970 (*MN* 2[3]: at L. Josephine, 1 on 3 Sep 2010 and 2 on 3 Aug 2014 (both WJS).

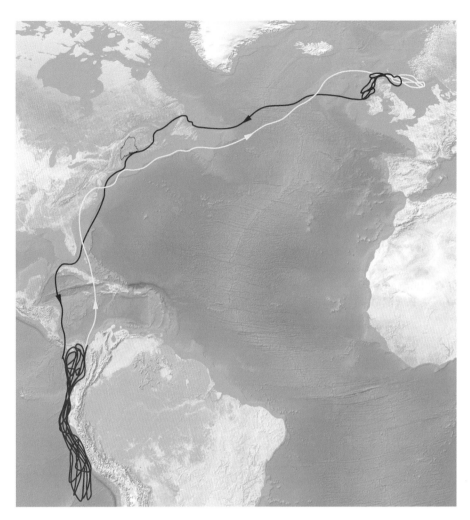

Map 15: Red-necked Phalarope Migration

Generalized migration routes of three Red-necked Phalaropes fitted with light-sensitive geolocators on their breeding grounds in Shetland, Scotland (one bird in 2012 and two in 2016). After leaving Shetland in midsummer, each migrated westward (red line), arriving at the Bay of Fundy in mid-August, where they stayed for three to five days before flying to Florida. Continuing south, they crossed the Isthmus of Panama to the Pacific Ocean by mid-September and went on to the coast of Ecuador by early October, where they remained (blue lines) until the first week of May, when they returned to Scotland (yellow line). Red-necked Phalaropes from the eastern Canadian breeding population, which once staged by the millions in Passamaquoddy Bay, are believed to follow the same track to the Pacific (Smith et al. 2018a, 2018b).

Piscataquis Co.: 2 at Carpenter Pond, T7 R11 WELS on 14 Aug 1988 (S. Ray, ph.). Penobscot Co.: 1 in Orono, 24 Aug 2003 (J. Markowsky); and 1 at Sebasticook L. on 26 Aug 2017 (S. Mierzykowski, eBird). York Co.: Sanford Lagoons: 5 on 2 Sep 2006 (L. Brinker), 1 on 19 Sep 2015 (K. Couture and A. Aldrich, eBird), and 1 on 18 Oct 2010 (A. Aldrich, eBird). Dozens of records along immediate coast. Latest: 8 birds at Scarborough Marsh on 17 Oct 2015 (T. Hannah, Z. Loman; eBird) and 1 on Passamaquoddy Bay, 20 Aug 2017 (D. Lovitch).

PDV and CDD

DEC: 50,000, 7 Oct 1999 (N. Famous); >10,000 on 7 other occasions Aug–Jan (fide J. Despres); 15,000 on 21 Aug 1977, and 10,000 on 24 Aug 1980 (PDV).

A detailed study of gulls from Campobello and Deer Is., NB, to Eastport found Bonaparte's Gulls "peaking rather abruptly" in Aug with 5,000–10,000 present. Counts then remained steady at 2,000–5,000 through Oct. (Braune and Gaskin 1982). Regular sightings of hundreds to thousands of Bonaparte's Gulls in late autumn over the past decade suggest this pattern continues (C. Bartlett, pers. com.). This is in stark contrast to the disappearance of the enormous numbers of Red-necked Phalaropes, which also occurred in these waters until the mid-1980s.

Elsewhere in ME, >100 Bonaparte's Gulls frequently reported in Aug. Peak numbers inland occur from mid-Sep (300 on Scarborough Marsh, 12 Sep 2001, PDV) to mid-Oct with ~350 reported in 2 years in Scarborough on 6 Oct 1999 (PDV) and Ferry Beach, Saco, 13 Oct 2008 (M. Iliff).

WINTER: Most winter reports coastal with <150 birds, but Eastport CBC frequently reports many hundreds of Bonaparte's Gulls and reported >1,000 on 4 occasions, including an exceptionally high count of 2,514 in 2016. Nonetheless, Eastport CBCs seem to miss the tens of thousands sometimes reported here in Dec (50,000, 3 Dec 2003; N Famous, fide J. Despres) or a few weeks later in Jan (20,000, 5 Jan 2002; N Famous, fide J. Despres).

CDD

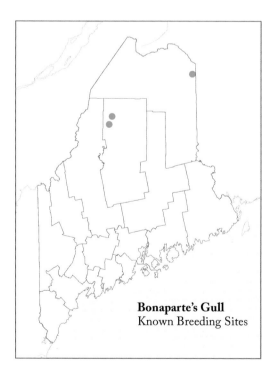

Bonaparte's Gull
Known Breeding Sites

Black-headed Gull
Chroicocephalus ridibundus

A handsome casual, but regular, visitor to harbors and nearshore waters

Status in Maine: Relatively recent additions to Maine's avifauna, Black-headed Gulls are casual visitors. Although not mentioned by Palmer, there are now records typically of one or two individuals in every month of the year and from the length of the Maine coast.

Global Distribution: Expanding. Historic range temperate Europe to Kamchatka. Colonized Iceland in 1911, began breeding in e. Canada as early as 1930s. Not recorded breeding in Greenland until 1969; first documented N. Am. nesting in NFLD in 1977. First U.S. nest discovered on Cape Cod in 1984 (Holt et al. 1986). Winters across w. Europe, south to equatorial Africa, coasts of Arabian Sea, and Pacific coast of Asia including Gulf of Thailand. In N. Am., several hundred reported on CBCs in NFLD and NS, up to 25 on ne. U.S. CBCs, and one to two birds as far south as NJ.

SPRING: One each: North End Launch Facility, Bath, 2 Mar 2010 (PDV, eBird); Wharton Pt., 4 Apr 2015 (G. Smith, eBird); Pine Pt., 25–27 May 2015 (m.ob., eBird); and one in alternate plumage seen on Laudholm Farm, Wells, 31 May 2003 (H. Wilson, eBird), was "noticeably larger than Bonaparte's Gulls with which it was roosting. Bill carmine-red rather than black."

SUMMER: Unpaired female incubated an egg on Petit Manan I. in 1986 (Drennan et al. 1987) and 2 pairs nested unsuccessfully there in 1991 (*AB* 46: 60–66). Few known summer records: 1 on Ship I., Hancock Co., 7 Jun 2015 (M. Baran, eBird); 1 seen at Rachel Carson NWR, on Timber Pt. Trail, 2 Jul 2015 (S. Keefer, eBird); and an unrecorded number on Matinicus Rock, 6 Jul 2010 (S. Hall, eBird).

FALL: One each: Ft. Foster Park, 22 Aug 2006 (M. Iliff, eBird); Straits of Alliquippa, Phippsburg, 1 Sep 2002 (PDV, eBird); Wells Beach, 17 Sep 2016 (J. Gamble, eBird); Scarborough Marsh, 17 Oct 2008 (PDV, eBird); and 21 Oct 2000 at Pine Pt. (H. Nelson, eBird). Phippsburg sightings: Spirit Pond, 19 Oct. 2013 (D. Suitor, eBird); Ft. Popham, 22 Nov 2013 (M. Fahay, eBird); and at Green Pt., 1 each on 11 Nov 2009, 30 Oct 2012, 1 Oct 2013 (all M. Fahay, eBird).

WINTER: An adult and immature in Rockland, 14 Feb 1952 (J. Monahan, ph.; *MASB* 9[3]: 48). Rockland Harbor hosted at least 3 Black-headed Gulls in early winter on 7 occasions in the

1990s. Highest count: 25 off Eastport, 3 Dec 2003 (N. Famous, fide J. Despres), although none were found there 3 weeks later on CBC. Twenty-two recorded on Dec 1995 Eastport CBC, all from Deer I., NB, section (fide J. Despres). Notable, 1 previous CBC recorded >3 individuals (6 birds, 1992); no subsequent CBCs recorded >3 individuals. None reported from Eastport CBC route again until 2011. Overall, CBC data suggest 1990s were peak of species' occurrence here. Nisbet et al. (2013) report similar findings for MA and tie decrease to elimination of raw sewage discharge into harbors in 1990s. Recent winter observations: 1–2 birds, Ft. Foster Park, intermittently 15 Nov–19 Dec 2005 (PVD, m.ob., eBird); 1, Cliff House, York, 23 Nov 2011 (L. Seitz, eBird); 1, Gilsland Farm, 2 Dec 2010 (E. Hynes, eBird); 1, Drakes I. Rd., Wells, 16 Jan 2011 (D. Hitchcox, eBird); 1, Riverbank Park, Westbrook, Cumberland Co., 3 Mar 2017 (B. Blauvelt, eBird).

CDD

Little Gull
Hydrocoloeus minutus

The smallest of all gulls

Status in Maine: Little Gulls are rare along the coast and often associated with Bonaparte's Gulls. Reported in all months except February and March, Little Gulls are most common between May and October. The highest reported count is six at Scarborough Marsh on 12 October 2003 (L. Brinker et al.). Only three Christmas Bird Counts have recorded Little Gulls: one on Mount Desert Island, 2 January 1971; one from Eastport on the Deer Island, New Brunswick, portion of the count on 26 December 1994; and three in the same location 26 December 2000, although it is unclear where in the count circle these were recorded.

Historical Status in Maine: Palmer provided the earliest historical records with two specimens and a sight report: adult males collected on 12 Aug 1904 near St. George, Knox Co., and on 20 Jul 1910 in Scarborough, and four individuals seen over several days in Sagadahoc Bay, Georgetown, Sagadahoc Co., Sep 1922.

Global Distribution: Palearctic. Enormous breeding range, nesting along freshwater marshes and lakes from n. Scandinavia, Baltics, and w. Russia east to Siberia. Disjunct N. Am. population, perhaps only 100 breeding pairs, in scattered locales around Great Ls., s. QC, and north to Hudson Bay. Although poorly documented, it is thought the species colonized N. Am. in 1930s (Nisbet et al. 2013).

After breeding, most Little Gulls in Old World move southward in small flocks (occasionally larger groups reaching into the thousands) to winter at sea primarily off w. Europe and nw. Africa, but also Mediterranean, Caspian, and Black Seas. Others migrate westward to U.S. coast from MA to SC.

SPRING: Recent observations: 1 at Pine Pt. Beach, Scarborough, 23 May–6 Jun 2015 (m.ob., eBird); 1 on Stratton I., 17 May 2015 (K. McOmber and R. Lambert, eBird).

FALL: Recent observations: 1 in Passamaquoddy Bay, 20 Aug 2017 (D. Lovitch); 1 at Flye Pt., Brooklin, Hancock Co., 16 Sep 2017 (T. McLane and K. Jones, eBird); 1 at Muscongus Bay, 25 Sep 2015 (S. Mirick, eBird); and 1 at Hills Beach, Biddeford Pool, 5 Oct 2015 (M. Resch, eBird).

CDD

Laughing Gull
Leucophaeus atricilla

Maine's only regularly nesting hooded gull, famous for its raucous call

Status in Maine: A summer resident in coastal Maine, Laughing Gull is most abundant near its few island breeding colonies. It is rare inland, infrequently venturing more than 10 miles (16 km) from the coast. Although historically known to nest in Maine, it was absent in the early 1900s, making a comeback since the 1950s. In recent years, Laughing Gulls have nested, or attempted to nest, in three to five managed tern colonies. Numbers peaked at 4,000 nests estimated in 2008 (Allen et al. 2012) but had dropped to an estimated 2,365 nesting pairs in 2017 (USFWS 2018c). Tern colony managers have recently been actively discouraging Laughing Gulls from nesting at the tern colonies, an impact on one species of concern for the sake of several more-threatened species.

Maine Conservation Status: Species of Special Concern.

Historical Status in Maine: Knight wrote the Laughing Gull formerly bred more extensively on ME coastal islands but that as of 1903 was known to breed at only one site, Metinic Green I., where eight birds were seen in Jun 1903. Palmer said it ceased breeding in ME prior to 1944 but was known historically to nest on at least nine islands. He noted two pairs nested on Machias Seal I., NB, in 1948. He considered the loss of breeding colonies a result of "human

SUMMER: Uncommon and local breeder, with <50 pairs estimated at 5 sites statewide in 2015. Messalonskee L., largest colony: 40 birds at boat ramp on 30 Jun 2014 (C. Ring, eBird), 26 at south end on 17 Jul 2016 (G. Hodgkins, eBird), and 6 on adjacent Great Pond on 31 May 2017 (J. Dunham and A. Haverstock, eBird); 24 on Carlton Pond, 5 Jun 2015 (T. Aversa, eBird); 9 on Plymouth Pond, 14 Jul 2015 (C. Todd, eBird); 9 Great Moose L., 10 Jul 2014, but only 2 seen there on 24 Jun 2016 (T. Aversa). There were 17 reported on Pearl Pond, Ebeemee Twp. on 20 Jul 2014 (S. Guare) and nesting confirmed in 2016 (D. D'Auria, MDIFW). A single pair exhibiting defensive behavior seen at Portage L., an historic nesting site, 23 Jun 2011 (WJS). A. Gilbert (pers. com.) cautions that Black Terns are only loosely colonial and fluid in site selection, so colony presence and size vary year to year. Single Black Terns occasionally seen in company of other tern species on inland lakes and on Machias Seal and Petit Manan Is.

FALL: Departure from colonies complete by third week of Aug (eBird). Postbreeding dispersal to coastal areas: maximum 24 in Biddeford Pool, 28 Aug 2011 (D. Hitchcox, eBird); easternmost 2 in Eastport, 27 Aug 2011 (m.ob., eBird), and 1 there 5 Sep 2013 (C. Bartlett). Virtually all are gone by end of first week of Sep; latest records, 1 each: 14 Sep 2004, Halfway Rock, Casco Bay (A. Stackhouse, fide J. Despres); Lubec, 20 Sep 1998 (N. Famous, fide J. Despres); and in Monmouth, Kennebec Co., 7 Oct 1958 (Fernalds, fide J. Despres).

PDV and CDD

White-winged Tern
Chlidonias leucopterus

An Old World tern drops in for a visit

Status in Maine: Accidental. White-winged Terns are recorded annually in eastern North America but are rare in New England and the Canadian Maritime Provinces. This Old World tern has been observed three times in Maine.

Global Distribution: Primarily Africa, e. Europe, Cen. Asia, S. Pacific Is., and portions of Australia. No N. or S. Am. populations but recorded in QC, NB, ME, MA, and VT.

SUMMER: An adult in breeding plumage sighted from Pine Pt., 19 Jul 2000 (R. Toochin). Another adult in breeding plumage ph. at Little R. mouth, Wells, 13–14 Jun 2003 was accepted by ME-BRC (G. McElroy, ph.; m.ob., S. Mirick; *BO* 35: 156–157). An adult in alternate plumage was seen at close range between Otter Creek and Seal Harbor on Mount Desert I., 13 Aug 2005 and carefully described (A. Klein). The description is as follows:

"[A]pproximately 8 to 10 inches in length, similar in shape to Black Tern (*Chlidonias niger*), but NOT Black Tern; black head, throat, breast and belly; black axillaries and under wing coverts; white primaries and secondaries; white flanks, undertail coverts and tail. Unable to see feet or legs. First spotted about thirty feet away; flew within fifteen or twenty feet of me at eye level before gaining a bit more altitude as it opened the distance from me. Adult breeding plumage. Bill appeared black, but at distance, not 100% positive. This bird could easily be confused with a Black Tern except for the white primaries and secondaries that, in this particular case, were easily observed."

PDV

Roseate Tern
Sterna dougallii

An endangered species, almost always found in the presence of Common Terns

Status in Maine: Roseate Terns are uncommon breeders on Southern and Midcoast Maine islands and rare Downeast, arriving early May and mostly gone by late August. They are colonial breeders currently occupying five coastal islands: Pond (two pairs in 2018), Eastern Egg Rock (82), Jenny (24), and Stratton (GOMSWG 2018, 128).

Maine Conservation Status: Endangered. Roseate Terns are included, with Common and Arctic Terns, in the category of island-nesting terns (MDIFW 2007), with an objective of 300 pairs in ME by 2021; the 2018 total of 236 remains below that target.

Roseate Terns

Historical Status in Maine: First recorded in 1879 with a small flock in outer Casco Bay. Norton (1925) described a marked increase by 1925, which Palmer attributed to the fact that Roseate Terns nest in dense ground cover, which naturally expands without disturbance and for which there is little competition from other tern species. By 1931, there were 552 individuals (276 pairs) breeding on Bluff I. in Casco Bay and on N. and S. Sugarloaf Is. off Popham Beach. The total dropped to 85 pairs by 1972, the species then primarily breeding on N. Sugarloaf and, much farther Downeast, on Petit Manan I. By 1983, the colonies on Sugarloaf Is., Petit Manan I., and Bluff I. were long abandoned by all island-nesting terns, although several other islands held 93 nesting pairs of roseates. ME's Roseate Tern population reached its zenith in 1999 with 288 pairs, including 28 once again on Petit Manan I., 100 on Stratton I., and 144 on E. Egg Rock, all with active management to deter gull nesting and predation. While none have nested on Petit Manan in recent years, a small number visit the colony each summer. Not surprisingly, observations Downeast have also become rare with the loss of the closest nesting island.

Palmer noted that he found no records of inland occurrence.

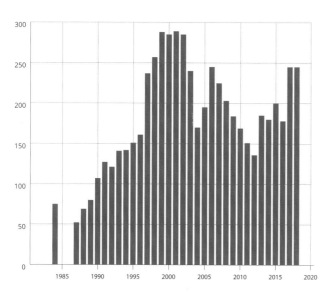

Figure 9. Roseate Tern Nests

Declared endangered in Maine in 1986, the number of Roseate Tern nests increased following listing and active nesting colony management, peaking in 1999. Numbers fell subsequently but are now rebounding. Note: no censuses performed in 1985 or 1986. (S. Kress, National Audubon Society).

Global Distribution: In N. Am., Roseate Terns breed from e. Long I., NY, to ME with a few nesting in NS. They formerly bred in VA, MD, and NJ. There is a discrete population in s. FL (particularly the Keys), Bahamas, and Caribbean. All populations winter in tropical waters of S. Am., especially the east coast of Brazil. In Europe, they breed on British Isles coasts, in both nw. and Mediterranean France, Madeira, and the Azores. Also breed in temperate waters of Japan, w. Australia, S. Africa, and tropical w. Pacific and Indian Oceans. Temperate-zone breeders winter in tropical waters; wintering location of tropical breeders is unknown (Nisbet et al. 2013).

Global Conservation Status: ESA: Endangered (northeastern breeding population); **Threatened** elsewhere, including FL, U.S. Virgin Is., and PR.

Remarks: All Roseate Tern nests in ME are currently on islands managed by National Audubon Society and USFWS.

SUMMER: Arrival end of first week of May; e.g., 6 May 2010, Stratton I., (Project Puffin, eBird). Commonly reported through season in s. ME and Midcoast, rarely Downeast, One at W. Quoddy Head S.P., 17 Aug 2010 (S. Fason, eBird).

FALL: Most gone by end of Aug, but numerous records into mid-Sep. Late occurrences: 1 or 2 at Scarborough Marsh, 20 Sep 1983 (PDV), and 8 on Jenny I., 28 Nov 1993 (Project Puffin, eBird).

CDD

Common Tern
Sterna hirundo

The tern most likely to be seen on the coast and nearshore islands

Status in Maine: Common Terns are abundant summer residents of the Maine coast where they breed colonially on coastal islands. Smaller but sometimes significant numbers (hundreds) breed or have bred on inland lakes in northern Maine. These inland nesting populations are considered to be underestimated and neglected as a conservation priority for both censusing and protection (JVW, pers. com.). There were an estimated 9,500 breeding pairs in 14 coastal colonies in 2018 (GOMSWG 2018).

Maine Conservation Status: Species of Special Concern. Discussed with Roseate and Arctic Terns in the species assessment and management plan for island-nesting terns (MDIFW 2007).

Historical Status in Maine: Palmer's valuable historical summary indicates that Common Terns were numerous breeders in the 1850s, with >75 ME colonies. In the 1880s, terns were slaughtered for the millinery trade, which wiped out some colonies entirely. A hunting party killed >1,100 terns, mostly Common Terns, in a single 1887 trip to Penobscot and Jericho Bays. The feathers they collected earned $340 (>$9,000 current dollars). Although ME passed legislation in 1889 to protect terns, hunting continued illegally to 1900, when only 23 coastal colonies remained. Protection, both by legislation and by guardians from the newly created National Association of Audubon Societies, proved effective but also benefited Herring Gulls, which pushed terns to more marginal breeding sites.

In 1936, 6,000 Common Tern pairs nested in 25 colonies (Kress and Hall 2002). Palmer (1949, 265) considered this species to be "common to abundant" on ME's coastal islands with a few pairs nesting on inland lakes in several counties. By the late 1970s, statewide populations were suffering from predation by rats, sheep pasturing on islands, continued encroachment by gulls, picnickers' dogs, and even free-roaming house cats at a U.S. Coast Guard Station. As a result, they were only half of the 1930s estimates: 2,095 pairs in 18 colonies (McCollough, updated by Tudor 2006).

Thanks in large measure to restoration efforts for this species, along with Roseate and Arctic Terns, the coastal population rebounded to 5,547 pairs of Common Terns in 22 colonies by 2004 and to more than 9,500 pairs by 2018 (GOMSWG 2018). While the population is growing, the number of colonies has declined to 14 currently; all but two, with one nest each, are on managed islands.

Global Distribution: Breeds in temperate and subarctic latitudes of the Holarctic, migrating to temperate and tropical oceans for winter. In W. Hemisphere, Common Terns breed along the Atlantic Coast from NL to NC and inland across Canada east of the Rocky Mtns. Also, small, partially migratory populations in Caribbean. Winters from s. Florida and Caribbean along both coasts of Mexico, Cen. Am., and S. Am. to n. Chile on the Pacific and s. Patagonia on the Atlantic.

Remarks: Although it seems to have fallen out of colloquial speech, Palmer mentions that ME fishermen used the term "medrick" for any species of coastal tern.

SPRING: In recent years, Common Terns arrive in s. ME as early as May (eBird), approximately a week earlier than Palmer reported.

SUMMER: Common on ME coast, over beaches, islands, and bays. Interior lakes with double-digit counts in the past two decades include Portage and Fish R. Ls., Aroostook Co., with 40 at the latter on 23 Jun 2011 (WJS, eBird); and Allagash L. and Allagash R. at John's Bridge, Piscataquis Co., on 8 Jun 2014 (PDV and WJS, eBird). Notable recent reports: 180 adults and 45 juveniles on 12 Aug 2007 at Long L., and 30 pairs breeding there the following year (WJS, fide J. Despres).

FALL: While most Common Terns depart by early Sep, individuals are sometimes seen into Oct. Notable late occurrences of large numbers include 1,500 in Scarborough, 22 Sep 1907 (Norton, fide Palmer 1949), and 350 on Jenny I., 28 Nov 1993 (Project Puffin).
CDD

Arctic Tern
Sterna paradisaea

The world's greatest migrant returns from Antarctica annually to breed on Maine's offshore islands

Status in Maine: Arctic Terns are common summer residents of the outer Maine coast where they breed colonially on islands. In 2018, there were ~2,550 breeding pairs in eight coastal Maine colonies, as well as 450 on Machias Seal Island (GOMSWG 2018). The Gulf of ME Arctic Tern population has decreased by 41% since 2008, a decline that appears to be echoed at colonies around the globe (USFWS 2018b).

Arctic Tern

**Maine Conservation Status:
Threatened.** Included, along with
Roseate and Common Terns in the
species assessment and management
plan for island-nesting terns
(MDIFW 2007).

Historical Status in Maine:
This species was a common to
abundant breeder on marine
islands east of Casco Bay (Palmer
1949) arriving May 16–22, ~7–10
days later than current arrival
dates. Fall departure typically
prior to end of Aug. The number
of Arctic Tern nests was estimated
at 2,900 in the 1970s and grew to
more than 4,000 in 2007–2008,
when many terns that nested
on Machias Seal I. relocated to
ME. By 2011, the number of nests
in ME declined to fewer than
3,000 (Allen et al. 2012). (See
also *Historical Status in Maine*
in Common Tern account, pp.
276–277.)

Global Distribution: Breeds in
Arctic and subarctic areas of N. Am.,
Europe, and Asia south to MA and
Brittany, migrating over the Atlantic
and Pacific Oceans to Antarctic
waters.

SUMMER: Arrival at colonies in early
May: 6 May 1995, Petit Manan I. (fide
J. Despres); 6 May 2015, Seal I. (K.
Yakola, eBird); 7 May 2012, Stratton I.
(R. Lambert, eBird). First U.S. record
of banded Arctic Tern from Iceland was
a second-year bird recorded at Seal I.
NWR, 4 Jul 2016 (K. Yakola, pers. com.).
Largest breeding colonies in ME during
2018: Seal I. (829 pairs), Matinicus Rock
(717 pairs), Metinic I. (522 pairs), and Petit
Manan (374 pairs; GOMSWG 2018). The
Gulf of ME Arctic Tern population has
decreased by 41% since 2008, a decline
that appears to be echoed at colonies
around the globe (USFWS 2018).

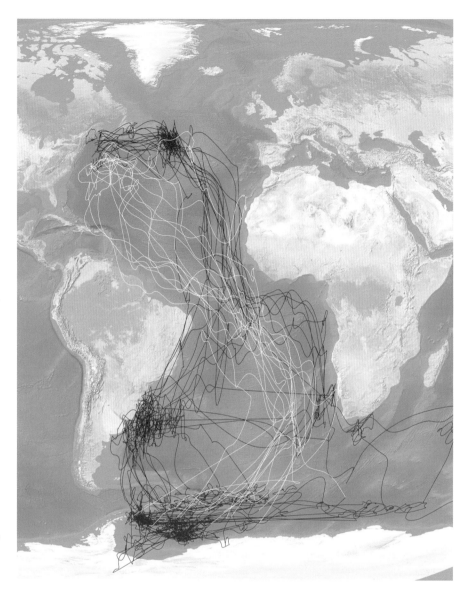

Map 16: Arctic Tern Migration

*The aggregate tracks of 14 Arctic Terns, fitted with geolocators in 2010 by USFWS and
National Audubon Society researchers on Eastern Egg Rock and Metinic Island, show
three migration patterns from the mid-North Atlantic (red tracks). After departing the
breeding grounds (green) half flew south to the Patagonian Shelf on the east coast of
South America. The others traveled down the West African coast, some continuing south
around the Cape of Good Hope to the Indian Ocean; the remainder went west to the
Patagonian Shelf. After five months in Antarctic waters (blue), all flew along roughly
the same path (yellow), returning to breeding colonies in the Gulf of Maine (USFWS,
unpublished data).*

FALL: Most Arctic Terns leave by late
Aug, though occasional stragglers as noted
by two eBird reports from Pine Pt.: 3
individuals, 25 Sep 2010 (J. Mays), and
1 juvenile on 30 Sep 2013 (F. Mitchell).

Exceptional observation, 1 bird on 24 Nov
2005, Biddeford, (P. Moynahan, fide J.
Despres).

CDD

Forster's Tern
Sterna forsteri

A rewarding late-summer sight for careful observers in southern Maine

Status in Maine: Forster's Terns are postbreeding wanderers in coastal Southern Maine. Although rare from late August through October, occasional one-day counts of 10 or more have been recorded. They are casual in other seasons and at all times Downeast.

Historical Status in Maine: Palmer mentioned only three sight records, all juveniles, in late summer: one in Muscongus Bay, 16 Aug 1937; another one there 26 Aug 1946; and two on Pemaquid Pt., 2 Sep 1946.

Global Distribution: Endemic to N. Am. Breeds in interior freshwater marshes from w. Mexico to AB and Great Ls., and in salt marshes of Gulf and s. Atlantic Coasts, rarely north to MA and Maritime Provinces. Winters primarily on Pacific and s. Atlantic Coasts of U.S., Gulf Coast, inland TX and AR, s. to Cen. Am. and Caribbean.

SPRING: Individuals reported: Sanford Lagoons, 10 Apr 2017 (J. Fecteau, eBird); Biddeford Pool, 16–18 Apr 2010 (m.ob., fide J. Despres); Prout's Neck, 5–7 May 2010 (m.ob., fide J. Despres).

SUMMER: Casual to rare, mostly in s. ME. Six records at tern nesting colonies, earliest record at Seal I. NWR, 23 May 2015 (K. Yakola, eBird), and latest on Stratton I., 19 Jun 2001 (Project Puffin). More numerous in Jul and early Aug but not recorded annually: 4 in Back Cove, Portland, 7 Aug 1984 (PDV), 2 on Popham Beach, 18 Aug 2016 (P. Moynahan, N. Houlihan, and M. Fahay); 1 in Biddeford Pool, 11 Jul–3 Aug 2014.

FALL: Rare but regular, occasionally in small groups, coastal s. ME to Midcoast, typically peaking in early Sep: 1 on Cape Elizabeth, 21 Sep 2017 (M. Ocampo and N. O'Reilly; eBird); about 23, Biddeford Pool, 9 Sep 2010 (D. Lovitch); "at least" 19 at Popham Beach S.P., 8 Sep 2010 (M. Fahey). Easternmost records: Cutler Naval Base, Washington Co., 7 Aug 1985 (W. Petersen et al., fide J. Despres); Eastport, 12 Aug 1991 (A. Wells and JVW, fide J. Despres); Cobscook S.P., Washington Co., 5 Sep 2010, after remnants of Hurricane Earl (J. Mays, eBird); Roque I., Jonesport, 10 Sep 2011, joined by second bird following day (E. and N. Famous, fide J. Despres). Single inland record: 2 in Richmond, 19 Oct 2011 (M. Fahay).

WINTER: 1 each, fide J. Despres: Kettle Cove, 21 Jan 2006 (G. Carson); Scarborough, 2 Feb 1984 (B. Hancock); and Biddeford Pool, 4 Feb 1984, (G. Sharpe). One ph. at Pine Pt., 20 Feb 2017 (R. Garrigus, eBird).

CDD

Royal Tern
Thalasseus maximus

A large, sleek tern of southern coastal waters

Status in Maine: Royal Terns are casual in Maine, first reported following the passage of Hurricane Donna in September 1960: one bird examined in the hand in Yarmouth was later released in Back Cove, Portland (D. Edgerton, E. Dana, et al.), and four were seen from Pemaquid Point (M. Libby). The species was not reported again until 1965. Since these early records, they have become increasingly regular with three reports in the 1970s, 10 in the 1980s, and eight in the 1990s. Most appear during summer months and, since 2000, Royal Tern records are nearly annual with as many as eight separate reports in 2006 alone. Most frequently seen near large sand beaches and offshore tern colonies; the majority of sightings occur between York and Sagadahoc Counties.

Historical Status in Maine: Neither Knight nor Palmer reported Royal Terns as occurring in ME. This is surprising given the species' regularity since 1980 and its regular occurrence following hurricanes.

Global Distribution: Nearctic. Breeds from VA to FL and Gulf Coast to s. TX, irregularly in Caribbean and locally in S. Am. In the Pacific, from s. CA to Baja California; Atlantic birds winter in NC through Caribbean, Cen. Am. and coastal S. Am. Species has occurred in coastal New England, Maritime Provinces, and NFLD.

SPRING: Spring reports for Royal Tern: the only Apr record and earliest ME occurrence, 1 in Manset, Hancock Co., 24 Apr 1978 (W. Russell et al.; Russell and Witt 2009); 1 at Port Clyde, 2 May 1985 (S. Cook, *AB* 39: 272); 1 at Hills Beach, Biddeford, 28 May 2001 (P. Moynahan); 1 in York, 22 May 2002 (ME Audubon, fide W. Townsend, *Guillemot* 32[3]: 25); and 1 at Matinicus Rock, 22 May 2003 (Project Puffin, eBird).

SUMMER: Summer reports in Jun and Jul usually involve individuals that dispersed north without the aid of tropical disturbances: 3 Jun occurrences of 2 terns: 2 off Seawall Beach, 22 Jun 2002 (PDV); 2 at Popham Beach, 22 Jun 2006 (B. Schmoker, eBird); 2 off Richmond I., Cape Elizabeth, 29 Jun 2012 (J. Delcourt). Multiple Jul occurrences on southern coast to Phippsburg. Jul records >1 tern: 3–4 individuals on Hills Beach, Biddeford, 6–12 Jul 2014 (P. Moynahan, D. Doubleday, N. Gibb, et al.); 2 in Rachel Carson NWR, 18 Jul 2015 (J. Garrett). Recent reports: 1 each, Popham Beach, 16 Jul 2017 (D. Lovitch);

Seabird Nesting Islands: Numbers of Breeding Pairs

Island (from east to west)	Atlantic Puffin	Razorbill	Common Murre	Laughing Gull	Roseate Tern	Common Tern	Arctic Tern	Leach's Storm-Petrel
Machias Seal[1]	5700[a]	2825[a]	400[a]			26	450	200[b]
Old Man[2]		120[c]						
Pulpit Rock[2]		10[c]						
Freeman Rock[2]		55[c]						
Petit Manan[3]	62	3		766		903	374	
Ship[3]						519		
Little Duck[4]								2800[d]
Great Duck[5]	2–4							5000[e]
Three Bush[6]						59		
Seal[7]	565	59				1204	829	724[d]
Matinicus Rock[7]	500	425[a]	8	1		268	717	706[d]
Metinic[8]						320	522	
Eastern Egg Rock[9]	178			1	82	1021	86	173[f]
Western Egg Rock[10]				800				
Pond[11]					2	1065	11	
Jenny[12]					24	1426	1	
Outer Green[12]						1553		
Stratton[13]					128	1206	8	
Total number of pairs	7008	3497	408	1568	236	9570	2998	9603

Owned/managed by if different from owner; those in italics are not managed. **1.** Canadian Wildlife Services; **2.** USFWS, not managed; **3.** USFWS; **4.** NAS; **5.** TNC, MDIFW, COA, and private; **6.** Private ownership; **7.** USFWS/NAS; **8.** USFWS and private/USFWS; **9.** MDIFW/NAS; **10.** NAS; **11.** USFWS/NAS; **12.** MDIFW/NAS; **13.** NAS. Unless otherwise noted, data GOMSWG 2018; other data sources: **a.** T. Diamond, CWS, and P. Shannon, NAS, 2016 data; **b.** Bird Life International, 1998–1999 data; **c.** Allen et al. 2012, 2006 data; **d.** Chilelli 1999, 1994–1996 data; **e.** COA, 2000; **f.** P. Shannon, pers. com., 2018.

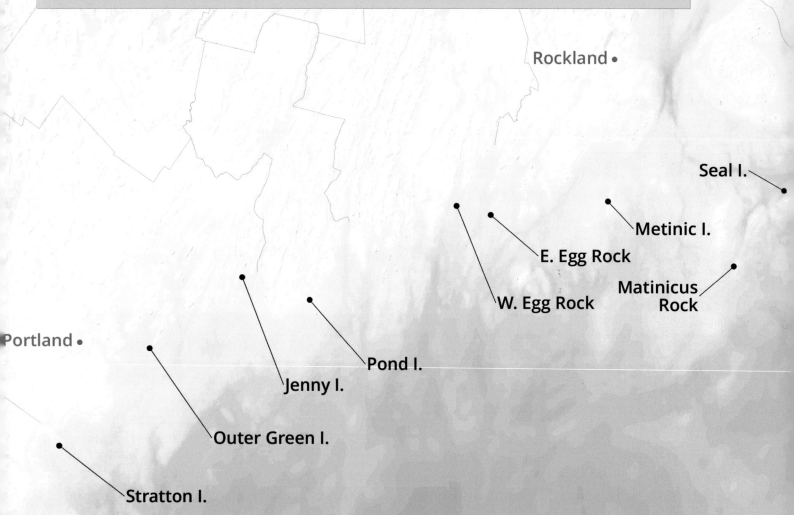

Rockland •

Seal I.

Metinic I.

E. Egg Rock

Matinicus Rock

W. Egg Rock

Pond I.

Portland •

Jenny I.

Outer Green I.

Stratton I.

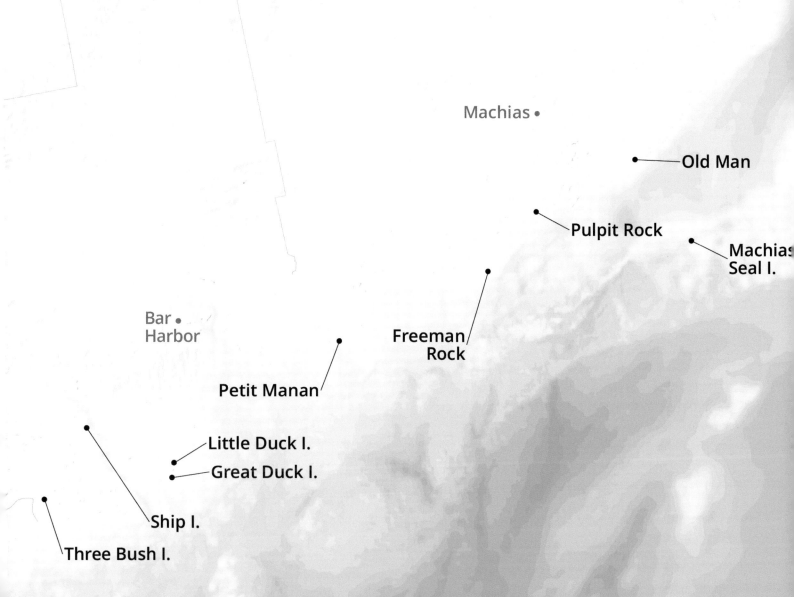

Machias •

Old Man

Pulpit Rock

Machias
Seal I.

Freeman
Rock

Bar •
Harbor

Petit Manan

Little Duck I.

Great Duck I.

Ship I.

Three Bush I.

SEABIRD NESTING ISLANDS: NUMBERS OF BREEDING PAIRS

Laudholm Beach, York, 20 Jul 2017 (W. Sweet; eBird); and Laudholm, Wells Reserve, 19 Aug 2017 (D. Lovitch).

More than 5 reports from Hancock Co., all on Mount Desert I. and Mount Desert Rock in Washington Co., single Royal Terns at Petit Manan NWR, 23 Jul 2002 (R. Hildreth, Guillemot 32: 37), 24 Jun 2003 (fide P. Garrity), and 9 Jul 2003 (Stanton Bird Club, Guillemot 33: 26). Only inland record: Moosehorn NWR, Baring Plt., 3 Jul 1996 (J. Dunn, CDD).

FALL: Late Aug and Sep reports occasionally involve sightings of multiple birds, usually following tropical storms or hurricanes. Previously noted, 4 birds on Pemaquid Pt., 13 Sep 1960, appeared after passage of Hurricane Donna (M. Libby). In 1991, a major flight of Royal Terns at Seawall Beach followed Hurricane Bob: 10 individuals on 20 Aug 1991, 3 additional terns on 21 Aug, and 3 more on 22 Aug (PDV). A few lingered briefly during this flight; most seen flying steadily southwest. At least 5 others reported at this time including 1 in Georgetown, Sagadahoc Co., 21 Aug 1991 that was banded near Lola, NC, 24 Jun 1991 (M. Libby, J. Weske). Additional reports of multiple terns not connected to tropical disturbance: 3 at Otter Pt., Bar Harbor, 17 Sep 1992 (M. Sharp; Witt and Russell, unpublished); 2 on Scarborough Marsh, 25 Aug 2011 (D. Hitchcox); 2, Dam Cove, Sagadahoc Co., 1 Aug 2012 (M. Fahay, eBird). A Royal Tern on Monhegan I., 27 Sep 2009 was the latest date for ME (MDIFW, CDD).

PDV

Sandwich Tern
Thalasseus sandvicensis

A powerful crested tern of more southerly coasts

Status in Maine: Since 1960, Sandwich Terns have been casual vagrants to Maine's coast from June through September. They have primarily, but not exclusively, appeared following tropical storms and hurricanes. There are approximately 15 records.

Historical Status in Maine: Perhaps surprisingly, neither Knight nor Palmer reported Sandwich Terns in ME.

Global Distribution: E. Nearctic and w. Palearctic. Breeds from VA to SC, along the Gulf Coast, to Yucatán Peninsula and Caribbean, Venezuela to Argentina. Winters from FL, Gulf Coast, south through Caribbean, Cen. to S. Am. Also breeds in Europe from Great Britain and Norway to Black Sea and Caspian Sea. Winters along coastal Africa and Mediterranean Sea. This species reported from all New England states except VT, and in all Maritime Provinces.

Hurricane-related sightings: The first Sandwich Tern in ME was observed at Pemaquid Pt., 13 Sep 1960, following Hurricane Donna (M. Libby); several Sooty Terns were also reported. At least five Sandwich Terns reported following Hurricane Bob in 1991: one at Seawall Beach, 20 Aug 1991 (PDV, ph.; AB 46: 65); one at Petit Manan NWR, 20 Aug 1991 (R. Widrig, MBN 5: 28); one found dead on Merchant I., Isle au Haut, 23 Aug 1991, was banded as a nestling in NC, 26 Jun 1984 (fide D. Bystrak; AB 46: 64, MBN 5: 28); one on Stratton I., Saco, Aug 1991 (Guillemot 20: 37); one in Wells, late Aug 1991 (D. Shealer, Guillemot 20: 37). An adult at Mount Desert Rock, 19 Sep 1999, was presumably a Hurricane Floyd vagrant (L. Brinker et al.; NAB 54: 29).

Non-hurricane-related sightings: In 1989, P. Kleinholz observed and carefully described a Sandwich Tern at Hen Cove, Harpswell, 27 Jul 1989 (MBN 3: 19, AB 43: 1290), the second ME record. In 1994, a single bird reported intermittently at Hills Beach, Biddeford, and Scarborough, 5–29 Jul 1994 (P. Moynahan, L. Brinker; MBN 7: 42, FN 49: 23). In 1997, an adult ph. at same locality, 8 Jun 1997 (L. Brinker, ph.; FN 51: 973). Sandwiches reported from Stratton I., 18 Jun 2001 (P. Moynahan, NAB 55: 413) and 21 Jun 2006 (R. Lambert). In 2003, one on Seal I., 30 Jun 2003 (V. Lane). Most recent records: one on ME Audubon trip, Stratton I., 1 Jul 2012 (D. Hitchcox), and one reported by kayakers a week later near Basket I. sandbar, Biddeford, 8 Jul 2012 (M. Zimmerman and P. Moynahan).

PDV

Black Skimmer
Rynchops niger

A southern coastal species that no longer depends on hurricanes for a visit

Status in Maine: Black Skimmers were first reported in Maine in 1879 following a hurricane, and this pattern of post-hurricane dispersal was repeated with at least seven additional fallouts. Since 1973, Black Skimmers have been found along the southern coast during the summer and early fall despite the lack of any strong tropical weather systems.

Historical Status in Maine: Palmer listed a number of post-hurricane records, including "hundreds at Blue Hill, Hancock County," 16 Sep 1944 (Palmer 1949, 279). He also anticipated that this species would become

immature bird was photographed in Edgecomb, Lincoln County, 2 September 2004 (ph., *MASB* 34: 1).

Historical Status in Maine: Palmer listed two specimen records. The first was shot in Berwick, York Co., 16 Jul 1896 and is now in the Bates College collection. The second stork was collected in Cundy's Harbor, Harpswell, 10 Aug 1922, and is currently in the Bowdoin College collection. There are apparently no records 1922–1984.

Global Distribution: Primarily Neotropical and s. Nearctic. Widespread in S. Am., Cen. Am., and Mexico. In N. Am., breeds locally in FL, GA, and SC and winters within breeding range. Reported from NB, NS, MA, RI, CT, and VT, and hypothetical in NH.

Global Conservation Status: ESA: Threatened.
PDV

ORDER SULIFORMES

Frigatebirds (Fregatidae)

The largest and the smallest of the world's five species of frigatebirds have found their way to Maine. Primarily tropical, two species are restricted to their own islands, and the fifth is found in the Indian and Pacific Oceans. Unequalled soaring birds that breed every other year, sexual maturity is not attained until females are about nine and males about 11 years old.

Lesser Frigatebird
Fregata ariel

An Old World tropical species chose Vacationland for its first North American visit

Status in Maine: Accidental. A single record. A male off Deer Isle on 3 July 1960 was captured on film serendipitously while the observer, B. Leadbetter, was filming a Bald Eagle; the bird was carefully identified by examination of enlarged single frames from the film footage by Alexander Wetmore (Snyder 1961). The following is quoted from the original *Auk* article:

"On 3 July 1960 Bertram Leadbetter of Beverly, Massachusetts, was photographing a Bald Eagle (*Haliaetus* [sic] *leucocephalus*) on the rocks of Deer Isle, Hancock County, Maine, when a large bird soared overhead. Swinging his movie camera up, he was lucky enough to get some six feet of 16 mm film of the bird. His companions, Henry S. Lewis and John E. Walsh, watched the bird for several minutes as it glided nearby, and recognized it as a Frigate-bird.

"Mr. Leadbetter kindly showed me the film in August. Noting a marked white patch on the side under the wing, I turned to the cut of *Fregata ariel* in Murphy's *Oceanic Birds of South America*. We ran through the film again and noted that, as one of the observers said, the white patch looked like 'a playing card placed on the body slightly on a slant.' After looking at skins at the Museum of Comparative Zoology, Harvard, it was obvious that only the adult male of *F. ariel* matched the pictures. The film was sent to Dr. Alexander Wetmore.

"Dr. Wetmore writes that he examined it under a magnifier that allowed study of single frames, and through the courtesy of the laboratory of the National Geographic Society, obtained blow ups of four of the clearest frames. 'These show the light spot clearly and indicate without question that the species photographed was *Fregata ariel* (G.R. Gray). This species ranges in the Pacific from the Philippines and coast of China to Australia; in the western Indian Ocean; and to South Trinidad I. in the Atlantic [700 miles east of Victoria, Brazil]… The supposition would be that the bird seen in Maine was from the South Trinidad colony, although there is no absolute certainty regarding this. At any rate, it is a species that has not been found earlier in our North American region.'"

"All authorities agree as to the essentially sedentary nature of frigate-birds, which are rarely seen out of site [sic] of land. It is amazing that *Fregata ariel*, seldom observed in the Atlantic, and little known away from its island homes of South Trinidad and Martin Vas, not only visited our coast, but was photographed. Negatives and prints are on file at the Peabody Museum (PMS-k 17)."

Global Distribution: Native to the tropics. Breeds in equatorial Pacific and Indian Ocean waters and in a small coastal area of Brazil. Frigatebirds are typically nonmigratory. There are only four records of this species in North America.
PDV

Magnificent Frigatebird

Fregata magnificens

A familiar shape in the tropics, this species is unexpected in Maine

Status in Maine: Accidental. The most recent sighting, and the only one reviewed and accepted thus far by Maine Bird Records Committee, was a bird in immature plumage seen from Stratton Island (Z. Smith, ph.; eBird) and Prout's Neck (m.ob. ph.; eBird) on 12 June 2017. There are at least five additional reports in the past 30 years: an adult female Magnificent Frigatebird was "observed for 10 minutes" on Monhegan Island, 26 September 2003 (R. Schutsky, *Guillemot* 33[5]: 44). On 5 August 2005, an adult female frigatebird, presumably a magnificent, was reported over the Bar Harbor waterfront (Z. Klyver). A male frigatebird "presumed magnificent," was reported from Wolfe's Neck Woods State Park, Freeport, on 6 August 2005 (L. Seitz, ph.; eBird). On 20 May 2006, an adult female was reported on Casco Bay and, on the same day, an adult male was reported at Cape Elizabeth (*NAB* 60: 349).

Historical Status in Maine: Palmer lists two specimen records, but neither was preserved. One specimen was taken in Boothbay in ~1871, and D. French of Jonesport shot a specimen in 1893 "as it was flying over Libby Island off Machiasport."

There are several records from the late 20th century, including a female off Monhegan I. on 21 May 1978 (PDV). Another bird was seen on Allen I., Muscongus Bay, 16 Aug 1984, where its "large size, forked tail, very long narrow wings, and black color looked like ones we have seen on the Keys, the Caribbean, and off Mexico" (H. and M. Damon, R. and D. Pope). This is likely the same individual "seen by 26 people as it spent 10 minutes hovering in the wind" two days later at Otter Pt., Mount Desert I., on 18 Aug 1984 (L. Winter, fide W. Townsend; *MBL* 6[4]: 66).

Global Distribution: Tropical and largely sedentary. In Atlantic from GA through Gulf Coast, south through Mexico and Cen. Am. to Uruguay and throughout Caribbean. In Pacific, CA to Ecuador and Galapagos Is.
RDP

Gannets and Boobies (Sulidae)

Three genera and 10 species make up this family of colonial, plunge-diving seabirds. Built for high-speed dives, gannets and boobies have reinforced bills, nostrils that open into the mouth, and four webbed toes on each foot. Whereas Brown Boobies, like most sulids, only rarely appear north of subtropical waters, Northern Gannets breed in the North Atlantic.

Brown Booby

Sula leucogaster

Clumsy on land, this tropical sulid is an agile flier and diver

Status in Maine: Accidental. There are three records. The first record was an adult photographed 12 miles (19 km) east of Portland, 12 August 2011 (ME-BRC #2011-007; J. Delcourt, ph. arch.). This bird was floating on a log and was photographed by a member of a whale-watching excursion. Its appearance in Maine was not associated with any major tropical weather systems. A second bird, seen 16 July 2013 from Eastern Egg Rock, was also accepted by Maine Bird Records Committee. The most recent bird was seen by many observers off Schoodic Island, Hancock County, on 2 June 2018 during the Downeast Birding Festival.

Historical Status in Maine: Unrecorded in ME prior to 2011.

Global Distribution: Pantropical. In N. Am., breeds on keys throughout Caribbean; also breeds in the Pacific, in Gulf of California, and Hawaii. Disperses after breeding season. Brown Boobies have been documented twice in MA and once in NS.
PDV

Northern Gannet

Morus bassanus

The plunge-diving expert of the North Atlantic

Status in Maine: Northern Gannets can be seen in Maine's coastal waters at any time of year. Nonetheless, reports of 10 or more are curiously few between January and May, when birds move from southerly winter quarters to Canadian colonies in mid-April (adults) and May (subadults). By late July, reports of more than 100 gannets are more routine.

Pond Marsh, Penobscot Co., 15 Jan 2005 (WJS, eBird); and 1, Presque Isle, 7 Feb 2006 (S. Pinette, fide WJS).

Overwintering birds often immature, 1 bird each, all fide eBird: "immature bird" at Falls Bridge, Phippsburg, 10 Feb 2016 (M. Fahay); immature at Laudholm Farm, Wells, 18 Feb 2012 (K. Janes); immature in Ellsworth, 7 Jan 2016 (K. and D. Lima); and "immature" by the Spurwink R., Cumberland Co., 2 Jan 2012 (M. Illiff).

RVJ

Great Egret
Ardea alba

This elegant wader is a common summer visitor to Maine's coastal marshes

Status in Maine: The Great Egret is a common sight in coastal marshes during migration stopovers and late-summer dispersal. The first migrants arrive in late March and early April, but sightings reach a peak during postbreeding dispersal from late July to mid-September, when they are often found congregating with other waders. Most frequently seen foraging alone, Great Egrets occasionally form large flocks up to 60 birds. Rare but regular inland, they are most frequently found there in late summer. From one pair in 1994, a breeding colony on Stratton Island expanded to 52 nests in 2015, 33 in 2016, 43 in 2017, and 49 in 2018 (MDIFW survey data). Only two nesting pairs have been sighted outside of this colony. Three winter records likely indicate stragglers rather than a pattern of overwintering.

Historical Status in Maine: Palmer described the Great Egret (at that time called American Egret), as rare in spring and uncommon in late summer and early fall along the coast, as well as rare inland. He noted only seven reports from 1854–1910, with abundance increasing thereafter until a large flight in 1948 (see *Remarks*). This could have been a result of nascent conservation in the U.S. After the decimation of egret populations in the late 19th century, public pressure culminated in the regulation of commercial plume hunting in the early 20th century and the 1901 Audubon Model Law which outlawed plume hunting in FL. In 1903, Theodore Roosevelt established what became the first national wildlife refuge at Pelican I., a frequent Great Egret breeding site. These early efforts by state Audubon societies catalyzed creation of the National Audubon Society in 1905 with the Great Egret as its crest (McCally 1999).

Global Distribution: Cosmopolitan. Breeds along coast and in isolated inland pockets s. ME, s. MA, n. NY, and s. QC, west to e. SD, and south to AR, OK, Gulf Coast, Caribbean, Mexico, and S. Am. Scattered breeding populations in ID, OR, WA, n. NV, and cen. CA. Wide postbreeding dispersal: ME and s. QC, west to e. ND, and south to S. Am. West of Rocky Mtns., postbreeding movement from s. ID and s. WA south through NV, AZ, and NM. Winters along both coasts s. NJ and w. WA, south to Gulf Coast, Caribbean, Mexico, and S. Am.

Remarks: "In August 1946, there was a flight, about 20 individuals being seen by various observers. Some of these went as far east as Acadia National Park on Mt. Desert I . . . In 1948 at least three times as many occurred as in 1946, with birds noted from July 14 to October 10. Relatively high numbers were present throughout August and most of September. Most were seen in coastal York and Cumberland Counties, but some went considerably farther eastward and northward…[Later reports indicate that perhaps nearly 200 individuals were present.]" (Palmer 1949, 51).

SPRING: At least 28 Mar records. Early reports: 1, at Scarborough Marsh, 22 Mar 2007 (L. Woodard, fide T. Duddy); 1 at Ogunquit, 23 Mar 2003 (N. McReel); 1 at Pine Pt., 23 Mar 2004 (G. Carson, fide K. Gammons); 2 at Scarborough Marsh, 24 Mar 2007 (L. Seitz, L. Brinker); 1 at Spurwink Marsh, Cape Elizabeth, 24 Mar 1999 (G. Carson, *MBN* 11[1]: 23); 1 at Crescent Beach, Cumberland Co., 24 Mar 2005 (fide D. Lovitch); 1 at Granite Pt., Biddeford, 24–25 Mar 2007 (J. Briggs). Palmer listed 1 sighting before 23 Apr. Late arrivals: 1, Scarborough Marsh, 14 Apr 1995 (S. Pollock, *MBN* 9[1]: 2) and 1 at Pine Pt., 23 Apr 1990 (J. Despres, *MBN* 4[1]: 2). Most spring records of individuals or pairs, larger flocks of Great Egrets occasionally appear, all at Scarborough Marsh: 4 on 6 Apr 2006 (D. Lovitch), 7 on 15 Apr 2005, and 6 on 11 Apr 2007 (both N. Famous). At Jones Creek Marsh, Scarborough, 6 sighted 20 Apr 2004 and 12 sighted 9 Apr 2006 (both G. Carson, fide K. Gammons). Flock of 7 at Weskeag Marsh, 26 Apr 2007 (N. Famous). Spring records from coastal counties, with 5 inland records: 1 in Livermore, Androscoggin Co., 12–14 Apr 1985 (P. Cross, *Guillemot* 14[2]: 14); 1 at Messalonskee L., 22 Apr 2003 (N. Famous, fide K. Gammons); 1 in Orrington, Penobscot Co., 26 Apr 2006 (fide J. Smith); 1 in Linneus, Aroostook Co., 10 May 2000 (S. Young); 1 along Androscoggin R., Lewiston, 12 May 1992 (D. Haines et al.; *MBN* 6[1]: 2); and 1 at a Great Blue Heron colony in Gray, Cumberland Co., 16 May 2017 (D. D'Auria).

SUMMER: Breeding records primarily from Stratton I., including pair with 2 young on 31 Jul 1994 (fide National Audubon Society) and pair with nest on 31 Jul 2001 (L. LaCasse, fide K Gammons). This colony grew from 1 successful nesting attempt in 1994 to 43 successful breeding pairs in 2015–2018 (fide MDIFW). Two recorded breeding confirmations outside of Stratton I.: 1 nesting pair on Appledore I. in 1994, and 2 pairs on Ram I. in 2014 (fide MDIFW).

FALL: Approximately 175 fall records. Northernmost: 1 bird at Roque Bluffs S.P., 6 Nov 2016 (C. Todd, eBird). Latest fall records: 1 bird, Laudholm Farm, Wells, 21 Nov 2015 (F. Hopper, N. Hall; eBird), and 1, Kennebunkport, 23 and 29 Nov 2003 (K. Harder).

WINTER: Two winter records: 1 in Wells, 6 Dec 2005 (N. McReel, fide K. Gammons); 1 at Parsons Beach, Kennebunk, 5 Dec 2005 (B. Crowley et al.).

IM

Little Egret
Egretta garzetta

An Old World wader that must like the view

Status in Maine: Accidental. A Little Egret, likely the same individual, has summered in Maine sporadically since 2011. A second individual arrived in 2019.

Maine's first Little Egret was observed and photographed at Scarborough Marsh, 29–30 June 2011 (D. Hitchcox), possibly the same bird seen on Plum Island, Massachusetts, in July of that year (*AB* 65: 596). Remarkably, a single Little Egret was seen again at Scarborough Marsh a year later (K. Kelly and D. Hitchcox); it lingered 8 July–18 August 2012 (Persons et al. 2015). Maine Bird Records Committee accepted both records.

Several other records of single birds, possibly the same individual, 2015–2018 not yet reviewed by Maine Bird Records Committee: Gilsland Farm and Back Cove, Portland, 8 June–20 July 2015 (m.ob.); Stratton Island on 7 August 2015 after no longer being seen at Back Cove area, marking the first York County record; 23 April–27 July 2016 (R. Garrigus and m.ob., respectively; eBird), then at Scarborough Marsh, 5–12 August (obs. unk.). The same or another was at Biddeford Pool–Great Pond, Biddeford, 2 August–23 September 2016 (m.ob., eBird); 11 July (B. Bunn) to 11 August 2017, and again after absence, 16 September

2017; and 24 May–3 September 2018 (D. Hitchcox et al. and m.ob., respectively; eBird).

Remarks: In 2019 a second Little Egret briefly joined the first in the Gilsland Farm area before one of them relocated to Scarborough Marsh.

Interestingly, the 2017 bird was missing one of its two head plumes by 11 Jul, while the Little Egret observed in 2016 molted its plumes 8–12 Aug.

Global Distribution: Old World. A bird of temperate and tropical wetlands of Europe, Africa, Asia, and Australasia, Little Egret expanded its range north into British Isles in the late 20th century and now breeds there. Also colonized New World, first breeding in Snowy Egret colonies in Barbados in 1994. A rare visitor to e. N. Am., May–Sep, ~15 records along Atlantic Coast, DE–NFLD (www.sibleyguides.com).

PDV

Western Reef-Heron
Egretta gularis

From coastal Africa and the Mediterranean to the New World

Status in Maine: Accidental. There is a single record of a Western Reef-Heron photographed in Kittery, 18–27 August 2006 (L. Brinker et al.; ph. arch.). This individual was also observed intermittently in adjacent New Hampshire, 19 August–21 September 2006 (S. Mirick et al.). Plumage anomalies of a bird reported in Nova Scotia in June and July that same summer were identical to the Kittery bird; thus, it appears this reef-heron traveled south from Nova Scotia to Maine and New Hampshire in August.

Historical Status in Maine: Not previously recorded in ME.

Global Distribution: Breeds in Africa, Azores, and Cape Verde Is., east to India. Recent vagrant to N. Am., first reported on Nantucket, MA (Jun–Aug 1983). Since 1984, species has been recorded in West Indies (St. Lucia, Barbados, Puerto Rico), where it is found with increasing frequency (Raffaele et al. 2003). Species recorded in NL (2005), NS (26 Jun–2 Aug 2006), NH (2006), NJ (2007), and NY (2007).

PDV

Black Vulture

Coragyps atratus

Despite its historical rarity, this species is now regularly seen wheeling across Maine skies

Status in Maine: Formerly casual, Black Vultures have become nearly annual since the 1990s. There are numerous spring and summer reports from as far north as Grand Isle and Houlton (N. Dodge). Fall reports occur primarily along the coast in September with a maximum of four individuals over Bath, October 2004 (M. Mahnke, W. Robbins). There have been consistent winter observations since the first December record in 1988.

Historical Status in Maine: Black Vultures were casual prior to 1950. Palmer listed 10 primarily fall records: two specimens from Calais area, first around 1868 and second probably in 1882; one in Whitefield, Lincoln Co., 25 Sep 1897; one in Eliot, York Co., no date provided; one near Dover, Piscataquis Co., 20 Aug 1901; one shot in Lubec, 26 Aug 1904; one shot on Monhegan I., 6 Jul 1909; one at Scarborough, 11 Jul 1915; one in Springfield, prior to Apr 1939; one shot in Milo, Piscataquis Co., late Oct 1941. Knight wrote he received a letter from G.A. Boardman, a naturalist from the Calais area, Washington Co., who reported six Black Vulture records there. An unknown number of these reports came from NB. Boardman (1906, *JMOS* 8: 21–22) said this species was "not uncommon some seasons," but the limited number of reports appears to contradict this assertion.

Global Distribution: Neotropical and s. Nearctic. Resident from NJ and se. PA, WV, TX, and s. AZ, south to FL, Mexico, Cen. Am., and S. Am. Expanding north and recently bred in e. MA. Species recorded in all New England states and Maritime Provinces.

SPRING: Near-annual spring migrants since 1990s, primarily in York and Cumberland Cos. In 2010, as many as 7 reported from as many localities, 10 Apr–17 May. Most appear Mar–May, peaking in Apr: 7 Mar reports, >20 in Apr, and at least 13 in May. Early reports: 1 in Biddeford, 11 Mar 2006 (E. Hynes), 3 in York, 16 Mar 2002 (*Guillemot* 32: 19). In Cumberland Co., 1 at Bradbury Mtn., 11 Apr 2017 (D. Lovitch). In Whiting, Washington Co., single bird with injured foot captured 25 Mar 1986; treated and released 24 May 1986 (CDD, *AB* 40: 443). Second individual reported in Whiting, 24 Mar 2004 (F. Hartman, *Guillemot* 34: 13). In n. ME, Black Vulture videotaped

in Grand Isle, 27–28 Apr 2003, provided first Aroostook Co. record (J. Dionne, fide WJS). Species observed 45 mi. (72 km) north of Bangor on I-95, 3 May 2003 (S. Otto). In Knox Co., single birds reported from Rockland on 11 Apr 1998 (S. Benz, *FN* 52: 304) and 17 May 2010 (D. Reimer), and at Clarry Hill, Union, 1 May 2002 (M. Libby).

SUMMER: Since 1956, at least 17 summer observations. Farthest north in Aroostook Co. ph. in Houlton, 14 Aug 2010, for second county record (N. Dodge). Black Vultures generally avoid open water, so single bird particularly unusual on Ragged I., Criehaven Twp., 15 Jun 1997 (J. Drury). Closer to mainland, 1 on N. Haven, 31 May 2011 (T. Sprague); probably same individual on Vinalhaven, 3 May–12 Jun 2011 (D. Hitchcox).

FALL: More than 14 fall reports since 1956, 9 in Sep, all from coast. Recent observations, 1 each, fide eBird: Grant St., Bangor, 1 Aug 2017 (R. Ostrowski); Houlton, 10 Aug 2010 (N. Dodge); and Great Salt Bay Farm Wildlife Preserve, Damariscotta, 15 Sep 2014 (m.ob.). High count: 4 reported over Bath, 19 Oct 2004 (M. Mahnke, W. Robbins).

WINTER: First winter record in 1988. Other winter records, 1 bird each: in E. Machias, 13 Dec 1988–28 Feb 1989 (D. Craven; *AB* 43: 552, *AB* 43: 284); Lincolnville Ctr., Waldo Co., 21 Dec 1995–20 Jan 1996 (R. Underhill, L. Brinker; *FN* 50: 147); Scarborough, 3 Dec 1997 (G. Carson, *FN* 52: 170); Perkins Cove, Ogunquit, 7 Jan 1999 (D. Green, *NAB* 53: 144); Popham Beach, Phippsburg, 21 Jan 2002 (G. Pennington et al., ph.); Portland, 28 Feb 2002 (S. Pollock); Warren, 25 Jan–24 Feb 2008 (D. Suitor) and 29 Jan 2009 (M. Fahay); W. Falmouth, 10 Feb 2012 (C. Hynes); Gilsland Farm, 18 Dec 2014 (D. Hitchcox, eBird); Winter Harbor, 10 Feb 2016 (E. Gervais, eBird); Farmingdale, Kennebec Co., 27 Dec 2016 (D. Hitchcox, J. Fecteau; eBird); Newport, 4–7 Jan 2017 (m.ob. eBird).
PDV

Turkey Vulture

Cathartes aura

A striking silhouette common throughout the year

Status in Maine: Turkey Vultures have been increasing in numbers since 1976 and are present year-round in Maine. They are common spring and fall migrants, increasingly common breeders since the late 1970s, and nearly annual in winter, especially along the coast. This species is known to nest in a variety of habitats from mountain cliffs and forests to old buildings and can often be found circling near mountains such as Mount Agamenticus, York (L. Scott).

Historical Status in Maine: Knight listed only eight reports and Palmer noted a total of 14 records, chiefly along the coast. The earliest record appears to be a specimen from the Calais area prior to 1862 (Palmer 1949). Starting in 1949, Turkey Vultures became more regular in small numbers (one to four individuals) and were nearly annual: four birds seen in Midcoast ME, summer 1950 (A. Cruickshank 1950b, *BASM* 10: 63–64); Mercer, Somerset Co., 4 Jul 1956 (N. Davis, MASFC); Greenville, 20 May 1967 (MASFC); Farmington, Apr 1959 (W. Greer); and Langtown Twp., Franklin Co., Apr 1973 (MASFC).

Global Distribution: Nearctic and Neotropical. Widespread throughout much of s. N. Am., Caribbean, Mexico, Cen. Am., and S. Am. In N. Am., breeds from NB (occasional), ME, s. QC, and s. Canada through s. U.S., Caribbean, Mexico, Cen. and S. Am. Resident throughout much of its breeding range, though some northern populations (especially in w. N. Am.) highly migratory.

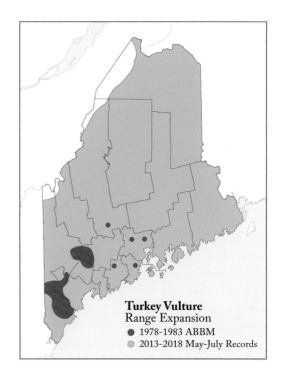

Turkey Vulture
Range Expansion
● 1978-1983 ABBM
● 2013-2018 May-July Records

SPRING: Increasing since 1976: >20 in s. ME spring 1977; >40 spring migrants in 1979; >28 in ME, spring 1982; "too numerous to list" in ME, spring 1985 (*AB* 39: 270); "everywhere" in ME, spring 1986 (*AB* 40: 443); "continue to be widely reported in Maine," spring 1987 (*AB* 41: 402). Prior to 1987, first spring migrants usually reported Apr–May. After 1987, several Mar reports: 1 in Bath, 1 Mar 1987 (*AB* 41: 254); 1 at Bear Mtn., Hartford, Oxford Co., 9 Mar 1987, and 21 at same locality, 25 Mar 1987 (B. Murphy); 2 in Farmington, 26 Mar 1987 (JVW). By 1990, first spring migrants arrived mid- to late Feb: 1 in Scarborough, 11 Feb 1990 (J. Despres); 2 in Scarborough, 29 Feb 1992 (D. Thompson, PDV); 1 in Kennebunk, 26 Feb 1994 (L. Brinker).

The pattern of vultures arriving earlier each spring reflected in Hunt's comments (*FN* 51: 729): "Turkey Vultures began migrating N into n. New England with the mid-February warm spell." Pattern continues with Feb reports in 2006, 2007, 2009, 2011–2014. In 2012, at least 17 Feb reports, 10 prior to 15 Feb, earliest: 1 in Bath, 5 Feb 2012 (M. Fahay), and 2 in Kennebunk, 6 Feb 2012 (S. Schulte). Notably, 6 vultures reported in Falmouth, 10 Feb 2012 (C. Hynes), and 10 seen in Biddeford, 25 Feb 2012 (P. Moynahan).

SUMMER: Given number of Turkey Vultures migrating into ME in late 1970s, nesting was anticipated to follow. Family unit of 3 birds (2 adults and a juvenile), over Dayton, York Co., provided first evidence of breeding in ME, Aug 1978 (S. Kenniston). Breeding confirmed when nest with 2 young found in Camden Hills S.P., Aug 1982 (B. Bochan, *AB* 36: 955). The *ABBM* (Adamus 1987) reported probable nesting in s. Oxford

and n. Cumberland Cos. Avian Haven, a bird rehabilitation center in Freedom, Waldo Co., receives nestling and fledgling vultures almost annually. Young birds admitted from Damariscotta (2003); Searsport (2005); Union (2007); Woolwich (2010); Bath (2011); Camden, Knox Co. (2012); Sebago (2013); Lewiston and Albion (2014); and in Somerset Co., from Sangerville (2010) and St. Albans (2013). When known, nest locations are usually inside abandoned buildings, cabins, barns, or trailers. Also, in Somerset Co., presumed nests found in abandoned structures in Solon and Canaan (W. Reid). In Piscataquis Co., Turkey Vultures found nesting above Fourth Debsconeag L., Rainbow Twp., in 2004 (T. Duddy, L. Woodard), and 2 adults, observed at N. Traveler Mtn., BSP, 26 Jun 1999, probably nesting (PDV). In Washington Co., nesting confirmed at Magurrewock Mtn. when juvenile vultures were heard hissing in Jun 2008 (R. Brown). Not surprisingly, BBS reported an 8.8% annual increase 1966–2015.

FALL: Prolonged fall migration starting mid- to late Aug, peaking in Oct, continuing in diminishing numbers to early Nov. On Mt. Agamenticus, high number of migrants seen by early Sep: 42 on 6 Sep 1988 and 11 on 8 Sep 1990 (S. Mirick et al.). Seasonal totals at this site: 104 in 1987 (*AB* 42: 233), and 100 in 1988 (*AB* 43: 62). At Clarry Hill Hawkwatch in Union, highest seasonal total recorded 504 vultures in 2013, peak daily counts of 103 on 8 Oct 2012 and 109 on 12 Oct 2014 (T. McCullough); latest date of 1 vulture on 13 Nov 2005 (M. Libby). Vultures often congregate at rich food sources: 35–40 birds observed at piggery in Arundel, York Co., Sep 1985 (*AB* 40: 255); >60 at Skowhegan Landfill, 29 Sep 1991 (M. K. Lucey); >100 at Turner Landfill, mid-Sep 1992 (W. Howes,

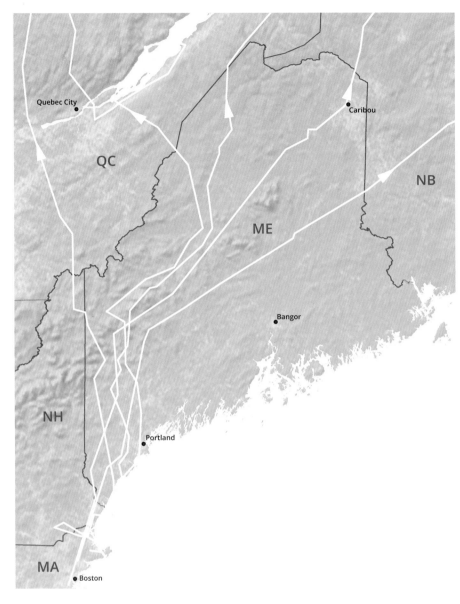

Map 21: Snowy Owl Migration Corridor

Five Snowy Owls tagged on the New England coast in 2016 and 2017 with GPS transmitters followed a surprisingly narrow route north along the uplands of western Maine before diverging widely. This narrow corridor holds several large wind farms, and tracking data show that one of the owls flew directly through the turbine fields. This is an example of how little we know about the nocturnal migration routes of many migrants (Project SNOWstorm).

Global Conservation Status: PIF: Watch List. IUCN: Vulnerable due to population declines and risks from climate change. However, purported declines in population, based on Partners in Flight Landbird Conservation Plan global estimates (Rosenberg et al. 2016) reflect change in estimate methodology, not any direct evidence of population trends.

Remarks: Palmer (1949, 311) clarified that Snowy Owls never bred in ME in post-glacial times: "Reports of this owl nesting in Maine began with Audubon and are, of course, erroneous." R. Eakin collected 61 pellets near the playing fields at Back Cove, Portland, over 12 winters 1978–2001. His identification of the remains, with T. French's help, provides insight into prey near urban areas in winter. "The majority of skeletal remains were those of *Microtus pennsylvanicus* [Meadow Vole] and *Rattus norvegicus* [Brown or Norway Rat]. One pellet (24 Jan 1997) contained bones of at least six *M. pennsylvanicus* and one *R. norvegicus*. Two pellets (27 Feb 1987 and 19 Mar 1988) contained bones of *Mus musculus* [House Mouse], and the one collected on 27 Feb 1987 also contained remains of *Sturnus vulgaris* [European Starling] as well as those of brown rats and meadow voles. One pellet (9 Feb 1997) contained bones of *Blarina brevicauda* [Northern Short-tailed Shrew]. Other avian prey included *Bucephala albeola* [Bufflehead], *Columba livea* [Rock Dove], and unidentified songbird bones. A pellet collected on 13 March 1980 contained skeletal remains of *Podilymbus podiceps* [Pied-billed Grebe]. Unidentified fish bones were found in a pellet collected on 23 Feb 1997" (R. Eakin, pers com.). Pellets collected on Appledore I., 2013–2014, included complete adult Muskrat remains, and bones of Common Eider and Red-throated Loon. Tracking data show that coastal wintering owls prey frequently on offshore waterbirds.

SPRING/SUMMER: Five migrating, GPS-tagged Snowy Owls from the New England coast (3 in Apr 2016, 1 in Feb 2017, and 1 in Apr 2017) followed a remarkably narrow route north through w. ME mountains in Oxford, Franklin, and Somerset Cos., suggesting a consistent migratory path through the region, and one which also passes through several major wind energy installations. Tracking data show that one of the owls flew, apparently unharmed, directly through turbines on Saddleback Mtn.

Several late-spring and summer records of immature birds: 1 in Cutler, 15 May 1988 (CDD, *AB* 42: 409); 1 immature banded in MA on Stratton I., 20–31 May 2002

(S. Hall, *NAB* 56: 286); 1 in Presque Isle, 30 May 1977 (*AB* 31: 975); an emaciated bird found harassing terns on Seal I., mid-Jun 1993, was captured for rehabilitation (*AB* 47: 1090); 1 in W. Paris, Oxford Co., 15 Jun 2014, a continuing bird from earlier (S. Galick, eBird); 1 immature in Madison, Somerset Co., 18 Jun 1992 (*AB* 46: 1121); immature bird on rooftop being harassed by gulls videotaped by a local news station in Westbrook, Cumberland Co., 21 Jun 1989 (*AB* 43: 1290); 1 in Trescott, Washington Co., 25 Jun 1969 (C. Dorchester); 1 in Brunswick, 17 Jul 1961 (*MFO* 6: 76); and 1 on Marginal Way, Ogunquit, 20 Jul 2014 (T. Fuller, eBird). This last record and the W. Paris one listed above are 2 of 5 sightings Jun–Jul 2014. One apparently summered on Cushing I., Casco Bay, ph. on 31 Jul 2017 (fide D. Hitchcox).

FALL/WINTER: Snowy Owls occur nearly annually in small numbers (1–5 per winter). Most frequently observed along coastal headlands, open fields, airports, and offshore islands, although reported from a variety of unexpected places; i.e., "seen while walking down Main Street in Brunswick." As noted by Palmer, first owls typically arrive mid-Oct to Nov in flight years, 6–8 weeks earlier than non-incursion years (late Nov–Feb). Recent records, fide eBird: 1 in Frenchville, Aroostook Co., 30 Oct 2014 (WJS); 1 on Monhegan I., 5 Nov 2014 (D. Cundy); 1 in Augusta, 10 Nov 2014 (R. Simpson); 2 at Sargent Mtn., ANP, 30 Nov 2015 (M. Good); 1 at Pineo Pt. Rd., Harrington, 6 Dec 2017 (M. and A. Archie).

PDV

FLIGHT YEARS

Major Snowy Owl flights usually occur on a three- to five-year cycle. Flight magnitude varies, but occasionally involves many hundreds or thousands of owls. Palmer (1949, 308) stated, "the larger flights come 'with a rush' in late fall, and birds tend to follow the coastline where they concentrate on islands and the mainland. In lesser flights, however, the birds appear later, and are more evenly distributed throughout." The 1945–1946 flight was remarkable as >1,000 owls were reported in ME with large numbers seen on offshore islands and at lighthouses: ~50 at Petit Manan Light; 25 on Isles of Shoals; ~50 at Matinicus Rock Light; ~25 Halfway Rock Light, S. Portland; 14 at Seguin I. Light (*BMAS* 2:79).

Flight year reports in Maine, first year of incursion winter given:

1878:	moderate flight (Palmer)	1953:	small flight >10 reported
1882:	sizable flight (Palmer)	1960:	>100 reported; first 1 in Brunswick, 31 Oct 1960 (MFO 5: 109)
1890:	moderate flight (Palmer)		
1892:	very large flight; >125 owls to taxidermists (Palmer)	1986:	moderate flight (*AB* 41: 256)
		1987:	>60 reported; first, 2 in Jonesport, 28 Oct 1987 (*AB* 42: 235 and 409)
1901:	large flight; >125 birds to taxidermists (Knight)		
1905:	>200 killed in ME (Knight); Palmer considered this a moderate flight	1991:	>30 (*AB* 46: 238); 1 landed on the MV *Bluenose*, 10 mi. (16 km) off coast
1912:	small flight (Palmer)	1992:	>14 (AB 47: 241–242)
1917:	small to moderate flight (Palmer)	2000:	small flight >26
1922:	moderate flight (Palmer)	2004:	small flight >16
1926:	major flight (Palmer)	2005:	small flight 14
1932:	moderate flight (Palmer)	2006:	small flight 15
1937:	moderate flight (Palmer)	2008:	small flight >30
1941:	moderate flight (Palmer)	2013:	exceptionally large flight, first records late Nov 2013
1945:	>1,000 reports (BMAS 2: 79); 247 received by taxidermists		
		2014:	small flight 20–30
1949:	>166 reported	2017:	moderate flight >50

Northern Saw–whet Owl

13 May 2000, and 49 individuals during an extensive nocturnal survey in Hancock and Washington Cos., 8 May 1999. In southern and coastal ME north to Farmington, Franklin Co., territorial calling starts in mid-Feb to mid-Mar. In Aroostook and Somerset Cos., calling begins ~2 weeks later (late Mar). Peak vocalizations occur throughout the state in Apr and May.

Breeding season is protracted: Palmer (1949) reported that F.H. Carpenter collected 2 eggs in Upper Magalloway, Oxford Co., 6 Apr of unstated year, and that he found 3 young in a nest at the base of Katahdin, 30 Apr 1881. The latest nesting record comes from Monson, Piscataquis Co., 6 Jul 1891: "four fresh eggs were taken from [the nest], another set of four having been taken a 'week or ten days previous,' and the brooding bird had to be removed from the nest by hand; the third clutch of four, subsequently laid, was left to hatch." This indicates that the first clutch was probably laid in early to mid-Jun. R. Long (1982, 14) actively searched for nesting saw-whet owls on Mount Desert I. and surrounding areas and reported, "On May 31, 1971 I found an old flicker cavity in a rotted stub on the edge of a cedar swamp containing three young Saw-whets and an addled egg. The hole was ten feet above the ground. The young left the nest in about a week. In the spring of 1981, a pair of Saw-whets nested in a flicker box at the edge of a cedar swamp in Seal Cove. The box was intentionally placed to attract Saw-whet Owls. On April 22 the nest contained five eggs. On several occasions the box contained six or more assorted mice and shrews. Single specimens of the White-throat, Yellow-rumped Warbler, and Palm Warbler were also found." In addition, Long reported 4 young and 1 addled egg in a flicker nest box on Mount Desert I., 19 May 1985, and young fledged before 26 May 1985; 5 eggs in a flicker nest box in Tremont, Hancock Co., 16 May 1987.

Other confirmed nesting records: 1 pair on Hog I., Bremen, 13 Jul 1952; 5 young banded on Cobboseecontee L., 19 May 1977 (MDIFW); a female and 3 young banded in Dresden, 19 May

1981 (MDIFW); 3 fledglings banded in a nest box at the head of Long Cove in Tremont on Mount Desert I., 19 Jun 1982 (W. Townsend); 2 adults at a nest cavity, Big Reed Pond, Piscataquis Co., in the 1990s (S. Rooney); a pair in a Wood Duck box in Camden, Knox Co., Apr 2006; a nest in Monroe, Waldo Co., 2008; young found in a nest box, Dresden, 29 May 2009 (K. Sullivan). Given the difficulty of locating nests, it is unsurprising that the *ABBM* confirmed only 6 breeding records statewide, in York, Cumberland, Oxford, and Lincoln Cos. (Adamus 1987).

FALL: Banding records in Freeport (J. Camuso and S. Walker), Kennebunkport (J. Ficker), Petit Manan NWR (A. Leppold and D. Brinker), and a variety of island and mainland sites (Biodiversity Research Institute [BRI]) have clarified a great deal about this species' fall migration. Freeport banding station banded an average of 230 owls annually, 1997–2006, with maxima of 356 individuals in 1999 and 367 in 2000. The Kennebunkport banding station captured an average of 65–75 owls annually (J. Camuso, pers. com.). Petit Manan averaged 236 owls annually, 2014–2017, with a minimum of 56 in 2014 and a maximum of 428 individuals in 2016. One-night peak capture 73 on 26 Oct. 2016. The migration takes place late Sep to mid-Nov with a peak in mid-Oct. Most owls (>65%) were immature. The BRI effort was notable for showing the importance of coastal and overwater migration in this species; 829 owls were captured at 14 sites, 2010–2013, with captures significantly more frequent on island and coastal sites than those farther inland, suggesting this species routinely migrates across and along the Gulf of ME (BRI, unpub. data).

WINTER: Although found throughout the state at this season, it seems likely that survivorship is greater along the coastal plain than in interior parts of the state where the snow depth is usually much greater. However, it is possible that frozen crust may be more critical than snow depth for owl survival. Palmer (1949, 323) noted that "some winters many of these owls are found dead. A large proportion of those picked up are in good flesh [fat reserves present], which would rule out death from slow starvation." He suggested that a plausible explanation might be a sharp decline in the mouse population, causing an incursion of the owls: "During a period of lowered energy from lack of adequate nourishment, the birds might freeze in cold weather" (Palmer 1949, 323). It seems more likely that a combination of factors such as snow depth, snow condition (ice crust), prey availability, and temperature, all of which can differ annually and regionally, contribute to winter mortality. Regarding saw-whet owls in Aroostook Co., Chamberlain (1949, *BMAS* 5: 50) noted, "occasional birds brought in dead, usually in winter. Most of them found in barns." At least 6 individuals were found dead, apparently from starvation, in the Farmington area Feb 1954 and 7 were found beneath feeders in Mar 1956 during a difficult winter (*MB* 1: 39). In 1967, there were 8 reports of dead owls in Feb, several found in garages or on porches, and in winter

1986–1987, 10 were found dead, primarily in Jan–Feb (*AB* 41: 256). Saw-whet owls reported infrequently on CBCs, primarily singly and along the coast from Calais to Portland. Most often seen on Mount Desert I. (>8 times) and the Bath area CBCs (>9 times); recorded once in Misery Twp., Somerset Co.

PDV

ORDER CORACIIFORMES

Kingfishers (Alcedinidae)

North America is kingfisher-poor—of 114 species worldwide, only one lives north of Texas. The Belted Kingfisher's reliance on water is distinct from many of its family, which are terrestrial and do not eat fish.

Belted Kingfisher
Megaceryle alcyon

The fiercely territorial Belted Kingfisher's rattling call echoes across Maine waterways

Status in Maine: Belted Kingfishers are common throughout Maine, especially along rivers and lakes in spring, summer, and fall. As coastal winter residents, they are common in southern and Midcoast Maine but less regular Downeast.

Historical Status in Maine: The status of this species has not changed appreciably in the 70 years since Palmer (1949, 331) noted that it was "fairly common throughout; transient, common in spring and fall; winter resident, uncommon but regular, mainly coastwise from Hancock County westward."

Global Distribution: Nearctic. Breeds throughout most of Canada and U.S. (absent in the high Arctic), Labrador to Aleutian Is., south to FL, TX, and CA. Winters from southern coastal ME and Maritime Provinces throughout most of the U.S., north along AK coast, and south throughout Cen. Am., Caribbean, and rarely n. S. Am.

Remarks: Belted Kingfishers are often unwelcome predators at fish hatcheries. Modern hatcheries have covered raceways, but that was not the case in 1965 when 65 kingfishers were shot at one fish hatchery that summer (*MFN* 21: 12).

SPRING: Migrate north to ME late Mar–Apr, arrival undoubtedly linked to the severity of the spring and the amount of available open water. Early records, 1 bird each: Old Town, Penobscot Co., 10 Mar 1979 (P. Turnbull); Lincoln Ctr., 19 Mar 1979 (PDV); Farmington, 11 Mar 1980 (P. Cross); Capisic Pond, Portland, 5 Mar 1999 (G. Sharpe). In 2000, Vassalboro, Kennebec Co., 4 Mar (H. Wilson); Scarborough, 5 Mar (C. Tubbesing); Machiasport, 9 Mar (A. Graham); Newport, 11 Mar 2002 (N. Famous); Durham, Androscoggin Co., 2 Mar 2008 (P. and D. McKeith); Middle R. causeway, Machias, 16 Mar 2010 (B. Southard, eBird); ME Ls. Resource Ctr., Belgrade, Kennebec Co., 8 Mar 2016 (L. Parker, eBird). In Aroostook Co., kingfishers generally arrive mid- to late Apr; thus, single birds notably early in Caribou on 24 Mar 2003 and 2 Apr 2006 (WJS).

SUMMER: Common in summer, nesting in long burrows in a variety of habitats but especially in sandbanks along rivers, lakes, and streams. The *ABBM* (Adamus 1987) confirmed breeding in every ME county. BBS data revealed no significant change in abundance in ME, 1966–2015, but a significant decline of 1.4% in the U.S. over the same timeframe.

FALL: Fall migration more protracted than spring. Disperses from breeding areas to suitable feeding sites throughout late Jul–Aug, generally moving to coastal areas in Sep–Oct. Kingfishers do not aggregate into flocks; thus, never numerous at any one site. In Aroostook Co., 6 individuals seen in Caribou, 21 Aug 2005 and 5 along the Aroostook R., Caribou, 30 Aug 2006 (both WJS). By Sep, more seen along coast: 4 in York, 10 Sep 2000 (B. Coullon); 24 at various points around Frenchman Bay, 13 Sep 2001 (W. Townsend); and 12 in Merrymeeting Bay area, Sagadahoc and Lincoln Cos., 14 Sep 2002 (R. Duddy).

Kingfishers linger in northern and western counties into Oct but are occasional thereafter. Late kingfishers in Aroostook Co., 1 bird each: Presque Isle, 18 Dec 1971 (*MN* 4: 6) and at same locality 30 Dec 2001–2 Jan 2002 (WJS); Ft. Kent, 30 Nov 2009 (C. Kesselheim); and St. Agatha, 28 Nov 2010 (WJS, eBird). Regular throughout fall after 15 Oct, but generally occur singly; 4 birds were somewhat unusual at Seawall Beach, 11 Oct 1999 (PDV).

WINTER: Winters annually along coast in small numbers since 1980s with some reports continuing through Jan–Feb. CBC results, 2013–2017, indicate kingfishers are occasional to rare in Washington Co., none recorded on Calais or Danforth counts for these years; in Eastport reported 1 in 5 years. Uncommon in Hancock Co., both Schoodic Pt. and Mount Desert I. observed birds 1 in 5 years. Annual or nearly annual along central and southern coast (Thomaston–Rockland, Pemaquid–Damariscotta, Bath–Lower Kennebec, Freeport–Brunswick, Portland, Biddeford–Kennebunk, and York Co.). Not in Lewiston, 26 Dec 1954 (obs.unk.) and 31 Dec 1996 (J. Scher). Penobscot R.: 1 dark variant in Enfield, Penobscot Co., 7 Jan 1966 (*MFN* 22: 45); 1 in Milford, 27 Feb 1992 (M. Hunter, A. Calhoun); 1 in Bangor, 2 Dec 2004 (*Guillemot* 34: 57). Other inland occurrences: 1 in Fryeburg, 5 Jan 1968 (fide C. Packard, *NMAS* Jan 1968); 1 in Bradford, Penobscot Co., 12 Jan 1987 (D. Tarbet); 1 in Dixmont, Penobscot Co., 3 Dec 1988 (B. Barker, *AB* 43: 285); 1 in Ft. Kent, 22 Feb 1994 (*Guillemot* 24: 4). From eBird: 2 southern coastal record blocks and 1 Downeast, Jonesboro-region block, Dec–Feb 2007–2017.

PDV

Peregrine Falcon

Falco peregrinus

Gone by the 1960s, peregrines have now recovered and continue to increase

Status in Maine: Since 1988, small numbers of Peregrine Falcons have nested in Maine on steep cliff sites inland and on the coast. Fall migrants are seen widely across all of Maine, but most are concentrated along the coast and outer islands. Uncommon in spring, they are most frequently reported March to May. Spring migration of peregrines tends to be via interior flyways, similar to shorebirds. Common and sometimes numerous during fall migration; the peak occurs late September to mid-October. On days with strong northerly winds, it is possible to see more than 20 individuals at preferred strategic stopovers, such as Monhegan Island, where juvenile falcons, especially, can efficiently hunt migrant prey. Adult peregrines breeding in Maine seem to be year-round residents, as in much of the Northeast. ANP documented wintering peregrines near nests as each pair set up residence starting in 1988. Even in January at far northern locations, like Kineo (Piscataquis County), ice fishermen see peregrines near their nests. This species now winters regularly along the coast and, more recently, on major rivers.

Maine Conservation Status: Endangered (breeding population only).

Historical Status in Maine: Knight said that a few pairs of e. Peregrine Falcons (*F. p. anatum*) nested in the mountains of w. ME, and that the species was common along the coast in Oct. Palmer also considered these falcons rare breeders in ME, noting there were probably <10 pairs, and that this species did not breed in cities. This latter point has changed considerably since the 1980s, as peregrines now nest in several ME cities. Widespread use of organochlorine pesticides, 1940s–1970s, caused eggshell thinning and subsequent reproductive failure (White et al. 2002). By 1960s, peregrines no longer bred in the Northeast; last known nest reported from ANP, Mount Desert I., was in 1962 (MDIFW 2003b). From 1984–1997, MDIFW released 153 young captive-bred peregrines at historical eyries. First successful nest was documented in Oxford Co. in 1988, and since then pairs have nested at 37 different sites in ME (MDIFW 2003b). The breeding population has increased to about 30 pairs (MDIFW 2003b).

Peregrine Falcon

Global Distribution: Global. In W. Hemisphere, breeds from Greenland, Arctic and subarctic Canada and NL to AK, uncommonly throughout Maritime Provinces and New England to Mid-Atlantic states and w. U.S. and n. Mexico. Winters from Maritime Provinces and s. Canada, New England south through Caribbean and S. Am.

Remarks: Captive-bred Peregrine Falcons released in the Northeast, 1984–1997, were not exclusively eastern peregrines (*F. p. anatum*) but instead reflected an assortment of subspecies, including the nominate subspecies, *F. p. peregrinus*, a native of Eurasia.

SPRING: Regular spring migrants. Passes north in small numbers: Bradbury Mtn. Hawkwatch averages 4/spring,

2004–2018 (D. Lovitch et al.). Four birds an unusual high over Mt. Agamenticus, 20 Apr 1980 (L. Phinney). Nearly annual on Monhegan I. since 2010, daily counts 1–2 (eBird). Spring migration starts in Mar, increases late Apr–early May, diminishes by end of month.

Early migrants typically local breeders; adults occur regularly at nesting cliffs by Mar. Male at Champlain Mtn. breeding site, Bar Harbor, first seen on 13 Mar 1996 (B. Connery) and joined by female on 30 Mar 1996 (M. Sharp); 2 birds seen from Precipice Trail Overlook, both called, joined to chase an eagle and returned to their perches, 20 Mar 2016 (N. Gormley, eBird); and 2 birds on 14 Apr 2017 (E. Barkdoll, eBird). Nesting pair at Beech Cliffs, Mount Desert I., present by 31 Mar 1996 (M. Libby); pair in Lewiston, 30 Mar 2007 (M. Knight). In Aroostook Co., single adult along Aroostook R., Caribou, 17 Mar 2009, exceptionally early (WJS).

Later migrant records peak late Apr–early May, likely peregrines that nest in Arctic. Late migrants on outer islands and along coast: Monhegan I., 1 chasing Red-necked Phalaropes on 26 May 1984 (JEP), 1 on 5 Jun 2001 (W. Boynton), and 2 on 27 May 2017 (m.ob., eBird). On Appledore I., 1 bird each: 26 May 1991 (D. Holmes), 16 May 2013 (W. Nichols, eBird), and 17 May 2017 (P. Ackerson, R. Suomala; eBird). One on Mount Desert Rock, 24 May 2007 (W. Townsend); 1 on Little Cranberry Isle, Hancock Co., 25 May 2007 (C. Kesselheim); 1 at Biddeford Pool, 25 May 2004 (P. Moynahan) and 20 May 2014 (J. Shorty and D. Doubleday, eBird). Single peregrine unusual at Messalonskee L. on 22 May 2008 (K. Lindquist), 22 Apr 2014 (D. Suitor, eBird), and 22 May 2016 (F. Kynd, K. Lima, and D. Hitchcox; eBird).

SUMMER: By far, the largest Peregrine Falcon nesting concentration is in mountains surrounding Androscoggin Valley in w. ME (s. Oxford Co., especially Bethel–Rangeley region). With >5 eyries, Mount Desert I. and surrounding islands support second largest concentration of peregrines in ME; they nest regularly on Beech Mtn., Champlain Mtn., and Penobscot Mtn., at Echo L., and on Ironbound I. in Frenchman Bay (B. Connery). Adults usually return to eyries by Mar but some winter locally and are seen at nest sites in Feb: 2 at Champlain Mtn., 28 Feb 2003 (W. Townsend). Usually incubate in May, fledglings seen mid- to late Jul (W. Townsend et al.). Known to use bridges and buildings for nesting and found in Portland (m.ob.); Bath (PDV); Brunswick (J. Royte); Bucksport (J. Smith); Lewiston (M. Knight); Brewer; Old Town, Penobscot Co.; Winslow, Kennebec Co.; Westbrook, Cumberland Co., and Kittery (C. Todd, pers. com.). Also documented nesting on quarry walls in Sagadahoc and Kennebec Cos. and on inland cliffs, notably Mt. Kineo, Piscataquis Co., and Evans Notch, Batchelder's Grant, Oxford Co. (G. Wallace). Peregrines now nest at >5 cliffs historically used by nesting Golden Eagles.

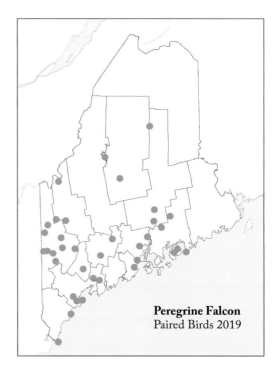

Peregrine Falcon
Paired Birds 2019

FALL: Disperse from breeding areas late Jul–early Aug, now regular in small numbers along coast. Especially common where waterfowl and shorebirds congregate, including Biddeford Pool, Scarborough and Weskeag Marshes, Seawall and Popham Beaches, east to Lubec Bar: 1 at Weskeag Marsh, S. Thomaston, 31 Jul 2001 (D. Mairs), 23 Jul 2010 (E. Fink, eBird), 15 and 22 Jul 2015 (C. Caron and M. Fahay, eBird), and 2 on 13 Jul 2016 (m.ob., eBird). Main migration takes place along coast and outer islands late Sep to mid-Oct; diminishing numbers continue through Nov–early Dec: 1 in Scarborough, 1 Dec 2006 (E. Woodin); 1 in Augusta, 3 Dec 2007 (M. Smith). Uncommon inland, occurs along major rivers and lakes.

Peregrine Falcons not regular or numerous in 1960s–1970s, when organochlorine pesticides reduced populations in Northeast and Arctic. Six to 8 birds on Monhegan I. late Sep–early Oct 1978 considered a good flight then (DWF et al.); these numbers considered low for weekly counts in 2000. Recovery evident by 1980s when >10 peregrines daily on Monhegan I. under favorable NW winds: 11 on 28 Sep 2017 (B. Barker, eBird), 14 on 26 Sep 1981 (PDV et al.), 25 on 30 Sep 1989 (B. Nikula), 22 on 25 Sep 1996 (PDV et al.), 30 on 30 Sep 2008 (D. Lovitch et al.), 39 on 11 Oct 2010 (J. Trimble, eBird). Barnes I., Hawkwatch documented population increase: 1970s seasonal average, 9.1 individuals increased to 26.2 falcons/fall in 1980s (daily high count 41 on 6 Oct 1985), 35.9 in 1990s, and 40.8 in 2000s (G. Appell, P. Donahue et al.). Peregrine Falcons regularly observed during pelagic trips: 8 reported at sea, New Harbor–York Harbor, 4 Oct 1954 (M. Libby).

WINTER: Rare in winter prior to 1995; now annual along coast to ANP. Unusual Washington Co. report: 1 in Machiasport, 1 Jan 2011 (C. Bartlett, eBird). Early reports, 1 bird each: Phippsburg, 2 Jan 1956; Enfield, Penobscot Co., 6 Dec 1963 (Potter, *MFN* 20: 13); Eaton, Washington Co., 13 Dec 1965

Global Distribution: Neotropical. Breeds in Argentina, s. Brazil, Paraguay, and s. Bolivia. Winters in n. S. Am. in n. Brazil, Guyana, Trinidad and Tobago, Venezuela, and Columbia. This subspecies has a long history of reverse migration, flying north instead south to S. Am. for the austral breeding season. Spring vagrants are presumably a result of individuals migrating north beyond their wintering grounds. Has occurred in all New England states, Maritime Provinces, QC, ON, and NFLD.

SPRING–SUMMER: 5 spring and early-summer records: 1 adult in heavy molt ph. at Ft. Foster, 18–31 May 1994 (J. Trull, L. Brinker, ph.; *FN* 48: 277). Individual associated with flock of 10–20 Eastern Kingbirds. Second bird ph. on Kennebunk Plains, 27 Jun 1994. This bird "appeared to be in fresher plumage and sported a longer tail than the bird present in Kittery one month earlier. Perhaps this was the same Kittery bird only further advanced in its molt process" (J. Bear, ph.; B. O'Toole, P. Dugan, fide L. Brinker). One at Ft. Foster, 24 Jun 2000 (P. Moynahan, eBird). Immatures observed at Kittery Pt., 12 Jul 2005, and on Stratton I., 6–8 May 2006 (R. Lambert, S. Sanborn, ph.). One seen at Pennellville Rd., Brunswick, 22 Jun 2012 (D. Hitchcox, eBird).

FALL: At least 12 fall records in ME, 11 since 1970. Nearly all records reported from along or near coast with 2 inland occurrences: 1 in Monroe, Waldo Co., 10 Oct 1985 (J. McQuilkin, fide B. Barker; *MBN* 1: 24, *AB* 40: 258), and 1 full-tailed individual in Manchester, Kennebec Co., 27 Nov 2010 (J. Timm). Coastal records, 1 bird each: 1 collected in Marion, 1 Dec 1908 (Palmer 1949; see above); Biddeford Pool, 6–11 Sep 1970 (K. Elkins et al.; *AB* 25: 29, ph.); adult in Whiting, Washington Co., 14–25 Sep 1975 (C. Dorchester et al., ph.); Tenants Harbor, Knox Co., 9–15 Sep 1976 (S. Cooke); Goose Rocks Beach, 1–8 Oct 1976 (*AB* 31: 232, ph.); Bailey I., Harpswell, 24–27 Oct 1984 (E. Schneider et al.; *AB* 39: 28); 1 in Cape Elizabeth, 23 Aug 1985 (obs. unk.); Cutler, 30 Sep 2007 (ph., fide N. Famous); Belfast, 23 Sep 2010 (J. Rose, ph.); Stratton I., 2–3 Sep 2011 (L. Seitz, eBird, ph.). Recent record: 1 at Gilsland Farm, 16–19 Sep 2017 (m.ob., eBird).

PDV

Olive-sided Flycatcher
Contopus cooperi

A large flycatcher whose distinctive "Quick-three-beers!" song is no longer heard on Maine's southern coast

Status in Maine: The Olive-sided Flycatcher is one of the shortest-staying breeding bird species in Maine. It was historically a local breeder throughout the state, but there are no recent records of nesting in southern coastal counties. This species is now more commonly encountered at higher elevations in the western mountains and the northern half of the state. Olive-sided Flycatchers declined by 2.9% in Maine, and more than 3.3% in North America, per year between 1966 and 2014, resulting in a cumulative decline of 81% (Sauer et al. 2017). It is an uncommon spring and fall migrant.

Maine Conservation Status: Species of Special Concern due to long-term annual decline in ME.

Historical Status in Maine: Knight listed the Olive-sided Flycatcher as common throughout most of the state. The species was considered a fairly common summer resident throughout Maine including the coast (Palmer 1949), breeding at Westbrook, Cumberland Co. (Norton 1890), and Mount Desert I. (Tyson and Bond 1941), among other nearby islands.

Global Distribution: Nearctic. Breeds from NL, NS, NB, ME through n. New England, south to Catskill Mtns. of NY and locally along Appalachian Mtns. in WV, e. TN, and w. NC. Breeding extends west through James Bay to w. AK and south at higher elevations in CA, AZ, and NM. Winters primarily in S. Am.

Global Conservation Status: IUCN: Near Threatened; PIF: Watch List due to population declines and moderate to high threats.

Remarks: In addition to Eastern Wood-Pewee and other flycatchers causing identification confusion, a number of late-season reports of Olive-sided Flycatcher pertain to young Cedar Waxwings, another species that hawks insects from prominent perches in autumn and has a "vested" appearance when viewed from below.

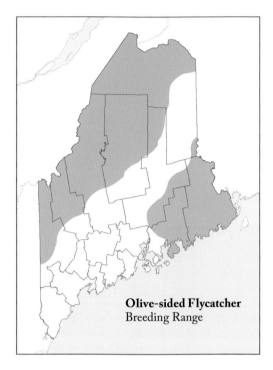

Olive-sided Flycatcher
Breeding Range

SPRING: Typically begin to arrive in ME mid-May, peak movement near end of May–first week of Jun. Migration continues through mid-Jun. Early season records, 1 bird each: Pine Tree State Arboretum, Augusta, 14 May 1988 (G. Therrien et al.); Cumberland, Cumberland Co., 14 May 1996 (L. Brinker); Hinckley Park, S. Portland, 16 May 2009 (B. Marvil); and Cyr Plt., Aroostook Co., 17 May 2010 (WJS). Recent late-spring records: a singing male at Capisic Pond, Portland, 12 Jun 2006 (G. Neavoll), and another at Hidden Valley Nature Center, Jefferson, Lincoln Co., 21 Jun 2014 (D. Suitor, G. Smith, Merrymeeting Audubon).

SUMMER: Vocal, prefers to sing from prominent perches; relatively easily detected on breeding territory. Breeds in coniferous forest openings and edges including bogs, flowages, and clear-cuts with clear airspace for foraging flights. Currently breeds locally western mountains to north and Downeast northward. Though ABBM confirmed breeding along immediate coast from Cumberland to Washington Cos., there is no recent documented nesting there. Recent evidence of coastal breeding is scant but includes: 2 (1 singing) at Lobster Cove Meadow Preserve in Boothbay Harbor on 29 Jun 2000 (M. Libby).

FALL: Earliest southbound birds appear where they are presumed not to breed by early Aug. Recent early records, 1 bird each: Eastern Promenade, Portland, 2 Aug 2004 (G. Neavoll); Evergreen Cemetery, Portland, 11 Aug 2012 (N. Gibb); and Rachel Carson NWR, 12 Aug 2013 (D. Hitchcox, P. Moynahan et al.). Peak movement of postbreeding adults occurs mid-Aug (north) to earliest Sep (south and coastally). Latest fall records occur last days of Sep and beginning Oct. Young of the year typically found on coastal islands and southern locations. Latest

records on Monhegan I.: 1 at Gilsland Farm Audubon Ctr., 9 Oct 2017 (D. Hitchcox, eBird), 1 juvenile on 7 Oct 2000 (L. Brinker, *NAB* 55: 29), and 1 late Sep–2 Oct 2005 (J. Trimble, D. Lovitch et al).

WJS

Western Wood-Pewee
Contopus sordidulus

A cryptic visitor from the West, confirmed thanks to photos and audio recordings

Status in Maine: Accidental. A single bird was carefully described, photographed, and sound-recorded by W. Hutchison on Roque Island, Jonesport, on 12 June 2018 (eBird). The bird was singing and calling as if territorial but could not be relocated the following day. Accepted by the Maine Bird Records Committee (#2018-016).

Global distribution: Breeds in w. N. Am., from se. AK to cen. Honduras. Winters in nw. S. Am. south to cen. Bolivia. Fewer than 10 East Coast records, most of these in fall.

CDD

Eastern Wood-Pewee
Contopus virens

A common forest flycatcher named for its song, which is heard into late summer

Status in Maine: Eastern Wood-Pewees continue to be common breeders throughout Maine despite an apparent 3.5% annual decline on Breeding Bird Surveys 1966–2015 (Sauer et al. 2017). The species occupies a variety of woodland habitats but is most numerous in open deciduous and mixed forests. It is less common in northern and eastern areas where young coniferous regeneration associated with commercially managed forestland dominates the landscape. Pewees are late-spring migrants, generally arriving from mid- to late May into early June. Fall migration takes place mid- to late August, peaking in early September. In migration, pewees are found almost anywhere deciduous trees occur. The earliest spring report is of a bird seen and heard in Bath, 24 April 1961 (*MFO* 6: 40), and the latest fall record was photographed on Bailey Island, Harpswell, 2 Nov 2013 (L. Bevier).

previous page: Olive-sided Flycatcher

Maine Conservation Status: Species of Special Concern.

Historical Status in Maine: Knight considered Eastern Wood-Pewees common breeders in open mixed and deciduous forests. Palmer (1949, 357) said this species was "uncommon but regular throughout on the mainland, except rare in areas of relatively unbroken forest." He also said that available data indicated "it was more plentiful as a breeder in the previous century than it is in the present."

Global Distribution: E. Nearctic. Breeds from Maritime Provinces and s. Canada west to SK, south to FL and e. TX. Winters primarily in n. S. Am. south to Brazil and Bolivia.

SPRING: Arrives mid- to late May, peaks last week of May: on Monhegan I., 10 on 29 May 1983 and 15 on 30 May 1987 (both PDV, eBird); 8 on 29 May 2010 (W. Sweet); 9 on 30 May 2013 (R. Lambert); 11 on 29 May 2015 (J. Trimble, B. Nikula; eBird); 12 on 28 May 2016 (J. Offermann, J. Trimble; eBird). Unusually early reports, 1 bird each: seen and heard in Bath, 24 Apr 1961 (*MFO* 6: 40); Bowdoinham, 5 May 1967 (F. Holmes); Boothbay Harbor, 8 May 1968 (M. Johnson); Petit Manan NWR, 5 May 1989 (R. Widrig); Scarborough, 6 May 1989 (G. Carson); and Lewiston, 9 May 1989 (D. Haines et al.). Migration continues through early Jun, stragglers appearing on outer islands into mid-Jun: 17 banded on Appledore I. first week of Jun 1985 (D. Holmes, *AB* 39: 888). On Outer Green I., late stragglers reported on following dates: 1 on 24 Jun 2002, 2 on 15 Jun 2003, 1 on 15 Jun 2006, 2 on 9 Jun 2007, 1 on 10 Jun 2009 (all Project Puffin, eBird). Arrive in Aroostook Co. last week of May, earliest observations reported in Woodland, 23 May 2010, and in Presque Isle, 23 May 2013 (both WJS). A wood-pewee that arrived in T5 R8 WELS, n. Penobscot Co., 6 Jun 1967, notably late (C. Jones).

SUMMER: Generally common in deciduous and mixed forests and pine woodlands throughout ME. Confirmed breeding from s. York to n. Aroostook Cos. (Adamus 1987). Although it continues to be common, species has declined by 3.5% per year, 1966–2015 (Sauer et al. 2017). Unlike many other flycatchers, adults often remain on territory well into Aug.

FALL: Attenuated fall migration. Suspected southbound migrants begin appearing in early Aug in coastal locations where they are not known to breed. Migration occurs mid- to late Aug, peaks in early Sep, and diminishes later in the month. On Monhegan I., large counts reported only in early Sep: 8 on 3 Sep 1983, 11 on 7 Sep 1985, 12 on 5 Sep 1987 (all PDV). Pewees depart Aroostook Co. early Sep, the latest reported in Woodland, 10 Sep 2014 (WJS). At least 12 Oct records, primarily the first week: 1 banded on Appledore I., 1 Oct 1995 (D. Holmes, S. Morris et al.). Late reports: 1 in Falmouth, 16 Oct 1956 (*MFO*

1: 117); 1 in Carmel, Penobscot Co., 12 Oct 1970 (*MN* 2: 31); 1 ph. on Monhegan I., 28–30 Oct 2013 (PDV, JEP); 1 at Johnson Cove Rd., Birch Pt., Washington Co., 29 Oct 2017 (J. Hand, eBird); 1 ph. on Bailey I., 2 Nov 2013 (L. Bevier); and 1 on Morse Mtn., 11 Nov 2017 (E. Raynor, eBird). Later reports either undocumented or do not eliminate possibility of similar Eastern Phoebe, which is known to occasionally linger into Dec.

WJS

Yellow-bellied Flycatcher
Empidonax flaviventris

A breeding bird of boreal forests, one of Maine's most distinctive empids

Status in Maine: The Yellow-bellied Flycatcher is a fairly common breeder in boggy spruce, fir, and cedar forests in western, northern, and eastern Maine and Downeast islands. It is an uncommon migrant in spring and fall.

Historical Status in Maine: The status of this species has changed little since Knight (1908, 317), who knew it to breed "on many of the larger thickly wooded islands along the coast, such as Deer Isle, Mount Desert, Islesboro, Isle au Haut, and in the deeper recesses of the moist interior forests of the northern, western, and eastern portions of the state." He wrote it was a common but under-detected migrant in s. ME that usually arrived around 1 Jun and departed by the start of Sep. This assessment was echoed by Palmer.

Global Distribution: Nearctic. Breeds in boreal coniferous forest from NL west through cen. QC, n. ON, n. MB, n. SK to cen. BC, south to Maritime Provinces and west through n. New England to n. cen. NY and ne. PA. Isolated breeding in WV. Winters in Cen. Am. from s. Tamaulipas, Mexico, to w. Panama.

SPRING: Later-arriving migrant with brief period of passage. Typically, first detected in s. ME third week of May and following week in n. and e. ME. Some years' arrival dates nearly simultaneous across state, suggesting migration route from west rather than along coast. Peak numbers encountered last week of May–beginning of Jun with lingering individuals through mid-Jun detected at locations where species is not known to breed. Earliest birds, 1 each: Kittery, 11 May 2014 (D. Akers); Winterport, Waldo Co., 12 May 1980 (B. Bochan); Lubec, 13 May 2000 (N. Famous); Woodland Bog, Woodland, 15 May 2004 (WJS). High counts along coast: 13 banded at Appledore I. on 1 Jun 1997 (25 banded from 20 May–8 Jun that spring; D. Holmes et al.); 26 at Biddeford Pool, 30 May 2013 (M. Iliff).

Later migrants away from known breeding locations, 1 bird each: Canaan, Somerset Co., on 19 Jun 1999 (W. Sumner); Peaks I., Portland, 18 Jun 2015 (D. Lovitch); Unity on 17 Jun 2012 (T. Aversa); Colby College, Waterville, on 16 Jun 2005 (R. Duchesne).

SUMMER: Breeds in dense bogs and mossy coniferous forest including alpine and coastal habitats. Breeding confirmed from cen. Oxford Co. east to Deer Isle–Mount Desert I. in Hancock Co., coastal Washington Co., and north through western mountains to Canadian border (Adamus 1987). Can be common in poorly-drained boreal forests in n. ME. Favors dense regeneration in wet areas of harvested stands of spruce, fir, larch, and Northern White Cedar. First documented nesting in ME in Houlton, 18 Jun 1878 (Purdie 1878). Local juvenile and adult parents banded at Woodland Bog, Woodland, on 13 Jul 1996 (WJS). Singing males observed in late Jun and Jul at isolated boggy habitats in Kennebec, Lincoln, and Knox Cos. but breeding unconfirmed. Breeding pair ph. at ANP, Tremont, on 17 Jun 2015 (M. Good et al).

FALL: Quiet and uncommonly detected during fall migration. Movement away from breeding areas occurs by mid-Aug, continuing through Sep. Numbers peak at south coastal locations last week of Aug–beginning Sep. Maximum of 22 banded at Appledore I. on 4 Sep 1986 (*AB* 41: 59). Last dates at known breeding locations: 1 at Aroostook NWR, Limestone, on 15 Sep 2012 (WJS), and 1 at Woodland Bog, Woodland, on 1 Sep 2015 (WJS). One banded on Metinic I., 10 Oct 2009 (A. Leppold). A notably late record on Matinicus I., 15 Oct 1996 (D. Mairs, M. Libby).

WJS

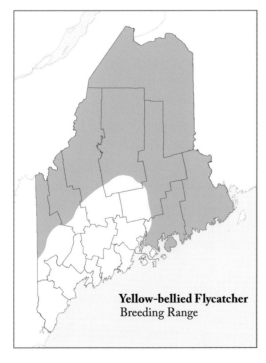

Yellow-bellied Flycatcher
Breeding Range

Acadian Flycatcher
Empidonax virescens

Casual in Maine, but a regular visitor to Appledore Island

Status in Maine: The first Acadian Flycatcher reported in Maine was banded in Brunswick, 11 September 1960 (C. Livesay, H. Tyler). The species was next observed and heard singing in Scarborough, 27 May 1967 (D. Perry). It has been a nearly annual spring migrant on Appledore Island since 1984, with as many as 12 individuals banded in late May and June 2007 alone. The Acadian Flycatcher is rare in summer and fall.

Historical Status in Maine: Neither Knight nor Palmer listed Acadian Flycatcher as occurring in ME.

Global Distribution: Nearctic. Breeds from w. VT, MA, CT, west to s. WI, south to FL and TX. Winters from e. Nicaragua to n. S. Am.

SPRING: On Appledore I., first Acadian Flycatcher banded in late May 1976 (E. Phinney); second record collected 26 May 1978 (D. Abbott, UNH bird collection). By 1984, nearly annual spring migrant on Appledore I., usually with 1–3 banded birds, 21 May–6 Jun; high counts: 5 banded in 1998, 6 in 2000, 5 in 2002, 5 in 2006, 11 in 2007 (S. Morris et al.). Three banded on Metinic I. in late May 2011 (A. Leppold). Surprisingly few spring records elsewhere in ME, 1 bird each: in Portland, singing male, 5 May 2000 (PDV, *NAB* 54: 262); 1 calling, 21 May 2005 (JEP, PDV); 7 Jun 2008 (E. Hynes, eBird). On Monhegan I.: 1 banded, 6 Jun 1984 (M. Plymire); 22 May 2011 (R. Lambert, eBird); 26–30 May 2013 (L. Seitz et al., eBird). In Kittery Pt., 1 was heard and observed, 21 May 2013 (D. and J. Lovitch, D. Hitchcox; eBird).

SUMMER: Rare in summer, few records include: 1 banded on E. Egg Rock, 11 Aug 1978 (fide S. Kress); 1 in Yarmouth, 9 Jun 1992 (L. Brinker, *AB* 46: 1121); 1 singing in Scarborough, 19 Jun 1995 (L. Brinker, *FN* 49: 910); 1 banded at Laudholm Farm, Wells, 18 Jul 1998, and also on 21 Aug 2013 (J. Ficker); 1 singing in Kennebunk, 19 Jun 1999 (S. Mirick); 1 singing on Monhegan I., 6 Jul 2011 (T. Magarian, eBird). Two remarkable reports from n. ME, both recorded: 1 in T4 R11 WELS, Piscataquis Co., 8 Jun 1983 (P. Adamus); 1 in Stockholm, 25 Jun 2012 (J. Grenzke, D. Kroodsma; eBird).

FALL: Few fall records, but very likely this species is overlooked at this season: 1 banded in Brunswick, 11 Sep 1960 (C. Livesay, H. Tyler); 1 individual on Mount Desert Rock, 20 Aug 1977 (W. C. Russell); 1 at Kittery Pt., 18 Sep 1983 (PDV, D. Abbott); 1 banded in Steuben, 27 Sep 2011 (fide B. Southard); 1 on Machias

Blue-headed Vireo

Vireo solitarius

An early-spring migrant with bold white spectacles, a blue-gray cap, and yellow sides

Status in Maine: The Blue-headed Vireo is widespread but never abundant in Maine. It breeds in medium-aged to mature mixed-wood and coniferous forests with extensive understory. In deciduous forest-dominated landscapes, Blue-headed Vireos are typically found along cool streams with mature hemlocks. Breeding Bird Surveys show an increasing long-term trend in Maine and in North America, though the population data show a non-significant decline in Maine, 2005–2015. A common early-spring and fall migrant, the species typically arrives by early April, continuing through mid-May. In fall, migrants appear in mid-August and continue through October with occasional November records and one December record.

Historical Status in Maine: Knight considered the Blue-headed Vireo a common and widespread spring and fall migrant throughout the state. A rare summer resident in s. ME, he considered it locally distributed even in n. ME where it was more common. Palmer wrote that it was a common summer resident except in sw. ME and on some coastal islands, where it was rare and local. He considered it a common spring and fall migrant.

Global Distribution: Nearctic. Breeds from sw. NFLD, s. QC, New England, and NY west to se. YT, s. NT, and ne. BC, south to AB, n. MN, WI, and MI, through Appalachian Mtns. Winters from coastal VA and NC south, across Gulf States and into Mexico and Cen. Am. to Guatemala.

SPRING: A common but never abundant early-spring migrant, early Apr to mid-May. Earliest records, 1 each: 3 Apr 1942 in Portland (Palmer 1949); 10 Apr 1992 in Scarborough (G. Carson); 13 Apr 2017 in Auburn, Androscoggin Co. (G. Jarvis, eBird); all on 14 Apr: in 2006 in Evergreen Cemetery in Portland (S. Walsh), 2010 at Bradbury Mtn. S.P. in Pownal (N. Lund, eBird), and 2017 at Capisic Pond in Portland (J. Lorenc, eBird); both on 15 Apr: 2015 at Gilsland Farm (E. Hynes, eBird) and 2017 in Windham (M. Tucker, eBird); both on 16 Apr: 2003 in Augusta (N. Famous) and 2005 in Readfield, Kennebec Co. (R. Spinney). Exceptionally early arrival date of 3 Apr 1942 aside, Palmer's dates were 26 and 29 Apr, suggesting arrivals in recent years generally earlier than previously. Since 1950, at least 60 arrival records in ME before 26 Apr. Typically, 1–2 birds at single location during migration, occasionally higher numbers

recorded. Maximum spring migration counts: 30 on 12 May 1996 and 18 on 11 May 1996 at Phippsburg (PDV); 18 on 5 May 2006 at Evergreen Cemetery, Portland (D. Lovitch); 16 on 1 May 2010 in Falmouth (L. Seitz); and 15 on 13 May 1997, Monhegan I. (PDV, D. Abbot). Spring peak based on highest number of eBird checklists week of 8 May, when reported on 20% of checklists.

Blue-headed Vireo

SUMMER: Widespread and common but not abundant in ME, preferring coniferous dominated forests, often along stream corridors with hemlocks. Widespread breeding species across state (Adamus 1987), but never reaching abundance of deciduous forest songbirds like Red-eyed Vireo, which is 8 times more abundant in ME (BBS data). BBS data suggests ME has highest relative abundance (4.5 per route) of Blue-headed Vireo of all U.S. states, exceeded in N. Am. only by NB and NS. Maximum BBS numbers all from 2 Washington Co. routes: 74, 70, 52, 47, and 44 on Northfield BBS in 1980, 1979, 1976, 1981, and 1977; 40, 39, and 31 on Cooper BBS in 1979, 1978, and 1981. At least 20 recorded 27 times on BBS routes in ME since 1966. BBS trend for ME shows 1.4% statistically non-significant increase per year, 1966–2015, and a non-significant decline of 2.5% per year from 2000–2015. N. Am. BBS trend increasing, 1966–2015 (Sauer et al. 2017).

FALL: Fall migration mid-Aug to Oct, peaking mid- to late Sep, occasional migrants into Nov. Species reported from highest percentage of ME eBird checklists (15%) week of 22 Sep. Highest fall counts: 15 on 21 Sep 2004, Monhegan I. (L. Bevier); 15 on 26 Sep 2006 in Oakland, Kennebec Co. (D. Mairs); and 13 on 10 Oct 2011 at Sandy Pt., Cousin's I. (R. Speirs, eBird). Species regularly persists through late Oct (>50 records 15–31 Oct); at least 14 Nov records. Latest Nov records: 1 on 17 Nov 2007 at Back Cove, Portland (S. Baron, eBird); 1 on 11 Nov 1999 at Middle Rd., Cumberland, Cumberland Co. (L. Brinker); 1 each on 11 Nov at Pine Pt., 2003 (G. Carson), and at W. Falmouth, 2005 (L. Seitz).

WINTER: Single winter record: 1 Dec 2002 at Holmes Rd., Scarborough (J. Stevens). Dec records in MA, VT, NH, QC, NS, and NB.

JVW

Plumbeous Vireo

Vireo plumbeus

A denizen of Southwestern pine forests, this species has been recorded in Maine once

Status in Maine: Accidental. Maine's only Plumbeous Vireo record is a bird photographed on Matinicus Rock, 11 June 2005 (S. Smith, ph.; Maine Bird Records Committee).

Global Distribution: Sw. Nearctic. Breeds primarily in dry montane forests of NV, UT, WY, CO, south to NM, AZ, Mexico, Guatemala, and El Salvador. Winters from Mexico to El Salvador, with small numbers in s. CA and s. AZ. Vagrant on Atlantic Coast with records in ON and NS. Species has not been recorded elsewhere in New England.

PDV

Philadelphia Vireo

Vireo philadelphicus

One of northern Maine's specialty breeding birds, and avidly sought during migration

Status in Maine: Restricted to northern and western Maine in summer, breeding Philadelphia Vireos are one of Maine's most difficult breeding vireos to detect. Breeding Bird Surveys show increasing population trends in Maine and elsewhere in North America. A rare spring migrant seen from mid-May through early June, it is an uncommon fall migrant from mid-August through October with exceptional records of birds as late as November.

Historical Status in Maine: Knight (1908, 476) characterized the Philadelphia Vireo as a rare and local summer resident and suggested, "future search will doubtless show that it breeds regularly and perhaps even commonly about the ponds and lakes of northern and eastern Maine." It was a rare to uncommon and local summer resident in northern counties, according to Palmer, whose southern limits in the state were unknown. He considered it an uncommon but probably often overlooked spring

and fall migrant. Both authors noted difficulties in detecting the species because of similarities between its song and that of the more abundant and co-occurring Red-eyed Vireo.

Philadelphia Vireo
Breeding Range

Global Distribution: Nearctic. Breeds from s. NFLD (possibly with an isolated population in Labrador), s. QC and ME, west to sw. NT and ne. BC, south to n. U.S., east to ND. Winters from s. Mexico south through Cen. Am. to Panama.

SPRING: Rare to uncommon spring migrant; reports of >1 bird at a location unusual. Migration mid-May to early Jun; migrant birds banded or observed on islands where they do not breed in early Jun. Earliest records, 1 each: 5 May 2015, Viles Arboretum, Augusta (J. Lazzaro, eBird); 9 May 2000 at Capisic Pond, Portland (G. Carson); 12 May 2005, Monhegan I. (H. Nielson); 12 May 2012, Green Pt. WMA, Dresden (M. Fahay); 12 May 2014, Evergreen Cemetery, Portland (D. Hitchcox et al., eBird); 13 May 1997, Laudholm Farm, Wells (fide K. Gammon); 13 May 2001 at Hinckley Park, S. Portland (L. Brinker). Spring peak week of 22 May when reported on 2% of eBird checklists. Maximum migration counts: 4 on 25 May 2000, Monhegan I. (T. Duddy); 4 on 26 May 1983, Cherryfield (J. and V. Layton); 3 on 27 May 1984 at Ft. Kent (G. and S. Flagg); 3 each on Monhegan I., same day, 28 May 1989 and 2005 (JVW and A. Wells; L. Brinker, respectively).

SUMMER: Restricted to n. and w. ME. One of least widespread and least abundant breeding vireos in ME, typically occurring in young to mid-successional deciduous and mixed forest. Species breeds in few n. and w. ME blocks, no records

and occasionally in back dunes in southern York and Cumberland Counties, and probably elsewhere. The species became less widely distributed in the late 19th and early 20th centuries. Both Forbush (1927) and Palmer listed numerous towns where larks bred, but it seems the species no longer occurs at many of those sites. Horned Larks breed regularly in potato fields and agricultural areas of Aroostook County. Inexplicably, it is not known to breed regularly, if at all, in eastern Maine; this is all the more curious given the extensive sandy habitat provided by vast blueberry barrens in Washington and Hancock Counties. In winter, Horned Larks are regular in small numbers along the southern coast and inland farmlands in central Maine. The species is occasional to rare in northern and eastern Maine at this season.

Maine Conservation Status: Species of Special Concern (breeding population only).

Historical Status in Maine: Palmer (1949, 361) noted that "Prairie" Horned Lark (*E. a. praticola*) was an "occasional" summer resident in s. ME and that it was more common in the "northern third of the state." He considered both the prairie and the northern subspecies (*E. a. alpestris*) to be regular in spring, fall, and winter.

Global Distribution: Holarctic. In N. Am., breeds in high Arctic from NL and Baffin I. west to AK, throughout much of the continent in unforested areas south to GA, TX, and Mexican highlands, and locally in Colombia. In winter, withdraws from most of Canada to U.S. and Mexico. The prairie subspecies of Horned Lark spread eastward from the Great Plains into New England in late 19th century and was not known to breed in ME or New England prior to this period.

SPRING: Common migrant; arrives late Feb, most numerous in Mar, continues in diminished numbers Apr–May. Small flocks (4–30) typical in spring, occasional larger counts of 40–100 birds. High counts of >200 birds: 200 in Wells, 27 Mar 1973, increased to 1,000 on 4 Apr 1973 (L. Phinney); 200 in Cutler, 22 Mar 1979 (N. Famous); 200 in Barnard Twp., Piscataquis Co., 29 Mar 1997 (M. Hunter); 400 in Turner, 16 Apr 1999 (J. Despres). Larger flocks presumably primarily darker and more yellow northern subspecies; however, Palmer reported paler "Prairie" Horned Lark also arrived in ME by late Feb–Mar. Given that most observers do not distinguish between subspecies, they are considered here together.

Early migrants reported in Turner: 15 on 24 Feb 1988, 4 on 22 Feb 1996, 4 on 19 Feb 1997 (all J. Despres). At Popham Beach,

30 on 27 Feb 1998 (D. Mairs). In Aroostook Co., early migrants noted in Presque Isle: 3 on 13 Mar 1982 (M. Holmes), 1 on 20 Feb 1983 (M. Trombley); and in Bancroft, 2 on 1 Mar 1999 (J. MacDonald). Late migrants linger into May in Turner: 41 on 4 May 1995, 1 on 26 May 1997, 10 on 9 May 1998, 50 on 12 May 1999 (all J. Despres). In Aroostook Co., WJS recorded 120 birds in Presque Isle, 10 May 1995; 70 in St. Agatha, 1 May 2011; and 19 in Ft. Fairfield, 4 May 2014. Late migrants elsewhere: 2 in Augusta, 22 May 1992 (H. Wilson); 1 on Monhegan I., 29 May 1994 (S. Surner); 1 on Outer Green I., 29 May 2005 (Project Puffin); 3 at Biddeford Pool, 25 May 2010 (B. Marvil).

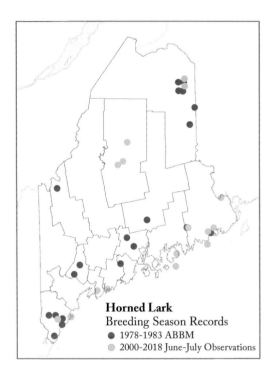

Horned Lark
Breeding Season Records
● 1978-1983 ABBM
● 2000-2018 June-July Observations

SUMMER: "Prairie" Horned Lark breeds locally at airports, in sand dunes, and on grassland barrens in s. and cen. ME, and in agricultural fields in n. ME. Curiously, largely unknown as nesting species in Washington Co. despite abundant habitat on blueberry barrens (N. Famous). In York Co., Larks bred in dunes along Harbor Rd., Wells, 1970s–1980s: many in Jun 1971 (*MN* 3: 6); 4 on 31 Jul 1973 (L. Phinney); 1 male in flight song, 10 May 1982 (PDV). Species bred, at least occasionally, at Wells Barren: male in flight song on 19 Jun and 1 Jul 1985 (PDV); and 1–2 pairs found at Sanford Airport, 20 Jul 1988, 17 Jul 1995, and 18 Jun 1996 (PDV, JVW, L. Brinker, respectively).

Species nested regularly at Kennebunk Plains. In 1984, during intense blueberry management, ~10 singing males, 31 May 1984 (PDV, JVW). As management of grassland habitat shifted from commercial blueberry cultivation to more natural prescribed burns, number of larks diminished to 1–4 pairs. No larks observed in 1995, but 2–3 pairs present once more in 1996 (PDV). Most recently, juvenile observed on 26 Jul 2008 (B. Herrgesell). Elsewhere, short-tailed juvenile observed at

Biddeford Pool, 13 Aug 1978 (PDV, JEP). In Cumberland Co., 1–3 pairs of Horned Larks nested at Brunswick Executive Airport (formerly Brunswick Naval Air Station) ~1985–1991 (PDV, JVW). In Gorham, Cumberland Co., nest with 3 eggs found on 13 Apr 1952 (W. Smart). In Kennebec Co., Horned Larks resident at Augusta Airport in 1988, 6 on 14 Aug (G. Therrien). Historically, larks also nested in Manchester, Kennebec Co. (Apr 1903), Clinton (Apr 1901), and China, Kennebec Co. (May 1906, Palmer 1949). In n. Penobscot Co., 2 territorial larks at Millinocket Airport, early Jun 1976 and 1977 (PDV). In Aroostook Co., Horned Larks have nested in potato fields since 1920s (Chamberlain 1949). Species remains regular and fairly common summer resident in agricultural portions of e. Aroostook Co. Recent summer observations, fide eBird: 2 in Presque Isle, 13 Jun 2013 (WJS); 1 west of Telos, Penobscot Co., 3 Jun 2013 (J. Mays); 1 Great Wass I. Preserve, 22 Jun 2017 (D. Jones); 2 at Biddeford Pool, 29 Jun 2014 (m.ob.).

FALL: Protracted migration Aug–early Dec. Main flight late Sep–Oct. Reports of Aug migrants: 2 at Back Cove, Portland, 19 Aug 1982 (PDV); 1 in T19 MD BPP, Washington Co., 23 Aug 2006 (PDV); 2 in Bar Harbor, 26 Aug 2011 (C. Ahern). In Turner, J. Despres maintains longest, most consistent lark observations, accurately reflecting species' fall movements. Earliest arrivals: 12 Sep 1994 (5 birds) and 11 Sep 1998 (1 bird, both J. Despres). Largest numbers in Turner typically found late Oct–early Nov: 600 on 20 Oct 1981; 125 on 18 Oct 1989; >400 on 10 Nov 1990; 200 on 23 Oct 1994 diminishing to 150 on 8 Nov 1994; 150 on 4 Oct 1995; 400 on 25 Oct 1998; 90 on 5 Nov 1999 (all J. Despres). Migrants occasionally linger into Dec: 50 on 1 Dec 1994 and 100 on 4 Dec 2001 (both J. Despres).

Early Sep migrants in Aroostook Co.: 25 in Eagle L., 13 Sep 1977 and 5 at Marcum Pond, 6 Sep 1977 (both J. Gibson); 30 in St. Agatha, 13 Sep 2014 (WJS). Early birds at Scarborough Marsh: 9 on 14 Sep 2005 (L. Brinker). Early reports elsewhere: 6 at Bangor Airport, 5 Sep 1978 (PDV); 8 at Seawall Beach, 14 Sep 1985 (PDV); 1 on Appledore I., 8 Sep 1990 (D. Holmes); 3 in Gouldsboro, 6 Sep 1996 (N. Famous); 1 in Machiasport, 13 Sep 1998 (N. Famous). Agricultural fields of Aroostook Co. often produce large counts; in St. Agatha: 600 on 30 Sep 2007, and 170 on 13 Oct 2008; in Caribou, Presque Isle, and Easton, 200 at each location on 18 Oct 2007; in Limestone, 120 on 13 Oct 2007 (all WJS). In Piscataquis Co., 150 reported from Katahdin Twp., 12 Oct 2002 (T. Griset); in Kennebec Co., 100 in Clinton, 30 Oct 2008 (D. Mairs et al.); in York Co., 100 at Seapoint Beach, Kittery, 15 Nov 2008 (P. Augusta); and 35 at Goose Rocks Beach, 2 Dec (J. Junker).

WINTER: Locally distributed throughout Maine, generally rare to occasional in n. and e. ME, largely absent from forested parts of w. and cen. ME. In s. cen. ME, small flocks of 5–20 Horned Larks found in open habitats, beaches, and agricultural fields. Larger counts (60–100) regularly reported at several locations: 100 in Turner, 27 Dec 1998 (J. Despres); 115 in Clinton, 28 Dec 2012 (M. Viens). Large counts on coastal CBCs: 112 on Biddeford–Kennebunkport CBC, 28 Dec 1976; 101, Portland Area, Dec 2004; Bath–Lower Kennebec, 106 in Dec 2000 and 219 in Dec 2003. Additional large counts: 75 individuals in Cutler, 5 Dec 1978 (N. Famous), and 78 at Popham Beach S.P., 23 Dec 2007 (M. Fahay).

PDV

Swallows (Hirundinidae)

Superior aerial maneuvering and efficient flight in this globe-spanning family of about 90 species of insectivores allows for niche feeding among mixed flocks hunting at different heights. Populations of the six swallow species that breed in Maine are in decline—as are populations worldwide—as flying insect numbers plummet.

Bank Swallow
Riparia riparia

Maine's most severely declining species of bird

Status in Maine: Though still fairly widespread in southern Maine, the Bank Swallow is becoming an increasingly uncommon and locally breeding species in the rest of the state. Breeding Bird Survey results show a steep decline 1966–2017 in Maine to less than 1% of its 1966 population—as throughout North America, a trend seen in all swallows and most other aerial insectivores. Bank Swallows are regular spring migrants in April and May, and uncommon fall migrants July through September.

Historical Status in Maine: Knight considered Bank Swallows common summer residents throughout the state. Palmer wrote that the species was an uncommon and declining colonial breeder throughout the state and "fairly common" in spring and fall migration (1949, 366).

Global Distribution: Nearctic. Extensive breeding range covering much of N. Am.: NL and cen. QC west to AB, n. NT, and YT to interior and s. AK, n. BC to e. WA and OR and n. CA; south to coastal VA, Midwest, n. NV, UT, and NM; also in s. TX and ne. Mexico. Winters primarily in S. Am. but small numbers have been recorded in winter from s. Mexico through Panama. Also breeds in Europe and Asia.

SPRING: Still widespread, but rapidly decreasing spring migrant. Migration late Apr–late May. Earliest records: 2 on 10 Apr 2001 at Abagadasset R. mouth, Bowdoinham (PDV);

Bank Swallows

1 on 15 Apr 1993 in Scarborough (L. Brinker); 1 on 18 Apr 2017 at Sanford Lagoons (J. Fecteau); 2 on 22 Apr 1990 at Mt. Agamenticus (L. Phinney); 1 on 22 Apr 2006 at Hinckley Park, S. Portland (N. Schwarzel); and 1 on 23 Apr 1994 at Scarborough (L. Brinker). Arrival dates indicate birds arriving earlier than decades prior to 1949, as Palmer found arrivals during first 8 days of May. However, Knight (1908) noted spring arrival 19–25 Apr near Bangor; these dates are earlier than those recorded decades later by Palmer, who surmised that earlier arrival dates at the turn of the century were because Bank Swallows were more numerous then. Spring peak based on eBird checklists in weeks of 15 and 22 May, when species appeared on 3.3% and 3.5% of checklists, respectively. Maximum spring counts: 1,000 on 19 May 2000 at Sanford Lagoons (PDV, JEP et al.); 250 on 23 May 1957 and 200 on 18 May 1959 at Leeds Ctr., Leeds, Androscoggin Co. (Ramsdell; *MFO* 4[3]: 48, *MFO* 2[6]: 59); 150 on 23 May 2008 at L. Josephine (WJS); 120 on 22 May 1957 at Warren (Lord, *MFO* 2[6]: 59); 60 on 28 May 1997 at Gibson Rd., Scarborough (K. Gammons). Note: counts from Leeds, Warren, and Scarborough are from breeding colony locations, although recorded during spring migration.

SUMMER: A widespread but uncommon breeding bird, declining over last 50 years to less than 1% of its 1966 population, as estimated by BBS (Sauer et al. 2017). In 1980s, widespread outside of remote n. and w. ME and interior Washington Co. (*ABBM,* Adamus 1987). Maximum numbers at or near colonies, Jun and Jul: 246 banded from ~360 active nesting burrows, 21–24 Jun 1988, Lubec Flats, Lubec (M. Plymire); 150 on 6 Jul 1998 at Lubec Flats (N. Famous); 146 on 15 Jul 1957 at Cape Elizabeth (R. Payne, *MFO* 2[8]: 83); 100 through Jul 1958 at Livermore, Androscoggin Co. (Stetson, *MFO* 3[8]: 85). Maximum BBS numbers: 140, 110 in 1980 and 1971 on Otisfield BBS (Oxford

Co.); 131 in 1981, Cooper (Washington Co.); 121 in 1973 on E. Troy BBS (Waldo Co.). Fifty or more birds recorded on individual BBS routes in ME 29 times since 1966, but only once after 2000. Subsequent years produced lower counts: Otisfield BBS recorded no Bank Swallows in 19 of 21 years, 1995–2015; no count above 10 birds since 1988. On Cooper BBS conducted 16 years, 1989–2016, 11 counts produced no Bank Swallows; 1 count had 20 birds; 2–4 birds remaining 4 years. E. Troy BBS completed 6 of 12 years, 2005–2016, no Bank Swallows recorded. Only recent BBS route with >50 Bank Swallows was in 2005. N. Am. and ME BBS show decreases of 5.3% and 11.2% per year 1966–2017, respectively (Sauer et al. 2017).

FALL: Uncommon fall migrant Aug–Sep, peaks Jul–Aug. Adult and juvenile swallows form postbreeding flocks beginning Jul creating highest seasonal numbers, then gradually taper off through fall. Reported from highest percentage of ME eBird checklists (5%) weeks 8–22 Jul. Maximum migration counts: 5,000 on 19 Aug 1998 in Benton, Kennebec Co. (W. Summer); 400 on 6 Sep 1998 in Turner (J. Despres); 200 on 22 Aug 1984 in Ft. Fairfield (M. Trombley); 150 on 7 Sep 1998 in Turner (J. Despres). Late records: 16 at Annis Rd., Ft. Fairfield, 23 Aug 2015 (WJS, eBird); 11 on 10 Sep 2014 at Wyman Rd. farm, Benton (L. Bevier); 1 on 16 Sep 2015 at Scarborough (N. Gibb); 1 each, 17 Sep 2013 and 2016 (D. Hitchcox and A. Gilbert, respectively) at Biddeford Pool; 1 on 19 Sep 1992 at Appledore I. (S. Morris); 1 on 26 Sep 1987 and 2 on 13 Sep 2015 on Monhegan I. (PDV and K. Yakola, respectively; eBird). Reported on Machias Seal I., 28 Sep 2006 (R. Eldridge). In Aroostook Co., 1 Bank Swallow "extremely late, with Tree and Cliff Swallows, hurricane blown + returning south?" 9 Sep 2010 (WJS, eBird).

WINTER: No ME records Dec–Feb.
JVW

Tree Swallow
Tachycineta bicolor

One of the most frequent occupants of backyard and garden nest boxes

Status in Maine: Although its populations have experienced tremendous declines in recent decades, the Tree Swallow is still one of Maine's most common and widespread breeding swallows. Breeding Bird Survey results show a substantial decrease in numbers in Maine and throughout North America, a trend seen in all swallows and most other aerial insectivores. Tree Swallows remain common spring and fall migrants with spring migration from March–April. Fall migration extends July–November, rarely into December.

Maine Conservation Status: Species of Special Concern.

Historical Status in Maine: Knight considered the Tree Swallow a common summer resident in Maine. Palmer wrote the Tree Swallow was "common to numerous" throughout the state and a "numerous" spring and fall migrant (1949, 363).

Global Distribution: Nearctic. Extensive breeding range from NL and QC to n. AK, south to coastal NC, through s. cen. U.S., ne. TX to n. CA. Winters from coastal SC west to Baja California and south to coastal e. Cen. Am. including most of Costa Rica.

SPRING: Common and widespread early-spring migrant, mid-Mar to early May. Earliest records: 1 on 10 Mar 2012 at Wharton Pt. (W. Nichols); 1 on 11 Mar 2006 at Seawall Beach (PDV); 5 on 14 Mar 2016 at Gardiner, Kennebec Co. (JVW); 3 on 15 Mar 1930 at Deering, Cumberland Co. (Palmer 1949); 2 on 15 Mar 2014 in Warren (W. Nichols). Spring peak, week starting 8 May when 32% of submitted eBird checklists report species. Maximum migration counts: 6,400 on 10 May 1999 at Abagadasset R., Bowdoinham (PDV); >5,000 on 19 May 2000 at Sanford Lagoons (PDV, JEP); 4,000 and 2,500 on 14 May 2004 and 19 May 2007, respectively, at Christina Reservoir (WJS); and 2,400 on 19 May 2009 at L. Josephine (WJS).

SUMMER: Common and widespread across state but, like most other swallows and aerial insectivores, experienced decline over past 50 years. Species once nested exclusively in tree cavities, typically near water, but adapted to nesting in variety of human-made structures. Norton (1908) mentioned Tree Swallows nesting in hollow fence rails, barn crevices, and bridges, once in an abandoned locomotive. Still found regularly nesting in natural cavities but more often in nest boxes, especially when boxes are regularly cleaned and maintained. The *ABBM* (Adamus 1987) shows species evenly distributed across ME. Maximum BBS numbers: 163, 156, and 137 on Forest Station BBS (Washington Co.) in 1977, 1982, and 1979; 149 in 1982, Otisfield (Oxford Co.); and 132 in 1978, S. Arm (Oxford Co.). Sixty or more birds recorded on individual BBS routes in ME 45 times since 1966, all but 4 before 1999. The most recent BBS with >60 Tree Swallows occurred in 2011. Based on BBS data, highest abundances in world: ME, NB, NH, NS, and VT. ME BBS show significant decreases of 4.5%, 1966–2017 (Sauer et al. 2017).

Tree Swallows

FALL: Common fall migrant, Jul–Nov, peak numbers usually Sep. Species reported from highest percentage of ME eBird checklists (11%) week of 8 Aug. Maximum migration counts: 5,000, 17 Sep 2016 at Biddeford Pool (A. Gilbert, G. Hodgkins); 2,970 on 6 Sep 2016 at Great Pond, Cape Elizabeth (G. Smith); 2,000 on 24 Jul 1991 at Christina Reservoir (WJS); 1,500 on 6 Sep 2012 at Scarborough Marsh (C. Caron); 1,000 on 19 Aug 1987 at Fryeburg Harbor (P. Richards); 1,000 on 5 Sep 2001 at Ogunquit Beach (N. McReel); 1,000 on 10 Sep 2016 at Richmond I., Cape Elizabeth (N. Hall, F. Hopper); 1,000 on 6 Sep 2016 at Higgins Beach, Cumberland Co. (B. Bunn); and 900 on 28 Sep 2015 at Pine Pt. (PDV). Latest records: 3 on 30 Nov 2015 at Biddeford Pool (M. and W. Schackwitz); 1 on 29 Nov 2014 at Granite Pt. Rd., Biddeford (M. Zimmerman); 1 on 28 Nov 2005 at Ogunquit Beach (D. Lovitch); 2 on 28 Nov 2014 at Seawall Beach (D. Jones); 1 on 26 Nov 2006, Eastern Rd., Scarborough (fide D. Lovitch); 2 on 26 Nov 2015 at Fortunes Rocks, Biddeford (M. Morales); 1 on 19 Nov 2005 at Reid S.P. (PDV); 2 on 16 Nov 2014 at Head Beach, Phippsburg (M. Fahay).

WINTER: 3 winter records in ME: 2 ph. on 27 Dec 2014 at Basket I. causeway, Biddeford (on Biddeford–Kennebunkport CBC, J. Fecteau and R. Watson); 1 on 17 Dec 2005 at Spurwink Marsh, Cape Elizabeth (on Greater Portland CBC, fide D. Lovitch); 3 on 6 Dec 2015 at Timber Pt., Biddeford (J. Fecteau). *JVW*

Violet-green Swallow

Tachycineta thalassina

An unexpected visitor from the West

Status in Maine: Accidental. A single bird reported at Salisbury Cove, Mount Desert Island, on 14 April 2018, was found and photographed by N. Dubrow (eBird) and seen by many (fide D. Hitchcox).

Global Distribution: Migratory breeding population from s. AK to nw. Mexico, east to MT, WY, CO, NM, and w. TX. Resident population in cen. Mexico. Wintering population south to Nicaragua. At least seven e. U.S. records.

Remarks: P. Pyle's analysis of photos suggests this bird was a second-year or after-second-year female. *CDD*

Northern Rough-winged Swallow

Stelgidopteryx serripennis

The state's most uncommon and geographically restricted breeding swallow

Status in Maine: Expanding into Maine in the 1940s and 1950s, Northern Rough-winged Swallows are an uncommon and patchily distributed breeding species near rivers and lakes in the southern half of the state. The species is seen in small numbers in spring and fall migration but normally vacates the state by August, with only a handful of records in September.

Maine Conservation Status: Species of Special Concern.

Historical Status in Maine: Knight did not record Northern Rough-winged Swallows in ME at the time of his book. The species began expanding its breeding range into NY and New England in the late 1800s, continuing across MA in the early 1900s (Veit and Peterson 1993). Palmer recounted the first confirmed breeding record in Ogunquit in 1941, where it possibly continued breeding through 1946. He noted another sight record of a bird in Damariscotta on 27 Jun 1947.

Rough-wings were documented breeding or were observed during breeding season in 1957 in Old Town, Penobscot Co.; Skowhegan; Gorham, Cumberland Co.; and Newry, Oxford Co. (*MFO* 2[6]: 59, 3[6]: 61), and northeast to Ellsworth by 1959 (*MFO* 4[6]: pp. unk.). Bond (1971) noted a pair nesting in an old kingfisher burrow in a gravel pit between Somesville and Town Hill, Mount Desert I., in Jun 1964.

Global Distribution: Breeds from s. ME and e. NB west across s. QC and s. Canada to n. cen. BC, south to Mexico and interior Cen. Am. Winters on southern tip of Florida, Gulf Coast, s. CA, northeastern and southwestern coastal Mexico through Cen. Am.

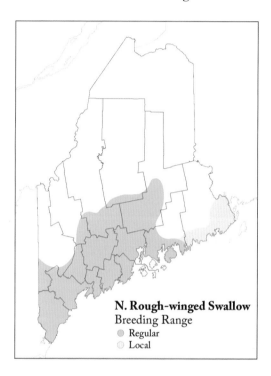

N. Rough-winged Swallow
Breeding Range
● Regular
◌ Local

SPRING: Uncommon spring migrant in southern third of ME, never in large numbers. Migration early Apr–early May. Earliest records, 1 bird each: exceptionally early 10–16 Mar 2012 at Wharton Pt. (m.ob., ph.); 3 Apr 2015 at Scarborough Marsh (M. Iliff, G. Smith); 4 Apr 2002 in Biddeford (P. Moynahan); 4 Apr 2006 in Saco (S. Pollock); 8 Apr 2007, Phippsburg (fide D. Lovitch); 8 Apr 2009, Florida L., Freeport (W. Laverty); 10 Apr 2014, Gilsland Farm (D. Hitchcox); 10 Apr 2012 at Florida L. (S. Walsh). Spring peak based on eBird checklists weeks of 1 and 8 May, reported on 2.5% of submitted checklists. Largest number reported in ME an unusual concentration of 150 birds at Union R. Dam in Ellsworth, 1 May 1981. From May 1-26, the number of birds fluctuated from 75 to 150 and several were observed defending territory beneath the powerhouse (W. Townsend). Other high counts: 20 on 20 May 1984 at Farmington (W. Howes); 15, 12 May 1979, Salisbury Cove, Mount Desert I. (C. Jellison); 12, 17 Apr 2001 in Biddeford (P. Moynahan); and 12 on 1 May 2012 at Capisic Pond, Portland (N. Gibb).

SUMMER: Uncommon breeder in s. ME, always near water—distribution closely tracks watersheds. In N. Am., species most abundant in Southeast and West. Species showed northward breeding range expansion over last 150 years, and like most other swallows and other aerial insectivores, a decline in N. Am. since late 1960s, perhaps leveling off in recent decades.

Species patchily distributed in southern third of ME along coast and s. Androscoggin, Kennebec, and Penobscot R. Watersheds (*ABBM*, Adamus 1987). Confirmed breeding in three atlas blocks in s. Washington Co. One isolated confirmed breeding record along St. John R. in northernmost ME along NB border. Maximum BBS numbers: 17 on now-discontinued Benton BBS (Kennebec Co.) in 1972; 9 in 1989, Otisfield (Oxford Co.); and 8 in Freedom (Waldo Co.) in 1976. Single location breeding season highs: 20 on 12 Jul 1999 at Union R. Dam, Ellsworth (W. Townsend); 20 on 18 Jul 2014 at Scarborough Marsh (J. McGowan, L. Santana, and A. VonNorstrand); 12 on 13 Jul 2016 at Livermore Falls, Androscoggin Co. (K. Brown).

ME BBS trend shows non-significant decline. N. Am. BBS shows significant decrease of 0.53% per year, 1966–2015, but a stable trend from 2005–2015.

FALL: Rare to uncommon fall migrant, Aug–Sep (1 exceptional record in Nov), peak late Jul–early Aug. Adults and juveniles congregate in postbreeding flocks in Jul, reach seasonal high numbers, then gradually taper off through fall. Species reported on highest percentage of ME eBird checklists (0.6%) week of 8 Aug. Numbers in fall migration typically <10, most often <5 per location. Maximum counts: 20 on 19 Aug 1991 at China L., E. Vassalboro, Kennebec Co. (B. Brown, H. Wilson), and 20 on 1 Aug 1999 at Goose Rocks Beach (M. Powers).

Exceptionally late sight record, 21 Nov 2009 at Thornhurst Farm, N. Yarmouth (S. Billerman, T. Lenz, B. Walker et al.). Other late records, all Sep: 1 on 11 Sep 1979 in ANP (A. Chartier); 1 on 7 Sep 2007 at Higgins Beach, Cumberland Co. (N. Lund); 1 on 4 Sep 2017 at Sanford Lagoons (T. Duddy). No known photographs documenting species in ME after Aug.

WINTER: No winter records in ME.

JVW

Purple Martin
Progne subis

This iridescent colonial nester is, like many aerial insectivores, in precipitous decline

Status in Maine: Purple Martins have diminished throughout the state. The species formerly nested locally, but statewide, in communities but has disappeared from northern and eastern parts of the state. Its range is now restricted to southern Maine

north to Kennebec, southern Somerset, southwestern Penobscot, and eastern Knox Counties. By 2015, there were fewer than 20 active colonies in Maine. Given this widespread contraction in the species' range, it is not surprising that the Breeding Bird Survey detected a 5.7% annual decline in Maine, which now holds just 6.5% of its 1966 martin population (Sauer et al. 2017). Continent-wide, martins have experienced an approximate 0.5% annual decline, 1966–2015.

Maine Conservation Status: Species of Special Concern.

Historical Status in Maine: Knight (1908, 52) said that Purple Martins were "found in nearly every section of the state" and it "is essentially a bird of civilization at present, and in Maine only occurs near human dwellings, and is of local distribution." Palmer (1949, 374–375) had a similar opinion, saying the species was "common at scattered localities (colonial breeder) in settled areas." He went on to state, "there is considerable evidence that at one time [in the late 19th century] Martins were very common in the state."

Global Distribution: Nearctic. Breeds from NS (local), ME, s. QC west to cen. AB, south to FL and TX, locally along Pacific Coast from WA to CA, also AZ, NM, to n. and cen. Mexico. Winters in S. Am. east of Andes Mtns. from Colombia and Venezuela south to Brazil and Argentina (rare).

Remarks: As noted by Palmer, construction and maintenance of martin houses might enhance ME's dwindling population. This was demonstrated in 2016 in Belgrade, Kennebec Co., where new martin houses and gourds resulted in a marked increase of martin numbers over the previous year (D. Lovitch et al.). It seems possible that similar efforts, especially in reasonable proximity to existing colonies, would benefit Purple Martins in ME. Such actions would not, however, address underlying declines in insect populations.

SPRING: Like Tree Swallows, Purple Martins are early-spring migrants, generally arriving late Apr to mid-May, continuing to end of month. Consistent observations at Belgrade colony reveal first martins appeared last week of Apr in 13 different springs; earliest observation, 17 Apr 1982 (P. Cross). Palmer reported 3 early observations: 1 in Lewiston, 12 Apr of unstated year; 1 in Norway, Oxford Co., 16 Apr 1914; and 1 in Androscoggin Co., 18 Apr 1946. Other early records: 7 in Raymond, Cumberland Co., 15 Apr 1958 (O. Smith); 6 in Denmark, Oxford Co., 10 Apr 1979 (P. Richards); 1 in Palmyra, Somerset Co., 15 Apr 1982 (M. Lucey); 1 over Bradbury Mtn., 8 Apr 2014 (J. Lovitch). Species no longer breeds in Aroostook Co., where birds arrived

1899, and a separate report from Winnegance, W. Bath, 21 Oct 1937, cited in Eliot (1938). We concur with Palmer that the circumstances surrounding both these possible reports are inadequately documented to constitute credible sight records.

Global Distribution: Nearctic. Primarily sw. U.S. and Mexico north through CA to WA and BC; formerly bred to s. cen. PA. Bewick's Wren reported from NS, NB, QC, MA, NH, VT, and RI.
PDV

Gnatcatchers (Polioptilidae)

Closely related to wrens, 19 species of gnatcatchers in three genera live in North and South America. Among the smallest songbirds anywhere, insectivorous gnatcatchers are largely tropical and sedentary, inhabiting a range of habitats from dry scrub to tropical forest. The migratory Blue-gray Gnatcatcher, found in Maine, is the only temperate-zone species.

Blue-gray Gnatcatcher
Polioptila caerulea

A tiny bird with a high-pitched, buzzy song, and a notably long, gray-and-white tail

Status in Maine: Among Maine's smallest birds, Blue-gray Gnatcatchers are regular, though never numerous, spring and fall migrants in southern coastal Maine and on the outer islands, but seldom inland. With range expansion into Maine in the 1970s, the first breeding record for the state was confirmed in 1979. The species has been a regular (although local) breeder since, occurring regularly in specific southern Maine locations, notably Brownfield; Gray, Cumberland County; New Gloucester, Cumberland County; and, more recently, Dresden. In Maine, breeding Blue-gray Gnatcatchers are generally confined to lowlands, especially near rivers and lakes where they prefer moist areas with deciduous trees, often near habitat edges. They usually nest in open wooded or scrubby areas. Spring migrants arrive in late April and are most widespread the first two weeks of May. Fall migration occurs primarily in late August and early September, but there are as many as 11 November records.

Historical Status in Maine: Knight (1908, 619) considered this species a "mere casual straggler to Maine," listing two records from Cape Elizabeth:

one on 29 Aug 1880 and one on 18 Apr 1896. Palmer reported ~15 individuals observed, 1878–1948, and said that the species was expanding its range north.

The status of Blue-gray Gnatcatchers changed from the 1950s to 1970s, when they became nearly annual, then expanded their breeding range into ME from the 1970s into the early 1990s. The first confirmed nesting was reported in Berwick, York Co., in 1979 (*ABBM*, Adamus 1987). The expansion has since ceased, and the species appears to be less regular now. The BBS reported an annual decline of 5.1% for gnatcatchers in New England and the Mid-Atlantic Coast since 1999 (Sauer et al. 2017), but no statistically significant trend could be detected in Maine, most likely because of insufficiency of data.

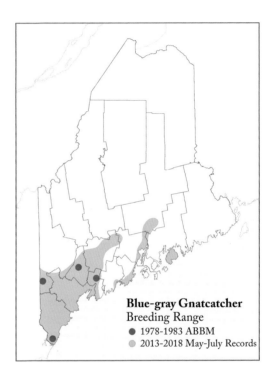

Blue-gray Gnatcatcher
Breeding Range
● 1978-1983 ABBM
● 2013-2018 May-July Records

Global Distribution: Nearctic. Breeds from s. ME, cen. NH, s. QC to MN south to FL and TX; largely absent from Great Plains states; farther west, from w. CO to NV and CA south to Mexico, Belize, and Honduras. Winters from coastal NC to FL, Cuba, TX, w. AZ, and se. CA to Mexico, south to Nicaragua.

Remarks: Forbush (1929) published an observation of a female Blue-gray Gnatcatcher feeding two young in s. ME sometime prior to 1929. This report was certainly known to Palmer who chose to ignore it. Given the vagueness of Forbush's account and that gnatcatchers were first found breeding in s. New England in the 1950s (Veit and Petersen 1993), it is difficult to give this report credence.

SPRING: First migrants arrive in coastal and s. ME mid- to late Apr, peak early May. Notably early records: in Cape Elizabeth, 1 on 6 Apr 1998 (K. Gammons) and 1 on 14 Apr 2006 (R. Harrison); 1 at Pemaquid Pt., 13 Apr 2006 (M. Libby); 1 in Falmouth, 14 Apr 1991 (G. Therrien); 1 at Biddeford Pool, 15 Apr 2006 (M. Dauphin). Late 19th century record in Cape Elizabeth, 18 Apr 1896 (*Auk* 13: 264). Migration continues through May with occasional reports into Jun: 1 on Appledore I., 1 Jun 1988 (D. Holmes). Spring migrants north and east of usual range: 1 in Orono on 25 Apr 1993 (J. Markowsky); 2 in Old Town, Penobscot Co., 19 May 2002 (A. White); 1 in Mattawamkeag Wilderness Park, Mattawamkeag, Penobscot Co., 18 May 1983 (PDV); Petit Manan NWR, 2 on 16 May 1988 (R. Widrig); 1 in Addison, 7 May 1981 (N. Famous); 1 in Eastport, 29 Apr 2009 (C. Bartlett).

SUMMER: First confirmed nesting in ME when family unit observed in Berwick, 10 Jun 1979 (*MB* 1: 36). From 1978–1983, *ABBM* (Adamus 1987) confirmed species at 4 localities: York; Berwick (record mentioned above); Turner with a nest with 2 young, 17 Jul 1983, young fledged 24 Jul (J. Despres); and east to Richmond, family unit of 4 birds observed 13 and 23 Jul 1982 (PDV). Additional reports during 1980s: family group of 4 in Auburn, Androscoggin Co., 10 Jul 1984 (N. Holler and P. Ledlie); 2 adults nest building at Gray Meadow, Gray, 29 May 1986 (K. Gammons). Species regular in this area and nearby in Intervale area of New Gloucester for past 30 years (W. Hancock).

At Evergreen Cemetery, Portland, nesting activity observed in 1990s and early 2000s with 2 nesting pairs: 1 pair nest building, 12 May 1999 (D. Ladd) and nest found 2 May 2001 (T. Rousseau). It appears species no longer nests at this locality. Several pairs observed at Brownfield Bog since 1987, where they remain regular: female on nest, 28 May 2005 (T. Duddy); 2 nest building on 11 May 2008 (M. Fahay); 1 nest building on 9 May 2009 (J. Potter). Pairs of gnatcatchers observed annually and likely breeding at Green Pt. WMA, Dresden (M. Fahay, D. Suitor, and PDV). Given wide range in breeding activity from early May nest building to mid-Jul family units, likely Blue-gray Gnatcatchers produce 2 broods at least occasionally. Single gnatcatcher in Masardis, Aroostook Co., 4 Jul 1979 (J. Greenlaw) unusually far north and remains only county record (*AB* 33: 845).

FALL: Extended fall migration begins mid-Aug with occasional earlier arrivals: 1 at Pine Pt., 5 Aug 2003 (G. Carson). Greatest numbers appear late Aug to mid-Sep in Midcoast ME. Regular on outer islands: 17 observed on Appledore I., 14 Aug–22 Sep 1994 (D. Holmes, *FN* 49: 23), and seen annually on Monhegan I., 2009–2017 (eBird), including 4 on 18 Sep 2016 (D. Mahlstedt) and 2 on 10 Sep 2017 (JVW).

Species never numerous; uncommon to observe more than 1 or 2 individuals in a day. High counts: 5 on Monhegan I., 25 Sep 1983 (DWF), 4 at same locality, 27 Sep 2012 (J. Trimble and B. Nikula, eBird); and 7 on Great Duck I., 29 Aug 1986 (PDV). Uncommon migrants inland and in e. ME. Notable inland records: 1 in Lincoln Ctr., 2 Sep 1979 (PDV); 1 in Canaan, Somerset Co., 23 Aug 1998 (W. Sumner); in Kennebec Co., 1 in Benton, 9 Sep 1988, and 1 at same locality, 6 Sep 1995 (W. Sumner); 1 in Fairfield, 3 Oct 1999 (D. Mairs); 3 records from Wilton, Franklin Co., latest on 23 Oct 2001 (J. Dwight). In Washington Co., several records from Petit Manan NWR; 1 from Roque I., Jonesport (R. Milardo, N. Famous); and 2 records from Lubec, 1 on 30 Aug 1984 and 1 on 29 Aug 1990 (W. Howes). Surprisingly, at least 9 Nov records, primarily from south coastal ME, as far east as Roque I., 15 Nov 1992 (R. Milardo and N. Famous, *AB* 47: 66). Late records: 1, Hallowell, Kennebec Co., 21 Nov 2006 (JVW); 1, Shore Path, Bar Harbor, 4 and 22 Nov 2017 (S. Mroz and J. Potter, respectively; eBird); 1 in Portland, 11 and 22 Nov 2013 (N. Gibb, eBird); 1 on Saco Riverwalk, 20 Nov 2014 (D. Thompson, eBird).
PDV

Kinglets (Regulidae)

Among the smallest songbirds, two of the seven species in this monotypic family are found in North America and both live in Maine. A rapid metabolism means these insectivorous birds are constantly foraging. Although tiny, Ruby-crowned Kinglets are the largest member of the family. Golden-crowned Kinglets, Maine's smallest breeding songbirds, overwinter here.

Golden-crowned Kinglet
Regulus satrapa

This tiny but tough Maine resident occurs in varying numbers in winter

Status in Maine: The Golden-crowned Kinglet is the smallest passerine breeding in Maine; only Ruby-throated Hummingbirds are tinier. The species nests commonly in coniferous forests and pine groves throughout most of Maine but is an uncommon and local nester in York and Cumberland Counties. It is a common but somewhat inconspicuous spring migrant, appearing in small numbers from mid-April through May. Kinglets tend to be conspicuous fall migrants mid-September to October. Kinglet numbers vary substantially in winter; CBC data indicate that approximately every five years large numbers remain in Maine. The species is generally more numerous along the coast.

in Windham, 30 Jun 2006 (E. Eklund), represented first broods. Gray Catbirds often produce double broods: in Kennebunk, an adult observed carrying food on 10 Aug 1999 (S. Richardson); in Berwick, York Co., adults feeding young on 6 Aug 2000 and a tailless juvenile seen 16 Sep 2011 (S. Richardson); in Brunswick, second broods remained until mid-Sep 2014 (S. Walker). At Avian Haven, a bird rehabilitation center in Freedom, Waldo Co., late nestlings admitted annually from late Jul–24 Aug 2010 (D. Winn). In Yarmouth, juvenile Gray Catbirds banded into Sep 2014 (S. Walsh).

FALL: Protracted fall migration mid-Aug to Sep, continues in diminishing numbers through mid-Oct. On Monhegan I., major flights >10 individuals reported as early as 17 Aug 2006 (15 birds) and 4 Sep 1983 (12); fall maximum of 20 birds on 26 Sep 1981 (all PDV). Late count of 15 observed on 8 Oct 2012 (J. Trimble). In Aroostook Co., catbirds generally depart in Sep; latest report from Easton, 17 Oct 2007 (WJS). Small numbers of late migrants linger on southern coast through Nov. On Appledore I., 237 individuals banded in fall of 2001 an above-average count (D. Holmes, *NAB* 56: 31).

WINTER: Palmer did not record Gray Catbirds as wintering in ME, noting a record from Cape Elizabeth on 16 Nov 1916 was late. He apparently ignored the report of a catbird that wintered in Portland through at least 23 Feb 1946 (A. Ghering, *BMAS* 2: 53). Species rare in 1950s–1960s with 3 reports: 1 in Portland, 3 Feb 1951 (G. Reeves, *BMAS* 7: 36); 1 in Lewiston, 7 Jan 1962 (Rock, *MFN* 18: 27); 1 in Fryeburg, 20 Dec 1969 (obs. unk.). CBC reports by decade reveal general increase along coast since 1970s: total of 6 catbirds reported in 1970s, 9 in 1980s, 4 in 1990s, and 19 in 2000s. Since 2000, 1–5 Gray Catbirds occur along the coast almost annually. Exceptional number of Gray Catbirds reported during winter 2005–2006: >30 individuals observed in coastal regions with a number successfully overwintering. During this winter, CBCs reported following: Portland (5 birds), Pemaquid–Damariscotta (3), Thomaston–Rockland (2), Biddeford–Kennebunkport (1), York (1), Mount Desert I. (1), Machias Bay (1). Other notable observations: 3 in Biddeford, 6 Jan 2006 (fide D. Lovitch), and 2 in Portland, 22 Jan 2006 (D. Lovitch).

Noteworthy inland CBCs, 1 bird each: Farmington, 17 Dec 1983; Lewiston–Auburn, 17 Dec 2011; Orono–Old Town, 23 Dec 1972; Sweden, Dec 1993; Waterville, 16 Dec 2001. Catbirds on Washington Co. CBCs, 1 each: Calais, 30 Dec 2004; Eastport, 23 Dec 1979; Machias Bay, 31 Dec 1988, 2 Jan 2006, and 14 Dec 2008. Northernmost winter records: Stockton Springs, Waldo Co., 22 Dec 2015 (K. Kravik, eBird), and Houlton, 1–14 Jan 2003 (L. Little).

PDV

Brown Thrasher
Toxostoma rufum

A declining, inconspicuous species of thickets and shrublands in southern Maine

Status in Maine: Brown Thrashers are locally regular in dry shrublands, near power lines, and in sandy blueberry barrens. Thrasher populations have suffered a significant decline in Maine according to Breeding Bird Survey data, 3.6% annually from 1966–2015 (Sauer et al. 2017). Spring migration starts in late April and peaks in early May, approximately a week earlier than reported by Palmer. The species breeds regularly but locally in southern Maine. It is regular on blueberry barrens in Washington and Hancock Counties and local along agricultural margins in Aroostook County. Brown Thrashers migrate south in September and October, the peak occurring the last 10 days of September. A small number remain resident through winter. Given the profound population decline, it is not surprising that this species has become rare on Maine Christmas Bird Counts.

Maine Conservation Status: Species of Special Concern.

Brown Thrasher

Historical Status in Maine: Both Knight and Palmer considered Brown Thrashers regular in s. ME west of the Kennebec R. Palmer called the species "fairly common, though diminishing in numbers," and reported only two records for Washington Co. (1949, 410). In n. Oxford Co., Brewster (1925) observed this species on four different occasions from May 1881–Sep 1905.

Global Distribution: E. Nearctic. Breeds from n. ME and NB, where irregular, to s. QC, ON, west to AB, south to FL and e. TX. Winters primarily from s. NJ and IN south to FL and TX.

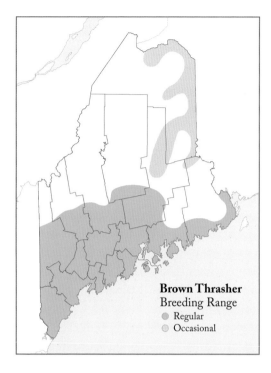

Brown Thrasher
Breeding Range
● Regular
◉ Occasional

SPRING: First arrive on territory last week of Apr, ~1 week earlier than reported by Palmer. Most thrashers appear first 2 weeks of May. On Monhegan I.: 4 on 13 May 1997 (PDV and D. Abbott) and 5 on 14 May 2011 (T. Magarian). Migration continues in diminishing numbers through May. At least 13 occurrences 17–30 Apr. Notably early migrants, 1 each: Peaks I., Portland, 23 Mar 2007 (fide J. Walker); Scarborough, 4 Apr 1997 (G. Carson); Skowhegan, 8 Apr 1905 (Palmer 1949); Portland, 9 Apr 1911 (A. Norton, in Palmer 1949); S. Portland, 16 Apr 2009 (D. Lovitch). Early thrashers at northern range limit, 1 each: Canaan, Somerset Co., 26 Apr 1995 (W. Sumner); Dexter, Penobscot Co., 26 Apr 2007 (A. Larrabee); Anson, Somerset Co., 26 Apr 2007 (G. McElroy). Uncommon and local in Aroostook Co., arrives more or less simultaneously with birds in s. ME, generally 4–24 May. Single thrasher in Ft. Fairfield notably early on 27 Apr 2013 (D. Smith).

SUMMER: Occurs locally in dry shrubby areas, especially along power lines, in secondary growth bordering fields, and sandy blueberry barrens. Although Brown Thrashers can be locally common (12 at Kennebunk Plains, 27 Jun 2006; R. Heil), species declining at precipitous rate. *ABBM* (Adamus 1987) confirmed breeding in s. ME north to cen. Franklin Co., and s. Somerset to n. Penobscot Co. (Lincoln), east through Washington Co., where found in brushy areas bordering blueberry barrens. Species largely absent from Piscataquis and cen. Somerset Cos. Rare and local in Aroostook Co.: Wade in 1979 and 1980 (A. and G. Robbins); confirmed nesting in Estcourt Station, Big Twenty Twp., 29 May 2001 (G. Flagg); Ft. Kent in 2002 (G. Flagg); Houlton in 2002, 2005, and 2006 (L. Little); Presque Isle in 2005 and 2009 (WJS); in 2007 in Masardis, Easton, and Portage L.

(all WJS); Bancroft in 2008 (M. Ballanger).

Typically breeds May–Jun: downy fledgling with adult at Kennebunk Plains, 15 Jun 2007 (B. Herrgesell); nest at Kennebunk Plains, 29 Jun 2001 (D. Tucker), possibly second breeding attempt. Family unit of 5 birds in Brunswick, 27 Aug 2000 (J. Perotta), also likely second nesting attempt. Recent nesting records: 6 at Biddeford Pool, 25 Jun 2002 (J. Suchecki); 4 in Dover-Foxcroft, 7 Jun 2006 (A. Larrabee); 4 birds in Bath, 26 Jun 2008 (M. Fahay); 2 on Monhegan I., 7 Jun 2007 (K. Lindquist); in Washington Co., 5 at Montigal Pond, T19 MD BPP, 21 Jun 2005, and 4 in Columbia Falls, 28 Jun 2005 (both N. Famous); 1 adult carrying food in Bangor, 28 May 2012 (L. Bevier); a family unit in Chelsea, Kennebec Co., summer 2014 (JVW).

FALL: Migration second week of Sep–Oct, peaks late Sep. On Monhegan I., Brown Thrashers noted as early as 28 Aug 2001 (possibly resident; W. Boynton), 10 Sep 2010 (T. Magarian), 12 Sep 2006 (PDV), 12 Sep 2016 (H. Merker, eBird), 2 individuals noted on 13 Sep 1980 (PDV), and 3 on 18–19 Sep 2016 (W. Russell, eBird). Nine or more daily counts of 3–4 birds from 19–29 Sep (eBird). Oct daily counts maximum 3 birds (eBird). One Nov report: 6 Nov 2001 (W. Boynton). Late migrants away from coast, 1 bird each: Lincoln Ctr., 22 Oct 1977; Orono, 11 Oct 1979 (both PDV); Brewer, 10 Oct 1988 (M. Lucey); Clinton, 10 Oct 2013 (L. Bevier); E. Machias, 14 Oct 1988 (CDD); Steuben, 7 Oct 1989 (R. Widrig); 1 in Lubec, 5 Oct 2008 (F. Pierce). In Aroostook Co.: 1 at Cross L. on 1 Sep 2014 (J. Hadley, eBird); 1 in Woodland, 25 Oct, 11 and 29 Nov 2015 (WJS, eBird). At least 20 records in sw. ME, latest in Biddeford Pool, 24 Nov 1991 (L. Brinker); 1 in Kennebunk, 26 Nov 2005 (N. Rich); 1 on Unity College campus, Unity, 29 Nov 2014 (D. Potter, eBird).

WINTER: Palmer listed only 3 winter reports though Brown Thrashers were regular on CBCs in 1970s–1980s; few reports since 1990. In 1970s, a total of 15 birds tallied on CBCs statewide. In 1980s, number diminished to 10 birds. Three thrashers reported in each decade, 1990–2000, and 7 thrashers recorded on CBCs, 2010–2016. In Washington Co., Thrashers reported from Danforth (26 Dec 1969), Machias Bay (3 CBCs, latest 27 Dec 1994), Jonesport (Dec 1990), and Schoodic Pt. (4 different CBCs, latest 1 Jan 2006). Northernmost report from Dover-Foxcroft, 2 Jan 1988.

Notably, Mount Desert I. CBC recorded Brown Thrashers in 1958; on 6 different CBCs in 1960s, with high counts of 3 birds on 3 separate counts; and on 2 counts in 1980s; but none 1987–2016. Two Aroostook Co. records: 1 in Easton, 1 Jan 2013, and 1 in Woodland, intermittently 25 Oct 2015–1 May 2016, "continuing in my yard. Day #187" (WJS, eBird). Brown Thrashers now rare in coastal s. ME; fewer than 10 reports since 2000: 1 in Kennebunkport, intermittently 16 Dec 2016–19

Feb 2017 (K. Donahue, eBird). Noteworthy observations from cen. ME: 1 at Unity College, 3 Dec 2014 (A. Vilag, eBird); 1 in Winterport, Waldo Co., 4 Feb–31 Mar 1998 (J. Wyatt); 1 in Brooklin, Hancock Co., 19 Dec 2008 (fide E. Hynes); in Bar Harbor, 1 on 31 Dec 2008–27 Feb 2009 (W. Townsend); 1 on 7 Jan 2013 in Mount Desert I. (M. J. Good); 1 in Orono, 13 Feb 2017 (K. Lena, eBird); 1 in Veazie, Penobscot Co., 21 Mar 2009 (J. Mays).

PDV

Sage Thrasher
Oreoscoptes montanus

The smallest thrasher leaves the "sagebrush sea" for a trip East

Status in Maine: Accidental. There is a single record of this western thrasher seen at Cape Neddick. The bird was first identified and photographed on 17 November 2001 and remained in the immediate area until 12 December 2001 (*NAB* 56: 29; PDV, ph. arch.). Other regional Sage Thrasher records include a bird banded and photographed on Kent Island, New Brunswick, 20 July 1999; one seen on Plum Island, Massachusetts, 26 October 1965 (Veit and Petersen 1993), and another there 6 November 2005 (fide D. Larson); and two records from New York, April 1942 and 18 October 1958 (Levine 1998).

Global Distribution: Breeds from southernmost SK, AB, and BC south through Great Basin to n. NM, AZ, and s. CA. Winters in desert southwest to cen. Mexico. Considered a sagebrush (*Artemisia* spp.) obligate, it is dependent upon large patches and expanses of sagebrush steppe for successful breeding.

PDV

Northern Mockingbird
Mimus polyglottos

The flash of this bird's white wing patches is increasingly common in southern Maine

Status in Maine: Northern Mockingbirds are not particularly well-studied in Maine, though the species is now more common than it was historically. Records suggest that mockingbirds arrive in early May to breed throughout the state, but primarily on the southern coast. The birds appear to withdraw from the northern edges of their breeding range in late September and early October, but migration may be protracted. This species regularly winters in southern coastal Maine.

Historical Status in Maine: Knight considered most Northern Mockingbird reports from ME likely to be escaped cage birds, despite the fact that the species bred, at least occasionally, in MA in the late 19th century (Griscom and Snyder 1955). Knight did consider a mockingbird in Portland Jan–Feb 1897 a likely natural vagrant. Palmer (1949, 406) rejected the escaped cage bird theory, reporting that this species was "resident, of regular, though rare and local occurrence." He further noted there were >80 records from 1871–1947, with at least three nesting records: Leeds, Androscoggin Co., 1885; Bangor in 1930; and Corinna, Penobscot Co., in 1944. Interestingly, though probably a matter of inadequate reporting, there were apparently no observations of nesting in southern Maine at this time. Wright (1921) documented an increase in mockingbirds along the northern edge of the range in ME, n. New England, and Maritime Provinces in 1900–1920.

Global Distribution: Nearctic. Resident and breeding from NS, s. NB and ME, s. ON, east to n. CA, south to FL, Mexico to Isthmus of Tehuantepec, and Greater Antilles. Withdraws from northern fringe of breeding range in winter.

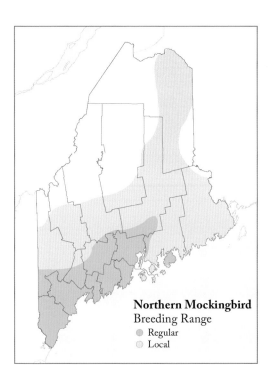

Northern Mockingbird
Breeding Range
● Regular
○ Local

SPRING: Appears to migrate or spread into n. ME in May as there are no eBird records for Mar–Apr and few other spring reports for the region. In Orono, J. Markowsky reported a "small migrant group [3 birds] heading north along the Penobscot River edge," on 9 May 1987, noting the species is "clearly migratory at the northern edge of its range." Typical May records: Piscataquis Co.: 2 in BSP, 15 May 2006 (T. Gordon); n. Penobscot Co.: 1 in Lincoln Ctr., 25 May 1977 (PDV); 1 in Mt. Chase, 15 May 2009 (J. Getchell).

SUMMER: *ABBM* (Adamus 1987) confirmed nesting primarily in s. cen. ME west and south of Bangor; nesting confirmed north to Aroostook Co. (Presque Isle and Mapleton), and east to Washington Co. (Machias). In Aroostook Co., 2 pairs also reported in Ashland, 11 May 1981 (G. Stadler), and nest with 4 young found in Masardis, 23 Jul 1995 (J. Greenlaw). In Washington Co., nest with 2 young observed in Columbia, 20 Jul 1985 (R. Long), and a pair seen at Cobscook Bay S.P., 22 May 1989 (G. Farthing). Species usually produces 2 broods. Fledglings attended by adults in Augusta, 30 May 2008 (M. Smith), clearly first brood. Whereas adults feeding young in Saco, 23 Jul 1957; 2 adults and 3 young in Newcastle, 15 Jul 1991 (J. Hamlin); and fledgling in S. Portland on 31 Jul 2007 from second broods (M. Jordan). BBS indicates an annual, nonsignificant decrease of 1.1% in ME, 1996–2015, and 1.5% decline, 2005–2015 (Sauer et al. 2017).

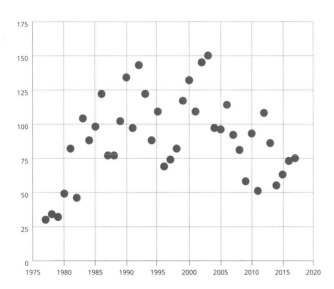

Figure 19. Northern Mockingbird on Christmas Bird Counts

Despite annual variation, there was a small increase in the average number of Northern Mockingbirds reported on representative southern coastal CBCs through the early 2000s; numbers have since declined. CBCs included: York County, Biddeford–Kennebunk, Greater Portland, and Thomaston–Rockland (NAS 2019a).

FALL: Fall movements difficult to discern. Most observations on Monhegan I. involve 1–3 birds in late Sep. High counts include: 12 on Monhegan I., 14 Sep 1981 (PDV), and 8 on 7 Oct 1990 (S. Surmer).

WINTER: Regular in winter in settled areas of coastal s. ME east to Waldo Co. Occurs regularly along Kennebec R. north to Waterville and along the Penobscot R. north to Bangor and Orono. Mockingbirds appear to withdraw from n. ME with few winter records: 1 in Millinocket, 1 Feb 2003 (J. Markowsky); 1 each on Presque Isle CBCs, Dec 1981, 1982, 1983, and 1986 (2 birds); and 1 on Caribou CBC in Dec 2010. A review of CBCs by decade reveals that mockingbirds did not increase on all CBCs; increases were largely restricted to several south coastal counts. Highest counts in 2000s in Portland (maximum of 89 birds, Dec 2003), Biddeford–Kennebunkport, and Bangor–Bucksport; high counts in 1980s included Augusta, Mount Desert I. (none reported since 1998), and Thomaston–Rockland; high counts for 1990s included Orono–Old Town and York Co. BBC high count for ME 2000–2017: 127 birds in 2012.
PDV

Starlings (Sturnidae)

Apparently originating in Asia, the starling family later expanded into Africa and Europe, and now encompasses more than 100 species worldwide. From an estimated 100 birds released in New York in 1890 to more than 200 million today, the European Starling has had a negative impact on native cavity nesters with which it competes.

European Starling
Sturnus vulgaris

A gregarious invasive species of human-altered habitats

Status in Maine: Introduced. European Starlings are found throughout the state, though at low densities in areas with extensive forest. This species also has been reported from offshore islands such as Monhegan and Matinicus Rock.

Historical Status in Maine: European Starlings were introduced to Central Park in New York City in 1890 (Cabe 1993). According to Palmer, starlings were reported from Rumford, Oxford Co., in Jan 1913, and were breeding across Maine by 1930.

Global Distribution: In N. Am., from NL to s. AK, south to n. Mexico. In native range, ne. Mongolia to Scandinavia and Iceland, south to n. India, n. Saudi Arabia, and Mediterranean coast of Africa. Also introduced in the Río Plata region of S. Am., s. Africa, Australia, and New Zealand.

Remarks: Starlings, along with House Sparrows, Rock Pigeons, and Mute Swans, are exempt from state and federal protections offered by the Migratory Bird Treaty Act.

SPRING: Although European Starlings occur year-round in ME, seasonal northward movements occur Mar–Apr, as well as what Palmer called "a dispersal of winter residents into rural areas and elsewhere" (1949, 438). Spring migration difficult to detect; 20 "deemed migrating" at Bradbury Mtn., 27 Mar 2007 (D. and J. Lovitch).

Starlings produce multiple broods/year. Egg-laying occurs mid-Apr to mid-May. Breeding observations include the following: 1 gathering nest material at Leonard St., Portland, 12 Apr 2011, and in Turner "first nestlings of the season," 16 May 1995, and "first nestlings peeping" on 16 May 2001 (all J. Despres). Young fledge late May–early Jun. First of year fledgling observations by J. Despres in Turner include 3 Jun 1997; 28 May 1998; 1 Jun 2000; and "1st proper mob of fledglings" on 9 Jun 2001.

SUMMER: Records from North Woods: 1 northwest of Saint Francis L., Somerset Co., 2 Jun 1981 (J. Cherry, eBird), and 22 in BSP, 18 Jun 2005 (A. MacKinnon), corroborate Palmer's observation that in summer, starlings can be found in "many places remote from occupied human habitations, such as forest clearings" (1949, 438).

High count for York Co.: ~3,500 at Wells National Estuarine Research Reserve, 23 Jul 2012 (C. Wintanley, eBird).

FALL: Palmer said fall movements occurred early Sep to mid-Nov, "with starlings gradually concentrating in urban areas". Fall high counts: ~6,500 starlings at pastures and feedlots at Langley Farm, Aroostook Co., 7 Oct 2013 (WJS), and ~2,500 in Scarborough, 6 Nov 2014 (N. Perlut, eBird).

WINTER: Palmer cited starlings as numerous to abundant in all population centers in winter and present in all villages, including islands such as Monhegan I. In 2010, total of 14,168 starling records on 27 of 29 CBCs in ME. In 2017, high counts in Caribou (2,505), Presque Isle (2,101), and Augusta (1,877); lowest on coastal CBCs in Schoodic (23) and Matinicus (20), although York Co. CBC reported 732.

RVJ

Waxwings (Bombycillidae)

One genus and three species, two of which occur in North America and Maine, are the sum total of this family spanning Eurasia, Asia, and North and Central America. The exquisite plumage of these fruit- and berry-eating birds makes them a favorite. Not true migrants, their nomadic and irruptive movements are difficult to predict.

Bohemian Waxwing
Bombycilla garrulus

Now a frequent winter resident, with large flights in central Maine every two to three years

Status in Maine: Since 1975, Bohemian Waxwings have become more regular in winter and are now reported almost annually. Waxwing numbers have increased since 1980, especially during irruption winters, which typically occur every two to three years. It is now common for several thousand birds to appear during irruptions; e.g., 3,000–5,000 birds reported in Bangor and environs, 16 February 1991 (*AB* 45: 252). The first waxwings typically appear in October, but there are two September reports. Numbers generally peak December–March, the last birds departing in April and, more rarely, in May and June.

Historical Status in Maine: Knight (1908, 463) noted "it has been years since there has been any definite report of the occurrence of this species in Maine." Palmer (1949, 431) considered this species to be an "incursion visitant" and did not report any flocks >100 individuals. He also commented on the general pattern of this species appearing in ME every three to five years, a pattern also noted by Knight (1909). Chamberlain (1949, 53) considered this species to be a "very rare winter visitor" in Aroostook Co.

Global Distribution: Holarctic. Breeds in N. Am. regularly from MB west to AK and south to BC and AB, and recently confirmed in NS (rare; Erskine 1992) and cen. QC (rare; WJS). In winter withdraws from northern areas. Notably irruptive, now occurring with regularity from NL, Maritime Provinces, and n. New England, to MI, CO, and e. OR. More consistent and numerous in Northeast since 1975.

Bohemian Waxwing

SPRING: Often lingers into mid- to late Apr following major flight years: >1,000 in Appleton, Knox Co., 7 Apr 1992 (*AB* 46: 396); 200 in Augusta, 21 Apr 2000 (D. Ladd, *NAB* 54: 262); 70 in Sabattus, Androscoggin Co., 27 Apr 1996 (D. Reimer, *FN* 50: 256); 80 in Bangor, 26 Apr 2011 (B. Cole); 65 in Falmouth, 28 Apr 2011 (R. Lambert); 25 on Beech Mtn., ANP, 25 Apr 2013 (M. Good, eBird); 10 in Essex Woods, Bangor, 30 Apr 2016 (S. Mierzykowski, eBird); 12 in Cooper, Washington Co., 16 Apr 2017 (K. Holmes, eBird). More rarely, small numbers found into late May–Jun: 1 in Northport, Waldo Co., 29 May 1919 (Palmer 1949); 1 in flock of Cedar Waxwings on Monhegan I., 9 Jun 1998 (W. Boynton, *FN* 52: 437); 1 in Gouldsboro, 14 May 2008 (D. Pluym); 1 in Corea, Hancock Co., 24 May 2008 (D. Santoni); 12 on Little Androscoggin R., 5 May 2017 (M. Fahay, eBird); 29 on Bangor Waterfront, 6 May 2017 (J. Smith, eBird).

FALL: In flight years, Bohemian Waxwings often arrive last week of Oct, and can be numerous by mid-Nov: >1,000 in Orono, 17 Nov 1993 (R. Milardo, *FN* 48: 184); >1,000 in Roque Bluffs, late Nov 2000 (N. Famous, *NAB* 55: 29). Early Oct observations: 40 in S. Bristol, 9 Oct 1976 (M. Libby); 3 in Roque Bluffs, 19 Oct 1989 (I. Balodis, P. K. Donahue, *AB* 44: 59); 3 in Orono, 23 Oct 1989 (J. Markowsky); unreported number first week of Oct 1995 (*FN* 50: 24); unreported number in n. ME, 19 Oct 1999 (*NAB* 54: 29); 1 in Woodland, 11 Oct 2004 (WJS); 20 in Presque Isle, 8 Oct 2007 (WJS); 30 in Washburn, Aroostook Co., 20 Oct 2012 (WJS); 3 at Schoodic Pt., Winter Harbor, 21 Oct

2014 (S. Benz); 1 at Saxl Park, Bangor, 5 Oct 2016 (R. Ostrowski). Exceptionally early records: 1 in Corea, 3 Sep 1993 (*AB* 48: 89); 1 in Brewer, 14 Sep 1977 (N. Famous, *Guillemot* 6: 41); 1 in Greenville, 20 Sep 2006 (N. Famous).

WINTER: Frequent, occasionally numerous, winter visitors. Major flights generally every 2–3 years, (see Figure 20), although there are some consecutive years of large flights; only small numbers in intervening years. Before 1985, Bohemian Waxwing total on 7 long-term CBCs did not exceed 200 individuals. CBC data shows species first surpassed 1,000 (1,499 birds) on 1986–1987 CBCs. Frequency and magnitude of high counts have increased since.

CBCs show Bohemian Waxwings primarily concentrated along Penobscot R. on Orono–Old Town (maximum 781 in Dec 2001) and Bangor–Bucksport CBC (maximum 2,016 in Dec 2007, state high count for single CBC), and to lesser degree along Kennebec R. in Augusta (maximum 693 in Dec 2007) and Waterville (453 in Dec 2007) CBCs. Bohemians less regular and numerous in coastal s. ME and Washington and Hancock Cos.: maximum number on Mount Desert I. CBC, 78 birds in Dec 2010. High counts on 2007–2008 CBCs in this region: Thomaston–Rockland (513), Freeport–Brunswick (145), Portland (76), Biddeford–Kennebunkport (35), York Co. (4). Pemaquid–Damariscotta CBC recorded maximum of 456 birds in Dec 1993, unusual for Midcoast ME.

PDV

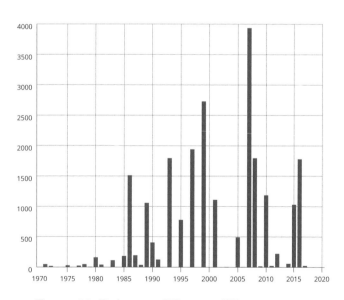

Figure 20. Bohemian Waxwing Winter Irruptions

Total number of Bohemian Waxwings counted on representative Maine CBCs, 1976–2017, show an irregular irruptive pattern. CBCs included: Augusta, Bangor–Bucksport, Greater Portland, Orono–Old Town, Thomaston–Rockland, and Waterville (NAS 2019a).

Cedar Waxwing
Bombycilla cedrorum

The sweet, cricket-like song of this demure species may be heard practically any time of year

Status in Maine: Cedar Waxwings breed commonly in a wide variety of habitats throughout Maine. The short spring migration takes place primarily in late May and early June when flocks of 30–400 individuals can be found, especially on outer islands. The fall migration is more protracted, from August through mid-October. Cedar Waxwings were historically irregular in winter but have become more numerous on Christmas Bird Counts since the 1980s and 1990s (e.g., a maximum of 2,740 individuals was tallied on the 2008–2009 Christmas Bird Count).

Historical Status in Maine: Knight noted that Cedar Waxwings were common in summer in the Bangor area where they arrived in late May, and indicated they were irregular in winter. Palmer concurred with Knight, reporting that this species generally arrived 23–30 May and was a common summer resident throughout the state.

Global Distribution: Nearctic. Widespread from NL, cen. Canada to se. AK, south to VA, n. GA, CO, and n. CA. In winter, withdraws from northern areas to ME, s. Canada, south to FL, Cen. Am., and irregularly, the Caribbean.

SPRING: Brief, punctuated spring migration. Birds arrive throughout ME in large numbers last week of May and first days of Jun: e.g., 3 arrivals in Presque Isle, 28 May 1991 (M. Trombley). On Monhegan I., T. Magarian observed 2 individuals on 24 May but reported 90 or more Cedar Waxwings the following day, 25 May 2011. Review of Monhegan eBird records in May and Jun reveal numerous counts >100 last week of May–early Jun. High counts there: 400 on 26 May 2010 (E. Hynes); 450 on 27 May 2012 and 530 on 30 May 2012 (R. Lambert); while only 8 seen on 25 May, 250 observed on 26 May 2014 (B. Nikula); 385 on 28 May 2014 and 303 on 26 May 2015 (J. Trimble); 120 on 1 Jun 2008 (J. Scott). No eBird reports of >50 after first week of Jun.

SUMMER: Breeding status of Cedar Waxwings unchanged since Knight's and Palmer's reports. Breed commonly in secondary growth, shrublands, road margins, and along lakes and other waterways across ME (*ABBM*, Adamus 1987). Nest building begins mid-Jun; adults carrying nesting material in Falmouth, 18 Jun 2009–Jul and Aug with fledglings in

Falmouth, 20 Aug 2009 (E. Hynes). Given species' proclivity for fruit and berries, not surprising that waxwings have a prolonged nesting season; 2 adults with 1 young observed in Sheepscot, 2 Sep 1991 (J. Hamlin); 3 late nestlings noted in Tenants Harbor, Knox Co., 7 Sep 1988, found dead 9 Sep 1988 (R. Palmer, *AB* 43: 66). Apparent first nesting on Appledore I. confirmed when adults observed feeding young on 13 Aug 1997 (D. Holmes). Significant long-term decline of 1.7% in ME 1966–2015; this does not appear to be a continental trend (BBS).

FALL: Protracted fall migration. On Monhegan I., species is common, often in large numbers, late Aug to mid-Oct. Earliest concentration: 250 birds on 31 Aug 2014 (JEP). Early Sep concentrations: 400 on 5 Sep 1980, 800 on 7–10 Sep 1984, 400 on 4 Sep 1987 (all PDV). Late Sep–Oct flocks of 150-400 birds nearly annual on Monhegan I. (J. Trimble, L. Seitz, E. Hynes, A. Wagner, B. Marvil, JEP, eBird). Waxwing numbers diminish to flocks of 15–40 by late Oct and Nov.

WINTER: Historically, irregular and uncommon in winter, appearing sporadically at orchards and ornamental plantings. Currently regular from Mount Desert I. south and inland south of Old Town, Penobscot Co. CBC numbers increased in 1980s. Since 1990, counts increased substantially on CBCs from s. Penobscot Co. to York Co. In 1980–1989, Cedar Waxwing numbers averaged 44.6 birds/winter with a maximum of 145 birds in 1984–1985. Since 1990, Waxwings average 564 birds, maximum of 2,740 counted on 2008–2009 CBCs. Numbers generally diminish Mar–Apr, presumably result of diminished fruit abundance. Moderately large flocks late Mar–Apr: 100 in Farmington, 31 Mar 1983 (P. Cross); 200 in Bangor, 11 Apr 1983 (B. Barker); 150 in Saco, 1 Apr 1997 (P. McGowan). This species continues to be unusual and irregular in Aroostook and Washington Cos. and western mountains, fide eBird: 28 in Eastport, 26 Dec 2016 (C. Bartlett); 76 in Charlotte, Washington Co., 29 Dec 2015 (W. Gillies); 1 in Lincoln, 14 Jan 2016 (B. Way); 5 in Moosehead area, Piscataquis Co., 19 Jan 2008 (B. Porter); 35 in Stacyville, Penobscot Co., 8 Feb 2005 (WJS); 50 in Houlton, 13 Feb 2015 (K. Hogan); 2 in Woodland, 16 Feb 2005 (WJS); 17 at Garnet Head Rd., Pembroke, Washington Co., 18 Feb 2017 (W. Gillies).

PDV

Old World Sparrows (Passeridae)

House Sparrows are one of 43 species of true sparrows native to Europe, Africa, and Asia. Old World sparrows typically live in open landscapes, nesting in small colonies and gathering in immense flocks outside the breeding season. Primarily seed-eaters, sparrows have an extra bone in their tongues to help manipulate seeds. Two species have been established (only one widely) in North America.

House Sparrow
Passer domesticus

This adaptable urban species is now a nearly ubiquitous resident of Maine

Status in Maine: Introduced. This Old World sparrow is a common nonmigratory resident in most parts of the state, especially near urban centers in winter. This species occurs north to the St. John River valley and eastern Aroostook County farm country but does not occur in northern forests away from human habitation. Although Palmer did not report House Sparrows on coastal islands, they now occur on all inhabited islands.

Historical Status in Maine: House Sparrows were introduced in NY in 1850 to control a Snow-white Linden Moth (*Ennomos subsignaria*) infestation. In ME, the species was introduced in Portland in 1854 and again in 1855 by T.A. Deblois. Following several other liberations in Portland, Lewiston, and Bangor, the species became an established breeder by 1875 and reached as far as Houlton and Eastport by 1886 (Palmer 1949). Palmer said the population peaked in the early 20th century and that at the time of his writing was still abundant but declining due to the replacement of horses by cars, and the decline of agriculture, especially grain-growing, in ME.

Global distribution: Global. Considered "the most widely distributed wild bird on the planet" (Anderson 2006). Originated in the Middle East and Europe and now found on every continent except Antarctica, usually associated with urban, suburban, and wheat-growing areas, but rarely in tropics or the Arctic. In W. Hemisphere, ranges from NL west to s. BC, south across U.S. to n. S. Am. and s. Brazil to Chile and Argentina. Resident in Iceland, attempted introductions to Greenland failed.

Remarks: House Sparrows are early cavity nesters, nesting as early as Mar and continuing with multiple broods. As a result, they often preempt or even evict native songbirds like Eastern Bluebirds from nest boxes. In fact, the increasing sparrow population has been identified as a primary cause of the historic decline in bluebirds. Because they are common and ubiquitous, House Sparrows have been subject to an enormous array of biological and ecological studies. BBS surveys show 84% decline in N. Am. since 1966, likely due to agricultural industrialization. Similar declines have occurred in the species' native range in Europe.
BSV

Pipits (Motacillidae)

Of the 65 species of pipits, wagtails, and longclaws, pipits are the most cosmopolitan; longclaws are strictly tropical African birds and wagtails are primarily found in the Old World, with two Alaskan breeding species. Primarily insectivorous and noted for their exceptionally long hind toes, there are also three pipit species in North America, of which only the American Pipit breeds in Maine.

American Pipit
Anthus rubescens

This state-listed endangered species nests only on Mount Katahdin

Status in Maine: American Pipits are common spring and fall migrants. The main spring flight takes place in April and May, and the fall flight occurs primarily late September to mid-October. Pipits breed regularly in small numbers on Mount Katahdin. Formerly rare in winter, pipits are now regular in small numbers in York and Cumberland Counties.

Maine Conservation Status: Endangered (breeding population).

Historical Status in Maine: Knight said that American Pipits were rare spring migrants and common in fall, but he did not comment about the possibility of this species nesting in ME. Palmer (1949, 430) noted pipits were uncommon summer residents on Katahdin and that nesting was rare: "apparently occurrence there in summer is irregular, and breeding a rare event." Palmer and Taber (1946) reported that American Pipits were seen occasionally in summer on Katahdin, possibly as early as 1900. They indicated that nesting was confirmed in 1939 when an unhatched egg was removed from a nest and identified as that of an American Pipit at the American Museum of Natural History.

FALL: Early arrivals late Sep–early Oct: 20 on Roque I.,
Jonesport, 29 Sep 1993 (N. Famous, *MBN* 7[1]: 15); female in
Windham, 14 Oct 2012 (B. Briggs); 12 on Mount Desert I., 14
Oct 2010 (M. Good); 1 in Belfast, 15 Oct 2003 (fide N. O'Brien);
7 at Tenants Harbor, Knox Co., 19 Oct 1957 (Logan, *MFO* 2[11]:
118); 2 on Vinalhaven, 20 Oct 2008 (N. Famous); 1 in Lubec,
25 Oct 2012 (F. Pierce, eBird); 1 on Aroostook R., 26 Oct 2012
(WJS); 2 in Kennebunk, 26 Oct 2012 (S. Schulte, eBird); 3 at
Biddeford Pool, 27 Oct 2005 (E. Hynes). But by Nov, there are
observations of small flocks statewide. An early larger flock was
30 on 5 Nov 2012 at Biddeford Pool (D. Rankin, eBird).

WINTER: Recorded on 10 CBCs 1913–1957, Common Redpolls
considered "local and exceedingly rare" when 90 birds recorded
in Scarborough on 26 Dec 1956 (McCord et al.). Recorded
on 56 CBCs 1958–2016. High and low CBC counts by decade:
1960s, 1,915 in 1969 and 2 in 1963; 1970s, 2,901 in 1977 and 20 in
1970; 1980s, 3,863 in 1981 and 1 in 1982; 1990s, 5,117 in 1999 and
3 in 1996; 2000s, 5,917 in 2003 and 31 in 2006; 2010s, 6,012 in
2012 and 55 in 2013. J. Despres' >20 years' observations include
first-of-season birds in Turner: 1 on 30 Oct 1981; 12 on 22 Nov
1985; 8 on 15 Dec 1986; undetermined number, "my first of the
entire year," 10 Dec 1991; 1, 29 Oct 1993 (*MBN* 7[1]: 15); 25 on 28
Oct 1997; 1 on 29 Oct 1999; >2 on 28 Oct 2001 and first flock of
20 a week later on 4 Nov 2001 (all J. Despres). First of season
elsewhere: 2 at Kennebunk Plains, 6 Nov 2012 (D. Rankin,
eBird); 15 in Sapling Twp., Somerset Co., 7 Nov 2011 (R. Speirs,
eBird); 1, Presque Isle, 18 Nov 2003 (WJS); 150, Owl's Head,
Knox Co., 18 Nov 2003 (S. Kauffman); 22 in Portland, 22 Nov
2003 (L. Brinker); 7, "first I've seen here since the irruption a
couple winters ago," Holmes Bay, Machiasport, 27 Dec 2002
(H. Fogel). High counts: 2,000, Roque Bluffs, 3 Dec 1986 (fide
W. Townsend, *AB* 41: 258); 700, Cutler on 28 Nov 1986 (CDD,
AB 41: 60); 500, UMaine, Orono, 24 Feb 1994 (fide A. Bacon,
MBN 7[1]: 25); 400 in ragweed patch, Turner, 5 Dec 1999 (J.
Despres); 365 on Presque Isle CBC, 2 Jan 2002 (WJS, fide K.
Gammons); 250, Black Stream, Carmel–Hermon, Penobscot
Co., 18 Jan 1998 (J. Smith); and 130, Long L., Aroostook
Co., 15 Nov 2015 (WJS, eBird). Winters without Redpolls are
notable: "No Pine Siskins or Redpolls this winter at all," New
Sweden, 2 Mar 2014 (N. Hudak); undetermined number heard
in flight in Turner, "My only record of the season," 19 Mar 1996
(J. Despres); 1 in Richmond, "first in several years, it seems,"
25 Oct 1993 (PDV, *MBN* 7: 15); 1 in E. Machias, 1 Dec 1991,
"Redpolls have been scarce or absent the past three winters,"
(CDD, *MBN* 5: 45); only 2 reports, Dec 1992–Feb 1993, 1 in Ft.
Kent on 8 Dec 1992 and 20 in Gray, Cumberland Co., 5 Feb
1993 (fide ME Audubon).

TE

Hoary Redpoll
Acanthis hornemanni

An occasional paler flash among flocks of winter finches

Status in Maine: A regular but uncommon winter
visitor with an irregularly irruptive cycle, the Hoary
Redpoll is often seen with Common Redpolls. It is
found at feeders across Maine, although less often in
the central and western mountains. First appearing in
late November, hoaries sometimes linger as late as April.
The species is regularly recorded in small numbers on
Maine Christmas Bird Counts in irruptive years.

Historical Status in Maine: Palmer acknowledged
a 1909 specimen identified by Norton, and that
contemporary published sight records of Hoary
Redpolls in flocks with Common Redpolls existed.
However, he cautioned that accepting sight records was
inadvisable due to difficulty distinguishing the species
from Common Redpolls. He also acknowledged that
Norton recognized a hoary in a flock of commons two
days before the 1909 specimen was taken.

Global Distribution: Nearctic. Breeds in Canadian
high Arctic, NU, NT, YT, and n. AK, Arctic Ocean
islands, e. and w. Greenland, and Siberia. Winters
from NL, Gaspé Peninsula, south to Great Ls., west
to AB, NT, YT, and AK. Irruptive south to ME, NJ,
PA, west to IA, WY, and WA.

Remarks: Two subspecies have been reported in Maine.
The "Southern" Hoary Redpoll (*A. h. exilipes*) and the
larger nominate subspecies "Hornemann's" Hoary
Redpoll (*A. h. hornemanni*). Most records pertain to *A.
h. exilipes*. Hoary Redpolls reported as "Hornemann's":
one "large" bird in Orono, 27 Feb 2000 (J. Markowsly),
and one large, pale individual seen and photographed
with at least three *A. h. exilipes* birds and more than 150
Common Redpolls, 10 Mar–13 Apr 2013, Woodland
(WJS). Recent genetic research, however, has found
little genetic divergence even between Hoary and
Common Redpolls, suggesting they (along with Lesser
Redpolls in Europe) be treated as a single, circumpolar
species (Mason and Taylor 2015).

FALL: One bird at Wainwright Field, S. Portland, 11 Nov
2012 (N. Gibb, F. Mitchell, and D. Hitchcox, eBird); 1, Flood
Brothers Dairy, Clinton, 17 Nov 2012 (L. Bevier, eBird); 1, Bay Pt.
Rd., Georgetown, Sagadahoc Co., 25 Nov 2007 (J. Frank).

WINTER–EARLY SPRING: Seen infrequently across ME
and throughout winter, Hoary Redpolls most readily seen in

irruptive years Dec–Mar: 2–4 at feeders on May St., Portland, 9 Feb–4 Mar 1987 (E. Stanley); 15–20, Ft. Kent, week of 19 Jan 1994 (fide ME Audubon, *FN* 48: 185); 1 in a flock of ~100 Common Redpolls at Land of Nod Rd., Windham, 24 Jan 1994 (fide ME Audubon); 1 in Northport, Waldo Co., 8 Feb 1994 (fide ME Audubon); 1 "classic" Hoary with "hoard [sic] of Commons" in Waterville, 4 Dec 1999 (L. Bevier); 5 in Machiasport, 14 Jan 2000 (H. Fogel); 1 male at feeders daily with Commons, Pembroke, Washington Co., 13 Jan–13 Mar 2000, joined by a female, 13–14 Feb (D. Feener); 1, Phippsburg, 21 Dec 2003 (M. Dauphin, fide J. Frank); 1 in Belfast with >50 Commons, 24–25 Jan 2004 (J. Walker); 3 in Caribou, 3 Feb 2004 (fide WJS); 1, Woodland, 20 Dec 2005 (WJS); 2 in Presque Isle, intermittently 18 Jan–1 Feb 2005 (fide WJS); 1 in Eastport, 23 Dec 2007 (fide E. Hynes and S. Walsh); 3 at Griffin Ave., Hampden, Penobscot Co., 8 Feb 2015 (B. Cole, eBird). Late season birds: 1 in Phillips, Franklin Co., 4 Apr 2000 (P. Donahue, fide K Gammons); 1 in Belgrade, Kennebec Co., 22 Apr 2000 (D. Mairs); 1 with ~70 Commons, at Beechwood Ave., Old Town, Penobscot Co., 8 Apr 2004 (B. Duchesne); 2 in Woodland, 13 Apr 2004 (WJS); 1 with ~70 Commons, Orono, 11 Mar 2004 (S. Smith); 1, Fairfield, 29 Mar 2005 (L. Bevier); 1, "the first in two years" at Pushaw L., Old Town, 26 Mar 2006 (B. Duchesne); female in Fairfield, 25–27 Apr 2011 (L. Bevier); 1 at Slab City Rd., Lovell, Oxford Co., 4 Apr 2015 (M. Zimmerman, eBird). Recorded on CBCs every other year 1993–2007, not again until 2012. Most CBC reports in 2003, 8 birds in 5 circles.

TE

Red Crossbill
Loxia curvirostra

A wanderer throughout Maine's coniferous forests

Status in Maine: The Red Crossbill is a highly nomadic species that travels widely in search of bumper cone crops. This bird and the White-winged Crossbill are among the most irregular of the irruptive finches. Red Crossbills breed in the coniferous forests of Maine's central and western mountains and along the Downeast coast. However, timing and location of breeding varies year to year depending on the availability of seed cones. Flocks appear sporadically throughout Maine in all seasons. Most significant movements into southern Maine occur in the winter, with visiting flocks sometimes lingering late into spring.

Historical Status in Maine: The overall occurrence pattern of Red Crossbills in ME has not noticeably changed over the past century. Knight considered crossbills to be common residents in coniferous forests

of n. and e. ME, and Palmer (1949, 540) thought them most regular in n. counties. Both authors noted irregular movements of this species and its potential to occur in coniferous forests anywhere in the state at any time of year. Palmer wrote, "after raising one brood, and very likely two sometimes, in one place, this species may not breed or even occur there again in any number of months or years." Palmer reported 3 records of *L. c. percna*, a now-scarce subspecies that breeds almost exclusively in NFLD.

Global Distribution: Holarctic. In N. Am., breeds in NFLD, Maritime Provinces, and n. New England west through s. AK. In east, breeds in high-elevation areas of Appalachian Mtns. south to n. GA. In west, breeds south along Sierra Nevada Mtns. into n. CA, through Rocky Mtns., into high elevation areas of Cen. Am. south to Nicaragua. In winter, highly nomadic northern-breeding populations occur from s. Canada south to cen. GA and west to nw. Mexico. Old World birds breed throughout Europe south into nw. Africa, east through s. cen. Mediterranean and n. Middle East. Also breeds on s. Tibetan Plateau.

Remarks: At least 10 types of Red Crossbill are identified in N. Am. based on flight call and bill size (Young and Spahr 2017). The most frequent type in ME is Type 10, although Types 1, 2, and 3, which also feed on spruce and pine cones, have been recorded. A type breeding in s. ID was recognized as a distinct species (Cassia Crossbill) by AOS in 2017.

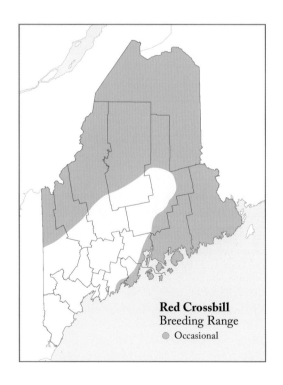

Red Crossbill
Breeding Range
● Occasional

SPRING: Individuals wintering south of typical breeding range seen late into spring; high counts include: 57 on Morse Mtn., 6 May 2012 (PDV, eBird); 38, Fryeburg Fairgrounds, 24 May 2015 (A. Robbins, eBird); 15, 29 Apr 2015, Evergreen Cemetery, Portland (T. Duddy, eBird). Sometimes breed before returning north: pair seen feeding young at nest in Shapleigh, York Co., 29 Mar 2015 (L. Waters, eBird).

SUMMER: Confirmed breeding on Mt. Desert I. and s. Lincoln Co., and noted possible breeding throughout Downeast coast and central and western mountains. (*ABBM*, Adamus 1987.) Two modern breeding records: 5 adults and 3 juveniles at a feeder in Presque Isle, 8–9 Jun 2013, and a female with 3 juveniles at Collins Pond, Caribou, 11 May 2016 (both WJS). Palmer reported species was common in L. Umbagog, Oxford Co., in certain years. Although total number recorded in ME varies greatly year to year, BBS found an overall 2.2% annual increase in ME, 1966–2015. Notable summer high counts, all eBird reports: 15 at Trescott Twp., Washington Co., 27 Aug 1992 (S. Mlodinow); 15 on Harbor I., Lincoln Co., 19 Jun 2012 (T. Johnson); and 30 on Gott's I., Hancock Co., 16 Jun 2012 (M. Rosenstein).

FALL: In years of southern invasions, southward movement often begins in fall. Numerous fall records from locations south of normal breeding ranges. High counts: 14 at Moose Pt. S.P., Waldo Co., 1 Sep 2012 (N. Paulson, eBird). Many reported on Monhegan I., 12 Sep–7 Oct 2012, with high count of 21 on 19 Sep 2012 (PDV et al., eBird).

WINTER: Highly irregular. CBCs show variation across state, but less in winter abundance and smaller total numbers over past 50 years. More likely to appear outside typical breeding areas in winter. Palmer reported crossbills abundant in Cumberland Co. some winters. Recent high counts from s. ME, all eBird records: 32 at Raven Ridge, Kennebec Co., on 17 Feb 2011 (J. MacDougall); 30 on Little Bigelow Mtn., Somerset Co., 11 Feb 2012 (A. Gilbert); 15 at Newfield Rd, Shapleigh, 7 Feb 2015 (M. Zimmerman). Remains in n. ME year-round when food supplies are sufficient: 60 at Grand L. Stream, Washington Co., 13 Feb 2016 (C. Brown); 20 in Aroostook Co., 22 Dec 2001 (WJS); 25 in Sunkhaze NWR on 8 Jan 2009 (P. Corcoran); 18 at Foss Pond, Piscataquis Co., 11 Feb 2012 (J. Kelly; all records eBird). Regardless of location, species known to breed opportunistically in late winter when seed cones are abundant (Hahn 1998). Audubon (1838, in Palmer) mentioned reports of species nesting in midwinter; a pair was observed constructing a nest in Waterboro, York Co., on 14 Feb 2015 (N. Gibb, eBird).

PD

White-winged Crossbill
Loxia leucoptera

An irruptive finch with highly variable abundance

Status in Maine: The White-winged Crossbill occurs in coniferous forests throughout Maine. Like its congener, Red Crossbill, the White-winged Crossbill is specialized to feed on conifer seeds and occasionally wanders great distances in search of sizeable cone crops. Distribution in Maine varies year to year. Overall, the species is more regular in northern and coastal Maine with significant numbers moving south in some winters. There is tremendous variation in abundance nearly everywhere, and breeding can occur in almost any month. White-winged Crossbills generally occur in larger flocks than Red Crossbills; sometimes more than 100 individuals reported at once.

Historical Status in Maine: Knight considered this species a local resident in Aroostook Co., a rare and irregular breeder in Hancock, Kennebec, Knox, Oxford, Penobscot, Somerset, and Waldo Cos., and an irregular winter visitor in Androscoggin, Cumberland, Franklin, Piscataquis, and Washington Cos. He noted that White-winged Crossbills are similar to Red Crossbills with respect to variable migratory behavior; the two species sometimes occur together in flocks. Palmer similarly acknowledged the White-winged Crossbill's irregularity, saying the species could occur and even breed in any coniferous habitat throughout ME at any time of year. He wrote that the species was most likely never a permanent resident at any locality but indicated it was more regular on the north and eastern coasts. Palmer believed the White-winged Crossbill occurred in greater numbers than the Red Crossbill.

Global Distribution: Holarctic. Breeds from NL south to n. New England, west through Canada to s. NU, NT, YT, and cen. AK, also breeds locally in Rocky Mtns. south to NM. Winters throughout breeding range and, during irruption years, occurs south across cen. U.S. from VA to n. CA. In Old World, breeds from e. Scandinavia, east to se. Russia and ne. China.

SPRING: Most birds wintering in southern areas during irruptions typically move by late winter. Palmer reported that high numbers wintering in Cumberland Co. in 1882–1883 departed by 11 Mar. High spring counts in northern and coastal areas: 30 or more in Rangeley, Franklin Co., 16 Mar 1997 (PDV, eBird); 30 in Presque Isle, 10 Mar 2001 (D. Dunford and WJS);

>30 on Muscovic Rd., Stockholm, 4 May 2003 (WJS); and 40 on Monhegan I., 4 Apr 2008 (D. Hitchcox, eBird).

SUMMER: Confirmed breeding in Downeast, Midcoast, and extreme ne. ME, and evidence of possible breeding in cen. and n. ME (*ABBM* Adamus 1987). Most summer records from these areas, although some Jun, Jul, and Aug reports in nearly all ME counties (eBird). Even in areas with regular breeding, considerable variation in annual numbers. Summer high counts: 100 at ANP, 25 Aug 1977 (D. Overacker, eBird), and 250 at W. Quoddy Head S.P., Saco, 18 Aug 2006 (W. Wilson, eBird). Dramatic changes in abundance make assessing population trends difficult, but BBS reports an overall 1.9% annual decrease in ME, 1966–2015. Recent record: unreported number, 10 Jul 2017, BSP (D. Lovitch).

FALL: During irruption years, individuals begin to arrive in southern areas in fall. High counts, fide eBird: 50 in S. Harpswell, 27 Oct 1997 (M. Libby); 80 at N. Haven, 1 Sep 2004 (R. Oren, eBird); 61 in Gilsland Farm, 12 Nov 2004 (E. Hynes); 45 at Head Beach, Phippsburg, 12 Nov 2004 (M. Fahay); 60 near Nesowadnehunk L., Piscataquis Co., 19 Nov 2007 (D. Hitchcox); 150 at Monhegan I, 25 Oct 2008 (JEP); 35 at Hermit I., Phippsburg, 26 Oct 2008 (G. Smith et al.); 35 in Troy, Waldo Co., 29 Sep 2009 (D. Potter). High counts in n. ME: 50 on Muscovic Rd., Aroostook Co., on 25 Nov 2002, and >60 at Irving Lot, New Sweden, 18 Nov 2002 (both WJS). Palmer wrote singing behavior occasionally occurs in fall; singing males reported in Aroostook Co., 13 Nov 2005 (WJS).

WINTER: Most records in s. ME occur in winter. High counts, fide eBird: 26 reported on York Co. CBC at Ft. Foster, 20 Dec 1977 (PDV); 70 in Scarborough, Portland Area CBC, 13 Dec 2004 (C. Governali); 58, Freeport CBC at Mast Landing Bird Sanctuary, Freeport, 26 Dec 2004 (D. Suitor); 50 in Fairfield, Waldo, 13 Dec 2004 (D. Smith), 87 at Forks, Somerset Co., 30 Dec 1990 (B. Brown and W. Wilson); 35 at Morse Mtn., 25 Dec 2008 (G. Smith); 100 at Popham Beach S.P., 19 Dec 1993 (A. Gilbert); 115 at Small Pt., 18 Dec 1983 (PDV); >100 at BSP, Piscataquis Co., some singing males, 18 Jan 2008 (D. Suitor); 39, Old Town–Orono CBC, 13 Dec 2004 (J. Mays); 150, at Matinicus I. CBC, 3 Jan 2009 (M. Fahay). Monhegan I. high counts: 300, 29 Dec 1977 (PDV, eBird); 251, CBC, 26 Dec 1983 (PDV, eBird); 85, CBC, 4 Jan 2008 (D. Hitchcox et al., eBird). Winter highs in n. ME: >50 at Irving Lot, 20 Dec 2002 (WJS); 38 in Mapleton–Chapman, Aroostook Co., 29 Dec 2002 (M. Fahay, eBird); >30 in Aroostook NWR, Limestone, 27 Jan 2003; 44 on Beaver Brook Rd., Aroostook Co., 17 Jan 2006; and 50 at BSP, 10 Feb 1999 (last 3, WJS).

Like Red Crossbill, this species breeds opportunistically during winter. Knight reported winter breeding in Washington Co. Palmer wrote that species breeds as early as Feb, but cited

White-winged Crossbills

report of species breeding in mid-Jan in NB in 1868. There are reports of singing males in ANP, 11 Feb 2003 (C. Kesselheim, eBird).

PD

Eurasian Siskin
Spinus spinus

This small, sweet Palearctic species has visited Maine twice

Status in Maine: Accidental. This species has been recorded twice in Maine. The first report was a male captured in Kittery, 24 March 1962. The bird was kept in captivity at the University of New Hampshire until it died in November 1962 (Borror 1963). The specimen is now at the Museum of Comparative Zoology, Cambridge, Massachusetts (specimen #262138, *AFN* Aug 1962, p. 391). The second record was a bright male among a large flock of Pine Siskins observed for approximately 10 minutes in Richmond on 31 January 2009 (Persons et al. 2015).

Historical Status in Maine: Unrecorded in ME prior to 1962.

Global Distribution: Palearctic. Breeds widely across Eurasia, from United Kingdom and Europe east to Asia and e. Russia, n. China, and Japan. Winters irregularly in southern range, sometimes with large irruptions south of usual range. Eurasian Siskins observed in MA: Cambridge, Aug 1904; New Bedford, Mar–Apr 1969; Rockport, May 1983. Also observed in St. Pierre et Miquelon (French territory off coast of NFLD), Jun 1983; Etobicoke, ON, Feb–Mar 1988; Terra Nova N.P., NL, Feb 1980; and Bloomfield, NJ, Feb 1983 (McLaren et al. 1989).

PDV

Pine Siskin

Spinus pinus

High numbers visit southern Maine during irruption years

Status in Maine: Like many other finch species, the abundance and distribution of Pine Siskins varies from year to year in Maine. While it is most regular as a northern and eastern Maine resident, it can be found in coniferous and mixed forests throughout the state. Movements are driven by availability of spruce and pine seeds, and large numbers occur in the south some years. When such irruptions occur, migrants and overwintering birds are seen from September to May in southern Maine.

Historical Status in Maine: Knight (1908, 388) described Pine Siskins as an irregular and local resident in n. and e. ME and "occurring in sporadic abundance," Oct–Mar in s. ME. Both he and Palmer commented on the nomadic and erratic nature of the species. Palmer said it does not breed in the same locality two years in a row and that flocks can appear throughout ME in any season.

Global Distribution: Nearctic. Breeds from NL south to n. New England west through s. Canada into NT, s. YT, and s. AK extending south through Rocky Mtns. into Mexico, Guatemala, and Pacific Coast, to s. CA and n. Baja California.

Remarks: The fact that Pine Siskins at least occasionally migrate at night was documented through nocturnal flight call research in Maine (Watson et al. 2011).

SPRING: Known to breed in southern areas during irruption years before returning north, depending on seed availability. Fide eBird: fledglings found in Cumberland Co., 27 Apr 2005 (K. D'Andrea), and in Sagadahoc Co. on 8 May 2008 (M. Fahay). Forbush (1929) reported finding young almost ready to fledge on 19 Mar in VT. Palmer reported that, following irruption, species departs wintering grounds in Apr to sometimes early May. Late departures include: 29 May in Portland and 31 May in Newcastle in 1993 (*MBN* 6: 1). In such years, variable number of migrants seen throughout ME. First banded on Appledore I. on 24 May 1987 (D. Holmes, *MBN* 1: 1). Notable high counts include: 60 in E. Machias, 16 Mar 1980 (PDV, eBird); 110 in Bradbury Mtn. S.P., 15 Mar 2005 (D. Akers, eBird); 70 in Hersey, Aroostook Co., 15 Mar 2008 (WJS et al., eBird).

SUMMER: BBS reported a 2.2% annual decrease in ME, 1966–2015 (Sauer et al. 2017). Breeds most regularly in n. and e. ME; summer records from all ME counties. Nested in ANP in Jul 2011 (M. Good, eBird).

FALL: When large southward movements occur, migrants seen late Sep–early Nov: 100 in Lincoln Ctr., 14 Dec 1974 (PDV, eBird); >300 in Richmond on 13 Oct 1983 (PDV, eBird); 1,000 on Monhegan I., 28 Sep 1989 (*MBN* 3: 3); 100 on Seal I. on 6 Oct 2004 (Project Puffin, eBird); 300 on Hermit I., Phippsburg, 1 Nov 2004 (M. Fahay, eBird); 169 on Monhegan I. on 23 Oct 2006 (T. Magarian, eBird); 80 in Freeport on 25 Oct 2007 (D. Nickerson, eBird); 350 on Monhegan I. on 27 Sep 2008 (J. Trimble, eBird); at least 300 comprised of flocks of 15–40 at Seawall Beach, 10 Oct 2008 (PDV, eBird); at least 125 in Kennebunkport, 21 Oct 2008 (D. Doubleday, eBird); 80 on Sears I., 27 Sep 2010 (R. Ostrowski, eBird); at least 874, Monhegan I., 10 Oct 2010 (J. Trimble, eBird); 130 on Hermit I., comprised of flocks of at least 30 on 24 Oct 2010 (N. Gibb et al., eBird).

WINTER: Winter records throughout ME; species often congregates near feeders. Large numbers sometimes occur in s. ME during irruption years. High counts: 180 in Richmond, 11 Jan 1983 (PDV, eBird); 325 reported on Farmington CBC and 319 reported by Augusta CBC, 19 Dec 1987 (*MBN* 1: 4); 85 in Belfast on 31 Dec 2004 (S. Benz, eBird); 250 in Clinton, on 2 Jan 2005 (P. Blair, eBird); 170 comprised of flocks of 20–50 individuals at Sunkhaze Meadows, 2 Dec 2007 (G. Smith, eBird); 150 at Little Bigelow Mtn., Somerset Co., 10 Feb 2008 (A. Gilbert, eBird); 120 in 3 flocks, ANP on 5 Nov 2010 (S. Benz, eBird); 80 in downtown Orono on 19 Dec 2010 (B. Barker, eBird); 68 in Phippsburg, 29 Jan 2011 (R. Robinson, eBird); ~115 in Orrington, Penobscot Co., 29 Jan 2011 (J. Smith; eBird); ~100 in Kennebunk, 7 Feb 2011 (M. Zimmerman, eBird); 75 in St. Albans, Somerset Co., 16 Feb 2011 (B. and D. Witham; eBird); 40 at Sebasticook L., 27 Dec 2014 (T. Aversa, eBird).

PDV

Lesser Goldfinch

Spinus psaltria

A species of the desert Southwest finds the Northeast

Status in Maine: Accidental. The Lesser Goldfinch has been recorded three times in Maine. Two of these records have been accepted by the Maine Bird Records Committee. The earliest record, as yet unreviewed, is a black-mantled male photographed and observed by many in Georgetown, Sagadahoc County, from December 1992–April 1993 (Maine Bird Records Committee, ph. archive). The second record was reported 7 July 2009 at Parks Pond, Clifton, Penobscot County (J. Zievis, ph., ME-BRC #2009-009). A black-hooded male photographed and described at Whetstone Pond, Abbot, Piscataquis County, 5 August 2015, is the most recent report (E. Blanchard et al.; ph., eBird).

Global Distribution: Western N. Am. CO and NE, west to Pacific Coast, south to TX, NM, AZ, Mexico and Cen. Am. Occasionally found east of normal range; records from PA, NC, VA, KY (Sibley 2000), and ON.

PDV

American Goldfinch

Spinus tristis

A flash of gold and a taste for thistle

Status in Maine: American Goldfinch winter and summer ranges overlap in Maine; the common summer residents often initiate nesting from late June into August, and as late as early September. The species typically produces one brood, the timing of which seems to be related to thistle (*Cirsium* spp.) bloom and seed set. Unique among finches, goldfinches molt in spring as well as in the postbreeding season. Although many Maine breeders move south for colder months, goldfinches are common winter birds at feeders throughout the state, when residents may be joined by birds from farther north (McGraw and Middleton 2017).

Historical Status in Maine: Known by a variety of names from "wild canary" to "thistle bird," American Goldfinches were common in ME from May to Oct and led a "roving existence in small flocks" (Knight 1908). Griscom (1938) reported two wintering birds in Bethel in 1900 and at L. Umbagog in 1886. Palmer said that goldfinches were common summer residents throughout ME, late migrants, and winter residents locally. Nesting did not occur until Jul or later, and he noted at least one nest that was initiated as late as 5 Sep.

Global Distribution: Nearctic. Breeds from NFLD and NB west to n. AB, s. BC, south to GA, LA, west to OK and cen. NV. Breeding range overlaps winter range from New England south to n. LA and GA, west to NY, Great Ls., and WI, south to cen. NV, cen. WY, and MT. Winters from ME south to NC, e. cen. Mexico to Gulf Coast, and FL, west to OR and CA, south to U.S.–Mexico border in AZ and NM.

Remarks: Varying degrees of melanistic and leucistic coloring relatively common: a melanistic bird reported interacting well with the rest of the flock ("dark gray/black with light wingbars. Slight goldish tint on throat and face"), 2 and 5 Dec 2004, Presque Isle (A. Sheppard). Leucistic bird, seen periodically through Nov 2004, was "always alone" in Cozy Harbor, Southport, Lincoln Co. (N. Bither). A partial albino whose social status was not remarked upon ("Golden head and throat, dark wings, and the rest of it was white") was in S. Portland, 13 Mar 2002 (M. Jordan).

American Goldfinch

SPRING: Early birds: earliest record of song since 1991 in Portland on 7 Feb 2008 (J. Despres); goldfinches starting to "color up" in Aroostook Co., 14 Feb 2006 (fide WJS); 25, "A few goldfinches are nearly all yellow," Raymond, Cumberland Co., 14 Mar 2007 (S. Shanahan); "After a long winter absence…found my thistle feeders covered with goldfinches," Cape Neddick, 19 Mar 2006 (L. Scotland); 2, first of season after storm, Casco, 30 Mar 2002 (B. Dorr); "one male that is literally all yellow" in W. Falmouth, 31 Mar 2005 (L. Sietz); "some beginning to brighten up," on Hollywood Blvd., Whitefield, Lincoln Co., 4 Mar 2004 (B. Dalke, fide J. Suchecki); 2 arrived in S. Hiram, Oxford Co., 2 Apr 2006 (J. Potter); 3, "one of which was almost completely yellow," in Brunswick, 23 Apr 2004 (B. Bullock); "males at my feeder were fully molted into their alternate plumage," 23 Apr 2007 (R. MacDonald). Peak mid-May when 56% of ME eBird checklists include goldfinches. High numbers: 53, at feeders after big storm in W. Falmouth, 9 Mar 2005 (L. Seitz); 50 and 65 on N. Haven I., 15 Mar and 23 Mar 2007 (T. Sprague); 70 in Raymond, 26 Mar 2007 (S. Shanahan); 120 in Woodland, 18 Apr 2007 (WJS); 95, W. Falmouth, 4 May 2005 (L. Seitz). In Aroostook Co.: "still no sign of goldfinches…" as of 24 Mar 2004 (fide WJS); single goldfinches returning to feeders, Woodland, 18 Apr 2004 (WJS); "almost completely molted and males are starting to disperse from the winter's flocks and are singing," 24 Apr 2007 (WJS).

SUMMER: Typically produce single brood although nesting occurs throughout summer. J. Despres' extensive Jun–Sep nesting and fledging notes from Portland include: pair eyeing yarn on plant stakes, presumably nest material, 24 Jun 2016; female tugging at maypole yarn, 1 Jul 2017; "female grabbed a strand of the Chicory [*Cichorium intybus*] yarn in her bill and tried to pull it loose by jumping into midair, only to wind up hanging by her bill," 18–20 Jul 2009; female gathering nest material, 1, 8, and 15 Aug 2015, and 3 and 7 Aug 2016. First fledglings in Evergreen Cemetery, Portland: first calls, 31 Jul; first definite family group, 1 Aug 2010; unseen nestling/fledgling calling on 3 Aug 2016; first calls 9 Aug 2008 and 21 Aug 2005 (all J. Despres). Unseen fledgling calling at Leonard St., Portland on 3 Sep 2010, 5 Sep 2013, and 11 Sep 2015. In Turner, adult female collecting webworm tents presumably for nest material on 16 Aug 1993; on the same day in 2000, the first fledglings called (J. Despres). BBS data indicates small but significant decline in continental population 1966-2015 and a 3.6% but not significant decline in ME, 2005–2015 (Sauer et al. 2017).

FALL: American Goldfinch at lowest annual numbers in mid-Oct when recorded on 25% of ME eBird checklists. High counts: 200 at Dragon Fields, Portland, 5 Nov 2004 (M. Resch, fide J. Suchecki); 328, Cadillac Mtn., 7 Dec 2015 (M. Good, eBird). In Woodland: "finch species and numbers remain unchanged with Gold and Purple Finches common," 15–21 Sep 2004; following year, Purple Finches increasing while goldfinches "thinning out," 23 Sep 2003; visiting feeder after month's absence, 26 Oct 2004; and seen daily by 18 Nov 2003 (all WJS). Flocks of >50 in Caribou and Washburn, Aroostook Co., week of 24 Nov 2004 (WJS), and hundreds on White Oak timber lot in Stockholm, 6 Dec 2006 (WJS).

WINTER: Winter flocks common, often disappearing for extended periods before reappearing unexpectedly: S. Shore Dr., Rangeley Plt., Franklin Co., 2 Jan 2005, "we have been swamped with goldfinches for several weeks now" (J. Perry); 40 at feeders, Lewiston, 22 Feb 2005 (D. Marquis); "after a near absence of goldfinches for a couple of weeks, yesterday I counted a flock of 50+ on feeders," 17 Jan 2006 (T. Sprague); 140, W. Falmouth, 29 Jan 2006 (L. Seitz); 150 in Talmadge, Washington Co., 16 Feb 2007 (R. Follette). Aroostook Co.: flocks of 50–70 or more, Presque Isle and Woodland, mid-Jan to Feb 2005 (WJS); "Common Redpolls, Pine Siskins, and American Goldfinches are being seen together in unusually high numbers," 16 Feb–early Mar 2005 (WJS); "waves of finches in northern Maine show no sign of waning yet," 23 Mar 2005 (WJS). However, the biennial irruptive cycle of American Goldfinch in the East appears to be out of sync with that of Common Redpoll (Dougherty and Wilson 2018).

CBC surveys tallied 7,302 goldfinches on 24 CBC circles in 2000, 5,098 on 28 circles in 2010, and 8,091 on 33 counts in 2015. *TE*

Longspurs (Calcariidae)

Migratory ground-feeders of open landscapes and cold climates, four species of longspurs and two buntings comprise this family. Four members, including Maine's two accidentals, are strictly North American, whereas the ranges of Lapland Longspur and Snow Bunting span North America and Eurasia. Absent in summer, they enliven Maine during migration and winter.

Lapland Longspur
Calcarius lapponicus

An uncommon visitor from the tundra

Status in Maine: Uncommon but annual spring and fall migrants, Lapland Longspurs are found primarily along the coast and at a few inland localities. Uncommon to rare in winter, this species is most usually found in southern and coastal Maine.

Historical Status in Maine: Knight considered Lapland Longspurs rare, but noted, "recently they appear to occur regularly in limited numbers at Pine

Point, near Scarboro" (1908, 398). According to Palmer, longspurs were regularly reported in small numbers at Scarborough. Brown, who spent many years hunting in the Scarborough area, mentioned that "the longspur was really rare in the Portland region until 1882 at least," explaining, "Pine Point, where most examples have been taken or seen, was covered very thoroughly by myself during several years' collecting" with no sightings. However, "during the winter of 1912–13… I at once found Lapland Longspurs to be regular and prominent visitors" (Brown 1923, 131).

Global Distribution: Holarctic. In N. Am., breeds on open tundra from n. NL west and south along Hudson Bay, across Arctic Canada to AK. Winters from s. QC and s. ME to NJ, VA, and TX.

SPRING: Spring migration begins in early Mar, continuing to early Apr. During this period Lapland Longspurs reported from many townships, including many inland localities: e.g., 2 birds on Corn Shop Rd., Fryeburg, 1 Mar 2015 (S. Walsh and B. Marvil, eBird); 1 in Rockwood, Somerset Co., 6–7 Mar 1961 (obs. unk.); 1 male in Lincoln Ctr., 6–8 Mar 1977 (PDV); 4 in Clinton, 14 Mar 2000 (obs. unk.); 15 in Bowdoinham, 18 Mar 1961 (A. Smith), and 4 on 11 Mar 1981 (obs. unk.); 19 at Flood Brothers Dairy, Clinton, 19 Mar 2014 (M. Veins, eBird); 4 in Benton, Kennebec Co., 26 Mar 1997 (obs. unk.); 1 on Winter's Hill, Somerset Co., 28 Mar 2017 (M. Fahay, eBird). Single bird in Scarborough, 11 Apr 1956 (*MFO* 1[5]: 53), and 2 males in Scarborough, 24 Apr 1957, listed as late dates for ME (*AFN* issue unk.). In Turner, J. Despres registered longspurs 15–31 Apr no fewer than 13 years since 1970 and recorded small numbers (<5) in May in 10 different years (J. Despres). Late dates at this locality: 1 on 13 May 1996, 2 on 13 May 2002, 1 on 18 May 2002 (J. Despres). In Aroostook Co., longspurs reported rarely in spring; 1 at Presque Isle, 15 May 1966 was exceptional (M. Holmes). Finally, single male sighted at Bailey's Mistake, off the coast of Washington Co., 26 May 1986 (N. Famous).

FALL: Fall migration protracted: beginning in Sep, main flight occurs Oct–Nov, continuing through early Dec. Lapland Longspurs (<10) arrive in small numbers in Turner by late Sep, where species recorded regularly 24–30 Sep since 1975 (J. Despres). Unprecedented early report at Seal I. NWR, 28 Aug 2017 (I. Brofksy and K. Yakola, eBird). Other early records: Turner, several birds, 13 Sep 1976 (J. Despres); and in Lubec, single bird on 16 Sep 1997 (N. Famous). In Oct and Nov, single birds and small flocks (fewer than 10), often associating with Horned Larks and Snow Buntings, widespread in salt-marsh and dune habitat in s. and coastal ME: at least 15 sighted on Kennebunk Plains, 24 Oct 1993 (PDV). Two birds on Mount Desert Rock, 26 Oct 1998, and 10 in Searsport, 17 Nov 2003

(J. and K. Zeman), both unusual occurrences. Longspur numbers diminish through first weeks of Dec and species generally rare on CBCs. However, longspurs sometimes remain at preferred sites such as Turner (J. Despres). Flocks of 10–25 regularly reported from Scarborough Marsh, maxima: 60 birds on 11 Nov 2014 (PDV, eBird); more than 30 birds on 22 Oct 1989 (J. Despres, *AB* 44: 60); 25 birds, 30 Oct 1994 (obs. unk.); and 14 birds, 23 Dec 2003 (R. Eakin). Flock of 75 at Biddeford Pool, 29–30 Oct 1993, largest reported for ME (L. Brinker, *AB* 48: 90).

Lapland Longspurs appear uncommon and irregular in most inland localities; possibly due to inadequate observer effort since species recorded almost annually in Turner since 1975, and, more recently, 2 in Clinton, 18 Dec 1994, and 1 on 17 Dec 1997 (both W. Sumner), and 2 on 26 Dec 2000 (R. Joseph). Notable inland occurrences: 7 in New Gloucester, Cumberland Co., 6 Nov 2012, and 3 on Florida Ave., Bangor, 11 Nov 2016 (both R. Speirs, eBird); 12 at Clarry Hill, Union, 2 Nov 1999 (M. Libby); 5 in Wilton, 12 Nov 2003 (J. Dwight); 1 in Greenville, 1 Dec 1952 (I. Sherman); 2 in Fairfield, 18 Dec 1994 (PDV); 10 in Sabattus, Androscoggin Co., 24 Dec 1955 (fide D. Morse). In Aroostook Co., longspurs generally rare, or rarely reported; single birds reported with large flocks of Snow Buntings in St. Agatha, 6 Nov 2004, and in Presque Isle, 16 Dec 2004 (both WJS); and 2 birds with 1,900 Snow Buntings on 1 Dec 2013 (WJS, eBird). It is likely longspurs are present in small numbers from late Sep until deep snow cover obscures potato and other agricultural fields (WJS).

WINTER: Few Lapland Longspurs linger in ME after mid-Dec. CBC records reveal species is rare in winter and does not occur regularly on any counts. Interestingly, longspurs reported most consistently inland on Waterville CBC (13 occasions, maximum 13 birds). Seen on coastal CBCs in Bath and York Co. 6 times each (maximum: 8 birds in Phippsburg, 18 Dec 1993), inland on Danforth (Washington Co.) twice, and Farmington (Franklin Co.) CBC three times. Reported annually on CBCs since 2003.

Lapland Longspurs not reported annually in Jan. In Turner, 1–3 birds seen 9 different years, 1980–2004, including 11 on 13 Jan 1994 (J. Despres). Unusual concentrations: 10–25 birds in Thomaston, 5 Jan 1965 (obs. unk.); 15 at Popham Beach, 16 Jan 1990 (J. Despres); 22 in Biddeford, 22 Jan 1957 (*MFO* 2: 16). Small increase in numbers in Feb, especially during latter part of month: 11 in Hills Beach, Biddeford (*MFO* 2: 27), 1 Feb 1957; 24 in Durham, Androscoggin Co., 7 Feb 1961 (Vermette, *MFO* 6[2]: 21); 30 in Turner, 11 Feb 1967 (Litchfield, Kennebec Co., *NMAS* Feb 1967); 35 in Scarborough, 14 Feb 1956 (*MFO* 1: 30); 40 in Gouldsboro, 15 Feb 1991 (F. Young, *AB* 45: 253); 18 in Clinton, 24 Feb 2004 (*Guillemot* 34: 19); 6–10 birds in Farmington, 25 Feb 1977 (obs. unk.). Few Aroostook Co. reports, fide eBird: 4 in Limestone, 28 Jan 2007, and 1 at Presque Isle airport, same day 2016 (both WJS); 1 each in Easton on 13 Feb 2009 (C. Kesselheim), and in Masardis, 15 Feb 2016 (WJS).

PDV

Chestnut-collared Longspur
Calcarius ornatus

A striking endemic of the Great Plains

Status in Maine: Accidental. One historic specimen record and two sight reports from March 1993 and June 2012, both in south coastal Maine.

Historical Status in Maine: Knight listed one specimen reported by Goodale (1887) following a hunting trip on 13 Aug 1886 on Little R. marshes in Scarborough:

"I fired at it, as it rose from the grass before me, and had the pleasure to see it fall. I must confess that upon picking it up I was entirely at a loss to know what it was. I did not feel sure regarding it till some months later, when looking over one day, in company with Mr. Chadbourne, the large series of *Calcarius ornatus* in the Agassiz Museum in Cambridge, we discovered one bird which matched my bird in every particular. Mr. Brewster, to whom I showed it later, identified it as *ornatus* without doubt. It is apparently a young male, though the sex could not be positively determined."

Palmer indicated the specimen was still in the Goodale collection as of Feb 1904. The current disposition of this specimen is unknown.

Global Distribution: Nearctic. Breeds from Canadian prairies, southern AB, SK, MB, south to SD and CO. Winters in KS, AZ, TX, and Mexico. Reported in NFLD, NB, NS, MA, and CT.

Global Conservation Status: IUCN: Near Threatened; PIF: Watch List due to population declines and moderate to high threats.

SPRING: G. Carson observed a male Chestnut-collared Longspur in alternate plumage with a flock of Horned Larks at Scarborough Marsh, 27–30 Mar 1993. Her comments noted distinctive face pattern and yellow throat.

SUMMER: Individual sighted 22–28 Jun 2012 in coastal s. ME (Brown).

PDV

Smith's Longspur
Calcarius pictus

An accidental from the Arctic

Status in Maine: Accidental. One Smith's Longspur was observed in Norridgewock, 21–25 September 2011, and one bird in winter plumage was photographed at Crescent Beach, Cape Elizabeth, 2 January 1956, by Morse and Packard (ph. arch.). In their description, Morse and Packard noted, "especially striking was the white blotch on the wing coverts, the buffy underparts with their faint but distinct streaking, the strong facial markings and the white outer tail coverts" (*MFN* 12: 45–47).

Global Distribution: Nearctic. Breeds from nw. ON south along Hudson Bay westerly in a narrow band across Arctic Canada to cen. AK. Winters in Midwest (IA, IL, south to n. TX). Reported in all New England states, NS, and QC.

PDV

Snow Bunting
Plectrophenax nivalis

Males brave weeks of late winter in the Arctic to secure mate-luring rock crevices

Status in Maine: Snow Buntings are common to abundant spring and fall transients and winter residents. Large flocks of buntings move around the state's interior irruptively in winter, feeding in large, open flat areas where seeds or invertebrates can be gleaned from sand, soil, snow, or manure. Buntings typically appear in mid- to late October, with numbers growing to a late-November peak; some individuals linger until early April.

Historical Status in Maine: Palmer described Snow Buntings as common to numerous winter residents, especially on the coast and coastal islands in some years, and nearly absent in others. Inland numbers are more variable. Sometimes numerous to abundant in fall as a transient; Palmer noted that few, if any, birds pass through ME in spring. According to Palmer, buntings generally arrived 15 Oct to 12 Nov, with evidence of a few appearing as early as 24 Sep in Brunswick (Walch 1926, in Palmer). Knight reported a 10 Oct arrival as exceptionally early. Most of these fall birds were primarily coastal and apparently transient.

Snow Buntings

Global Distribution: Holarctic. In N. Am., breeds in high Arctic tundra from n. QC and Ellesmere I. west to n. AK. Winters from s. and cen. Canada and cen. U.S. throughout New England south to NJ.

Remarks: Although single flocks can be more than 800 birds, most Snow Bunting flocks are fewer than 100 individuals (PDV). Flock size seems linked to food availability. Buntings appear to migrate primarily along the coast, where they make use of Eelgrass (*Zostera* spp.) and Glasswort (*Salicornia europa)* seeds as a supplemental food source when upland seeds are snow-covered. Meanwhile, some flocks remain for the winter and occasionally move inland, where they feed voraciously on seeds from highland grasses (Palmer 1949).

SPRING: Small numbers of Snow Buntings linger from winter residency into early Apr. Largest spring flock >500 birds seen in Bangor, 5 Mar 1967 (French, *NMAS,* Mar 1967). Notable late-spring records: 1 on Brothers I., 26 May 2008 (L. Harter and D. Vander Pluym, eBird); 1 at Tri-Com Landfill, Caribou, 13 May 2011 (WJS); 1 in Durham, Androscoggin Co., 8 May 2014 (F. Aldrich, eBird); 1 at Mt. Agamenticus, 20 Apr 1985; 1 at Seapoint Beach, Kittery, 19 Apr 1989 (both L. Phinney); 1 in Turner, 27 Apr 1994 (J. Despres); 2 in Old Town, Penobscot Co., 17 Apr 1995 (E. Grew); 6 at Reid S.P., 15 Apr 1996 (fide A. Bacon); and an extremely late sighting of 3 birds in Dover-Foxcroft, 31 May 1967 (*NMAS* May 1967).

FALL: First migrating Snow Buntings appear in n. ME in mid- to late Oct. Numbers build through fall with largest concentrations in mid- to late Nov. Notable records include unusually early birds in Scarborough Marsh, 20 Sep 2009 (PDV, eBird); several in Nesowadnehunk Campground and 4 on Golden Rd., both in Piscataquis Co. and on 29 Sep 2012 (S. Pachulski, P. Blair, respectively; eBird); Yarmouth, 30 Sep 1992 (L. Brinker). Seasonal high counts: 2,000 on Tardiff Rd., Clinton, 17 Nov 2013 (P. Blair, eBird). In Oct 1970, 200 fall migrants on Smuttynose I., York Co., 28–31 Oct; 100 in Kittery, 29 Oct; and 100 in Wells, 31 Oct (all *MN* 2[4]: 32).

WINTER: Common to abundant winter resident in a variety of open habitats, notably salt marshes and sand dunes; also barrens and agricultural fields, especially if manure has been recently spread.

Depending on snow cover and food availability, moderately sized flocks (~100 birds) stay throughout winter with a fairly abbreviated pulse in late Mar–early Apr as birds move north. Flocks <100 birds recorded regularly on most CBCs throughout state, including w. and n. ME. In Farmington, Snow Buntings regular on CBCs (~50%), 2000–2017, with maximum of 102 birds seen on single count. In Aroostook Co., Presque Isle CBC averaged ~512 birds 2001–2017 and recorded largest numbers in ME: 1,058 birds in 2013 and 2,342 birds in 2010. Buntings recorded annually on ME CBCs since 2000. Numbers diminish Jan–Feb before northern movement occurs in Mar–early Apr.

PDV

New World Sparrows (Passerellidae)

Split from the Old World buntings in 2017, this family holds 27 genera and approximately 153 species. Typically inhabitants of shrubby environments, most species are well-camouflaged, brown, and stripy ground-feeders. Maine's wealth of Passerellidae includes 22 sparrows, towhees, and juncos, as well as the casual Lark Bunting and eight accidentals from western North America.

Cassin's Sparrow
Peucaea cassinii

A nomadic grassland sparrow of the Southwest, known for elaborate flight displays

Status in Maine: Accidental. There is a single photographic record of a bird on Mount Desert Rock, during the period 16–25 September 1986 (James 1990).

Global Distribution: This species normally occurs in arid grassland habitat in the sw. U.S. and cen. Mexico. Breeds in KS, CO, w. OK, TX, NM, and e. AZ. Northern populations migratory. Single records from NS, NY, and NJ, represent only other records from ne. N. Am.

PDV

Global Conservation Status: PIF: Watch List due to population declines and moderate to high threats.

Remarks: The account in *Maine BirdLife* (6[2]: 28) erroneously stated two birds were found in Maine in May 1984, one each at Moody and Wells. In fact, there was only one bird. Moody is not a separate town but is a community within the township of Wells.

SPRING: There are 3 spring records: 1 in Ft. Kent, May 1981 (PDV); an adult in Wells for ~2 weeks, May 1984 (*MBL* 6[2]: 28); and a bird on Monhegan I., 24 Mar–8 May 2012 (D. Hitchcox et al.).

FALL: Seven fall records. Earliest a single adult in Calais on 25–26 Aug 1958. This individual flew across the St. Croix R. to become a first NB record (Squires 1976). Three mid-Oct reports: 1 on Little Cranberry I., Hancock Co., 13–14 Oct 1972 (A. Stanley, *AB* 27: 30); 1 in Blue Hill, 14–15 Oct 1965 (*MFN* 21[5]: 17); and 1 immature in Orono, 15–17 Oct 1977 (N. Famous, PDV; *AB* 32: 180). Single Nov record: 17 Nov 2016 (S. McKeon) at a feeder in Belgrade, Kennebec Co., accepted by ME-BRC.

WINTER: A single bird wintered in Union, 1971–1972 (ME-BRC); an immature bird was found in Buckfield, Oxford Co., 5–22 Dec 1987 (*AB* 42: 231); and an adult was seen in Waldoboro, Lincoln Co., 26 Nov 2007 (J. Hassett, fide D. Reimer).
PDV

White-throated Sparrow
Zonotrichia albicollis

An irregularly abundant breeding sparrow with a pure song

Status in Maine: White-throated Sparrows are common to abundant in coniferous and mixed forest environments, usually in openings with thick, shrubby vegetation. They occur in especially high densities in recently harvested forest clearings. Common but late-spring migrants and common fall migrants, they often occur in flocks of 50–100 birds. This species regularly winters in Maine in small numbers along the coast and uncommonly inland to Aroostook County and toward the mountains.

Maine Conservation Status: Species of Special Concern.

Historical Status in Maine: Palmer considered White-throated Sparrows common throughout the state except perhaps southern York Co., and especially numerous at higher elevations. His reports of migrant

patterns were similar to what is seen today. He acknowledged some birds were found in winter but "not more than three birds . . . at any one place" (1949, 568). Palmer also noted that they are gregarious, most commonly associating with juncos, Song Sparrows, White-crowned Sparrows, and Hermit Thrushes.

Global Distribution: Nearctic. Breeds throughout ME, north to Labrador, west to NT, YT, AB, and BC, south to PA, MI, and MN. Species winters from coastal ME, New England to MI and s. MN, south to FL, TX, and n. Mexico.

Remarks: "White-throated Sparrows exhibit plumage polymorphism (white-striped and tan-striped morphs) during the breeding season, associated with a difference in their chromosomes. Such differences in plumage and genetic material are maintained by negative assortative mating—each morph nearly always mates with its opposite. These plumage differences are paralleled by differences in behavior, with white-striped males being more aggressive, territorial, and apt to seek matings outside the pair bond than their tan-striped counterparts, and with tan-striped females providing more parental care than their counterparts" (Falls and Kopachena 2010).

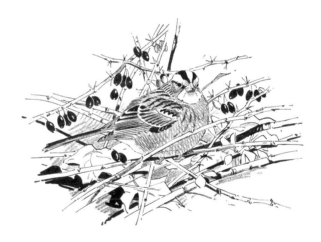

White-throated Sparrow

SPRING: First spring migrants usually arrive 15–30 Apr. However, recently appearing more regularly in Mar–early Apr; 1 bird each, unless noted, fide eBird: Carpenter's Boat Shop, Bristol, 2 Mar 2009 (D. Carlucci); Unity College, 6 Mar 2015 (T. Aversa); Belfast Harbor, 10 Mar 2017 (F. Kynd); 10 White-throated Sparrows on Monhegan I., 15 Mar 2011 (T. Magarian); Ripley Pond, Somerset Co., 21 and 24 Mar 2016 (K. Butler); Great Wass I., Cape Pt. Trail, 24 Mar 2009 (G. Watkevich); Bellamy R. Wildlife Sanctuary, Dover, Lincoln Co., 25 Mar 2010 (P. Brown). In 2006, sparrows in Saco (1), 2 Apr; Wilton (6), 6

Apr (J. Dwight); Bridgton (1), 11 Apr (J. Preis); and Lewiston (1), 12 Apr (D. Marquis). In Aroostook Co., sparrows generally arrive in Presque Isle and Ft. Kent late Apr–11 May (G. and S. Flagg, M. Trombley); birds on 12 Apr 1981 (J. Gibson) and 13 Apr 2008 (S. Seymour) exceptionally early.

The main migration passes through Maine late Apr to mid-May. In Turner, migrant numbers increased from 15 birds on 20 Apr 1996 to 50 on 21 Apr 2006 (J. Despres); >40 observed in Richmond on same date (PDV) and 25 on 29 Apr 2011 (D. Suitor, eBird). Flocks of 40–300 birds regular in s. coastal ME, 2–13 May: 40 in Georgetown, Sagadahoc Co., 2 May 2000 (J. Frank); in Portland, >35 seen on 30 Apr 2004 (L. Seitz), 40 on 3 May 2001 (PDV), >300 on 5 May 2006 (PDV, D. Lovitch), and >140, 11 May 1999 (PDV); 61 on Appledore I., 11–12 May 1996 (D. Holmes, FN 50: 256); on Monhegan I., 35 on 6 May 2017 (D. Hitchcox, eBird), 80 on 13 May 1997 (PDV, D. Abbott), and 48 on 17 May 2013 (K. Lindquist, eBird). Number of birds diminishes 24–31 May: 10 on Monhegan I., 26 May 1983, were unusual for the date (S. Tingley).

SUMMER: White-throated Sparrows are common "in coniferous and mixed forests, especially those with numerous openings with low, dense vegetation; areas of second growth after logging, fires, or insect damage; around edges of beaver ponds, beaver meadows, or open bogs" (Falls and Kopachena 2010). They also nest along edges of clearings made for cottages and roads. *ABBM* confirmed nesting throughout ME (Adamus 1987). BBS registered a 3.6% decline in ME, 1966–2015 (3.9%, 2005–2015). In 1979, 33–97 males recorded on 12 different routes in n. and w. ME. On 7 n. and w. routes for which there is data across the same years, total number birds recorded in 1998, 6–61; in 2009, 5–29; in 2017, 1–28. On Wilson Mills BBS (Oxford Co.), >50 birds recorded on 15 counts, 1983–2000, including 5 years >100 (high 138 in 1997); from 2001–2017, 2 years >50, with highest count 72 birds.

FALL: First fall migrants usually appear late Sep, main flight occurs end of month through mid-Oct, when large congregations sometimes conspicuous. Single bird on Appledore I., 18 Aug 1998 (D. Holmes), and two individuals on 9 Sep 2005 (S. Mirick), both notably early. High counts on Monhegan I.: 75 on 25 Sep 1982, 150 on 28 Sep 1983 (both DWF), 300 on 29 Sep 1995 (B. Nikula), 50 on 14 Oct 2003 (S. Mirick), 315 on 12 oct 2014 (L. Seitz et al., eBird). Flocks of 50–75 birds regular inland. In Turner, 200 birds on 7 Oct 1997 unusual but 1,000 birds at same locality, 26 Sep 1998 unprecedented (J. Despres, NAB 53: 34). Other notable coastal counts: 200 in Portland, 10 Oct 2003 (G. Neavoll); >200 in Yarmouth, 12 Oct 2004 (D. Lovitch); 30 at Roque Bluffs S.P., 25 Oct 2010 (D. Nickerson); 50 at Sandy Pt., Cousins I., 11 Oct 2017 (B. Marvil, eBird). Species remains in n. ME until early Oct: >8 seen in Woodland, 7 Oct 2004, and 28 on 14 Oct 2012 (both WJS, eBird). By late Oct, most sparrows

have flown south of ME; occasional flocks reported into early Nov: in Portland, 115 on 24 Oct 2005 (G. Neavoll), 125 on 29 Oct 2003 (D. Lovitch), 27 on 1 Nov 2006 (R. Eakin), and 45 on the Eastern Promenade, 16 Nov 2013 (N. Gibb, eBird); and on Monhegan I., 53 on 2 Nov 2010 (T. Magarian, eBird).

WINTER: White-throated Sparrows generally uncommon in winter, primarily found at feeding stations in coastal Maine where CBCs annually record small numbers (1–40 individuals). This sparrow occasionally remains in substantial numbers: hundreds reported on CBCs, winter 1976–1977: Biddeford (319), Portland (115), Jonesport area (192), Mount Desert I. (270). Unusually large numbers also reported 1980–1981 CBCs, largest counts on Mount Desert I. (145) and Machias Bay (146). In general, fewer sparrows reported from interior Maine: Orono–Old Town (61); Waterville (28); Augusta (47); Farmington (18); Danforth, Washington Co. (20); Calais (30); Eastport (19). Irregular farther north: Presque Isle (seen on ~10% of counts, maximum 4), Dover-Foxcroft (10%, 10). A single bird wintered in Greenville, Dec 1952–Mar 1953, unusually far north. Given this species' habit of remaining near feeders in populated areas, one in Dixmont, Penobscot Co., 29 Jan 1990 was "particularly interesting because this was a 'wild' bird, seen deep in the woods in its normal summer habitat. The nearest available feeder was 1 to 1-1/2 miles away" (B. Barker). Similarly, report of 8 individuals "in the wild" in a remote area of regenerating spruce-fir forest near W. Forks, Somerset Co., 25 Jan 2007, particularly unusual (T. Skaling). Few Aroostook Co. reports, 1 bird each, fide eBird: 4 Dec 2014 near Caribou (N. Hudak); 1 Jan 2016 on Hanson L. Rd., Presque Isle (obs. unk.); 31 Jan 2009 in Woodland (WJS). *PDV*

Vesper Sparrow
Pooecetes gramineus

Named for its sweet evening vespers to the setting sun

Status in Maine: Vesper Sparrows are an abundant summer resident on blueberry barrens in eastern Maine, and occur regularly on agricultural fields in Aroostook County. Local and uncommon in dry grassland habitats elsewhere. Uncommon spring migrants, they are generally seen in mid-April; during fall migration, they occur throughout September and into mid-October. The species is extremely rare in winter.

Historical Status in Maine: In the early 20th century, Knight felt Vesper Sparrows were common to abundant summer residents throughout ME. By 1949, Palmer thought this species was fairly common in Kennebec and Androscoggin Cos. only and was

Baltimore Oriole
Icterus galbula

Brilliant orange Neotropical songbird of hardwood forests

Status in Maine: Baltimore Orioles are a common breeding species in southern Maine, with fewer birds Downeast and in northern Maine, where they are most frequent along river valleys. Spring migration occurs in May; fall migration lingers late August–October. Some orioles, especially first-year birds, survive Maine's winters by frequenting bird feeders.

Historical Status in Maine: Knight described Baltimore Orioles expanding northward with European settlement in the 1800s, arriving in Bangor area "about 1860" and "at least north to Lincoln" by 1908 (1908, 352). Palmer (1949, 508) reported Baltimore Orioles as "fairly common in coastal counties to Penobscot Bay and north to include the southern parts of Oxford, Franklin, Somerset, Penobscot, and perhaps southern Piscataquis, uncommon but regular in a few settled areas east of the Penobscot drainage, and of rare occurrence (not known to breed) on a few larger islands; two winter records." Birds observed in Presque Isle area by 1942 (Chamberlain 1949).

It is unclear whether the drastic decline of the oriole's preferred nesting tree, American Elm (*Ulmus americana*), from Dutch elm disease (*Ophiostoma* spp.) in the late 1960s affected Baltimore Oriole populations in ME. However, they are now frequent nesters in other deciduous trees, often aspens, in riparian areas.

Global Distribution: Nearctic. Breeds from NS west to AB, south through Mississippi R. Basin and Appalachian Mtns. to GA, LA, and AR. Nonbreeding in FL, Cuba, Jamaica, and s. Mexico, south to Colombia and Venezuela.

Remarks: Hybridization with Bullock's Oriole caused dispute over Baltimore Oriole as a separate species, and from 1983–1995 the two were lumped together as Northern Oriole.

SPRING: Common in suitable habitat. Migration late Apr–May, peak during middle 2 weeks May. High counts: 60 over 9 hours on Monhegan I., 14 May 1997 (PDV, eBird); 25 at Totman Cove, Sagadahoc Co., 15 May 2007 (R. Robinson, eBird); >20, Windham, 13 May 2005 (fide D. Lovitch); 16 at Brownfield Bog, 14 May 2009 (M. Oyler, eBird); 15 over 3 hours at Ft. Foster, 8

May 2015 (D. Doubleday, eBird); and 14 over 2 hours at Gilsland Farm, 28 May 2016 (T. Mazerall, eBird).

Baltimore Oriole

Earliest record cited by Palmer, 17 Apr 1922, Brunswick. Regular Apr sightings since: 1 in Readfield, Kennebec Co., 4 Apr 1999 (R. Spinney); 1 at Salisbury Cove, Mount Desert I., 7 Apr 1983 (C. Jellison, fide WJS); 1 male in Falmouth, 10 Apr 1957 (D. Payne, *MFO* 2[5]: 48); and 1 Eight Rod Rd., Augusta, 11 Apr 2006 (N. Famous). Birds typically arrive in Aroostook Co. 3rd week May; notably early: 1 in Ft. Kent, 29 Apr 1998 (G. Flagg, fide K. Gammons; *MBN* 11[1]: 22).

SUMMER: Reported throughout ME in summer, but more frequent in human-altered habitats, and, especially in n. ME, in riparian habitats with deciduous trees. Not found in coniferous or upland habitats. Remote, forested location records: 1 Black Pond–Deboullie Public Land, Aroostook Co., 5 Jun 1980 (J. Gibson, eBird); 1 on BBS Route 059, Baker L., Somerset Co., 2 Jul 1996 (S. Mierzykowski, eBird); and 1 T9 R9 WELS, Piscataquis Co., 31 May 2009 (J. Toledano, eBird). Nest building in Saco, 20 May 2017 (R. Hussey, eBird). Palmer recorded nests with eggs on 3 and 5 Jun and freshly fledged young on 21 Jun (1949). Contemporary records: 1 fledged immature Capisic Pd., Portland, 1 Jul 2000 (M. Resch and D. Donsker); 2 fledglings, Sheepscot, 5 Aug 1990 (J. Hamlin); unreported number of adults with young, week of 11 Jul 2000 Houlton, (L. Little, fide J. Walker).

Baltimore Orioles do not appear to breed on ME's offshore islands, but some Jul records: 1 at Matinicus Rock, 12 and 15 Jul 2009 (Project Puffin Data, eBird); 1 on Monhegan I., 22 Jul 2008 (P. Folsom, eBird) and 7 Jul 2015 (J. Fischer, eBird); and 1 on Seal I. NWR, week of 31 Jul 2006 (S. Walsh, eBird).

FALL: Migration mid-late Aug–Oct, peaking in Sep, stragglers into Nov. Timing later than indicated by Palmer: "Migration occurs in August, the species being scarce during the last ten days of that month" (1949, 508). Island records indicate 1994 migration peak: 23 banded on Appledore I., 2 Sep–7 Sep 1994 (fide D. Holmes), and 25 on Monhegan I., 26 Sep 1994 (PDV, m.ob.). High counts: Monhegan I., 50 on 27 Sep 2011 (D. Hitchcox, eBird), 40 on 6 Sep 1985 (PDV, eBird), and 35 on 25 Sep 1995 (B. Nikula, *MBN* 8[1]: 30); and 19 on Machias Seal I., 19 Sep 2005 (R. Eldridge, eBird). Late northern reports: 1 in Lincoln, 17 Oct 1977 (PDV), and juvenile male in Caribou, 11 Nov 2006 (fide WJS).

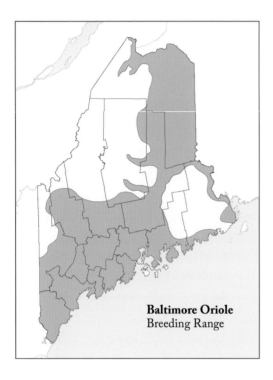

Baltimore Oriole
Breeding Range

WINTER: Palmer reported 2 winter records. Numerous s. ME observations since, mainly at bird feeders: bird visited J. Wyatt's feeder in Winterport, Waldo Co., 3 Nov 2012–23 Apr 2013. Species reported on 7 of 10 CBCs (2005–2016). Highest count in a year: 7 birds in 5 count circles.

RJV

Red-winged Blackbird

Agelaius phoeniceus

A loud, flashy harbinger of spring

Status in Maine: Red-winged Blackbirds are common breeding birds throughout Maine, with a preference for wetlands and open areas. A welcome messenger of spring, this species is one of the first migrants to return to Maine each year. Formerly entirely absent during winter, individuals now occasionally overwinter in the state. This familiar bird is declining at 2.6% annually on Maine Breeding Bird Surveys 1966–2017 (Sauer, pers. com.) and now is much less common than it once was.

Historical Status in Maine: Palmer (1949, 505) described Red-winged Blackbirds as "common to numerous" summer residents (except in densely forested parts of the interior) and "numerous" spring and fall migrants. Since Palmer's era, they arrive in ME earlier and depart later. Palmer listed 8–10 Mar as the earliest arrival dates and the latest known record as "one seen the week of the 14th [of November] in 1939, on offshore Monhegan (Mrs. J.A. Townsend)," making no mention of this species between Dec and Feb (1949, 506).

Global Distribution: Nearctic. Breeds from NL to YT and isolated patches in AK, south to NH, MI, n. WI and MN, MT, and interior BC. Year-round resident south to Costa Rica, with nonbreeding wintering population in nw. Mexico.

SPRING: First migrants appear mid-Feb; more typical arrival date early Mar. Adult males arrive first. Migration in n. ME occurs 1–4 weeks later, e.g.; Ft. Kent, 19 Mar 1982 (J. Gibson); compare: arrival Eliot, York Co., 4 Mar 1982 (N.B. Talbot). Notable: 1, Greenville, 15 Feb 1984 (P. Johnson and S. Roy); 6, Turner, 20 Feb 1981 (J. Despres); 3–4, Cherryfield, 21 Feb 1992 (J. Bush, fide G. Hazelton; *MBN* 5[2]: 45); and 4 males, Clinton, 27 Feb 2002 (W. Sumner). Aroostook Co. records: Houlton, 4 Mar 1979 (S. Rooney) and 5 Mar 2000 (L. Little, fide K. Gammons); and Presque Isle, week of 14 Mar 2006 (G. Flagg, fide K. Gammons).

Spring high counts include: 450, Sanford, 28 Mar 1957 (Prosser, *MFO* 2[4]: 36) and 500, Saco, 4 Apr 2014 (P. Moynahan, m.ob.; eBird).

SUMMER: Knight (1908, 346) wrote, "eggs are laid from as early as June first to as late as the first of July, usually in early June." Palmer added, "All data at hand indicate that, for the greater part, laying occurs during the first ten days of June throughout most of the state, although somewhat earlier in York and Cumberland Counties" (1949, 506).

Recent breeding records: 1 female ph. gathering nesting material at Capisic Pond, Portland, 19 May 2017 (R. Garrigus, eBird); 1 female observed carrying food in Brownfield Bog, 15 Jun 2016 (C. Nims, m.ob.; eBird); 1 female ph. carrying food in Bangor, 22 Jun 2017 (J. Smith, eBird); recently fledged individual ph. on Sanford Lagoons, 18 Jul 2017 (A. Aldrich, eBird); and 2 recently fledged birds ph. on Little Eddy Pond, Topsham, 22 Jun 2017 (M. Barker, eBird). A fledgling observed and ph. begging for food, Parsonsfield, York Co., 23 Jul 2017 (S. Wilcox, eBird).

In late summer, Red-winged Blackbirds sometimes form large foraging flocks: e.g., ~500 in cornfield in Turner, 20 Aug 1993 (J. Despres), and ~3,100 feeding in wild rice at mouth of Abagadassett R., Bowdoinham, 28 Aug 2017 (H. Heuer, eBird).

Orange-crowned Warbler

Leiothlypis celata

A northern boreal and western migrant

Status in Maine: Orange-crowned Warblers are occasional spring migrants in May and uncommon during fall in late September and October. Formerly casual in winter, the species is now more regular with at least 16 records since 1992. Earlier assertions of nesting in Maine are unsubstantiated and almost certainly incorrect (see *Remarks*). There are four subspecies but only the eastern form of Orange-crowned Warbler (*O. c. celata*) has been reported in Maine.

Historical Status in Maine: Knight listed Orange-crowned Warblers as hypothetical but provided no specific records. He suggested that Audubon was in error when he indicated this species bred in e. ME. Palmer listed three fall records.

Global Distribution: Nearctic. Eastern race breeds from cen. QC and s. NL to cen. ON and AK. Winters primarily south from VA, to Gulf Coast, cen. CA south to Guatemala and El Salvador.

Remarks: See Tennessee Warbler *Remarks*, p. 538, regarding genus classification.

There is no clear evidence Orange-crowned Warblers ever bred in ME, despite Audubon's (1834) and Chapman's (1907) assertions. Chapman (1907, 87) stated that the species was "once found breeding at Brunswick, Maine," apparently on the basis of a nest found in Brunswick. Knight (1908, 652–653) clarified these misconceptions: "Audubon records the species as breeding in eastern Maine, but it seems very likely it is a mistake, and subsequent writers have so regarded his statement. There is said to be a set of eggs in the Smithsonian Institution which were collected near Brunswick, Maine, and referred to as this species' but the data from the set seems to be lacking, and I am more inclined to believe that the Nashville Warbler is the really responsible species for our Orange-crowned Warbler records." A detailed study of N. Am. warblers (Dunn and Garrett 1997) shows the southern limit of the Orange-crowned Warbler's eastern breeding range to be north of St. Lawrence R. in cen. QC and NL, ~900 km (~560 mi.) north of Brunswick. The likelihood of breeding in Brunswick is remote.

SPRING: Occasional in spring in coastal ME east to Steuben. At least 40 records since 1952; 7 or more Monhegan I. records, with 3 birds recorded in 1997 (PDV et al.). Reported from Petit Manan NWR on 4 occasions, 1987–1996 (R. Widrig). Species usually observed throughout May, most common in latter half of month, 15–31 (>22 records). Three Apr records, 1 bird each: Waldoboro, Lincoln Co., 6 and 11 Apr 1998 (S. Russell, D. Mairs); Lisbon, Androscoggin Co., 19 Apr 1952; and Biddeford, 21 Apr 2001 (C. Dauphin et al.). Late migrant found dead in Ogunquit, 3 Jun 1956 (specimen in Portland Museum of Natural History). Unusually far north and inland records: 1, Pleasant R. Plt., Piscataquis Co., 26 May 1957 (*MFO* 2: 60); 1 singing in Lincoln Ctr., 25 May 1976 (PDV); 1 in Viles Arboretum, Augusta, 13 May 2015 and 9 May 2017 (D. Suitor and M. Veins et al., respectively).

FALL: Uncommon fall migrants, primarily along coast. First migrants appear early Sep, main migration takes place 20 Sep–Oct, diminishing by 10 Nov. Five recorded on Appledore I., 24 Oct 1972 (DWF); and 4 observed on Monhegan I., 30 Sep 1978 (DWF) and 13 Oct 1982 (PDV), with a total of 11 individuals seen 13–15 Oct 1982 (PDV), a fall when 20 were seen in NS and 23 in MA (*AB* 37: 158). Found on highest number of ME eBird checklists (2%) week of 8 Oct. Latest Monhegan I. record: 22 Nov 2011 (D. Hitchcox, eBird). Notably less common inland, particularly noteworthy first ME record reported by W. Brewster at Pine Pt., Magalloway Plt., Oxford Co., 2 Sep 1898 (Palmer 1949). W. Drury reported third ME record on Mt. Bigelow, Dead R. Plt., Somerset Co., 12 Oct 1941 (Palmer 1949). Other inland records: 1 captured in Bangor, 13 Oct 1934 (Palmer 1949), and another in Bangor, 9–10 Sep 1957; 1 at Duck L., Springfield, late Sep 1975 (PDV). One in Dixmont, Penobscot Co., 30 Sep 1988 (B. Barker); 1 in Turner, 4–5 Oct 2000 (J. Despres); and 2 in Wilton, 17–25 Sep 2001 (J. Dwight). Recent inland records from Brownfield Bog; Saxl Park, Bangor; and Unity. Late inland record: 2, Saxl Park, Bangor, 12 Nov 2015 (R. Ostrowski, eBird).

WINTER: At least 22 winter records since 1952. First winter record in Bar Harbor, Dec 1952–30 Apr 1953 (G. Berry, *MFN* 9[2]: 42). Species casual in winter prior to 1992 (6 records). Since 1992, species more regular and considered occasional; at least 16 records, primarily at feeding stations near coast, easternmost in Machias through Feb 1998 (P. Donahue). Particularly rare inland occurrences, 1 bird each: Auburn, Androscoggin Co., 1–17 Dec 1994 (T. Hayward, J. Despres); and Two-penny Bridge Trail, Kennebec Co., 11–12 Dec 2013 (L. Bevier, D. Mairs, M. Veins; eBird). Reported from 6 CBCs, 2009–2016, and York Co. CBC at Eldridge Rd., Wells, in 2017.

PDV

Nashville Warbler

Leiothlypis ruficapilla

A ground-nesting warbler of abandoned fields, clear-cuts, and second-growth forest

Status in Maine: Common spring warblers first appearing early to mid-May, Nashville Warblers breed throughout the state in a variety of habitats. Numbers may fluctuate with insect infestations and, while the North American population has not appreciably changed since 1966, there were significant decreases of Nashville Warblers in Maine, 1966–2015, and especially in the decade 2005–2015 (3.0% and 4.6%, respectively) after a Spruce Budworm outbreak subsided. Nashvilles are regular fall migrants through September. No December records prior to 2015.

Historical Status in Maine: Both Knight and Palmer considered Nashville Warblers common breeders throughout ME, and common spring and fall migrants. The status of this species in the state has not changed appreciably since Knight's writing.

Global Distribution: Nearctic. Disjunct breeding populations: eastern subspecies (*L. r. ruficapilla*) breeds in scrubby second-growth woodlands from s. QC and Maritime Provinces, west to MB and SK, south to New England and WV. Western subspecies (*L. r. ridgwayi*) breeds primarily from AB, w. MT, south to cen. CA. Winters from s. TX and Mexico to El Salvador.

Remarks: See Tennessee Warbler *Remarks*, p. 538, regarding genus classification.

SPRING: Common spring migrants, appearing early to mid-May, sometimes 3–12 birds/day. Most arrive s. and cen. ME 4–16 May. Found on highest number of ME eBird checklists (13%) week of 8 May. Migration in Aroostook and Penobscot Cos. somewhat later. At least 10 late Apr records, earliest: 3 in Fryeburg, 20 Apr 1968 (obs. unk.), and 1 in N. Berwick, 24 Apr 2011 (A. Aldrich, eBird). Unusual concentrations: 15 on Monhegan I., 17 May 2005 and 20 in E. Machias, 12 May 2005 (E. Raynor). Migrants on Monhegan I. seen as late as 30 May 2006 (B. Boynton).

SUMMER: Breeds throughout ME (*ABBM*, Adamus 1987) in variety of habitats: mixed forest, edges, and fields; borders of sphagnum bogs; in conifer clearings and groves, especially Balsam Fir ; and second-growth deciduous trees, such as birch and aspen.

Nashville Warbler populations can increase dramatically during insect infestations. BBS data reveal an annual increase of 8.7%, 1966–1979, during a significant Spruce Budworm outbreak in ME, n. New England, and surrounding Canadian provinces. In ME and NH in 1982–1983, Crawford and Jennings (1989) found Nashville Warbler stomachs contained an average of 3.5 budworms/stomach and estimated >10,000 budworms/ ha were consumed throughout nesting season. The budworm outbreak subsided in early 1980s; not surprisingly, Nashvilles declined annually by 1.9%, 1980–2005 (Sauer et al. 2017). Longer term Nashville populations in ME significantly declined by 3% annually but have not changed appreciably across N. Am (BBS data 1966–2015, Sauer et al. 2017).

FALL: Fall migration protracted, late Aug–early Oct. Species normally seen with other migrant warblers. Found on highest number of ME eBird checklists (7%) week of 22 Sep. In Bancroft, s. Aroostook Co., often most common fall warbler third week Aug–Sep, occasionally form single species flocks, and >8/day regularly observed (J. McDonald). In s. coastal ME, >4–6 birds uncommon in a day. On Monhegan I., 1–4 usually recorded daily in Sep, early migrant 29 Aug 2006 (B. Boynton). Six birds on 12 Sep 1982 (PDV) and 8 reported on 3 Oct 2003 (WJS). Earliest migrant in York Co.: Biddeford Pool, 23 Aug 2005 (B. Coullon). Main southward passage abates by Oct; minimum 30 late records notably: 3 on Hawk Mtn., Waterford, 18 Oct 1984 (P. Richards); 1 at Petit Manan NWR, 27 Oct 1988 (R. Widrig); and 1, Turner, 17 Oct 1996 (J. Despres). More than 20 Nov records, most in s. coastal ME. Notably late inland record: single bird in Augusta, 4 Nov 1989 (G. Therrien).

WINTER: 4 Dec records including 1 bird, Saco Riverwalk, York Co., 24 Nov–27 Dec 2015 (m.ob., eBird).

PDV and JVW

Virginia's Warbler

Leiothlypis virginiae

A southwestern warbler of piñon-juniper and oak woodland

Status in Maine: Accidental. There are four photographically documented records, all from Monhegan Island. An adult was photographed 21 May 1998 (G. Dennis, ph.; *FN* 52: 307 and 405, *MBN* 11: 18–19); a second individual seen 28–30 September 2006 (V. Laux; ph. L. Masters, image on file); a possible female, near Burnt Head, 8 November 2011 (D. Hitchcox, ph.with eBird checklist); and one at Lobster Cove Trailhead, 29–30 May 2014 (G. Willow, m.ob., ph. with eBird checklist).

Global Distribution: W. Nearctic. Breeds sporadically from w. WY and s. ID, south to w. TX, NM, AZ, UT, and s. CA. Winters in w. Mexico. There is one record each from RI (2006) and upstate NY (2016). No records for QC, Maritime Provinces, or NFLD.

Remarks: See Tennessee Warbler *Remarks*, p. 538, regarding genus classification.

Global Conservation Status: PIF: Watch List due to population declines and moderate to high threats.
JVW

Connecticut Warbler
Oporornis agilis

A geographically misnamed species of northern bogs and muskeg

Status in Maine: Connecticut Warbler is a casual spring and uncommon to occasional fall migrant, primarily along Maine's southern coast and outer islands. It has not been recorded in Aroostook County.

Historical Status in Maine: Knight and Palmer both listed nine records between 1878 and 1906. Palmer added a single record in Kennebunk, 7 Sep 1946. The first ME record was collected in Cape Elizabeth, 30 Aug 1878 (Knight 1908).

Global Distribution: E. Nearctic. Breeds locally in s. QC, west to ON, AB, and BC, south to n. MI, WI, and n. MN. Winters in S. Am., largely east of the Andes. Reported from all New England states, NFLD, and Maritimes Provinces.

Global Conservation Status: PIF: Watch List due to population declines and moderate to high threats.

Remarks: Often under-detected by field observers unfamiliar with the habitat preferences and skulking behavior of this species. Given that Palmer noted only a single report of this species, 1906–1949, and that there have been >100 subsequent observations, it seems the species was likely present, especially in fall, but unreported by observers of Palmer's era.

SPRING: A casual spring migrant; at least 8 records since 1954, all on coast. Appears as late migrant mid-May to early Jun. First record, a female banded in Bar Harbor, 4 Jun 1954 (obs. unk). One found dead in Ogunquit, 3 Jun 1956 (*MFO* 1: 75). Three Monhegan I. records since 1997: 1, 25 May 1997 (*Guillemot* 27: 28); 1, late May 1999 (*NAB* 53: 260); and 1, 17 May 2003 (R. Eakin, *Guillemot* 33: 29). Additional records: 1 male, Portland,

11 May 1991 (*AB* 45: 419); 1, Great Chebeague I., Cumberland, Cumberland Co., 15 May 2000 (C. Tubbesing); and 1, Brothers I., Washington Co., 9 Jun 2008 (L. Harter and D. Vander Pluym, eBird).

FALL: Nearly annual fall migrants, primarily along coast and outer islands. Reported 20 Aug–5 Oct, peak 5–20 Sep. Recent coastal records, fide eBird: 2, Machias Seal I., 28 Sep 2005 (R. Eldridge); 1, Metinic I., 3 Oct 2011 (a banding capture; N. Stryker); Monhegan I., 1 each, 7 Sep 2001, 21 and 23 Sep 2011, 21 Sep and 5 Oct 2016, and 28 Sep 2017 (m.ob.); and 1 Sandy Pt., Cousins I., 9 Sep 2017 (D. Lovitch). Since 1986, 3–9 individuals banded nearly annually on Appledore I.; peak 10–15 Sep (D. Holmes, S. Morris). Late records, all single birds: Scarborough, 11 Nov 2017 (N. Perlut); Monhegan I., 5–8 Oct 2001 (B. Boynton); and 3–5 Oct 2003 (D. Abbott, DWF). Maximum of 10 inland records: 1, Skowhegan, 19 Sep 1957; 1, Lincoln Ctr., 19 Sep 1977 (PDV); 1, Old Town, Penobscot Co., 18 Sep 1970; 1, Ward Hill, Unity, 18 Sep 2016 (T. Aversa, eBird); 1 banded in Orono, 16 Sep 1958 (*MFO* 3: 109); 1 in Turner, both 15 Sep 1991 and 16 Sep 2000 (J. Despres); and 1, Millinocket, 1–2 Sep 1973 (R. Conn).
PDV

MacGillivray's Warbler
Geothlypis tolmiei

A skulker from the western mountains

Status in Maine: Accidental. This often difficult-to-identify species is found in fall and early winter. The Maine Bird Records Committee has accepted four records of MacGillivray's Warbler. Maine's first, an immature bird found by E. Hynes, was extensively photographed and seen by many observers at Gilsland Farm from 19–22 December 2009. There are three records of immature birds mist-netted and photographed separately at banding stations, the first at Petit Manan Point on 12 September 2010 (C. Runco, Doran); one on 27 September 2010 and another not yet considered by the Maine Bird Records Committee on 28 September 2011, both at Metinic Island (A. Leppold). These September records represent early dates for vagrant MacGillivray's Warblers in the northeastern U.S. (Persons et al. 2015). The final record was a bird seen and recorded in Kettle Cove, Cape Elizabeth, 27–29 November 2015 (D. Lovitch, L. Seitz, D. Hitchcox et al., fide L. Bevier *BO*; 45: 103).

Historical Status in Maine: Neither Knight or Palmer mentioned this species.

Global Distribution: Primarily w. Nearctic. Breeds from s. YT south through s. coastal AK, BC, and sw. AB, south to CA, AZ, and NM; small, isolated breeding population in n. cen. Mexico. Winters from Mexico south to Costa Rica. Species has occurred as a vagrant across many e. U.S. states and Canadian provinces. Documented in MA, CT, NY, NS, and ON. *JVW*

Mourning Warbler

Geothlypis philadelphia

An early colonizer of disturbed habitat

Status in Maine: Given this species' proclivity for recently disturbed habitats in forested landscapes, Mourning Warbler populations have undoubtedly varied with natural disturbance events and Maine's forest management. In the late 1970s and 1980s, Mourning Warblers were common breeders throughout Maine except south of Bangor on the coastal plain. However, the species is now rare or locally common across its breeding range. Mourning Warblers are uncommon spring migrants and among the last to arrive, between 25 May and 5 June. Fall migration is more protracted, beginning in August, continuing through September, peaking 26 August–5 September. There are no winter records.

Historical Status in Maine: It is remarkable that Knight never saw or heard a Mourning Warbler himself (1908, 554). Citing various authorities, he indicated that the species was common in Aroostook Co., a rare summer resident in Franklin and Washington Cos., and rare in Cumberland Co., and "not uncommon" as a migrant in Sagadahoc Co. Palmer considered the species generally uncommon from Oxford Co. to Aroostook Co. and rare in e. ME. It should be noted that there were no recent major forest disturbances when Knight and Palmer were preparing their books.

Breeding abundance has changed substantially in ME in the past 30 years. Habitat in n. and e. ME altered dramatically as a result of Spruce Budworm outbreak in mid-1970s to mid-1980s, when larvae decimated many hectares of fir and spruce. Dead and moribund trees were harvested, leaving extensive clear-cuts quickly replaced by cherry trees and raspberry tangles. Mourning Warblers bred abundantly in successional habitats, becoming common in n., w., and e. ME. Around Moosehead L., they were common, especially

in regenerating deciduous and coniferous clear-cuts 5–10 years post-harvest. Currently uncommon to rare near Moosehead L. due to fewer clear-cuts, herbicide control of brambles and deciduous shrubs and trees, and spruce-fir regeneration.

Global Distribution: Nearctic. Breeds from NFLD, west through boreal Canada to ne. YT, south to cen. ME, cen. NH and VT, and in higher elevation sites of NY, PA, locally in WV. Winters primarily in Costa Rica, Panama, and n. S. Am.

Mourning Warbler

SPRING: Uncommon spring migrants usually seen individually and occasionally in small groups (2–3). Typically found in dense thickets and brushy areas, but males regularly sing from exposed perches. Particularly late migrants, most birds arrive late May–early Jun. Banding records on Appledore I. exemplify pattern: since 1983, 5 birds banded 5–20 May; 33 netted 21–25 May; >125 banded 26–31 May; >136 individuals 1–5 Jun; >42 individuals banded 6–10 Jun (all fide D. Holmes); and 13 birds on 1 Jun 1990 (D. Holmes, *AB* 44: 1115). Most frequently included on eBird checklists (1.4%) weeks of 22 May and 1 Jun. Palmer listed only 3 occurrences prior to 20 May, all 16–18 May. Since 1980, >11 records prior to 20 May, earliest 15 May, E. Machias, 1980 (N. Famous); and Portland, 2000 (P. Moynahan). Inland: 1 in Flint Woods, Farmington, 18 May 2018 (S. Cronenweth, eBird); Rangeley, 18 May 2017 (D. Lovitch); and 2, Colby Arboretum, Mayflower Hill, 20 May 2015 (P. Blair, eBird). Other late migrants south of known breeding range include: 1 female in Richmond, 13 Jun 2000 (PDV); 1 on Monhegan I., 7 Jun 2005 (B. Boynton); and 1 in Freeport, 9 Jun 2006 (D. Lovitch).

Mourning Warblers arrive throughout ME simultaneously, unlike many wood-warblers that have northward migrations of 7–10 days through ME. Early Aroostook Co. migrants: Woodland, 18 May 1999 (WJS); Ft. Kent, 24–29 May (G. and S. Flagg, no year provided); Caribou, 28–30 May 2004 (WJS); and Mapleton, 29 May 1985 (G. M. Stadler). Other migration records: Canaan, Somerset Co., 23–27 May 1999 (WJS); Turner,

21 May 2002 and 22 May 1995 (J. Despres). Species more local in e. ME but reported in E. Machias, 15 May 1980 (N. Famous); in Brooksville, Hancock Co., 22 May 2004 (L. Thorpe); and Winter Harbor, 24 May 2001 (W. Townsend).

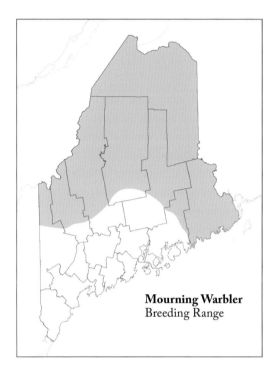

Mourning Warbler
Breeding Range

SUMMER: Breed in low brushy thickets, particularly raspberry tangles. Species quickly occupies forested areas that have been disturbed by fire, insect outbreaks, harvesting and wind damage. Confirmed breeding in 30 blocks in *ABBM*, primarily in Aroostook, n. Piscataquis, n. Somerset, w. Oxford, Washington, and e. Hancock Cos. (Adamus 1987). Confirmed south to Minot, Androscoggin Co. (Adamus 1987), and once a regular, but local, summer resident in Turner, where breeding was confirmed in 1982 (J. Despres).

Mourning Warbler is now local and uncommon throughout breeding range in ME, except in Aroostook Co., where more numerous but still local: 12 males recorded in Aroostook NWR, Limestone, 28 Jun 2005 (WJS). BBS data shows a non-significant decline for this species in ME and U.S., 1966–2015, but a significant 1.2% decline survey-wide during the same timeframe when data from Canada are included.

FALL: First fall migrants appear along coast in early Aug, main migration is protracted 16 Aug–15 Sep, with peak in late Aug–early Sep. Exceptionally early migrants, or wandering individuals, found by Cruickshank in Greenland Cove, Bremen, Lincoln Co., 29 Jul 1936 (Cruickshank 1950a) and also Muscongus, 23 Jul 1956 (A. Cruickshank). Appledore I. banding records show migratory peak 26–31 Aug (>110 banded) and 1–5 Sep (>90 banded). Found on highest number of eBird checklists (0.8%) week of 22 Sep. More likely seen in small concentrations in fall than in spring: 5 on Wreck I., Muscongus Bay, 25 Aug 1952, considered unusual (fide Cruickshank); and 10 on

Monhegan I., 16 Sep 1982 exceptional (DWF). Rare after 5 Oct; single bird in Turner, 7 Oct 1988, notable inland (J. Despres). Late records on Monhegan I.: 3 Oct 2014 (D. Hitchcox, eBird); 9 Oct 2001 and 14 Oct 2003 (both B. Boynton); 14 Oct 2012 and 2013 (both D. Hitchcox); 20 (2 birds) and 21 Oct 1918 (Jenney 1918). Late Matinicus I. record: 1 bird on 30 Sep 2017 (M. Fahay, eBird). Single bird on Roque I., Jonesport, 17 Oct 2003 (N. Famous), and in Lubec on 15 Sep 2017 (P. Janzen, eBird) unusually late for Washington Co.

PDV

Kentucky Warbler
Geothlypis formosa

A distinguished and bespectacled southern visitor

Status in Maine: Kentucky Warblers are casual spring and fall vagrants, with approximately 30 records for each season. Reported from coastal Maine east to Cutler, they are rare inland. There are only two summer records for Maine.

Historical Status in Maine: This species is not listed in Knight or Palmer.

Global Distribution: E. Nearctic. Breeds from s. NY, PA, west to MI, south to n. FL and TX. Winters primarily in Mexico, Cen. Am., and n. Colombia and Venezuela, uncommon in Caribbean. Reported from all New England states, Maritime Provinces, and NFLD.

Global Conservation Status: PIF: Watch List due to population declines and moderate to high threats.

SPRING: More than 30 spring Kentucky Warbler records since 1959, primarily along southern coast east to Stonington. One Apr record identified and described at W. Head, Cutler, 20 Apr 1996 (E. Kindahl et al., *MBN* 9: 27, *FN* 50: 257). Only other spring Washington Co. records: Petit Manan NWR, 24 May 1987 (*AB* 41: 404), and Seal I. NWR, 13 May 2017 (K. Yakola). About 10 records for early May, including 1 bird 6–7 May 2011 (T. Magarian). More typically appear 16–31 May; >20 records during this period. Late vagrants reported from Stonington, 4 Jun 1959 (obs. unk.), and male seen on Matinicus Rock, 9 Jun 2003 (fide V. Lane). Two inland records: 1 in Livermore, Androscoggin Co., 19–20 May 1959 (obs. unk.), and 1 specimen killed by a house cat in Dixmont, Penobscot Co., 1 May 1980 (spec. identification confirmed G. Freese, PDV).

SUMMER: 2 summer records, single birds, both inland: male, Big Lyford Pond, Kokadjo, Piscataquis Co., 9 Jul 1960 (obs. unk.); singing male in Canaan, Somerset Co., 17 Jun 1995 (W. Sumner, *FN* 49: 910).

FALL: Thirty or more fall records since 1952, mostly coastal. First ME record described in Saco, 12 Oct 1952 (*BMAS* 9: 70). At least 13 records, all in late Aug, from Appledore I.; 9 birds banded there since 1974 (D. Holmes). Remaining records reported primarily late Aug–15 Sep. Three records for Mount Desert I.; 2 banded in Somesville, 1 each in Aug 1974 and Aug 1975, and 1 at Sieur de Monts Spring, Bar Harbor, late Sep 1998 (*NAB* 52: 33). Other records for e. ME, all single birds: earliest presumed fall migrant record, Aurora, Hancock Co., 11 Aug 1980; Petit Manan NWR, 28 Aug 2015 (L. Cannon, A. Leppold. eBird); 1 banded in Cutler, 12 Sep 1996 (J. Broka, *FN* 1: 27). One, Hermit I., Phippsburg, Sagadahoc Co., 30 Aug 2017 (I. Turner, eBird); 1 lingered at Biddeford Pool, 6–10 Sep 2013 (m.ob., eBird). Only inland occurrence in fall was immature bird in Somerville, Lincoln Co., 25 Aug 1993 (J. Fiore, *Guillemot* 22: 35). A bird caught by a cat in St. George, Knox Co., 3 Nov 1976 (obs. unk.) constitutes the latest fall record.

PDV

Common Yellowthroat
Geothlypis trichas

Vociferous, black-masked balls of energy

Status in Maine: The Common Yellowthroat is a common to abundant summer resident in brushy, semi-open habitats, and a common spring and fall migrant. In winter, it is occasional along the south coast and rare along the central and eastern coast, but it has not been reported north of Bangor.

Historical Status in Maine: Both Knight and Palmer considered Common Yellowthroats to be common summer residents throughout the state, as they are currently.

Global Distribution: Nearctic. Breeds in boreal Canada from NFLD west to YT, throughout U.S., and cen. Mexico. Winters from NC and Gulf states, south to Caribbean and Cen. Am., west to CA.

SPRING: Migration more protracted than most warblers. Males arrive first week of May; main flight builds through May, peaking 21–31 May and diminishing first 2 weeks of Jun. On Appledore I., over a decade banded yellowthroats increased from >2,500 birds, 10–20 May; to >5,000 individuals, 21–31 May; decreasing to 600, 1–10 Jun. Highest inclusion on eBird checklists (46%) the week of 15 May. Exceptional flight: 1,000 birds, Machias Seal I., 6 Jun 2006 (R. Eldridge).

Earliest Apr records: 1, Cape Porpoise, York Co., 12 Apr 2004 (D. Doubleday); 1, Fryeburg, 20 Apr 1968 (obs. unk.); and 1, Cape Neddick, 20 Apr 2006 (L. Scotland). Unusually early

inland Apr records include: 1, Belgrade, Kennebec Co., 30 Apr 1994 (D. Ladd, L. Brinker); 1, Atkinson, Piscataquis Co., 23 Apr 1979 (P. Johnson); and 1, Mercer, Somerset Co., 30 Apr 1998 (W. Sumner). In Aroostook Co., birds arrive Presque Isle, 11–21 May (M. Trombley); Chamberlain reported early migrant on 9 May (Palmer 1949). As noted, migration continues late May–Jun; >20 individuals seen on Monhegan I., 29 May 1983 (S. Tingley); on Appledore I., 22 banded first week of Jun 1985 (D. Holmes, *AB* 39: 888). Spinney, the Seguin I. lighthouse keeper, reported "many" as late as 7 Jun (Palmer 1949, 492). Banded birds are regularly recaptured on Appledore I.: 1 initially banded as hatch-year male, 19 Aug 1990, was re-trapped 29 May 1992, 30 Aug 1992, 14 May 1993, and 9 Jun 1997 (D. Holmes). An adult banded Aug 1987 was re-trapped 10 Sep 1993, the oldest Appledore-banded yellowthroat ever recaptured there (S. Morris, D. Holmes, *AB* 48: 89).

Common Yellowthroats sometimes occur in substantial numbers. On Appledore I., 117 banded, 19 May 1992 (D. Holmes, AB 46: 396), and 186 banded with additional >50 birds released unbanded, 13 May 1993 (D. Holmes, *AB* 47: 396). At least 100 seen in Phippsburg, 12 May 1996, following major migratory fallout (PDV).

SUMMER: Abundant in wide variety of shrubby habitats, including wetlands, dry sandy areas, sub-alpine openings, peatlands, bogs, freshwater marshes, along river and lake margins, and in overgrown brushy pastures and openings in harvested forests throughout ME. Species less numerous, but still common, in heavily forested Aroostook, Piscataquis, Somerset, and Franklin Cos. Eighteen BBS in these counties recorded between 12–18 males in 1979 (D. Folger). One of 3 most common species confirmed by *ABBM* (Adamus 1987). BBS trend for 1996-2015 shows species has declined both in ME, 1.8%, and in N. Am., 1.0%.

FALL: Common, sometimes numerous, fall migrants in wide variety of brushy habitats. First migrants arrive on Appledore I. 10–20 Aug (550 or more banded during that period since 1992); migration remains steady 21 Aug–15 Sep with 360–510 birds banded per 5-day sampling period within those dates, before diminishing late Sep–early Oct. Reported from highest number of eBird checklists (20-22%) from 22 Aug through 22 Sep. Late birds on Monhegan I.: 20 birds, 25 Sep 1983 (D. Finch); 25, 26 Sep 1994 (PDV); and 25, 22 Sep 2004 (M. Iliff). Notable concentrations on mainland: 50, Ft. Kent, 1 Sep 1998 (G. Flagg); 50, Corea Heath, Gouldsboro, 6 Sep 1996 (N. Famous); and 19, Reid S.P., 23 Sep 2005 (C. Caron).

Palmer noted few Oct migrants but it is clear that the species occurs in small numbers along coastal ME through late Oct, even into Nov and Dec. Late inland records: 4 in New Sweden, Aroostook Co., 14 Oct 2006 (N. Hudak), and immature female, Canaan, Somerset Co., 3 Nov 1990 (W. Sumner). Notable Nov

in mature, thick coniferous forest. Palmer cited the summer status of Blackburnians as "uncommon to fairly common in all counties" (1949, 470). He considered it common in both spring and fall migration in w. ME, and common on the coast during spring migration but uncommon in the fall.

Global Distribution: Nearctic. Breeds from cen. AB, east to s. QC, south through ne. U.S. and Appalachian Mtns. to n. GA. Winters in n. S. Am. especially in mid-elevations of n. Andes.

SPRING: Relatively common and widespread migrant in small numbers. Migrates late Apr–late May. Small numbers continue to arrive on coast and offshore islands into first week of Jun. At least 5 Apr records: 1, S. Portland, 26 Apr 2011 (fide E. Hynes); 1, Oosoola Park, Norridgewock, 26 Apr 2014 (K. Brown, eBird); 1, Evergreen Cemetery, Portland, 27 Apr 2011 (S. Walsh, eBird); 1, Augusta, 29 Apr 2000 (N. Famous); and 1, Lovell, Oxford Co., 30 Apr 1990 (E. McNerney). More than 10 records first 5 days of May, 1980–2007. Palmer noted earliest arrival: 3 May 1942 in Brewer and 4 May 1905 in Portland and Skowhegan but normal arrival in s. ME ~8 May. From 1959–2007, >30 records of Blackburnian Warbler before 8 May. Spring maxima: 50 and 12, both on Monhegan I., 23 May 1999 (B. Boynton), and 27 May 2006 (L. Seitz); and 12, Stonington, 12 May 1959 (M. Hundley). Spring peak week of 22 May when 12% eBird checklists included this species.

Blackburnian Warbler

SUMMER: Widespread and locally common breeder, local in s. ME (*ABBM;* Adamus 1987). According to BBS, ME has third highest relative abundance in U.S. Highest counts: 45 and 37 on now-discontinued Northfield BBS (Washington Co.), 1980 and 1978; 37 on Cooper BBS (Washington Co.), 1978; and 35 on Wilson Mills BBS (Oxford Co., west of Rangely), 2008. Since 1989, Cooper BBS high count not above 5 birds. Wilson Mills recent highs: 10 birds, 2010 and 2014. ME BBS trends show slight decline of 0.7% per year 1966–2015. N. Am. BBS trends stable 1966–2015, 1.2% increase per year, 2005–2015.

FALL: Fall migration mid-Aug to Sep with occasional birds into late Oct. Reported from highest number of ME eBird checklist (3%) week of 15 Aug, highest counts weeks of 15 Aug and 1 Sep. Blackburnian Warblers typically counted during early morning crossing to mainland from Sandy Pt., Cousins I., ~0–3 (D. Lovitch et al.). Highest counts from Sandy Pt.: 15, 1 Sep 2009 (E. Hynes), and 8, 24 Aug 2013 (D. Lovitch). At other locations: 16 killed at ceilometer light, Portland airport, 17 Sep 1958 (C.M. Packard), and 15 in Petit Manan NWR, 15 Sep 1995 (R. Widrig). At least 20 Oct records, 1957–2018. Three latest Oct records: 2, Brewer, 23 Oct 1958 (Clish, *MFO* 3[11]: 120); 1, Monhegan I., 14 Oct 2003 (S. Mirick et al.); 1 East Pt., Biddeford Pool, 11 Oct 2005 (D. Lovitch, M. Iliff).

WINTER: A late Blackburnian Warbler on Saco Riverwalk, Biddeford, discovered 23 Nov, lingered to 27 Dec 2015 (N. Houlihan, J. Fecteau, m.ob.).

JVW

Yellow Warbler
Setophaga petechia

Widespread and well known, a sweet-singing warbler of shrubby edge habitats

Status in Maine: One of the most common and widespread breeding warblers in Maine, Yellow Warblers occur throughout the state in shrubby habitat, second-growth forest, and along rivers, streams, and lakes. Breeding Bird Survey data show a slight population decline in North America, 1966–2015. A significantly steeper decline occurred in Maine in the same period. Nonetheless, the Yellow Warbler remains a widespread and abundant spring and fall migrant. It is a relatively early spring migrant, arriving in late April and early May. In fall, migrant Yellow Warblers appear as early as July and are largely gone by September, though occasional individuals linger into October.

Maine Conservation Status: Species of Special Concern.

Historical Status in Maine: Knight considered Yellow Warblers one of the most common summer resident birds found throughout ME. Palmer wrote that the Yellow Warbler was a fairly common summer resident except "in areas of relatively unbroken forest" and that its numbers increased 1909–1949. Palmer also speculated that, "Before the forest was cut off, this warbler probably was restricted to nesting chiefly in young willows along watercourses and to sprout growth in burned-over areas" (1949, 458). He noted that both Carpenter (1886) and Bond (1947) considered Yellow Warblers to be most common around human settlements. Palmer considered it numerous in spring and fall migration.

Global Distribution: Nearctic. Breeding range encompasses most of N. Am.: AK (except North Slope), YT and NT, east to NL, south to n. GA, AL, and MS, and west to CA. Does not breed in TX and LA. Distinct "Mangrove" form breeds in s. FL. Many subspecies and forms breed from s. Mexico, across Caribbean. Winters from Mexico through Cen. Am. to n. S. Am. and Caribbean. Five Yellow Warblers fitted with light-level geolocators on Appledore I. in 2015 migrated to Columbia by way of Eastern Seaboard, Caribbean, and Cen. Am. (Witynski and Bonter 2018).

SPRING: Common and widespread spring migrant, often one of most abundant warbler species. Migration late Apr–late May. Many late Apr records. Although they may be correct, earliest reported observations (Apr 10, 11, 13, 20, 21) overlap with arrival of all-yellow eastern race of Palm Warbler and are not supported by any photos or other evidence. Earliest certain Yellow Warbler report: 2 birds on 25 Apr 2011, River Pt. Conservation Area, Falmouth (P. Keenan, R. Lambert; eBird). Maximum spring reports, all on Monhegan I. and, remarkably, all from 25 May over wide span of years: 50, 1990 (JVW and A. Wells); 40, 1983 (S. Tingley); and 25 on 25–26 May 2006 (D. Lovitch). Spring peak week of 15 May when highest number of ME eBird checklists (37%) include species.

SUMMER: Common and widespread breeding warbler in ME, occurs in shrubby field edges, along rivers, streams, lakes, and ponds, recently cut-over or burned forest, and abandoned hayfields with encroaching shrubs. Prefers low shrubs; will disappear from cutover forest as trees increase in size and from brushy fields if brush is removed. Along waterways, often found in low willows and alders.

Species ubiquitous along coast, in s. ME, and parts of St. John Valley in ne. ME; spotty distribution in areas with significant forest cover in western mountains, nw. ME, and interior Washington Co. Possibly related to less ABBM survey effort in nw. ME, no records from nearly entire w. Aroostook Co. and only a few records from n. Androscoggin Co. (Adamus 1987). Atlas of the Breeding Birds of Quebec (Gauthier and Aubrey 1996) shows similar spotty distribution of Yellow Warbler records in region bordering nw. ME. Representative maximum BBS counts: 35, in 1983, on Hermon BBS (Penobscot Co.); 30 in 1993, Boundary BBS (Aroostook Co.); and 26 in both 1993 and 1997 on Washburn BBS (Aroostook Co.). BBS trends for ME show significant decline of 3.3% per year from

1966–2015 and declining 5.2% per year 2005–2015. N. Am. BBS shows significant but less steep decline of 0.6% per year from 1966–2015.

FALL: Migration early Jul–Sep, peaks Aug–early Sep. Individual birds sometimes persist into Oct. Species reported from highest percentage of ME eBird checklists (15%) week of 1 Aug.

Maximum fall counts lower than many other warbler species with single location counts typically 1–5. Maxima: 15, Monhegan I., 25 Sep 1983 (DWF), and 15 in Turner on 19 Aug 1992 (J. Despres). Species found regularly lingering into Oct with at least 13 records. Latest records: 1, Cape Elizabeth, 25 Oct 2010 (PDV, J. Mays); 1 on Sandy Pt., Cousins I., 21 Oct 2000 (R. Garrigus, eBird); 6, Machias Seal I., 17 Oct 2005 (R. Eldridge); 1 on 13 and 18 Oct 1998 on Monhegan I. (B. Boynton). Palmer (1949) speculated late Yellow Warbler records may be a subspecies that nests in n. Canada. We are not aware of any research on whether this may be true of late ME Yellow Warbler records.

WINTER: 2 winter records, both Saco Riverwalk, Saco: 1, 8 Dec 2014 (N. Houlihan, eBird); 1–2 birds consistently 4–7 Dec 2015 and then 1 bird, 8–28 Dec 2015 (m.ob., eBird).
JVW

Chestnut-sided Warbler
Setophaga pensylvanica

A bird of early successional forest and shrubby edges

Status in Maine: The Chestnut-sided Warbler is an abundant breeding species throughout many scrubby edge habitats and forest openings in Maine, but has declined in abundance in the Northeast over the last 50 years. It is a common, and occasionally numerous, spring and fall migrant. Maine supports approximately 6% of the global breeding population of this species (Rosenberg and Wells 1995). There are no winter records in the state.

Maine Conservation Status: Species of Special Concern.

Historical Status in Maine: Both Knight and Palmer considered Chestnut-sided Warblers common breeders throughout ME. Palmer said that the species was apparently rare during Audubon's time and probably increased in abundance as mature woodlands were converted into the species' preferred second-growth, shrubby habitat.

Global Distribution: E. Nearctic. Breeds from s. QC and ON to cen. AB, south to n. IL, IN, and OH, through Appalachian Mtns. to n. GA and AL. Winters primarily in Cen. Am. from s. Mexico to Panama.

1 on 1 May 2004 at Boom Rd., Saco (L. Eastman); and 1 on 1 May 2004 at Brownfield Bog (J. Preis). At migration stopover sites, usually 1–2 birds at a time. Highest numbers at known or potential breeding sites: 15 on 6 May 2006 at Hurricane Rd., Falmouth (L. Seitz); 12 on 26 May 1998 along Rt. 236, Eliot, York Co. (B. Dorr); and 10 on 28 May 1992 at Kennebunk Plains (J. Despres et al.). Spring peak based on eBird checklists weeks of 8 May and 15 May, when 3–4% of checklists report species.

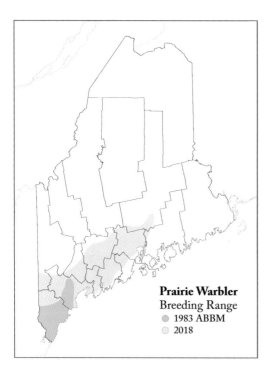

Prairie Warbler
Breeding Range
● 1983 ABBM
○ 2018

SUMMER: Southern breeding species, has rapidly expanded range northward through New England as part of larger trend of northward expansion noticed as early as 1930s in NY and continuing since (Nolan et al. 2014, Dunn and Garrett 1997, Bonney 1988, Palmer 1949). Species occurs in dry, Pitch Pine barrens and edges (e.g., Kennebunk Plains), and in shrubby powerline cuts, abandoned gravel pits, and similar habitats.

The 1987 ABBM showed species confined to ME's 2 southernmost counties and confirmed breeder in 9 atlas blocks (Adamus 1987). Singing male Prairie Warblers now found sparingly but regularly on territory from Naples, Somerset Co., to Turner and Sabattus, Androscoggin Co., eastward to Belgrade, Kennebec Co.; Sidney, Kennebec Co.; Augusta to Troy, Waldo Co., and south to Swanville, Waldo Co., and Belfast. Recently, males found along powerline cuts in Orrington, Penobscot Co., and N. Belfast (all fide eBird). Occasional in Somerset and Oxford Cos., fide eBird: unrecorded number at Fahi Pond WMA, Somerset Co., 29 Jun 2008 (J. Mays); 1 at Farrand Rd., Canton, Oxford Co., 17 and 19 Jun 2012 (both D. Wardwell); and 1 at Hastat Rd., Greenwood, Oxford Co., 3 Jun 2017 (J. Reddoch). Species recorded from 9 BBS routes with maximum of 7 on Westbrook (Cumberland Co.) in 2004 and 6 on Biddeford

(York Co.) in 1982 and 1988. Highest single location records, Kennebunk Plains: 34, 27 Jun 2006 (R. Heil), and 20, 30 Jun 1989 (JVW). Highest count elsewhere: 15 on 6 Jun 2006 along Hurricane Rd. power lines in Falmouth (L. Seitz). BBS trends show increase of 2.4% per year, 1966–2015, in ME, while N. Am. BBS shows significant decline of 1.85% per year, 1966–2015.

FALL: Migration primarily early Aug–Sep, with individual birds into Oct, 1 Nov record, and 3 Dec records. Reported from highest percentage of ME eBird checklists (2.4%) week of 22 Sep. Most records of just 1 or 2 birds. Higher counts: 18 on 27 Aug 2014 at Capt. William Fitzgerald Recreation and Conservation Area, Brunswick (G. Smith, fide eBird); 12, Mount Desert Rock on 8 Aug 1993 (T. Cole, fide Ann Bacon); 7 on 22 Sep 2003 (J. Walker); and 6 on 27 Sep 1997, both Monhegan I. (J. Markowsky). Few Prairie Warblers counted at Sandy Pt, Cousins I., where migrants cross to mainland in early morning; high of 7 on 10 Sep 2008 (obs. unk.). Species regularly found into Oct (>20 records), becoming rare after mid-Oct. One Nov record: 1, 10 Nov 1987 at Martinsville, Knox Co. (M. Plymire).

WINTER: 3 Dec records: 1 on 4 Dec 2005 at Ft. Foster (J. Walker); 1 on 18 Dec 1993 on Thomaston–Rockland CBC (fide W. Petersen); and 1 on 23 Dec 1996 on York Co. CBC (fide W. Petersen).
JVW

Black-throated Gray Warbler
Setophaga nigrescens

An almost monochromatic western bird with a dash of yellow

Status in Maine: Accidental. First recorded in 1936, the Black-throated Gray Warbler has made few appearances in Maine. There are certainly fewer than 10 records but there may have been more than three legitimate records in the last 30 years, making it possibly casual rather than accidental. The majority are fall observations.

Historical Status in Maine: Bagg and Eliot (1937, 784) provided the following details in their book *Birds of the Connecticut River Valley*, which appear to describe a male Black-throated Gray Warbler seen on Eagle I., Harpswell, on 18–19 May 1936. A. Marden "saw near his house a Warbler which he took at first glance for a Blackpoll, but he immediately noticed its black throat, the black below the eye, and white above the eye. Fetching his Portraits of New England Birds, he took it to the spot and got within five feet of the Warbler, clearly seeing 'the wee yellow spot by the eye.' Mrs. Marden corroborated the identification. They knew, of course, that they had never seen the species before, but did not know that it had never been recorded in Maine." It is noteworthy that Palmer (1949, 467) listed Black-throated Gray Warbler as hypothetical, writing, "of the Black-throated Grey Warbler, no later records have come to me than one on the Maine coast, May 18–19, 1936 (S. A. Eliot, Jr., 1938: 10). The manner in which this—the only alleged ME occurrence—is recorded in print is too vague and indefinite to accept unquestioningly." Palmer apparently ignored Bagg and Eliot (1937), as this volume is not cited in the bibliography to *Maine Birds*. In a Feb 1963 note from A.O. Gross, Bowdoin College ornithologist, to C. Packard, editor of *MFO*, Gross stated, "Palmer I know did not think much of the Birds of Conn. Valley by Bagg and Eliot so that may be the reason he ignored it. I must admit I overlooked it as I never thought of checking a Maine record in that book."

Global Distribution: W. Nearctic. Breeds from coastal AK and s. BC, to OR and s. WY, south to NM and n. Mexico. Winters primarily in Mexico. Reported from NFLD, NS, NB, QC, MA, CT, NH, and VT.

All records: Three photographic records: one at Biddeford Pool, 30 Sep 1998 (B. Schram, *NAB* 52: 33); one in Cape Elizabeth, 31 Oct–6 Nov 2005; and one, Appledore I., 8 Sep 2006 (S. Mirick, accepted by ME-BRC). A single bird on Mount Desert Rock, 31 Aug 1987, was carefully described by H. Corbett and from the description the warbler appeared to be an immature male: "Head dark gray—almost black, darker than back or tail which were dark gray; 2 white wing bars; black streaking at sides of breast; breast and belly white, no complete black breast band; white cheek patch and gular stripe… yellow lore spot [seen] on two occasions. Legs dark; eye was surrounded by black (the cheek patch was behind the eye). Probably a female (but not certain) as the black breast band was absent" (*MBN* 1: 35).

Additional sight records, one bird each: Waldoboro, Lincoln Co., 26 May 1952, seen at close range by J. Keene, probably valid but uncertain; immature, ME Coastal Is. NWR, Steuben, 10 Aug 2007, well described (*Guillemot* 37[4]: 38); and Cape Elizabeth, 1 Nov 2015 (P. Moynahan, B. Crowley, M. Zimmerman). *PDV*

Townsend's Warbler
Setophaga townsendi

A colorful treetop warbler from the Pacific Northwest

Status in Maine: Accidental. There are four fall and early-winter records in Maine for Townsend's Warbler, a distinctive wood-warbler that nests in the treetops of western North American forests. All records: male photographed on Monhegan Island, 13 September 1993 (H. Tetrault, T. Martin; ph. on file); female photographed at a feeder in Portland, 15 December 1993–5 January 1994 (*FN* 48: 184); juvenile male observed on Monhegan Island, 13– 21 September 1999 (H. Nielsen, T. Martin); and a bird in Winterport, Waldo County, 28 November 2012–March 2013 (J. Wyatt et al.; ph.).

A fifth record not accepted by the Maine Bird Records Committee is worth mentioning briefly. L. Seitz found what he believed to be a Townsend's Warbler among photos taken at Sandy Point, Yarmouth, on 26 September 2011. The photo is distant and somewhat blurry as the bird is moving and zooming causes graininess. Based on a single poor photo, the committee deemed the evidence too weak to support a definitive record. Nonetheless, the species is not well studied in the East. If more information becomes available, this record's credibility may change, and we would do well not to lose the data point.

Historical Status in Maine: Neither Knight or Palmer mentioned this species.

Global Distribution: Primarily w. Nearctic. Breeds in coniferous forests coastal and cen. AK, BC, s. AB to OR. Winters along Pacific coast of WA, OR, and CA to Mexico and Cen. Am. Species has occurred as vagrant in NFLD, NB, NS, MA, NH, RI, and VT, but has not been reported in QC or CT.
PDV

Hermit Warbler
Setophaga occidentalis

A rare visitor from Pacific coastal coniferous forests

Status in Maine: Accidental. There are two records: a young male photographed on Monhegan Island, 28 September–1 October 2008 (S. Surner, K. Lindquist, B. Marvil, et al.; ph. ME-BRC #2008-006), and a single bird in Harpswell, 18 November–13 December 2013 (Hewson, D. Lovitch).

IN, TN, TX, and CO, sporadically east to NY and PA. Winters primarily in Venezuela, also occurs in small numbers in n. coastal S. Am. and Mexico.

Remarks: Dickcissels bred in MA 1835–1877 (Veit and Petersen 1993), but there is no evidence they nested in ME during this period.

SPRING: Rare in spring; found most regularly on outer islands or along s. coastal ME. Early records, 5 Mar–Apr, probably individuals that joined migrant flocks of Red-winged Blackbirds and Common Grackles; 2 in Machias, 5 Mar 1970 (*MN* 1[10]: 7) particularly unusual. There are at least 10 Monhegan I. records of single birds between 26 Apr 1983 and 30 May 2017 (C. Lapierre, L. Seitz, and J. Trimble; eBird). There are 2 or more records for Appledore I., most recently, 17–19 May 1996 (D. Holmes). Rare inland records: 1 in Alexander, Washington Co., 3 May 1980 (J. Dudley); 2 in Bethel, 15 May 1983 (C. Gorman); 1 in Mt. Vernon, Kennebec Co., 2 Apr 2006 (J. Kinney); and 1 at Town Farm Rd., Thorndike, Waldo Co., seen intermittently 9–23 Mar 2016.

SUMMER: Few summer records: 1 in Brewer, 4 Jul 1954 (P. Clish, *BMAS* 10: 72); 1 in Camden, Knox Co., 12–22 Jul 1954 (*BMAS* 10: 72); and 1 in Lincolnville, Waldo Co., 18 Jun 1961 (Dailey, *MFO* 6: 66). Recent summer records, fide eBird: 1, Monhegan I., 17 Jul 2011 (T. Magarian); 1, Juniper Ledge, Yarmouth, 19 Jul 2011 (S. Walsh); and 1, Scarborough Marsh Pannes, 27 Jul 2016 (R. Lambert).

FALL: Migration begins mid-Aug. Early records: 1 in Falmouth, 7 Aug 2005 (C. Kent); 1 in Brunswick, 11 Aug 2005. Multiple records from 15–31 Aug with a maximum of 4 individuals in Cape Elizabeth, 21 Aug 1956 (*MFO* 1: 98). Numerous reports (usually 1–2 birds) from coastal ME in Sep–Nov. Small flocks on Monhegan I.: 7 in Sep 1956, 9 on 1 Sep 1957, 6 birds 25 Sep–2 Oct 1962, 18 birds 6–10 Sep 1970, >12 on 24 Sep 1995 (all V. Laux et al.), and 5 on 6 Oct 2005 (M. Iliff). More recent island reports: Monhegan I.: 1, intermittently, 11–27 Aug 2010 (T. Magarian, eBird), 29 Sep, and 1 Oct (both D. Lovitch); Seal I., 1, 8 Aug 2009 (Project Puffin, eBird), 1, 1–2 Aug 2015 (K. Yakola, eBird), and 2 on 24 Aug 2017 (I. Brofsky and K. Yakola, eBird).

An exceptional inland report from Wilton first 2 weeks of Sep 1965: "A flock of upwards of 50 Dickcissels were feeding upon an intervale field of ripening oats . . . I had not seen this species for several years, and because of the difficult nature of early-fall identification, was reluctant to believe our suspicions. However, after following the flock up and down the long narrow field on two different afternoons, we could accept no other possibilities" (J. Mudge et al. *MFN* 21: 17). Other inland records for single birds: in Gardiner, Kennebec Co., Nov 1976 and 14 Aug 2006 (JVW); in Bethel, 27–31 Oct 1965 and Nov 1976 (C. Gorman); in Gray, Cumberland Co., 2 Nov 1970 (obs. unk.); in Turner, Nov 1960 (2 birds, *MFO* 5: 123) and 22 Aug 2005 (J. Despres); in Patten, 22–25 Sep 1959 (*MFO* 4: 90); and in Unity, 29 Aug 2012 (T. Aversa, eBird).

WINTER: Rare in winter. First reported in 1949, when a male and a female appeared in Saco on 21 Jan and remained through winter (*BMAS* 5: 35). Regular but not annual thereafter, primarily along coast. CBCs reported Dickcissels from Mount Desert I. (9 times, 1 each), Portland (5, 1), York Co. (4, 1), Farmington (2, maximum 2 birds), Orono–Old Town (2, 1), and once each Bangor–Bucksport, Eastport, Pemaquid–Damariscotta, Thomaston–Rockland, and Monhegan I. Records for Danforth CBC not substantiated. A bird residing in Freeport, 2 Nov–15 Dec 2017, reported on Freeport–Brunswick CBC.

Notable inland records: 1 in Danforth, Washington Co., and 2 in Bethel from Oct 1967–Jan 1968; 1 in Hampden, Penobscot Co., Feb 1969; 1 in Augusta, Dec 1969–Feb 1970; 1 in Orono, 9 Jan 1968 (all obs. unk.); and 1 in Kenduskeag, Penobscot Co., 28 Dec 1988 (*AB* 43: 286); 1, Pleasant St., Clinton, 10 Dec 2016 (L. Powell, eBird); 1, Hermon, Penobscot Co., 6 Jan 2015 (E. Barber, eBird). A Dickcissel in Sherman Mills, Dec 1967–7 Jan 1968, likely succumbed to severe winter conditions, "very cold weather may have been too much for this bird" (Elwell, *NMAS* Dec 1967); this is apparently the only Aroostook Co. record. Recent winter records of note: 1 at a feeder in Prince's Cove Beach, Eastport, Washington Co., intermittently seen 19 Dec 2015–13 Feb 2016 (C. Bartlett, eBird).

PDV

Acknowledgments

The book, even more than is usual with such a massive undertaking, reflects the work, passion, expertise, and financial support of many, without whom it would have been impossible.

We are particularly grateful to the Nuttall Ornithological Club, especially David Larson and Allan Keith, for encouraging Peter Vickery's publication of this work, advising on its overall framework, providing financial support for its publication, and for reviewing the entire manuscript.

The editors and co-authors acknowledge with gratitude the ornithologists who contributed important portions of this book's text: Malcolm Hunter, Jody Despres, Jeremiah Trimble, Sara Morris, and Jan Pierson. We had the exceptional help of multiple research and editing assistants who also drafted a number of species accounts and sidebars: Rachel Prestigiacomo, Paul Dougherty, Isaac Merson, Heidi Franklin, Richard Joyce, Ian Carlsen, and Tamara Enz. (A special, heartfelt thanks to Tamara for applying her relentless eye for detail and passion for consistency of style, leavened with humor, to the project over two years of the editing process.) Alison Childs Wells also assisted with species account drafting.

A book such as this ultimately owes its existence to the careful record-keeping of myriad bird observers, as well as a much smaller number of unsung heroes who compile and edit all of those records. Jody Despres was the titan who compiled Peter's and his own species records, gleaned from many publications as well as Bird Alerts and e-lists, into a searchable database that became the basis for each species account. Stella Walsh transcribed all of Peter Vickery's and Mark Libby's field notes to eBird, from which additional data were gathered. We are deeply indebted to the reviewers, especially Chris Wood and Marshall Iliff, the editors of all the journals of bird records cited in the text, and the past and current members of Maine Bird Records

Committee who made the tough calls on acceptance of reports of accidental occurrences.

Thanks to the many people who provided information on particular species: George Appell, Chris Bartlett, Louis Bevier, Seth Benz, Don Dearborn, Mike Fahay, Norm Famous, Davis Finch, Jon Greenlaw, Karen Holmes, Steven Kress and the Project Puffin staff, Jerry Longcore, Derek Lovitch, Dan McCauley, Maurry Mills, Glen Mittelhauser, Julie Paquet, Jan Pierson, Ellen Robertson, Nancy Sferra, Paula Shannon, Bill Townsend, Diane Winn, Nat Wheelwright, and Herb Wilson. David Christie, Ralph Eldridge, and Anthony Diamond contributed information about gannets and alcids nesting in New Brunswick. Thanks to Rob E. Lambert for help in retrieving Mark Libby's field notebooks, and to Don Mairs for tracking down specimens in the Maine State Library and UMaine collections, and to the staff of those institutions who helped in that effort, Paula Work and Ann Diefenbacher-Krall respectively. Lena Usyk provided data on band recoveries from BandedBirds.org. Thanks to Delaware Species Conservation and Research Program for shorebird banding and resighting data.

We are indebted to the staff of Maine Audubon—to Andy Beahm and Dori Barnes for arranging the fiscal sponsorship that made our fundraising possible and for helping us keep the Birds of Maine, Inc., financial records straight; to Jeremy Cluchey for tracking down old journals; and to Sally Stockwell and Doug Hitchcox for advice along the way.

State and federal agency staff who were especially helpful include: from MDIFW, Lindsay Tudor, Brad Allen, Tom Hodgman, Danielle D'Auria, Kelsey Sullivan, Charlie Todd, Adrienne Leppold, Judy Camuso, and Brad Zitske; from MNAP, Kristen Puryear and Lisa S. Hilaire; and from USFWS, Kate O'Brien and Linda Welch. Staff in Senator Angus

King's office assisted in illuminating the international legal tangle surrounding Machias Seal Island.

Many thanks to those who provided information and data files for the migration tracking maps: Joseph Moore (American Woodcock); David Okill and Malcolm Smith (Red-necked Phalarope); Kevin Regan (Willet); Robert Ronconi (Great Shearwater); Fletcher Smith (Hudsonian Godwit and Whimbrel); Project SNOWstorm (Snowy Owl); Danielle D'Auria (Great Blue Heron); Michael Langlois (Arctic Tern); Lawrence J. Niles (Red Knot); Tom Rothe (Black Scoter); Michel Robert (Harlequin Duck); Phil Taylor ("Ipswich" Savannah Sparrow).

Additional spatial data for maps from *Atlas of Breeding Birds in Maine* 1978–1983; Cornell Lab of Ornithology; eBird Basic Dataset, November 2018; ESRI, Gulf of Maine Research Institute; Maine Departments of Agriculture, Conservation, and Forestry, Inland Fisheries and Wildlife, Marine Resources, and Transportation; Maine Natural Areas Program, Maine Office of GIS, Natural Earth, and The Nature Conservancy.

We thank those who reviewed species accounts, sidebars, and chapters for catching our errors of commission and omission and giving us the benefit of their enormous experience with Maine birds and natural history: Brad Allen, John Anderson, Chris Bartlett, Dave Brinker, Lysle Brinker, Rob Butler, Judy Camuso, Andy Cutko, Danielle D'Auria, Heather Deese, Jody Despres, Anthony Diamond, John Drury, Sue Gallo, Andrew Gilbert, Mac Hunter, Steve Kress, Adrienne Leppold, John Lloyd, Richard MacDonald, Don Mairs, Janet McMahon, Ed Minot, Glenn Mittelhauser, Larry Niles, Kate O'Brien, Brian Olsen, Wayne Petersen, Kevin Powers, Kristen Puryear, Don Reimer, Greg Shriver, Bob Steneck, Iain Stenhouse, Sally Stockwell, Lindsay Tudor, Charlie Todd, Herb Wilson, and Laura Zitske.

Thank you, Liz Pierson, for creating the *Birds of Maine* style manual and patiently responding to myriad additional questions of editorial style. Our able, efficient, meticulous, and patient copy editor was Jennifer Hanson.

We feel enormously fortunate to have had Charles Melcher and Margo Halverson of Alice Designs, with the help of Lucian Burg of LU Design Studios, work with us in designing this book. We appreciate their skill in bringing our vision to reality. We are also pleased with the good luck of newly retired Bill Hancock's availability to create our maps. His considerable GIS, cartography, and editing skills, ornithological knowledge, as well as imagination and an excellent design eye, made these maps a special feature of this book. Thanks to Dan Coker of TNC for providing GIS data to augment the Maine Office of GIS.

Susan Marsh provided valuable advice throughout regarding design and book production.

It is impossible to overstate our gratitude for the contributions made by our two extraordinary artists, Lars Jonsson and Barry Van Dusen; this work would have been vastly poorer without their graceful artwork. We extend an extra note of appreciation to Barry for donating the use of his ink drawings.

We are grateful to these fine photographers for contributing their images of Maine's iconic environments: Ian Patterson, Paul Cyr, Heather Perry, Patrick Higgins, Josephine Gingerich, Mark Berry, Josh Royte, John Andrew Rice, and Mike Fahay. We thank Lisa St. Hilaire and Tim Paul for helping to track down images from MNAP and TNC files. Thanks also to Desiree Butterfield-Nagy of the University of Maine Special Collections for assistance in retrieving a photo of Ralph Palmer. Finally, we thank Friends of Hog Island and the Stanwood Wildlife Sanctuary for historical photographs.

It was a pleasure to work with you all. We are also grateful for the patience and support of our friends and families as we took on significant and sadly unexpected responsibilities in finishing this book on top of multiple prior commitments.

Undoubtedly there are others we have inadvertently omitted whom Peter would have acknowledged if he were able to do so. We are certain he appreciated you all deeply.

Finally, we have been fortunate to work with Robert Kirk of Princeton University Press, who embraced this joint project with the Nuttall Ornithological Club with enthusiasm, and who has given us a great deal of freedom to produce the book Peter had long envisioned.

Nuttall Ornithological Club, the co-publisher, made a significant financial contribution to the book's production. In addition, more than 100 individuals and organizations contributed funds that helped defray the costs of editing, artwork, cartography, and the design of this work. We acknowledge gratefully the grant from the Maine Outdoor Heritage Fund; the advice of Kate Dempsey, Roger Milliken, Ellen Baum, and Thomas Urquhart; the technical assistance of Bill Kunitz; and the generosity of the following who contributed directly or indirectly to the Birds of Maine fund:

Phillip Ahrens
Deanna and Charles T. Akre
John and Meg Albright
Anonymous
Anonymous
Anonymous
George and Laura Appell
C.D. and Beth Armstrong
Jeanne Bamforth
Tom and Paula Bartlett
Ellen Baum and Jeffery Fischer
Margaret Betts
Jerry Bley
Kate Dempsey and Tim Blair
Dirk Bryant
Barry Burgason
Franklin and Susan Burroughs
Aram Calhoun and Mac Hunter
Diane Clay
Joyce and Les Coleman
John Cook
David Courtemanch
Robert P. Smith and
    Margaret Creighton
Doug and Shay DeAngelis
Jody Despres and Jan McDonough
Michael and Nancy Dickinson
Nancy and Dale Dorr
David Doubleday
Olivia S. and Alexander Dreier
Tamara Enz
Cindy and Michael Fahay
Davis W. Finch
Mark and Kathy Fulford
Janet R. Galle

William Ginn and June LaCombe
Sally and Tony Grassi
Michael Ware and
    Barbara Gravinese
Paul N. Gray
Babette Gwynn
Bill Hancock
Anne and Martin Hayden
Julie Henderson and Tony French
DeWitt and Jane John
Jack and Sally Ijams
Jody Jones and Jack Witham
The Kennebec Land Trust
William B. Krohn
William Kunitz
Bill and Lucy LaCasse
Tonia Laliberte
Roxanne Leighton
Clara and Bevis Longstreth
Tom Longstreth
Jay Levin
Janet McMahon
Nancy McReel
David Mehlman
Roger and Margot Milliken
J. Mason and Margaret C. Morfit
Sarah and Harvey Moseley
John W. and Catherine Norris
Bucky and Sue Owen
Wayne R. Petersen
Roger and Shirley Piasio
Liz and Jan Pierson
Bancroft Poor
Kristen Puryear
Josie Quintrell

Kent Redford and Pamela Shaw
Ala H. Reid
Michael Ridgway
Juanita Roushdy
Anne-Seymour St. John
Christopher and Eunice St. John
Michael St. John
Nathaniel St. John
Susan St. John
Evelyn Sawyer
Nancy Sferra
Gerald Smith
John and Sylvia Sowles
Rob and Sue Speirs
Stantec, Inc.
Bob and Joanne Steneck
Mitchell Stokes and
    Cristina Squeff
Beth Swartz
Ellen Theodores
Anna Marie and John E. Thron
Adelaide Trafton
Richard and Barbara Trafton
Thomas Urquhart
Ian Vickery
Sally Volkert
Scott Weidensaul
Joseph Wetherold
E. John and Kathryn White
Marc Payne and Diane Winn
Carol and Joe Wishcamper
Kent Wommack
Dan and Linda Wood
The York County Audubon Society
Sylvia Young

The Downeast coast is often enveloped in fog. Great Wass Island, Beals, Washington Co. (© Justin Schlawin)

Appendices

The appendices include a guide to frequently cited place names and the map on which they can be located; a comprehensive listing of conservation designations of Maine species by international, national, and state entities; and lists of those species whose occurrence in the state is considered hypothetical and those for which introductions failed.

Olive-sided Flycatcher

Appendix I
Geographic place names found in Birds of Maine text

Place names in text	Town	County	Map(s)
Acadia N.P. (ANP)		Hancock	E
Addison		Washington	E
Albion		Waldo	W, S
Allagash Lake	T8 R14 WELS T7 R14 WELS	Piscatquis	N
Allagash River Wilderness Waterway		Aroostook/ Piscataquis	N
Appalachian Trail			W, N, S
Appledore Island	Kittery	York	S
Aroostook NWR	Caswell/Connor Twp/ Limestone	Aroostook	N
Ashland		Aroostook	N
Attean Pond	Attean Twp.	Somerset	W
Augusta		Kennebec	W, S
Aziscohos Lake	Lincoln Plt.	Oxford	S
Back Cove	Portland	Cumberland	C
Bangor		Penobscot	W, S, E
Bar Harbor		Hancock	E
Baring		Washington	C
Barnes Island	Harpswell	Cumberland	S
Baskahegan Lake	Brookton Twp.	Washington	E, N
Bass Harbor		Hancock	C
Bath		Sagadahoc	S
Baxter S.P. (BSP)		Piscataquis	W, E, N
Belfast		Waldo	W, S, E
Belgrade Lakes	Belgrade	Kennebec	W, S
Bethel		Oxford	W, S
Biddeford		York	S
Biddeford Pool	Biddeford	York	S
Bigelow Mountain	Bigelow, Wyman, and Dead River Twps.	Franklin and Somerset	W, S
Blue Hill		Hancock	E
Blue Hill Bay		Hancock	E
Boothbay		Lincoln	S
Boothbay Harbor		Lincoln	C
Bowdoin		Sagadahoc	C
Bowdoinham		Sagadahoc	C
Bradbury Mountain S.P.	Pownal	Cumberland	S
Brewer		Penobscot	C
Bridgton		Cumberland	S
Brimstone Island	Vinalhaven	Knox	C

Blancher, P.J., K.V. Rosenberg, A.O. Panjabi, B. Altman, J. Bart, C.J. Beardmore, G.S. Butcher, D. Demarest, R. Dettmers, E.H. Dunn, W. Easton, W.C. Hunter, E.E. Iñigo-Elias, D.N. Pashley, C.J. Ralph, T.D. Rich, C.M. Rustay, J.M. Ruth, and T.C. Will. 2007. *Guide to the Partners in Flight Population Estimates Database.* Version: North American Landbird Conservation Plan 2004. Partners in Flight Technical Series No. 5. [www.partnersinflight.org]

Blockstein, D.E. 2002. Passenger pigeon (*Ectopistes migratorius*). Version 2.0. In *The Birds of North America* (A.F. Poole and F.B. Gill, eds.). Ithaca, NY: Cornell Lab of Ornithology. doi.org/10.2173/bna.611.

Blumton, A.K., R.B. Owen, Jr., and W.B. Krohn. 1988. *Habitat Suitability Index Models: American Eider (Breeding).* U.S. Fish and Wildlife Service Biology Report 82(10.149). 24 pp. [https://www.nwrc.usgs.gov/wdb/pub/hsi/hsi-149.pdf]

Boardman, G.A. 1862. Catalogue of the birds found in the vicinity of Calais, Maine, and about the islands at the mouth of the Bay of Fundy. A.E. Verrill, ed. *Proceedings of the Boston Society of Natural History* 9: 122–132.

Boardman, G.A. 1897. Naturally trapped water birds. *Forest and Stream* 49:167.

Boardman, S.L. 1903. *The Naturalist of the St. Croix.* C.H. Bangor, ME: Glass and Co. 351 pp.

Bocetti, C.I., M. Donner, and H.F. Mayfield. 2014. Kirtland's Warbler (*Setophaga kirtlandii*). Version 2.0. In *The Birds of North America* (A.F. Poole, ed.). Ithaca, NY: Cornell Lab of Ornithology. doi.org/10.2137/bna.19.

Bock, C.E., and L.W. Lepthien. 1976. Synchronous eruptions of boreal seed-eating birds. *American Naturalist* 110(974): 559–571. doi.org/10.1086/283091.

Boertmann, D., and M. Frederiksen. 2016. Status of Greenland populations of Great Black-backed Gull (*Larus marinus*), Lesser Black-backed Gull (*Larus fuscus*), and Herring Gull (*Larus argentatus*). *Waterbirds* 39 (Special publication): 29–35.

Bolgiano, N.C. 2004. Changes in boreal bird irruptions in eastern North America relative to the 1970s Spruce Budworm infestation. *American Birds* 58: 26–33.

Bonaparte, C.L. 1828. *American Ornithology.* 2 Vols. Philadelphia: Carey, Lea, and Carey. 95 pp.

Bond, J. 1940. Identity of the United States specimens of Fork-tailed Flycatcher. *Auk* 57: 418–419.

Bond, J. 1947. What has happened to the Vesper Sparrow? *Bulletin of the Maine Audubon Society* 3(1–2): 10–11.

Bond, J. 1971. *Native Birds of Mount Desert Island.* Second ed. Philadelphia: Academy of Natural Sciences. 29 pp.

Bonney, R. 1988. "Prairie Warbler." In *The Atlas of Breeding Birds in New York State*, edited by R.F. Andrle and J.R. Carroll, 388. Ithaca, NY: Cornell University Press.

Bookhout, T.A. 1995. Yellow Rail (*Coturnicops noveboracensis*). In *The Birds of North America* (A.F. Poole and F.B. Gill, eds.). Philadelphia and Washington, DC: Academy of Natural Sciences and American Ornithologists' Union. 16 pp.

Boone, R.B., and W.B. Krohn. 2001. Partitioning sources of variation in vertebrate species richness. *Journal of Biogeography* 27: 457–470. doi.org/10.1046/j.1365-2699.2000.00386.x.

Borror, A.C. 1963. European Siskin (*Cardulis spinus*) in Maine. *Auk* 80: 201.

Borror, A.C., and D.W. Holmes. 1990. *Breeding Birds of the Isles of Shoals.* Ithaca, NY: Shoals Marine Laboratory.

Bosakowski, T., and D.G. Smith. 1992. Comparative diets of sympatric nesting raptors in the eastern deciduous forest biome. *Canadian Journal of Zoology* 70: 984–992. doi.org/10.1139/z92-140.

Both, C., and M.E. Visser. 2001. Adjustment to climate change is constrained by arrival date in a long-distance migrant bird. *Nature* 411: 297–298.

Braune, B.M., and D.E. Gaskin. 1982. Feeding ecology of non-breeding larids off Deer Island, New Brunswick. *Auk* 99: 67–76.

Brewer, T.M. 1875. Catalogue of the birds of New England. *Proceedings of the Boston Society of Natural History* 17: 436–454.

Brewer, T.M. 1877. Breeding of Leach's Petrel on the coast of Maine. *Bulletin of the Nuttall Ornithological Club.* 2: 80–81.

Brewster, W.M. 1893. Some additional eastern records of Swainson's Hawk. *Auk* 10: 82–83.

Brewster, W.M. 1895. Notes on certain flycatchers of the genus Empidonax. *Auk* 12: 157–163.

Brewster, W.M. 1924. The birds of the Lake Umbagog region of Maine, Vol. 1. *Bulletin of the Museum of Comparative Zoology.* Cambridge, MA 66(1): 1–209. [https://www.biodiversitylibrary.org/item/26719#page/11/mode/1up]

Brewster, W.M. 1925. The birds of the Lake Umbagog region of Maine, Vol. 2. *Bulletin of the Museum of Comparative Zoology.* Cambridge, MA 66(2): 211–402. [https://www.biodiversitylibrary.org/item/26719#page/11/mode/1up]

Brewster, W.M. 1937. The birds of the Lake Umbagog region of Maine, Vol. 3. *Bulletin of the Museum of Comparative Zoology.* Cambridge, MA 66(3): 403–522.

Brinker, L., and P.D. Vickery. 1997. First confirmed nesting of Clay-colored Sparrow (*Spizella pallida*) in New England. *Bird Observer* 25: 204–208.

Brodkorb, P. 1960. Great Auk and Common Murre from Florida midden. *Auk* 77: 342–343.

Broley, C.L. 1947. Migration and nesting of Florida Bald Eagles. *Wilson Bulletin* 59: 3–20.

Brown, N.C. 1923. The standing of the Lapland Longspur in Maine. *Auk* 40: 131–132.

Brown, R.G.B. 1986. *Revised Atlas of Eastern Canadian Seabirds, Vol I. Shipboard Surveys.* Ottawa: Canadian Wildlife Service. 111 pp.

Brown, R.G.B., S.P. Barker, D.E. Gaskin, and M.R. Sandeman. 1981. The foods of Great and Sooty Shearwaters *Puffinus gravis* and *P. griseus* in eastern Canadian waters. *Ibis* 123(1): 19–30.

Brown, S., C.D. Duncan, J. Chardine, and M. Howe. 2010. Red-necked Phalarope Research, Monitoring, and Conservation Plan for the Northeastern U.S. and Maritimes Canada. Version 1.1. Manomet, MA: Manomet Center for Conservation Sciences.

Brown, S., C. Hickey, B. Harrington, and R. Gill, eds. 2001. The U.S. Shorebird Conservation Plan. Second ed. Manomet, MA: Manomet Center for Conservation Sciences.

Brown, W.H. 1963. Carolina Wren's ability to survive during severe winters. *Wilson Bulletin* 75: 449.

Brownson, W.H. 1903. Birds in the vicinity of Portland. *Journal of the Maine Ornithological Society* 5: 42–44.

Brownson, W.H. 1905. The first Hooded Warbler taken in Maine. *Auk* 22: 85.

Bucher, E.H. 1992. The causes of extinction of the Passenger Pigeon. *Current Ornithology* 9: 1–36.

Burgio, K. R., C.B. van Rees, K.E. Block, P. Pyle, M.A. Patten, M. F. Spreyer, and E.H. Bucher. 2016. Monk Parakeet (*Myiopsitta monachus*). Version 3.0. In *The Birds of North America* (P.G. Rodewald, ed.). Ithaca, NY: Cornell Lab of Ornithology. doi.org/10.2173/bna.monpar.03.

Butcher, G.S., and D.K. Niven. 2007. *Combining Data from the Christmas Bird Count and the Breeding Bird Survey to Determine the Continental Status and Trends of North America Birds.* New York: National Audubon Society.

Butler, R. 1992. Great Blue Heron (*Ardea herodias*). In *Birds of North America* (A.F. Poole and F. Gill, eds.). Philadelphia and Washington, DC: Academy of Natural Sciences and American Ornithologists' Union.

Byer, M., and A. Østhagen. 2016. Why does Canada have so many unresolved maritime boundary disputes? *Canadian Yearbook of International Law/ Annuaire Canadien de Droit International* 54: 1–62. doi.org/10.1017/cyl.2017.14.

C

Cabe, P.R. 1993. European Starling (*Sturnus vulgaris*). Version 2.0. In *The Birds of North America* (A.F. Poole and F.B. Gill, eds.). Ithaca, NY: Cornell Lab of Ornithology. doi.org.10.2173/bna.48.

Cadman, M.D., P.F.J. Eagles, and F.M. Helleiner, eds. 1987. *Atlas of the Breeding Birds of Ontario, 1981–1985.* Waterloo, ON: University of Waterloo Press. 617 pp.

Cadman, M.D., D.A. Sutherland, G.G. Beck, D. Lepage, and A.R. Couturier, eds. 2007. *Atlas of the Breeding Birds of Ontario, 2001–2005.* Toronto: Bird Studies Canada, Environment Canada, Ontario Field Ornithologists, Ontario Ministry of Natural Resources, and Ontario Nature. 706 pp.

Campbell, G. 2017. *High Elevation Landbird Program: Mountain Birdwatch 2.0 2016 Report.* Sackville, NB: Bird Studies Canada (Atlantic Region). Unpublished report.

Campbell, G. and R. Stewart. 2012. High Elevation Landbird Program 10-year Report. Sackville, NB: Bird Studies Canada (Atlantic Region). 19 pp.

Carlson, M., J. Wells, and M. Jacobson. 2015. Balancing the relationship between protection and sustainable management in Canada's boreal forest. *Conservation and Society* 13(1): 13–22.

Carroll, W.J. 1910. The Eskimo Curlew or doughbird. *Forest and Stream* 74: 372.

Cascade, J., B. Sorte, V.E. Davidson, M.C. Franklin, K.M. Benes, M.M. Doellman, R.J. Etter, R.E. Hannigan, J. Lubchenco, and B.A. Menge. 2016. Long-term declines in an intertidal foundation species parallel shifts in community composition. *Global Change Biology* 23: 341–352. doi.org/10.1111/gcb.13425.

Cawley, K.M., K.D. Butler, G.R. Aiken, L.G. Larsen, T.G. Huntington, and D.M. McKnight. 2012. Identifying fluorescent pulp mill effluent in the Gulf of Maine and its watershed. *Marine Pollution Bulletin* 64: 1678–1687.

Chamberlain, G.D. 1949. The birds of Aroostook County. *Bulletin of the Maine Audubon Society* 5(3): 43–58.

Chapman, F.M. 1907. *The Warblers of North America.* New York: D. Appleton and Company. 306 pp.

Chardine, J. 2015. "Ring-billed Gull." In *Second Atlas of Breeding Birds of the Maritime Provinces*, edited by R.L.M. Stewart, K.A. Bredin, A.R. Coutier, A.G. Horn, D. Lepage, S. Makepeace, P. D. Taylor, M.A. Villard, and R.M. Whittam, 230-231. Port Rowan, ON: Bird Studies Canada, Environment Canada, Natural History Society of Prince Edward Island, Nature New Brunswick, NB Department of Natural Resources, Nova Scotia Bird Society,

O

O'Connell Jr., A.F., F.A. Servello, and S.P. Whitcomb. 1995. Spruce Grouse on Mount Desert Island: Fragmented habitat complicates species management. *Park Science* 15(3): 10–11.

Ontario Shorebird Resighting Project and Delaware Bay Shorebird Resighting projects. 2017. Project Data. [bandedbirds.org]

Osberg, P.H., A.M. Hussey II, and G.M. Boone, eds. 1985. *Bedrock Geologic Map of Maine.* Augusta, ME: Maine Geological Survey.

Ouellet, H. 1993. Bicknell's Thrush: Taxonomic status and distribution. *Wilson Bulletin.* 105: 545–572.

P

Packard, C.M. 1955a. Magpies reported in Maine. *Bulletin of the Maine Audubon Society* 11(2): 29.

Packard, C.M. 1955b. Additional notes on magpies. *Bulletin of the Maine Audubon Society* 11(3): 53–54.

Palmer, R.S. 1949. *Maine Birds.* Cambridge, MA: Museum of Comparative Zoology. 656 pp.

Palmer, R.S. 1962. *Handbook of North American Birds: Vol. 1. Loons through Flamingos.* New Haven, CT: Yale University Press. 567 pp.

Palmer, R.S. 1976. *Handbook of North American Birds: Vols 2 and 3. Waterfowl (Parts 1 and 2).* New Haven, CT: Yale University Press. 556 pp.

Palmer, R.S., ed. 1988. *Handbook of North American Birds: Vol. 5. Diurnal Raptors (Part 2).* New Haven, CT: Yale University Press,. 448 pp.

Palmer, R.S., and W. Taber. 1946. Birds of the Mt. Katahdin region of Maine. *Auk* 63: 299–314.

Parker, J., and J. Parker. 1987. One-eye the owl. *Maine Fish and Wildlife* 29(3): 24–25.

Parmelee, D.F. 1992. White-rumped Sandpiper (*Calidris fuscicollis*). Version 2.0. In *The Birds of North America* (A.F. Poole, P.R. Stettenheim, and F.B. Gill, eds.). Ithaca, NY: Cornell Lab of Ornithology. doi. org/10.2173/bna.29.

Parmesan, C., and G. Yohe. 2003. A globally coherent fingerprint of climate change impacts across natural systems. *Nature* 421: 37–42. doi.org/10.2173/bna.29.

Parsons, K.C., and T.L. Master. 2000. Snowy Egret (*Egretta thula*). Version 2.0. In *The Birds of North America* (A.F. Poole and F.B. Gill, eds.). Ithaca, NY: Cornell Lab of Ornithology. doi.org/10.2173/bna.489.

Paruk, J.D., T.J. Cade, E.C. Atkinson, P. Pyle, and M.A. Patten. 2018. Northern Shrike (*Lanius excubitor*). Version 2.1. In *The Birds of North America* (P.G. Rodewald, ed.). Ithaca, NY: Cornell Lab of Ornithology. doi.org/10.2173/bna.norshr.4.02.1.

Paruk, J.D., M.D. Chickering, D. Long IV, H. Uher-Koch, A. East, D. Poleschook, V. Gumm, W. Hanson, E.M. Adams, K.A. Kovach, and D.C. Evers. 2015. Winter site fidelity and winter movements in Common Loons (*Gavia immer*) across North America. *Condor: Ornithological Applications* 117: 485–493.

Patterson III, W.A., and K.E. Sassaman. 1988. "Indian fires in the prehistory of New England." In *Holocene Human Ecology in Northeastern North America*, edited by G.P. Nichols, 107–135. New York: Plenum. 320 pp.

Peck, C.G., and R.D. James. 1998. Breeding birds of Ontario: nidiology and distribution. Vol. 1: passerines (First revision–Part C: tanagers to Old World sparrows). *Ontario Birds* 16: 111–127.

Perkins, A. 1935. Notes on some rare birds in southwestern Maine. *Auk* 52: 460.

Perlut, N.G., D.N. Bonter, J.C. Ellis, and M.S. Friar. 2016. Roof-top nesting in a declining population of Herring Gulls (*Larus argentatus*) in Portland, Maine, USA. *Waterbirds* 39(sp1): 68–73. doi. org/10.1675/063.039.sp113.

Pershing, A.J., M.A. Alexander, C.M. Hernandez, L.A. Kerr, A. Le Bris, K.E. Mills, J.A. Nye, N.R. Record, H.A. Scannell, J.D. Scott, G.D. Sherwood, and A.C. Thomas. 2015. Slow adaptation in the face of rapid warming leads to collapse of the Gulf of Maine cod fishery. *Science* 350: 809–812. doi.org/10.1126/science. aac9819.

Persons, T.B., L.R. Bevier, W.J. Sheehan, P.D. Vickery, and C.A. Bartlett. 2015. Fourth report of the Maine Bird Records Committee. *Bird Observer* 43: 21–37.

Peters, H.S., and T.D. Burleigh. 1951. *The Birds of Newfoundland.* St. John's, NL, and Cambridge, MA: Newfoundland Department of Natural Resources and Riverside Press. 431 pp.

Petersen, A., D.B. Irons, H.G. Gilchrist, G.J. Robertson, D. Boertmann, H. Strom, M. Gavrilo, Y. Artukhin, D.S. Clausen, K.J. Kuletz, and M.L. Mallory. 2015. The status of Glaucous Gulls (*Larus hyperboreus*) in the circumpolar Arctic. *Arctic* 68: 107–120.

Petersen, W.R. and W.R. Meservey, eds. 2003. *Massachusetts Breeding Bird Atlas* 1. Natural History of New England Series. Amherst, MA: University of Massachusetts Press. 434 pp. [https://www. massaudubon.org/our-conservation-work/wildlife-research-conservation/statewide-bird-monitoring/breeding-bird-atlases/bba1]

Pettingill, O.S. 1939. History of one hundred nests of Arctic Tern. *Auk* 56: 420–428.

Phillips, J.C. 1926. *A Natural History of the Ducks, Vol. 4.* Boston: Houghton Mifflin.

Piatt, J.F., and A.S. Kitaysky. 2002. Tufted Puffin (*Fratercula cirrhata*). Version 2.0. In *The Birds of North America* (A.F. Poole and F.B. Gill, eds.). Ithaca, NY: Cornell Lab of Ornithology. doi. org/10.2173/bna.708.

Pokagon, S. 1895. The wild pigeon of North America. *Chautauquan* 22: 202–206.

Pollet, I.L., A. Hedd, P.D. Taylor, W.A. Montevecchi, and D. Shutler. 2014. Migratory movements and wintering areas of Leach's Storm-Petrels tracked using geolocators. *Journal of Field Ornithology.* 85: 321–328.

Powell, A.N., and R.S. Suydam. 2000. King Eider (*Somateria spectabilis*). Version 2.0. In *The Birds of North America* (A.F. Poole, ed.). Ithaca, NY: Cornell Lab of Ornithology. doi.org/10.2173/bna.491.

Powell, L. 2008. *Rusty Blackbird (*Euphagus carolinus*) Breeding Ecology in New England: Habitat Selection, Nest Success and Home Range.* MS thesis. Orono, ME: University of Maine. 86 pp.

Powers, K.D. 1983. *Pelagic Distributions of Marine Birds off the Northeastern United States.* National Oceanic and Atmospheric Administration Technical Memo NMFS-F/NEC-27. Woods Hole, MA: National Oceanic and Atmospheric Administration, National Marine Fisheries Service, Northeast Fisheries Center.

Powers, K.D., and J.A. Van Os. 1979. A concentration of Greater Shearwaters in the western North Atlantic. *American Birds* 33: 387–429.

Powers, K.D., D.N. Wiley, A.J. Allyn, L.J. Welch, and D. Ronconi. 2017. Movements and foraging habitats of Great Shearwaters *Puffinus gravis* in the Gulf of Maine. *Marine Ecology Progress Series.* 574: 211–226. doi.org/10.3354/meps12168.

Preston, C.R., and R.D. Beane. 2009. Red-tailed Hawk (*Buteo jamaicensis*). Version 2.0. In *The Birds of North America* (A.F. Poole, ed.). Ithaca, NY: Cornell Lab of Ornithology. doi.org/10.2173/bna.52.

Probst, J.C., J.-F. Therrien, L.J. Goodrich, and K.L. Bildstein. 2017. Increase in numbers and potential phenological adjustment of Ruby-throated Hummingbirds (*Archilochus colubris*) during autumn migration at Hawk Mountain Sanctuary, Eastern Pennsylvania, 1990–2014. *Wilson Journal of Ornithology* 129: 360–364.

Project Feederwatch. Ithaca, NY, and Port Rowan, ON: Cornell Lab of Ornithology and Bird Studies Canada. [http://feederwatch.org]

Project Puffin. n.d. *Research Reveals Incredible Migratory Journey of Arctic Terns.* New York: National Audubon Society. [projectpuffin.audubon.org/news/research-reveals-incredible-migratory-journey-arctic-terns]

Purdie, H.A. 1878. The nest and eggs of the Yellow-bellied Flycatcher (*Empidonax flaviventris*). *Bulletin of the Nuttall Ornithological Club* 3: 166–168.

Pushcock, J. 2013. #ABArare—Fieldfare—Massachusetts. [http://blog.aba.org/2013/03/abarare-fieldfare-massachusetts.html]

Pyle, P. 1997. *Identification Guide to North American Birds Part I: Columbidae to Ploceidae.* Bolinas, CA: Slate Creek Press. 732 pp.

R

Raffaele, H.A., J. Wiley, O.H. Garrido, A. Keith, J.A. Raffaele, T. Pedersen, and K. Williams. 2003. *Birds of the West Indies.* Princeton, NJ: Princeton University Press. 216 pp.

Raftovich, R.V., S.C. Chandler, and K.K. Fleming. 2018. Migratory bird hunting activity and harvest during the 2016–2017 and 2017–2018 hunting seasons. Laurel, MD: U.S. Fish and Wildlife Service. 76 pp. [https://www.fws.gov/migratorybirds/pdf/surveys-and-data/HarvestSurveys/MBHActivityHarvest2016-17and2017-18.pdf]

Rand, A.L. 1947. Notes on some Greenland birds. *Auk* 64: 281–284.

Read, A.J., and C.R. Brownstein. 2003. Considering other consumers: Fisheries, predators, and Atlantic herring in the Gulf of Maine. *Conservation Ecology* 7(1): 2. [www.consecol.org/vol7/iss1/art2]

Recher, H.F., and J.A. Recher. 1972. The foraging behavior of Reef Heron. *Emu* 72: 85–90.

Renfrew, R.B., D. Kim, N. Perlut, J. Smith, J. Fox, and P.P. Marra. 2013. Phenological matching across hemispheres in a long-distance migratory bird. *Diversity and Distributions* 19: 1008–1019. doi. org/10.1111/ddi.12080.

Renfrew, R.B., A.M. Strong, N.G. Perlut, S.G. Martin, and T.A. Gavin. 2015. Bobolink (*Dolichonyx oryzivorus*). Version 2.0. In *The Birds of North America* (P.G. Rodewald, ed.). Ithaca, NY: Cornell Lab of Ornithology. doi.org/10.2173/bna.176.

Rich, T.D., C.J. Beardmore, H. Berlanga, P.J. Blancher, M.S.W. Bradstreet, G.S. Butcher, D.W. Demarest, E.H. Dunn, W.C. Hunter, E.E. Inigo-Elias, J.A. Kennedy, A.M. Mertell, A.O. Panjabi, D.N. Pashley, K.V. Rosenberg, C.M. Rustay, J.S. Wendt, and T.C. Will. 2004. *Partners In Flight North American Landbird Conservation Action Plan.* Ithaca, NY: Cornell Laboratory of Ornithology. 40 pp.

Rich, W.H. 1908. *Feathered Game of New England.* London: George G. Harrap and Company. 628 pp.

Rimmer, C.C., J.D. Lloyd, and J.A. Salguero-Faría. 2019. Overwintering Bicknell's Thrush *(Catharus bicknelli)* in Puerto Rico: Rare and local. *Caribbean Journal of Ornithology* 32: 34–38.

Rimmer, C.C., and K.P. McFarland. 2012. Tennessee Warbler (*Oreothlypis peregrina*). Version 2.0. In *The Birds of North America* (A.F. Poole, ed.). Ithaca, NY: Cornell Lab of Ornithology. doi.org/10.2173/bna.350.

Robert, M., G.H. Mittelhauser, B. Jobin, G. Fitzgerald, and P. Lamothe. 2008. New insights on Harlequin Duck population structure in eastern North America as revealed by satellite telemetry. *Waterbirds* 31(sp2): 159–172. doi.org/10.1675/1524-4695-31.sp2.159.

Roberts, D.L., C.S. Elphick, and J.M. Reed. 2010. Identifying anomalous reports of putatively extinct species and why it matters. *Conservation Biology* 24: 189–196.

Robertson, E.P., and B.J. Olsen. 2015. Behavioral plasticity in nest building increases fecundity in marsh birds. *Auk* 132: 37–45.

Robinson, S.K. 1994. Use of bait and lures by Green-backed Herons in Amazonian Peru. *Wilson Bulletin* 106(3): 569–571.

Rodenhouse, N.L., S.N. Matthews, K.P. McFarland, J.D. Lambert, L.R. Iverson, A. Prasad, T. S. Sillett, and R.T. Holmes. 2008. Potential effects of climate change on birds of the Northeast. *Mitigation and Adaptation Strategies for Global Change* 13(5–6): 517–540.

Ronconi, R.A., H.N. Koopman, C.A.E. McKinstry, S.N.P. Wong, and A.J. Westgate. 2010. Inter-annual variability in diet of non-breeding pelagic seabirds *Puffinus* spp. at migratory staging areas: Evidence from stable isotopes and fatty acids. *Marine Ecology Progress Series* 419: 267–282.

Ronconi, R.A., S. Schoombie, A.J. Westgate, S.N.P. Wong, H.N. Koopman, and P.G. Ryan. 2018. Effects of age, sex, colony and breeding phase on marine space use by Great Shearwaters *Ardenna gravis* in the South Atlantic. *Marine Biology* 165: 58.

Ronconi, R.A., and S.N.P. Wong. 2002. *Seabird Colonies of the Grand Manan Archipelago: 2001 Census Results and Guidelines for Surveys and Future Monitoring.* Grand Manan Whale and Seabird Research Station, Bulletin No. 4. Grand Manan, NB: Grand Manan Whale and Seabird Research Station. [www.gmwsrs.org]

Roosevelt, T. 1919. "My debt to Maine." In *Maine, My State*, edited by Maine Writers Research Club. Lewiston, ME: Author.

Root, T.L., J.T. Price, K.R. Hall, S.H. Schneider, C. Rosenzweig, and A. Pounds. 2003. "Fingerprints" of global warming on wild animals and plants. *Nature* 421: 57–60.

Rosenberg, K.V., A.M. Dokter, P.J. Blancher, J.R. Sauer, A.C. Smith, P.A. Smith, J.C. Stanton, A. Panjabi, L. Helft, M. Parr, and P.P. Marra. 2019. Decline of North American avifauna. *Science* 366: 120–124. doi:10.1126/science.aaw1313.

Rosenberg, K.V., J.A. Kennedy, R. Dettmers, R.P. Ford, D. Reynolds, J.D. Alexander, C.J. Beardmore, P.J. Blancher, R.E. Bogart, G.S. Butcher, A.F. Camfield, A. Couturier, D.W. Demarest, W.E. Easton, J.J. Giocomo, R.H. Keller, A.E. Mini, A.O. Panjabi, D.N. Pashley, T.D. Rich, J.M. Ruth, H. Stabins, J. Stanton, and T. Will. 2016. *Landbird Conservation Plan: 2016 Revision for Canada and Continental United States.* Ithaca, NY: Partners in Flight Science Committee. 119 pp.

Rosenberg, K.V., and J.V. Wells. 1995. *Importance of Geographic Areas to Neotropical Migrant Birds in the Northeast.* Final report. Hadley, MA: U. S. Fish and Wildlife Service, Region 5.

Rosenberg, K.V., and J.V. Wells. 2005. "Conservation priorities for terrestrial birds in the northeastern United States." In *Bird Conservation Implementation and Integration in the Americas: Proceedings of the Third International Partners In Flight Conference Vols. 1 and 2*, edited by C.J. Ralph and T.D. Rich, 236–253. USDA Forest Service, General Technical Report PSW-GTR-191, Albany, CA: U.S. Department of Agriculture, Forest Service, Pacific Southwest Research Station. 1296 pp.

Rosier. 1887. [Reprint of] *Rosier's Relation of Waymouth's Voyage to the Coast of Maine, 1605, with an introduction and notes.* By H.S. Burrage, D.D. Printed for Gorges Society. Portland ME. 176 pp.

Roth, A., and R. Robicheau. 2019. "Wildlife Implications on the Loss of Beech." University of Maine and Maine Department of Inland Fisheries and Wildlife joint presentation. [https://forest.umaine.edu/wp-content/uploads/sites/231/2019/04/Wildlife-implications-on-the-loss-of-beach-Roth-and-Robicheau-2019-1.pdf]

Rounds, W.D. 1957. Pileated Woodpeckers roosting in a barn. *Maine Field Naturalist* 13(1–2): 22.

Rusch, D.H., R.A. Malecki, and R.E. Trost. 1995. "Canada Geese in North America." In *Our Living Resources: A Report to the Nation on the Distribution, Abundance, and Health of U.S. Plants, Animals, and Ecosystems*, edited by E.T. LaRoe, G.S. Farris, C.E. Pukett, P.D. Doran, and M.J. Mac, 26–28. Washington, DC: U.S. Department of the Interior, National Biological Service. 548 pp.

Rush, S.A., K.F. Gaines, W.R. Eddleman, and C.J. Conway. 2018. Clapper Rail (*Rallus crepitans*). Version 2.1. In *The Birds of North America* (A.F. Poole, ed.). Ithaca, NY: Cornell Lab of Ornithology. doi.org/10.2173/bna.clara111.02.1.

Russell, W., and C. Witt. 2009. *The Birds of Mount Desert Island and Acadia National Park: Status and Distribution.* Unpublished manuscript.

S

Samuels, E.A. 1867. *Ornithology and Oology of New England.* Boston: Nichols and Noyes. 583 pp.

Sánchez-Bayo, F., and K.A.G. Wyckhuys. 2019. Worldwide decline of the entomofauna: A review of its drivers. *Biological Conservation.* 232: 8–27.

Santonja, P., I. Mestre, S. Weidensaul, D. Brinker, S. Huy, N. Smith, T. McDonald, M. Blom, D. Zazelenchuck, D. Weber, G. Gauthier, N. Lecomte, and J.-F. Therrien. 2019. Age composition of winter irruptive Snowy Owls in North America. *Ibis* 161: 211–215.

Sauer, J.R., D.K. Niven, J.E. Hines, D.J. Ziolkowski, Jr, K.L. Pardieck, J.E. Fallon, and W.A. Link. 2017. *The North American Breeding Bird Survey, Results and Analysis 1966–2015 Version 2.07.2017.* Laurel, MD: USGS Patuxent Wildlife Research Center. [https://www.mbr-pwrc.usgs.gov/bbs/bbs.html]

Sauer, J.R., S. Schwartz, and B. Hoover. 1996. *The Christmas Bird Count Home Page. Version 95.1.* Laurel, MD: Patuxent Wildlife Research Center. [https://www.mbr-pwrc.usgs.gov/bbs/cbc.html]

Schauffler, M., and G.L. Jacobson. 2002. Persistence of coastal spruce refugia during the Holocene in northern New England, USA, detected by stand-scale pollen stratigraphies. *Journal of Ecology* 90: 235–250. doi:10.1046/j.1365-2745.2001.00656.x.

Schorger, A.W. 1955. *The Passenger Pigeon: Its History and Extinction.* Norman, OK: University of Oklahoma Press. 424 pp.

Schreiber, R.W. 1967. Roosting behavior of the Herring Gull in central Maine. *Wilson Bulletin* 79: 421–431.

Seamans, M.E., and R.D. Rau. 2018. *American Woodcock Population Status, 2017.* Laurel, MD: U.S. Fish and Wildlife Service. [https://www.fws.gov/migratorybirds/pdf/surveys-and-data/Population-status/Woodcock/AmericanWoodcockStatusReport18.pdf]

Senner, N.R., W.M. Hochachka, J.W. Fox, and V. Afanasyev. 2014. An exception to the rule: Carry-over effects do not accumulate in a long-distance migratory bird. *PLoS ONE* 9(2): e86588. [https://journals.plos.org/plosone/article?id=10.1371/journal.pone.0086588]

Sherony, D.F. 2008. Greenland Geese in North America. *Birding* 40: 46–56.

Shifley, S.R., F.X. Aguilar, N. Song, S.I. Stewart, D.J. Nowak, D.D. Gormanson, W.K. Moser, S. Wormstead, and E.J. Greenfield. 2012. *Forests of the Northern United States.* General Technical Report NRS-90. Newtown Square, PA: U.S. Department of Agriculture, Forest Service, Northern Research Station. 202 pp.

Shriver, W.G., J.P. Gibbs, P.D. Vickery, H.L. Gibbs, T.P. Hodgman, P.T. Jones, and C.N. Jacques. 2005b. Concordance between morphological and molecular markers in assessing hybridization between Sharp-tailed Sparrows in New England. *Auk* 122: 94–107.

Shriver, W.G., T.P. Hodgman, and A.R. Hanson. 2018. Nelson's Sparrow (*Ammospiza nelsoni*). Version 1.1. In *The Birds of North America* (P.G. Rodewald, ed.). Ithaca, NY: Cornell Lab of Ornithology. doi.org/10.2173/bna.nstspa.01.1.

Shriver, W.G., A.L. Jones, P.D. Vickery, A. Weik, and J.V. Wells. 2005a. *The Distribution and Abundance of Obligate Grassland Birds Breeding in New England and New York.* n.p.: U.S. Department of Agriculture, Forest Service, General Technical Report, PSW-GTR-191.

Shriver, W.G., P.D. Vickery, T.P. Hodgman, J.P. Gibbs. 2007. Flood tides affect breeding ecology of two sympatric Sharp-tailed Sparrows. *Auk* 124: 552–560. doi.org/10.1642/0004-8038(2007)124[552:FTABEO]2.0.CO;2.

Sibley, D.A. 2000. *The Sibley Guide to Birds.* New York: Alfred A. Knopf. 544 pp.

Sidor, I.F., M.A. Pokras, A.R. Major, R.H. Poppenga, K.M. Taylor, and R.M. Miconi. 2003. Mortality of Common Loons in New England, 1987 to 2000. *Journal of Wildlife Diseases* 39: 306–315.

Skeel, M.A., and E.P. Mallory. 1996. Whimbrel (*Numenius phaeopus*). Version 2.0. In *The Birds of North America* (A.F. Poole, ed.). Ithaca, NY: Cornell Lab of Ornithology. doi.org/10.2173/bna.219.

Sklepkovych, B.O., and W.A. Montevecchi. 1989. The world's largest known nesting colony of Leach's Storm-Petrels on Baccalieu Island, Newfoundland. *American Birds* 43: 38–42.

Smallwood, J.A., M.F. Causey, D.H. Mossop, J.R. Klucsartis, S. Robertson, J. Mason, M.J. Maurer, R.J. Melvin, R.D. Dawson, G.R. Bortolotti, J.W. Parrish, Jr., T.F. Breen, and K. Boyd. 2009. Why are American Kestrel (*Falco sparverius*) populations declining in North America? Evidence from nest-box programs. *Journal of Raptor Research* 43: 274–282. doi.org/10.3356/JRR-08-83.1.

Smith, E. 1882. The Birds of Maine. *Forest and Stream* 19: 425–426.

Smith, J. 1630. *The Trve Travels, Adventvres and Observations of Captaine Iohn Smith, in Europe, Asia, Africke, and America: Beginning about the Yeere 1593, and Continued to This Present 1629.* Republished at Richmond, VA: Franklin Press 1891.

Smith, J.P., C.J. Farmer, S.W. Hoffman, C.A. Lott, L.J. Goodrich, J. Simon, C. Riley, and E.I. Ruelas. 2008. "Trends in autumn counts of raptors around the Gulf of Mexico, 1995–2000." In *The State of North*

Wells, J.V., and P.D. Vickery. 1990. Willet nesting in sphagnum bog in eastern Maine. *Journal of Field Ornithology* 61: 73–75.

Wetlands International. 2019. "Waterbird Population Estimates." [wpe.wetlands.org]

Whitaker, D. 2017. Expanded range limits of boreal birds in the Torngat Mountains of Northern Labrador. *Canadian Field Naturalist* 131: 55–62.

White, C.M., N.J. Clum, T.J. Cade, and W.G. Hunt. 2002. Peregrine Falcon (*Falco peregrinus*). Version 2.0. In *The Birds of North America* (A.F. Poole and F.B. Gill, eds.). Ithaca, NY: Cornell Lab of Ornithology. doi.org/10.2173/bna.660.

Whitman, A., A. Cutko, P. deMaynadier, S. Walker, B. Vickery, S. Stockwell, and R. Houston. 2013. *Climate Change and Biodiversity in Maine: Vulnerability of Habitats and Priority Species.* Report SEI-2013-03. Brunswick, ME: Manomet Center for Conservation Sciences in collaboration with Maine Beginning with Habitat, Climate Change Working Group. 96 pp.

Widrig, R.S. 1989. *The Birds and Plants of Petit Manan National Wildlife Refuge.* Milbridge, ME: Author.

Wiemeyer, S.N., C.M. Bunck, and C.J. Stafford. 1993. Environmental contaminants in Bald Eagle eggs—1980–84—and further interpretations of relationships to productivity and shell thickness. *Archives of Environmental Contamination Toxicology.* 24: 213–227.

Williamson, W.D. 1832. *History of the State of Maine: From Its First Discovery, AD* 1602, *to the Separation, AD* 1820, *Inclusive.* Vol. 2. Hallowell, ME: Glazier, Masters, and Co.

Wilson, A. 1812. *American Ornithology.* Vol. 5. Philadelphia: Bradford and Inskeep.

Wilson, E.O. 2016. *Half-Earth: Our Planet's Fight for Life.* New York: W.W. Norton and Company.

Wilson, W.H., Jr. 1999. Bird feeding and irruptions of northern finches: Are migrations short-stopped? *North American Bird Bander* 24: 113–121.

Wilson, W.H., Jr. 2017. The dynamics of arrivals of Maine migratory breeding birds: Results from a 24-year study. *Biology* 6(4): 38–55. doi.org/10.3390/biology6040038.

Wilson, W.H., Jr. 2018. Closing the loop: Autumn departure dates of Maine migratory breeding birds. *Environmental Analysis and Ecology Studies* 4(2): 1–9. doi.org/10.31031/EAES.2018.04.000584.

Wilson, W.H., Jr., and B. Brown. 2012. Fidelity and interseasonal movements of Purple Finches (*Carpodactus purpureus* (Gmelin)): Analysis of band re-encounter data. *Open Ornithology Journal.* 5: 61–72.

Wilson, W.H., Jr., and B. Brown. 2017. Winter movements of *Sitta canadensis* L. (Red-breasted Nuthatch) in New England and beyond: A multiple-scale analysis. *Northeastern Naturalist* 24(sp7). doi.org/10.1656/045.024.s716.

Wilson, W.H., Jr., A. Savage, and R. Zierzow. 1997. Arrival dates of migratory breeding birds in Maine: Results from a volunteer network. *Northeastern Naturalist* 4(2): 83–92.

Winne, J.C. 1998. History of Vegetation and Fire on the Pineo Ridge Blueberry Barrens in Washington County, Maine. MS thesis. Orono, ME: University of Maine. 57 pp.

Witham, J.W., and M.L. Hunter, Jr. 1992. "Population trends of Neotropical migrant landbirds in northern coastal New England." In *Ecology and Conservation of Neotropical Migrant Landbirds*, edited by J.M. Hagan III and D.W. Johnson, 85–95. Washington, DC: Smithsonian Institution Press. 609 pp.

Witt, C. 1997. First record of Swainson's Warbler (*Limnothlypis swainsonii*) in Maine. *Maine Bird Notes* 10: 1–2.

Witt, C., and W. Russell. 1987. *The Birds of Mount Desert Island and Acadia National Park: Status and Distribution.* Unpublished manuscript.

Witynski, M.L. and D.N. Bonter. 2018. Crosswise migration by Yellow Warblers, Nearctic–Neotropical passerine migrants. *Journal of Field Ornithology* 89(1): 37–46. doi:10.1111/jofo.12237.

Wootton, J.T. 1987. Interspecific competition between introduced House Finch populations and two associated passerine species. *Oecologia* 71: 325–331.

Wright, H.W. 1921. The mockingbird in the Boston region and in New England and Canada. *Auk* 38: 382–432.

Y

Young, M., and T. Spahr. 2017. "Crossbills of North America: Species and Red Crossbill Call Types." [https://ebird.org/news/crossbills-of-north-america-species-and-red-crossbill-call-types/]

Yukich, R., and J. Varella. 2000. Slaty backed Gull in Toronto. *Ontario Birds* 18(2): 73–77.

Z

Zumeta, D.C., and R.T. Holmes. 1978. Habitat shift and roadside mortality of Scarlet Tanagers during a cold wet New England spring. *Wilson Bulletin* 90: 575–586.

Mixed northern hardwoods and coniferous forests typical of northern Maine. Debsconeags Wilderness Area, Piscataquis Co. (© J. Gingerich)

Bird Species Index

Notes: Bold-faced numerals refer to main accounts for species. Page numbers followed by "s" refer to text sidebars. Page numbers followed by "t" refer to tables.